AF835837

CURRENT ISSUES IN SUCCESSION LAW

While Continental and comparative lawyers have recently rediscovered succession law as an area of immense practical importance deserving greater academic attention, it is still a neglected field in England. This book aims to reinvigorate the English debate. It brings together contributions by leading academics and practitioners engaging with currently topical issues as well as questions of fundamental importance in succession law and estate planning. The book will be of interest to both academics and practitioners working in the field, and to non-English comparative lawyers.

Current Issues in Succession Law

Edited by
Birke Häcker and Charles Mitchell

HART PUBLISHING
OXFORD AND PORTLAND, OREGON
2016

Hart Publishing
An imprint of Bloomsbury Publishing plc

Hart Publishing Ltd
Kemp House
Chawley Park
Cumnor Hill
Oxford OX2 9PH
UK

Bloomsbury Publishing Plc
50 Bedford Square
London
WC1B 3DP
UK

www.hartpub.co.uk
www.bloomsbury.com

Published in North America (US and Canada) by
Hart Publishing
c/o International Specialized Book Services
920 NE 58th Avenue, Suite 300
Portland, OR 97213-3786
USA

www.isbs.com

HART PUBLISHING, the Hart/Stag logo, BLOOMSBURY and the Diana logo are trademarks of Bloomsbury Publishing Plc

First published 2016

© The editors and contributors severally

The editors and contributors have asserted their right under the Copyright, Designs and Patents Act 1988 to be identified as Authors of this work.

All rights reserved. No part of this publication may be reproduced or transmitted in any form or by any means, electronic or mechanical, including photocopying, recording, or any information storage or retrieval system, without prior permission in writing from the publishers.

While every care has been taken to ensure the accuracy of this work, no responsibility for loss or damage occasioned to any person acting or refraining from action as a result of any statement in it can be accepted by the authors, editors or publishers.

All UK Government legislation and other public sector information used in the work is Crown Copyright ©. All House of Lords and House of Commons information used in the work is Parliamentary Copyright ©. This information is reused under the terms of the Open Government Licence v3.0 (http://www.nationalarchives.gov.uk/doc/open-government-licence/version/3) except where otherwise stated.

All Eur-lex material used in the work is © European Union, http://eur-lex.europa.eu/, 1998–2015

British Library Cataloguing-in-Publication Data
A catalogue record for this book is available from the British Library.

ISBN: HB: 978-1-78225-627-4
ePDF: 978-1-78225-629-8
ePub: 978-1-78225-628-1

Library of Congress Cataloging-in-Publication Data

Names: Häcker, Birke, editor. | Mitchell, Charles (Charles Christopher James), editor.

Title: Current issues in succession law / edited by Birke Häcker and Charles Mitchell.

Description: Oxford : Portland, Oregon : Hart Publishing, an imprint of Bloomsbury Publishing Plc, 2016. | Includes papers presented at a conference at All Souls College, University of Oxford, on 10–11 July 2015.—ECIP galley. | Includes bibliographical references and index.

Identifiers: LCCN 2016015040 (print) | LCCN 2016015640 (ebook) | ISBN 9781782256274 (hardback : alk. paper) | ISBN 9781782256281 (Epub)

Subjects: LCSH: Inheritance and succession—England—Congresses.

Classification: LCC KD1500.A75 C87 2016 (print) | LCC KD1500.A75 (ebook) | DDC 346.4205/2—dc23

LC record available at https://lccn.loc.gov/2016015040

Typeset by Compuscript Ltd, Shannon
Printed and bound in Great Britain by
TJ International Ltd Padstow, Cornwall

PREFACE

In the summer of 1818, the Scottish-born and London-based genre painter David Wilkie (1785–1841) received a commission from Maximilian I Joseph, King of Bavaria, to produce a painting 'as purely English as possible' (letter by Wilkie to A Raimbach, 2 July 1818). The resulting picture is reproduced on the cover of this book. Entitled *Reading of a Will (Die Testamentseröffnung)*, it was completed in 1820 and—after being exhibited to great acclaim at the Royal Academy—was despatched to Bavaria, where it was to grace the monarch's bedchamber at his Tegernsee summer residence until his death in 1825.[1] Today the original may be admired at the Neue Pinakothek in Munich; preliminary sketches are held, inter alia, by the Fitzwilliam Museum in Cambridge, the Ashmolean Museum in Oxford, and in various collections around London.

Whilst on display at the Royal Academy in 1820, the painting was accompanied by the following text printed in the catalogue:[2]

> Mr. Protocol, accordingly, having required silence, began to read the settlement aloud, in a slow, steady, business-like tone. The group around, in whose eyes hopes alternately awakened and faded, were straining their apprehensions to get at the drift of the testator's meaning through the mist of technical language, in which the conveyance had involved it.

The passage is attributed to the 'Author of Waverley' and thus—unbeknown to anybody at the time—to Sir Walter Scott. It is a (slightly amended) quote from Scott's successful novel *Guy Mannering or The Astrologer*, which had been published anonymously in 1815. In the book, the scene in question occurs after the funeral of an elderly lady, Mrs Margaret Bertram of Singleside. In Wilkie's painting, by contrast, the deceased seems to have been a man (possibly an army officer) leaving behind a young family. Today's observer will want to muse over the many fine details in the depiction of the room and the company gathered therein; yet when the painting was first exhibited, its style and popularity with the crowds

[1] For further details on the painting and its context, see eg F Dietrich, 'A Picture for the Bavarian King: David Wilkie's *The Reading of the Will* (1820)' (2003) 4 *British Art Journal* 37; N Tromans, *David Wilkie: The People's Painter* (Edinburgh, Edinburgh University Press, 2007), especially 48–51 and 122; AS Marks, 'Wilkie, Hogarth, and Hazlitt: *The Reading of a Will*, Its Origins and Legacy' (2009) 48 *Studies in Romanticism* 583. The present account is heavily indebted to these informative secondary sources.

[2] *The Exhibition at the Royal Academy, The Fifty-Second* (London, McMillan, 1820) 11.

elicited a scathing comment from the infamous Thomas G Wainewright, writing for *The London Magazine* under the pseudonym of Janus Weathercock:[3]

> [I]t offends me to the soul, to see a parcel of chuckleheaded Papas, doting Mammas, and chalk-and-charcoal-faced Misses, neglecting that beautiful eccentricity of Turner's yonder, in the mahogany frame, and crowding and squeezing, and riding upon one another's backs, to get a sight—not of the faces of the folks hearing the Will, but of the brass clasps of the strong box wherein was deposited the Will.

On the Continent, the bourgeois setting of Wilkie's *Reading of a Will* hit a nerve with a public increasingly interested in domestic matters as the so-called Biedermeier era progressed. Many an artist came to look at the painting, and it proved to be the inspiration for a whole spate of similar compositions. Even Englishmen on their travels flocked to see it. The lawyer-turned-author Wilkie Collins, for instance, whose painter father William Collins had been friendly with David Wilkie (the latter boasting to William Collins in 1827 that '[t]he sale of my picture at Munich made an impression at Rome among all descriptions of artists'),[4] reports of his father's tour of the Continent 1836–38:[5]

> It was ... from an expedition to the Royal Palace at Schleisheim, to see there Wilkie's celebrated picture, 'The Reading of a Will', that he derived his most genuine enjoyment while at Munich. He found his friend's work (which had been purchased by the King of Bavaria) in perfect preservation, holding its ground triumphantly against the old pictures which surrounded it, by its fine colour and *chiaroscuro*, and its strikingly dramatic developement of subject and character.

At about the time that William Collins was preparing to make his way back to England from Naples, via Rome, Venice, 'Innspruck', 'Saltzburg', Munich and the Rhine Valley, there came into force back home a statute that was intended to simplify the thitherto fiendishly complex legal regime governing wills. The Wills Act 1837 set out (amongst other things) uniform formality requirements for wills relating to personalty as well as devises of realty. With minor amendments and supplemented by the Land Transfer Act 1897, the Administration of Estates Act 1925 and other statutes, it remains a basic cornerstone of probate proceedings and the administration of estates to this day.

Although many social, economic and political parameters have changed since the days depicted in Wilkie's *Reading of a Will*, a large number of fundamental issues are as topical today as they were then: how best to ensure that the testator's final wishes are genuine, unimpaired and accurately expressed in the executed document; what formal requirements this document has to comply with to constitute a valid 'last will and testament'; to what extent provision is—or ought to be—made for the testator's family and dependants; etc.

[3] 'Janus Weathercock's Dialogue on the Exhibition at Somerset-House' in the newly revived *London Magazine* (January to June 1820) 700 at 701.

[4] WW Collins, *Memoirs of the Life of William Collins, Esq., R.A.*, (London, Longman Brown Green and Longmans, 1848) vol 1, 288.

[5] ibid vol 2, 153.

The law of succession was always and remains hugely important in practice. Rather surprisingly, however, it is (still) a neglected subject from the academic point of view. Few English universities offer courses on it, and hardly anyone engages in-depth with the fascinating questions raised by current developments. Comparative scholarship, on the other hand, has recently flourished, with a number of high-profile edited collections appearing in the space of just a few years.[6]

The marked mismatch between succession law's immense practical importance and its regrettable theoretical neglect led to the idea for a conference on 'Current Issues in Succession Law' bringing together people whose work relates to—or in some way overlaps with—English succession law, so as to reinvigorate academic interest and debate in the subject. The conference took place at All Souls College, University of Oxford, on 10–11 July 2015 and was attended by leading scholars and practitioners, Chancery judges, a member of the Court of Appeal and a representative of the Law Commission.

In terms of subject matter, the papers ranged from reviews of recent legislative reforms and analyses of topics which the Law Commission intends to tackle in the future, via problems raised by the interaction of the law of succession with other areas of law, to modern pensions and tax issues impacting on estate planning. Discussions were lively and sometimes controversial. Recurrent themes concerned the tension between promoting legal certainty on the one hand and achieving 'just and equitable' results for individual cases on the other, and the ambiguity latent within certain statutory provisions between giving effect to testators' typical or hypothetical intentions and pursuing wider public policy objectives.

Although fact situations involving, in one form or another, testamentary dispositions lie at the heart of many of the chapters, the present volume begins by looking at scenarios where the deceased has not—or at any rate not necessarily—made a will. Roger Kerridge thus critically assesses the recent revision of the law of intestacy contained in the Inheritance and Trustees' Powers Act 2014 in Chapter 1, while Rebecca Probert in Chapter 2 discusses the other leg of that statute, namely the reform of the family provision regime. Chapter 3, by Ian Williams, is devoted to the operation of the common law forfeiture rule which—he argues—differs from the 'deemed predecease' rule recently inserted into the Wills Act 1837. In Chapter 4, Ben McFarlane considers the extent to which the law governing proprietary estoppel could be said to undermine the law of succession. Ying Khai Liew's contribution in Chapter 5 is related insofar as he seeks to explain the mutual wills doctrine in part by an orthodox constructive trust and in part by an estoppel-type analysis.

Chapter 5 is also the first of three chapters engaging with topics that feature on the Law Commission's future reform agenda, the Commission having announced

[6] See, in particular, KCG Reid, MJ de Waal and R Zimmermann (eds), *Comparative Succession Law, vol 1: Testamentary Formalities* (Oxford, Oxford University Press, 2011) and *Comparative Succession Law, vol 2: Intestate Succession* (Oxford, Oxford University Press, 2015); A Braun and A Röthel (eds), *Passing Wealth on Death: Will-Substitutes in Comparative Perspective* (Oxford, Hart Publishing, 2016).

that it intends to 'review the law of wills, focusing on four key areas that have been identified as potentially needing reform: testamentary capacity, the formalities for a valid will, the rectification of wills, and mutual wills'.[7] In Chapter 6, prompted by the recent Supreme Court decision in *Marley v Rawlings*,[8] Birke Häcker examines the rules pertaining to the interpretation and rectification of wills (and in this context also their relationship with the formality requirements), while Penelope Reed in Chapter 7 reviews the case law on testamentary capacity and its relationship with the so-called doctrine of 'knowledge and approval'. Often connected with an alleged lack of capacity or a want of knowledge and approval is the problem of undue influence being brought to bear on testators. Brian Sloan explores this issue in the context of contemporary informal care scenarios in Chapter 8.

In Chapter 9, Lionel Smith asks whether and to what extent the actual or supposed principle against the delegation of testamentary power survives in the modern (English) common law. A different kind of delegation is addressed by Alexandra Braun's contribution in Chapter 10. She looks at the 'will substitute' practice of pension schemes allowing their members to nominate beneficiaries to receive death benefits when the member dies, while usually leaving the trustees of the scheme discretion as to the actual distribution. Pension scheme death benefits are thus a significant (albeit somewhat haphazard) factor when it comes to estate planning. Tax considerations are, of course, typically the prime mover here. The volume therefore concludes with Emma Chamberlain in Chapter 11 scrutinising the extent to which business property can effectively be exempted from inheritance tax through the availability of 'business property relief'. Her finding that the current UK regime contains many unjustified loopholes and anomalies, thereby increasing the complexity of estate and succession planning, is all the more topical as the equivalent German regime was recently held to be unlawful[9] and is now in the process of being reformed.

We, as the organisers of the conference, are extremely grateful to the Warden and Fellows of All Souls College for generously funding and hosting the event, and to all the presenters, session chairs and other participants for contributing to its success. Our thanks are also due to Bill Asquith and the whole team at Hart Publishing for publishing the proceedings in this collection and for securing the rights to reproduce Wilkie's painting on the cover.

Birke Häcker and Charles Mitchell
Munich/London, 20 November 2015

[7] See www.lawcom.gov.uk/project/wills/ (last accessed 20 November 2015).

[8] *Marley v Rawlings* [2014] UKSC 2, [2015] 1 AC 129, was a mirror wills case and potentially also a mutual wills case (though that question did not arise on the facts).

[9] Decision by the Federal Constitutional Court: BVerfG (17.12.2014) BVerfGE 138, 136.

CONTENTS

LIST OF CONTRIBUTORS

Alexandra Braun is an Associate Professor of Law at the University of Oxford and a Fellow and Tutor of Law at Lady Margaret Hall, Oxford.

Emma Chamberlain is a Barrister at Pump Court Tax Chambers, London.

Birke Häcker is a Senior Research Fellow at the Max Planck Institute for Tax Law and Public Finance, Munich, and a Fellow of All Souls College, Oxford.

Roger Kerridge is an Emeritus Professor of Law at the University of Bristol.

Ying Khai Liew is a Lecturer in Law at University College London.

Ben McFarlane is a Professor of Law at University College London.

Charles Mitchell is a Professor of Law at University College London.

Rebecca Probert is a Professor of Law at the University of Warwick.

Penelope Reed QC is a Barrister at 5 Stone Buildings, London.

Brian Sloan is a Lecturer and Fellow of Robinson College, Cambridge.

Lionel Smith is Sir William C Macdonald Professor of Law at McGill University, Montreal, and Professor of Private Law at the Dickson Poon School of Law, King's College London.

Ian Williams is a Lecturer in Law at University College London.

TABLE OF CASES

European Court of Human Rights

Domestic Courts

Australia

Canada

Germany

Ireland

New Zealand

South Africa

United Kingdom

United States

TABLE OF LEGISLATION

Treaties

National Legislation

Australia

Statutory Instruments

Canada

Germany

Ireland

New Zealand

Trinidad and Tobago

United Kingdom

1

Intestacy Reform in 2014—Unfinished Business

ROGER KERRIDGE*

1. Introduction

On 1 October 2014, the provisions of the Inheritance and Trustees' Powers Act 2014 came into force, but the theme of this chapter is that that Act represents unfinished business—unfinished in two senses. On the one hand, the 2014 Act, which enacted proposals contained in the Law Commission's 2011 Report on *Intestacy and Family Provision Claims on Death*,[1] succeeded for the most part in completing a programme begun by an earlier, 1989, Law Commission Report on *Family Law: Distribution on Intestacy*,[2] but it did this, in large part, by ignoring views with which the draftsmen of the two Reports were out of sympathy. It may be that this was inevitable, it may be that this difference of approach represents two opposed views of what, at the end of the day, is to be regarded as 'the family'. But, if this is so, the underlying problem remains. Those who drafted the two Reports almost certainly see themselves as representing not only the present, but the future, the direction of things to come. It may be that, in believing this, they could be wrong.

* This chapter draws and builds on an earlier contribution by the same author, to which the reader may also be referred, particularly for a discussion of the pre-1926 historical background: R Kerridge, 'Intestate Succession in England and Wales', ch 14 in KCG Reid, MJ de Waal and R Zimmermann (eds), *Comparative Succession Law*, vol 2: *Intestate Succession* (Oxford, Oxford University Press, 2015), especially 323–27.

[1] Law Commission, *Intestacy and Family Provision Claims on Death* (Law Com No 331, 2011) (hereinafter '2011 Report').

[2] Law Commission, *Family Law: Distribution on Intestacy* (Law Com No 187, 1989).

2. The Background

The rules which have applied to intestacies in England and Wales since 1926 are contained in Part IV of the Administration of Estates Act 1925, 'the 1925 Act'. They are based on the *rules of distribution*, the rules which had, before 1926, applied only to personalty and which had been codified in the Statutes of Distribution of 1670 and 1685. The principal effect of the 1925 Act was to get rid of the *rules of inheritance* which had until then applied to realty, to do away with the privileges given to the heir, to end the precedence of males over females and male primogeniture, and to create equality as between persons of the same degree. Eldest sons were the losers, widows the winners.

The code which took effect in 1926 has since been amended several times, but the majority of the changes have either been relatively unimportant[3] or have been linked with, or have resulted from, changes effected in other branches of the law.[4] Since 1926, there have been at most three occasions on which there have been significant changes to the intestacy code—these were in 1953, 1996 and 2014. There have been *at most* three occasions because the 1996 and 2014 changes are, to a considerable extent, linked. They result from two separate Law Commission Reports, but the 2014 changes follow on from those made in 1996 and could be viewed as an attempt to complete the task begun 20 years earlier—unfinished business left over from the earlier round. In order to put the 2014 changes in context, it may be helpful to consider, albeit briefly, the position in 1926, what happened in 1953 and then what did, and what did not, happen in 1996.

2.1. The Position in 1926

The 1926 rules were relatively straightforward. If the deceased left a surviving spouse, she[5] took (i) the personal chattels; (ii) the statutory legacy of £1,000; and

[3] The Family Provision Act 1966 provided that the statutory legacy to which the spouse was entitled could be increased from time to time by order of the Lord Chancellor. The Administration of Justice Act 1977 altered the way in which the capitalised value of the spouse's life interest was to be calculated. The Trusts of Land and Appointment of Trustees Act 1996 substituted a power of sale for what had previously been the personal representatives' implied trust for sale on intestacy.

[4] The Family Law Reform Act 1969 reduced the age of majority from 21 to 18 and also made changes to the rules applicable to illegitimate children. The Family Law Reform Act 1987 made further changes to the position of illegitimate descendants. The Civil Partnership Act 2004 equated civil partners with spouses for the purposes of intestacy.

[5] Strictly speaking, 'she' should, of course, be 'he or she' and 'her' (later on) should be 'his or her', but these phrases become clumsy, if repeated often. It is simpler to say 'she' and 'her' rather than to keep saying 'he or she' and 'his or her' and, as surviving spouses are marginally more likely to be women than men, it will be assumed (for brevity, and for no other reason) that where a married person dies intestate survived by a spouse, it is the husband who dies first, survived by a widow. If she remarries and then dies (see later examples), the third death in the sequence will be that of her widower.

(iii) a life interest in half the residue if there were issue, or a life interest in the entire residue if there were no issue but the deceased left a grandparent or the descendant of a grandparent.[6] If the deceased left a surviving spouse, but no issue and no grandparent or descendant of a grandparent, she took the entire estate. If the deceased left no surviving spouse, but did leave issue, the issue took the entire estate. If the deceased left no spouse and no issue, but did leave grandparents or their descendants, they would take his estate in a specified order.[7] If the deceased left no spouse, no issue and no grandparents or their descendants, the estate would pass to the Crown[8] as *bona vacantia*.

The personal chattels will be discussed further below.[9] The statutory legacy had had its origin in the Intestates' Estates Act 1890 which had provided that, where a man died totally intestate leaving no issue, his widow would take his entire estate if its value did not exceed £500, and that she would have a charge on his real and personal property for £500 if the value of the estate exceeded this sum. In 1926, the £500 had become £1,000, it was awarded both to widows and to widowers, it was to be paid whether or not there were issue, and it was to be paid also in cases of partial intestacy.

2.2. The 1953 Changes

The Intestates' Estates Act 1952, which came into force on 1 January 1953, was based for the most part on the recommendations of the *Report of the Committee on the Law of Intestate Succession*, usually referred to as 'the Morton Committee'.[10] The principal change effected by the 1952 Act was a huge increase in the spouse's statutory legacy. In 1953, the sum, which had been £1,000 irrespective of whether the deceased was survived by issue or by a grandparent or any descendant of a grandparent, was increased to £5,000 where there were issue, and to £20,000 where there were no issue. To compensate for these increases, an additional hotchpot rule[11] was introduced whereby a spouse had to account against her[12] entitlement to the statutory legacy for any benefits received in a partial intestacy.[13] There were no other changes in 1953 in cases where the deceased left a spouse and issue. The

[6] The residue went to the grandparents or their descendants in the order set out in n 7 immediately below.

[7] The order was (i) parents; (ii) brothers and sisters of the whole blood and/or their issue; (iii) brothers and sisters of the half blood and/or their issue; (iv) grandparents; (v) uncles and aunts of the whole blood and/or their issue; (vi) uncles and aunts of the half blood and/or their issue.

[8] Or to the Duchies of Lancaster or Cornwall.

[9] See Section 10.2.3 below.

[10] *Report of the Committee on the Law of Intestate Succession* (Cmd 8301, 1951). The Chairman of the Committee was Lord Morton of Henryton.

[11] For further explanation and discussion of 'hotchpot', see Section 8 below.

[12] The word 'her' is used as a shorthand for 'his or her': see n 5 above.

[13] Administration of Estates Act 1925, s 49(2), (3) and (4) added in 1952. These subsections were repealed in 1995 and do not apply to deaths occurring on and after 1 January 1996. See further Section 8.4 below.

spouse continued, as she had since 1926, to take the personal chattels, the now increased statutory legacy, and a life interest in half the residue, the issue took the remainder and the other half on the statutory trusts.[14]

If, after 1952, the deceased left a spouse and no issue, there were further changes. The spouse continued, as before, to take the personal chattels, but if the deceased left no parents or brothers or sisters of the whole blood or their descendants, the spouse now took the entire estate. Before 1953, the spouse took the entire estate only if the deceased left no grandparents or their descendants.[15] And, if he did leave grandparents or their descendants,[16] the surviving spouse had, before 1953, had only a life interest in the residue after taking the personal chattels and the £1,000 statutory legacy. If the deceased now left no issue, but left parents, or brothers or sisters of the whole blood or their descendants, the surviving spouse would now take, in addition to the personal chattels and the £20,000 statutory legacy, half the residue absolutely, rather than, as had been the case since 1926, the whole of the residue for life.

3. The 1989 Law Commission Report and the 1996 Changes

Apart from increases to the statutory legacy,[17] there were no significant changes to the intestacy rules between 1953 and 1988, but in that year the Law Commission produced a Working Paper and a survey of public opinion, and these were followed in 1989 by a Report *Family Law Distribution on Intestacy*[18] which made the following three recommendations for reform: (i) that—subject to (iii) below—a surviving spouse should in all cases take the intestate's whole estate; (ii) that the statutory hotchpot rules[19] should be repealed; and (iii) that a spouse should inherit under the intestacy rules only if he or she survived the intestate for 14 days.[20] The first of these was, of course, by far the most important and it has been at the heart of an on-going debate ever since. All other

[14] For the 'statutory trusts', see Section 10.3 below.

[15] *cf* the text accompanying and following n 6 above.

[16] ie parents, brothers or sisters of the whole or half blood and their descendants, grandparents, and uncles or aunts of the whole or half blood and their descendants.

[17] The statutory legacy was increased in 1952 to £5,000 where there were issue and £20,000 where there were no issue. It was then raised in 1967 to £8,750 with issue and £30,000 without; in 1972 to £15,000 with issue and £40,000 without; in 1977 to £25,000 with issue and £55,000 without; in 1981 to £40,000 with issue and £85,000 without; in 1987 to £75,000 with issue and £125,000 without; in 1993 to £125,000 with issue and £200,000 without; and in 2009 to £250,000 with issue and £450,000 without.

[18] Law Commission, *Family Law Distribution on Intestacy* (Law Com No 187, 1989).

[19] For further discussion of the hotchpot rules, see Section 8 below.

[20] The original proposal was 14 days—it was amended, to 28 days, in the Lords.

changes proposed in or since 1989 have either been linked with this, or have been relatively unimportant.

In the 100 years starting in 1890, 'progress' and 'reform' had always meant that the share of an intestate's estate given to his spouse was increased. The Intestates' Estates Act 1890, although described by JHC Morris as 'a timid half measure of reform',[21] established the notion of the statutory legacy *and*, in doing so, gave the widow a measure of precedence over the heir.[22] The 1925 Act applied to realty the rules formerly applicable to personalty. The 1952 Act hugely increased the size of the statutory legacy. The 1989 recommendation was the culmination of a century-long process, and it had the merit of being, in its application, a simplification. But did it go too far? There had always been fundamental differences of opinion as to how to divide up an intestate's estate between his spouse and his next of kin. These differences could be seen in 1951 when the Council of the Law Society suggested in their evidence to the Morton Committee that, where there were no issue, the surviving spouse should take the whole of an intestate's estate. By contrast, the General Council of the Bar, when giving their evidence to the same committee, suggested *no* increase to the statutory legacy; they would have retained it at £1,000, but they would have given the surviving spouse a life interest in the whole of the residue, above and beyond the personal chattels and the statutory legacy, in all cases, whether or not there were surviving issue. This was almost the opposite of the Law Society's suggestion—the Bar were drawing no distinction between the position where there were and where there were no issue, and the only way in which a spouse was better off after 1952 than before was in the case where the spouse *was* survived by issue. The recommendations of the Morton Committee, which were enacted in 1952 and came into force in 1953, steered a course between these extremes.

There are two interlinked questions here. The first is: with whom (if anyone) should the spouse share the intestate's estate? The second is: how much (or what percentage) should the spouse be awarded? From 1926 onwards, the spouse took the entire estate if the deceased left no surviving issue and no next of kin who were grandparents or their descendants.[23] From 1926 to 1952, the spouse's share of the estate was slightly smaller if there were issue than if there were no issue, but there were grandparents or their descendants, yet it made relatively little difference.[24] From 1953 onwards, the position where there were, and when there were not, issue, was radically different. In the latter case, unless the deceased left parents or brothers or sisters of the whole blood, or their descendants, the spouse now took

[21] JHC Morris, 'Intestate Succession to Land in the Conflict of Laws' (1969) 85 *LQR* 339 at 348.

[22] She took the first £500, so in the case of a small estate she took everything, whether the property consisted of realty or personalty.

[23] And if the deceased left no spouse and no next of kin who were grandparents or their descendants, the estate passed to the Crown as *bona vacantia*.

[24] In either case the spouse took the personal chattels and a £1,000 statutory legacy. If there were issue, she took a life interest in half the residue, and if there were no issue, but there were grandparents or their descendants, she took a life interest in the whole of the residue.

the whole estate; and even in cases where there were parents or such brothers or sisters or their descendants, the spouse now took a much larger statutory legacy (£20,000 as opposed to £5,000) than she would have been awarded had there been issue. So, where the deceased left a spouse, the effect of the 1953 changes was, in the vast majority of cases, to disinherit all next of kin except for issue.

But that brings us back to the question of the issue. From 1953 onwards, where a deceased left a surviving spouse, the issue were the only members of his family who were likely to share his estate with her. The proposal in the 1989 Law Commission Report to give the entire estate to the surviving spouse was one which would be of relatively little significance *except* where there were issue. So the question which needed to be asked was: how generously should issue be treated vis-à-vis a surviving spouse? Does it make sense simply to say that the surviving spouse should, in all cases, take the entire estate, or should the rights of the issue be to some extent preserved? In theory, one could of course draw all sorts of different lines according to the duration of the marriage on the one hand and the ages and closeness of the issue to the deceased on the other. What may seem to some to be a reasonably obvious dividing line may not appear so to others. One effect of the 1953 changes was to create a cut-off point for those of the next of kin who might share the deceased's estate with his spouse, between brothers and sisters of the whole blood and those of the half blood. This seems slightly arbitrary. The line between issue and non issue is easy to draw, but in terms of succession it may be suggested that the correct place to draw the line, when considering who should share with the spouse and how the shares should be measured, does not relate so much to the link between the deceased and the issue but, more importantly, to the link between the surviving spouse and the issue: ie is the surviving spouse the parent of the deceased's children? If rules are enacted which pass a large part of, or the whole of, the deceased's estate to his spouse in the case where he also left children or other issue, there will be a distinction between what are likely to be the longer term effects of this if the surviving spouse is the parent of the deceased's children, as opposed to what is likely to happen if she is not. There are, of course, all sorts of possibilities. At one extreme, the deceased's spouse may be the parent of his children, neither has any other children, and the survivor neither later remarries nor forms any meaningful attachment to anyone else. In this kind of case, the surviving spouse is highly likely, when she dies, to pass on the deceased's property or what is left of it to their issue. But, at the other extreme, there is the widow[25] who has children and grandchildren and who re-marries late in life someone who also has children and grandchildren. If this widow then dies and her property passes to her second spouse, it is unlikely that it will later pass back to her issue. There are, of course, intermediate situations—ones where the first spouse to die had some children in common with his surviving spouse and some from another union. And there are cases where the last spouse to die is childless. But, even in the

[25] 'Widow' is shorthand for 'widower or widow': see n 5 above.

latter case, property which passed to him on the earlier death (the second death in the series) will not pass back to that spouse's children (the childless survivor's step children) if this last death was intestate. It will go to the childless survivor's next of kin, probably the childless survivor's brothers or sisters,[26] or it will go to the Crown as *bona vacantia*.

If one dividing line is to be drawn, the most obvious place to draw it is between cases where a surviving spouse is the parent of none of the deceased's children and the case where she is the parent of some or all of them. The former example covers, in particular, marriages entered into late in life by those who were previously married, whose children are adults, and who now seek companionship in their declining years. The question as to how to deal with these cases is at the heart of attempts made to reform the English intestacy system during the past quarter of a century.

In 1989, the Law Commission proposed that the surviving spouse should, in all cases, take the entire estate. No special provision was suggested for the case where the deceased intestate left issue who were not issue of the surviving spouse. There was opposition to this proposal, almost all based on the need to protect such issue, and the end result was that the Law Commission's main proposal was not enacted. The Commission's other proposals, the abolition of hotchpot and the introduction of a survivorship period were enacted, but the principal proposal was not.

The Law Reform (Succession) Act 1995, which came into force on 1 January 1996, was a compromise, but it was not a happy one. The suggestion that hotchpot should be abolished had depended, in part, on the proposal that if there were a surviving spouse, she should take the entire estate. More will be said about hotchpot later in this chapter.[27] As far at the main proposal, to award the entire estate to the spouse, was concerned, the de facto compromise consisted in changing none of the principal rules—those who were entitled before 1996 continued to be entitled after, whether they were, or were not, issue; and whether, if there were issue, they were, or were not, issue of the surviving spouse. What *did* happen was that the statutory legacy was again increased. The principal change in 1953 had been the big increase in the statutory legacy, now there was another. There had, of course, been other increases in the intervening years, but in 1993,[28] there was an increase at about twice the general rate of inflation. The figures for the statutory legacy had last been raised in 1987, when they had been £75,000 if the deceased left issue and

[26] An example of this is *Re Callaghan* [1985] Fam 1, where property which came from the claimant's father and paternal grandfather passed to the claimant's mother, his father's widow; then, on her death intestate, to her second husband, the claimant's step father; and, on his death intestate, to the step father's sisters. So the effect of the intestacy rules was to bypass the claimant, passing property which came from his father's family to his step father's sisters.

[27] See Section 8 below.

[28] This 1993 increase, which came into force in December 1993, was effected by the Family Provision (Intestate Succession) Order 1993 (SI 1993/2906). It was technically separate from the Law Reform (Succession) Act 1995, but was part of the same package.

£125,000 if he did not. After the 1993 increase, they were £125,000 if there were issue and £200,000 where there were none.[29]

4. The 2005 Consultation Paper

Nothing further happened until June 2005, when the Ministry of Justice[30] produced a Consultation Paper entitled *Administration of Estates—Review of the Statutory Legacy*.[31] This seems to have been a thinly disguised attempt to re-enact the Law Commission's 1989 proposal that the surviving spouse should receive the whole estate. At the heart of this 2005 Consultation Paper was an account of the potential problems faced by surviving spouses who risked being evicted from their houses by the deceased's children. In order to overcome the problem, it was suggested that the statutory legacy should now be more than doubled in real terms, so that where the deceased had issue it would be raised from £125,000 to £350,000, and where there were no issue, it would go up from £200,000 to £650,000.[32] The authors of the Consultation Paper justified the suggestion that the statutory legacy needed to undergo such a huge revision by pointing to the rise in house prices; and implied that, unless the statutory legacy were increased in line with house-price inflation (as opposed to general inflation), there was a danger that the surviving spouses of deceased intestates would not be able to afford to remain in what had been their matrimonial homes. Visions were conjured up of aged widows and widowers being ejected from their houses by their granite-hearted offspring. What was interesting about this Consultation Paper was that (i) it contained erroneous statistics, and (ii) almost nobody noticed.

When attempting to calculate the statistical probability that the statutory legacy will, or will not, be sufficient to permit a surviving spouse to remain in what was the matrimonial home,[33] it will be necessary, inter alia, to calculate what

[29] Between 1987 and 1993, the retail prices index rose by about 33%. The 1993 increases to the statutory legacy were close to 66%.

[30] In 2005, the body which began the consultation process was called 'The Department for Constitutional Affairs'. It had been created in 2003 to replace the Lord Chancellor's Department and then, in 2007, it was enlarged and was renamed 'The Ministry of Justice'. To avoid confusion, it is in the main text referred to as 'Ministry of Justice' throughout.

[31] Department for Constitutional Affairs, *Administration of Estates—Review of the Statutory Legacy* (CP 11/05, 7 June 2005).

[32] This was a tripling in nominal terms, and more than a doubling in real terms. Between 1993 and 2005, the retail prices index had risen by about another 33% (*cf* already n 29 above). The rate of inflation was now lower than it had been in the period before 1993.

[33] One could, at this point, enter into a discussion as to whether it is generally beneficial to attempt to give widows and widowers a chance to remain in what were previously their homes, after one of them has died, or whether it might not assist in replenishing the housing stock if the survivor were encouraged to move. This is probably not the place for that discussion, but the assumption that a widow or widower should, for some reason, be encouraged to stay on in what might now be an unnecessarily large dwelling is not necessarily one which should go unchallenged. Those who wrote the Consultation Paper appeared to have had no appreciation of this point.

percentage of cases involve deceased married intestates who were the sole owners of the houses in which they lived, because these are the cases where the survivor is likely to find that the statutory legacy will be insufficient to cover the value of the house. The Consultation Paper stated—correctly—that the price of housing had, since 1993, risen by much more than the general rate of inflation. But the problem with this argument in favour of another huge rise in the statutory legacy was that it pre-supposed that the deceased, and he alone, owned the matrimonial home. The Consultation Paper made it seem as though approximately 35 per cent of married persons who died intestate in England and Wales were the sole owners of the houses in which they lived. This was nonsense: the correct figure was approximately six per cent. The analysis of the calculations which demonstrated this error was set out in an article written shortly after the Consultation Paper appeared[34] and the Ministry of Justice, when publishing their Response[35] to the 2005 Consultation, had to admit the mistake. The corrected figures showed that 80 per cent of those who die intestate are, in fact, beneficial joint tenants.[36] If a married couple are beneficial joint tenants of the house in which they live at the time when the first of them dies intestate, the survivor will take the house before any calculation needs to be made as to his or her entitlement to the statutory legacy. The statutory legacy will, in the vast majority of cases like this, considerably exceed the value of the part of the deceased's estate which passes under the intestacy rules, because it will not include the jointly owned property. So, a proper examination of the figures produced for the Consultation Paper ended up by demonstrating almost the exact opposite of what it had set out to prove. The vast majority of surviving spouses living in owner-occupied housing were, because of the inter-action of the *jus accrescendi* with the intestacy rules, getting a very generous deal.

The 2005 Consultation Paper had been designed to prepare the way for a huge increase in the statutory legacy. Those who had drafted the Paper had wanted to increase it from £125,000 to £350,000 where there were issue, and from £200,000 to £650,000 where there were no issue. After the discovery of the errors in the mathematics, the statutory legacy was raised, in February 2009,[37] to £250,000 where there were issue and to £450,000 where there were no issue.

[34] R Kerridge, 'Reform of the Law of Succession: the Need for Change, Not Piecemeal Tinkering' (2007) 71 *Conv* 47.

[35] There is a three-page Appendix B to the Response to the Consultation Paper in which the Ministry of Justice acknowledged that their figures had been misleading. How the errors came to be made was never properly explained. Lawyers in England are notoriously bad at sums, but it is surprising (i) that such serious errors were made in the first place and (ii) that they almost escaped notice. The figures in the Consultation Paper were complicated, but whoever compiled them should have seen what was wrong.

[36] The corrected figures, agreed in a three-page Annex B to the Ministry of Justice Response to the 2005 Consultation (itself undated, but published in 2008), showed that approximately 80% of those who died married and intestate were beneficial joint tenants of the houses in which they lived, only 6% were sole owners, another 6% were tenants (non-owners), 5% were beneficial tenants in common, and 3% were non-owners survived by spouses who were sole owners.

[37] By the Family Provision (Intestate Succession) Order 2009 (SI 2009/135).

The 2009 rises in the statutory legacy were much smaller than the Ministry of Justice had originally suggested.[38] But this led on to the next round of suggested reforms. The Ministry then asked the Law Commission to consider a project to review the law of intestacy and family provision. A Law Commission Consultation Paper was published in October 2009,[39] and this was followed in December 2011 by a Report, *Intestacy and Family Provision Claims on Death*.[40]

5. The Surviving Spouse's Entitlement—The Law Commission's 2011 Report

As in 1989, the principal focus of the Law Commission's 2011 Report was on the spouse's entitlement. In 1989, the Commission had recommended that the spouse should, in all cases, inherit the entire estate. That recommendation had not been adopted. This time, as well as making recommendations in relation to cohabitants[41] and as well as suggesting a number of minor reforms,[42] the Law Commission took a different approach. It now recommended that, where there were no issue, the spouse should take the entire estate. So, the spouse would no longer share with the deceased's parents, or brothers or sisters. But where there were issue (whom the Law Commission, using more up-to-date English, preferred to call 'descendants'), it suggested that the existing system should continue, except that the spouse should take her half of the balance of the estate absolutely, rather than for life.

The real problem area remained, as it has always been, the case where the issue are not the issue of the surviving spouse. The 2011 proposals included no special provision for dealing with this; all they did was to make things very slightly worse.[43] There is no doubt that many of those who responded to the Law Commission's 2009 Consultation Paper were unhappy, and a number of different alternative ways of dealing with the problem were suggested. One way of dismissing them was to make them sound both too varied and over-complicated. It is true that there are many ways in which one could, in theory, give some sort of extra priority to issue who are not issue of the surviving spouse, but listing them separately and then dismissing each, one at a time (making the whole exercise seem tedious),

[38] General inflation in the period between 1993 and 2005 had been about 33% (*cf* n 32 above), and in the period between 1993 and 2009 it was roughly 50%. In 2009, the statutory legacy was doubled (ie 100% increase) where there were issue and more than doubled where there were no issue. These were large real increases, but not remotely as large as the Consultation Paper had called for.

[39] Law Commission, *Intestacy and Family Provision Claims on Death: A Consultation Paper* (Law Com CP No 191, 2009).

[40] 2011 Report (n 1 above).

[41] See Section 11 below.

[42] See Section 10.2 below.

[43] Very slightly worse, in that the spouse was now getting a very slightly enhanced entitlement—with no special provision made for the case where she was not the parent of the deceased's children.

was the tactic adopted by the Law Commission when—as it seems it had always wanted to—it discarded them. In doing this, it had also to disregard the findings of a survey of public opinion (the Nuffield Survey) which it had itself commissioned, but this will be discussed further below.[44]

If it were to be suggested that different rules might apply where the surviving spouse is not the parent of the deceased's children (or not of all of them) it would first have to be decided whether to differentiate between the case where some of the children were not those of the survivor, or whether a line should be drawn at the point where none of the children were hers, or whether two separate lines should be drawn. It has been suggested above[45] that if one line is to be drawn (and it is suggested that *at least* one should be), it should be between the case where some or all of the children are hers on the one hand, and where none of them are on the other. Once the line has been drawn, the question then becomes: how might the widow who is not the parent of any of the deceased's children be treated differently from one who is the parent of some of them?

There are a number of ways of treating the spouse who is not the parent of the deceased's children less generously than one who is, and two of these are relatively straightforward. One is to give such a spouse a smaller statutory legacy. A version of this is to be found in the United States' Uniform Probate Code (the 'UPC') which differentiates between (i) the case where the deceased and his surviving spouse have issue in common and neither has any other issue; (ii) the case where all the deceased's issue are issue of his surviving spouse, but she also has other issue; and (iii) the case where the deceased leaves issue who are not issue of the surviving spouse. This division (into three categories, rather than simply two, as was suggested above) could appear to be over-complicated, but the Code gives the entire estate to the surviving spouse in case (i) above (ie where the deceased and his surviving spouse have issue in common and neither has any other issue), and so its operation in this case (i) is as simple as possible. Taken as a whole, therefore, the UPC system is not complicated. The Law Commission's Report referred to the Code but did not explain properly how it operated and emphasised what the Report suggested were the difficulties attached to case (ii). A slightly simpler version of the UPC scheme was proposed to the Law Commission by Farrer & Co, a leading firm of solicitors in the field of private client work.[46] The two proposals should have been discussed together, but the Law Commission's Report discussed Farrer & Co's proposal in paragraph 2.72 (the same paragraph in which

[44] The Nuffield Survey is discussed in Section 7 below. And it is not only the views of respondents to surveys which demonstrate that second marriages cause particular problems. There have been two recent mutual wills cases where the courts have gone out of their way to find mutual wills, almost certainly to protect the interests of the issue of an earlier union: *Fry v Densham-Smith* [2010] EWCA Civ 1410, [2011] WTLR 387; *Shovelar v Lane* [2011] EWCA Civ 802, [2012] 1 WLR 637. The courts, like the respondents to the survey, appear to understand that interests of the issue of an earlier marriage should not be entirely subordinated to those of a later spouse. Mutual wills are discussed by Ying Khai Liew in Ch 5 of this volume.

[45] See Section 3, especially the text around and following n 25 above.

[46] Some would say *the* leading firm. The identity of Farrer's best known client gives the firm particular cachet.

it discussed a quite different proposal by the writer of the present chapter),[47] and then went on to discuss the Uniform Probate Code in paragraph 2.78. Whether or not this was designed to confuse the reader, it must have had that effect.

The Law Commission's Report not only downplayed the significance of the Uniform Probate Code and of the fact that a number of American States have now adopted rules which give a smaller share of an intestate's estate to the spouse who is not the parent of his children than to one who is, but it also failed to note that the principle of distinguishing between the surviving spouse of a deceased who is the parent of (some of) his children and one who is not, and of giving the latter a smaller share of the estate, has been adopted in Australia (with New South Wales taking the lead), by the Nordic countries (particularly Sweden), by France and by the Netherlands. These countries are all facing up to the problems created by what one writer has called 'the multiple-marriage' society.[48] Their approach is neither old fashioned, nor discriminatory, and references in the Commission's Report to 'penalising'[49] the surviving spouse who is not the parent of the deceased's children were tendentious. If, whether under a will or on intestacy, it is decided that, for some reason, X should get more, and that therefore Y should get less, that is not a question of penalties. A sensible discussion involves weighing up the probable wishes of the deceased, the needs of the members of his family who survive him, and the probabilities as to the likely future destination of the property involved.

It was said above that there are at least two ways of treating the spouse who is not the parent of the deceased's children less generously than one who is. The first of these has just been discussed; it is to give the non-parental spouse a smaller statutory legacy than that given to the parental spouse. The other way was suggested, 20 years ago, by the present writer when discussing the Law Commission's 1989 Report. The writer suggested then that, where someone died intestate leaving a spouse and issue, but none of the issue were the issue of the spouse, the spouse should take only a life interest.[50] The objection to this approach is that it is said to be complicated. Maybe—but second or subsequent marriages, where there are issue from earlier unions, always lead either to complications or to unfairness.

In 1989 the Law Commission proposed giving the spouse the entire estate in all circumstances. That proposal met with opposition and was not adopted. But the movement since has been in the direction of getting to the same result by a more roundabout route. The Law Commission's 2011 Report proposed that the surviving spouse should (i) where there are no surviving issue, take the entire estate; and (ii) where there are surviving issue, take (as before) the personal chattels and the statutory legacy, and also an absolute interest in half the residue,

[47] See n 50 and accompanying text below.
[48] See fn 42 on p 41 of the 2011 Report (n 1 above) para 2.67.
[49] See ibid para 2.77.
[50] R Kerridge, 'Distribution on Intestacy: The Law Commission's Report' (1990) 54 *Conv* 358.

as opposed to taking only a life interest in half the residue, as he or she had taken since 1953. How much difference do these two changes actually make?

There were a number of things missing from the 2011 Report, and one of them was statistics. It is, of course, possible that the errors in the statistics in the 2005 Consultation Paper[51] led those who were drafting the Report into a form of self-denying ordinance. As the compilation of statistics could involve errors, there would be no more statistics. If the Ministry of Justice could not be trusted to get them right, the Law Commission would avoid them. But compiling inaccurate statistics at one stage in a debate is hardly an excuse for avoiding all statistics at a later stage in the same debate. Accurate statistics are important; they help to put suggested reforms in context.

6. Some Statistics

There are three sets of statistics which should be of assistance in any discussion concerning the reform of the intestacy rules. First, it would be useful to know what percentage of those who die each year in England and Wales die testate and what percentage die intestate. Then, given the way in which the intestacy rules have been operating, given their possible reform, and given that the spouse might (or might not) be asked to share with other members of the deceased's family, it would be helpful to be know what percentage of deceased persons who die leaving surviving spouses have estates of a size which require the survivor to share with others. In other words, at the time of the 2011 Report, what percentage of intestates who died leaving a spouse and issue left estates which were big enough to give the issue an interest? And what percentage of intestates who died leaving a spouse and no issue, but leaving parents or brothers or sisters (or their issue), left estates which were big enough to give the parents, or brothers or sisters, an interest? The Law Commission's Report did not set out any of these figures.

6.1. What Percentage of Those Who Die, Die Intestate?

Although the Law Commission's 2011 Report did not set out any of these figures, it is possible to attempt a rough calculation as to what percentage of those who die each year in England and Wales die testate, and what percentage die intestate. It seems generally to be assumed that a significant majority die intestate, but the assumption appears to be wrong. The latest statistics are for 2013, but the percentages have been much the same each year for the past few years. In 2013, 506,790 deaths were registered, but there were only 203,546 grants of probate,

[51] See Section 4 above.

17,496 grants of letters of administration with wills annexed, and 39,927 ordinary grants of letters of administration. A grant of probate means that the deceased left a will, appointed executors, and that they obtained probate. A grant of letters of administration with a will annexed means that he failed to appoint executors, or that the executors failed to act, but it means that he *did* leave a will. The grants of probate should be added to the cases of letters of administration with wills annexed, because these are all correctly classified as 'with a will' cases. So there were a total of 221,042[52] cases where the deceased died leaving a valid will. Then there are the 39,927 cases where the deceased died intestate and letters of administration were obtained. That makes a grand total of 260,969.[53] What happened to all the others? 260,969 is just over 50 per cent of the 506,790 who died that year. Of course, someone may die in one year, and probate or letters of administration may be obtained a year or so later, but this does not explain a distortion on this scale. Some will be those whose only property was held by them as beneficial joint tenants and so passed by way of the *jus accrescendi*,[54] they are a group at the size of which it is difficult to guess. Again, some cases where there has been a failure to obtain probate or letters of administration may involve attempted tax evasion. But the overall impression must be that the missing cases (the missing 50 per cent odd) generally represent deceased persons who had little or no property to leave. One may assume that the vast majority of them died intestate, but *also* that they had little property (apart from what they held as beneficial joint tenants).[55] If one then turns back to look at the 50 per cent odd in respect of whom probate or letters of administration were taken out, the surprise is that the overwhelming majority of them died testate, 221,042 left wills and a mere 39,927 were confirmed intestacies. So, almost 85 per cent of those in respect of whose estates grants of probate or letters of administration were taken out died testate.

Contrary to what seems generally to be assumed, the vast majority of those who, in England and Wales, die leaving property of any significant value, choose to make wills. Intestacy is relatively unusual for those who have property of value. It is true that, within the population as a whole, most people have not made wills, but those who have not made them include both those who have nothing much to leave and those who are unlikely to die in the near future. In spite of the fact that both the Law Society[56] and charities[57] spend much time and money in reminding

[52] 203,546 + 17,496 = 221,042.

[53] 221,042 + 39,927 = 260,969.

[54] Someone who acquires property as a beneficial joint tenant, and who has been properly advised (all those who acquire as beneficial joint tenants should understand the succession effects) is, when he acquires the property, engaged in creating a form of will substitute.

[55] The only property which should pass without a grant of probate or letters of administration will be (i) jointly owned property, (ii) chattels, and (iii) low value property passing under a statutory nomination (rare nowadays). Pension rights have to be regarded as a special case because, largely for tax reasons, a would-be pensioner does not usually have a beneficial interest in his share of his pension fund. For a discussion of pension death benefits, see Alexandra Braun's contribution in Ch 10 of this volume.

[56] The Law Society has an interest in promoting the preparation of wills by its members.

[57] Charities in England promote will-making in the expectation that testators will leave property to them.

the public about the dangers of intestacy, and about how prevalent it is, much of what they say is misleading. When the 2014 Bill was being discussed in a House of Commons Committee on 3 March 2014, the Minister of State at the Ministry of Justice, in answer to a question from a member of the Committee, said that one third of deaths in England were 'registered as intestate',[58] but it was not clear how he arrived at this figure. It is somewhere between the figure for confirmed intestacies and the figure for those who have not obtained probate or letters of administration with wills annexed. There were no clear calculations, and such figures as were disclosed to the Committee were out of date. In any case, even if the figure for intestacies were as high as this, it seems to be a much lower one than most commentators would have assumed. What does seem to be clear is that most of those who die in England and Wales and who are the owners of property of value do not die intestate.[59] That is not a reason for suggesting that it does not matter how the intestacy rules operate, but it may indicate that most of those who die with estates worth inheriting do not believe that the intestacy rules would accurately reflect their intentions.

6.2. What Percentage of the Spouses of Deceased Intestates Do Not Inherit their Entire Estates?

Then there is the question as to what percentage of spouses who survive their intestate husbands or wives have to share the deceased's estate with anyone else. There were no statistics in the Law Commission's Report but, when the 2014 Bill was being discussed in Commons Committee on 3 March 2014, the Minister of State told the Committee that about 10 per cent of those who died intestate did so leaving property worth more than £250,000 and about two per cent left property worth in excess of £450,000.[60] The figures of £250,000 and £450,000 were the figures for the statutory legacy: £250,000 if there were issue, and £450,000 if there were no issue. What the Minister of State was saying was that in less than 10 per cent of cases where the deceased left a spouse and issue would the issue take anything, and in less than two per cent of cases where the deceased left a spouse and no issue would anyone other than the spouse take anything. Put another way, the change whereby the estate of a deceased who leaves a spouse and no issue will pass in its entirety to the spouse after the 2014 changes have taken effect is likely

[58] Second Reading Committee, 3 March 2014, Simon Hughes MP at cols 10–11. Minutes of the committee meeting are available online via: www.publications.parliament.uk/pa/cm201314/cmpublic/inheritance/140303/pm/140303s01.htm (last accessed 20 November 2015).

[59] See also fn 2 in Ch 2 of this volume, where Rebecca Probert notes that two thirds of those over the age of 65 in this country *have* made wills.

[60] Second Reading Committee (n 58 above), Simon Hughes MP at cols 5 and 13. It seems that, at this stage, the Minister was anxious to assure the Committee that the changes to the intestacy rules were not going to amount to much.

to impact on less than two per cent[61] of those who do die leaving a spouse and no issue, and the change to the rules which apply where the spouse has died leaving a spouse and issue will be likely to affect less than 10 per cent of those who so die. The change which was proposed by the Law Commission in 2011 to cover the situation where the intestate left a spouse and no issue was virtually no change at all. The statutory legacy had already reached such a figure that more than 98 per cent[62] of those who were in theory affected were in practice not so affected.

7. The Nuffield Survey

Before moving away from statistics, it is appropriate to say something about the Nuffield Survey. Prompted by the wish of the Commission to have up to date information on public attitudes to intestacy and inheritance, the Nuffield Foundation funded a programme of research and this involved seeking the views of over 1,500 respondents to a series of questions about what should happen to someone's property if he died intestate.[63] When considering the results of the Survey, the Law Commission stated that, in the case where the deceased leaves a spouse and also children who are not the spouse's children, '[i]t is only where there are no children from the second marriage that support [from respondents to the survey] for prioritising the second spouse falls below 50 per cent'.[64] That was literally correct, but misleading. Where there were no children from the second marriage, only 15 per cent of the respondents would have given all to the second wife;[65] 31 per cent would have given priority to the wife; 35 per cent would have wanted the wife and children to share (presumably, more or less equally); 13 per cent would have given priority to the children; five per cent would have given everything to the children; and one per cent would have opted for 'other'. So, only 15 per cent of respondents would have favoured giving all to the spouse. But the figures supplied to the Commons Committee by the Minister of State in March 2014 show that that is what is going to happen in 90 per cent of cases.[66]

[61] The figure is 'less than' 2% because, even before the 2014 changes took effect, not all those of the 2% who died leaving a spouse but no issue also left next-of-kin eligible to share with the spouse. At a rough guess, the correct figure was probably close to 1%.

[62] Why 'more than' 98%? See the comment in n 61 immediately above. And the fact that the figure was nearer 99% when the statutory legacy stood at £450,000 must mean that it would have been much more still had the figures in the 2005 Consultation Paper been enacted. To suggest that the 2005 Consultation Paper was primarily designed to give the spouse everything does not seem to be an exaggeration.

[63] See A Humphrey, L Mills and others, *Inheritance and the Family: Attitudes to Will-Making and Intestacy* (Report published by the National Centre for Social Research, London, August 2010), Executive Summary and Tables 4.7 and 7.3. The respondents' answers varied according to the ages of the children and the ages of the respondents themselves. The respondents who were most pro-second spouse were the middle aged; those who were older or younger tended to be more biased towards the children.

[64] 2011 Report (n 1 above) para 2.82.

[65] She is described as 'a wife' not 'a spouse'.

[66] The Law Commission seemed to give greater emphasis to the findings of the Nuffield Survey in relation to the entitlement of cohabitants than in relation to the entitlement of children of earlier unions.

The 2011 Law Commission Report, and the enactment of its proposals relating to spouses in 2014, *were* therefore the finishing of unfinished business left over from 1989. But that brings us back to something else which was proposed in 1989, was enacted in 1995, and which would—it is suggested—have been better not enacted: the abolition of hotchpot.

8. Hotchpot

Where someone died totally or partially intestate, on or before 31 December 1995, three hotchpot rules might have applied. The principle behind hotchpot was that beneficiaries should not benefit more than once. The first of the three rules was ancient and its inclusion in the Administration of Estates Act 1925 was confirmation of it. The second rule was added in 1925, and the third in 1952.

8.1. Hotchpot on Total or Partial Intestacy—Lifetime Advancements to Children

The first and main hotchpot rule—which applied on total or partial intestacy—was based on the maxim that 'equality is equity' and that children should not take the same benefit twice. The rule had a long history and went back to the time before the enactment of the Statute of Distribution 1670. It was given statutory form as section 3 of the 1670 Statute, and re-enacted as section 47(1)(iii) of the Administration of Estates Act 1925. It required 'any money or property which, by way of advancement or on the marriage of a child of the intestate, ha[d] been paid to such child by the intestate' to be brought into account on the division of his residuary estate into shares under the statutory trusts. This rule applied only to gifts to *children*, and it applied only where the gift was *by way of advancement or on the marriage of the child.* A gift by way 'of advancement' implied that it was to make permanent provision for the child.

8.2. Hotchpot on Partial Intestacy—Benefits Given by the Will to the Issue

Section 49(1)(a) of the Administration of Estates Act 1925[67] required beneficial interests acquired by 'any *issue* of the deceased' *under his will* to be brought into hotchpot on a partial intestacy. The section was badly drafted,[68] and there was a

[67] As amended by the Intestates' Estates Act 1952.

[68] 'As bad a piece of draftmanship as one could conceive, in many respects': *Re Morton* [1956] Ch 644 (Ch) 647 (Danckwerts J); 'great difficulties of language': *Re Grover's Will Trust* [1971] Ch 168 (Ch) 174 (Pennycuick J). See also EC Ryder, 'Hotchpot on a Partial Intestacy' (1973) 26 *Current Legal Problems* 208.

particular problem[69] where the intestate had bequeathed property to one of his grandchildren under his will and that grandchild had a brother or sister who had not benefited under the will.[70]

8.3. Hotchpot on Partial Intestacy—Benefits Given by the Will to the Surviving Spouse

Section 49(1)(aa) of the 1925 Act—inserted by the Intestates' Estates Act 1952 to compensate for the significant increase in the statutory legacy payable to the spouse—enacted that a surviving spouse who acquired any beneficial interests under the deceased's will (other than personal chattels) was not entitled to the full amount of the statutory legacy under the intestacy rules. Instead, the surviving spouse took the statutory legacy *less* the value, at the deceased's death, of such beneficial interests.

The application of the hotchpot rules was excluded by a contrary intention on the part of the deceased, 'expressed or appearing from the circumstances of the case'.[71]

8.4. Abolition of the Hotchpot Rules

The 1989 Law Commission Report recommended that all three hotchpot rules should be repealed. This recommendation was carried into effect by section 1(2) of the Law Reform (Succession) Act 1995 which applies to all intestates dying on or after 1 January 1996. But did it make sense to repeal these rules?

The hotchpot rules appear, during the latter part of the twentieth century, to have been regarded as complicated, and largely irrelevant, remnants from an earlier age. But there were three separate rules, and insofar as there were proposals for modification or repeal, it is submitted that the three rules should have been considered separately. The main hotchpot rule was a fundamentally sensible rule based on the intestate's presumed intention and on the maxim that 'equality is equity'. It is true that it would apply only where there were significant lifetime gifts (or gifts on marriage) followed by the donor's intestacy, and that donors who make significant lifetime gifts are not the kind of people who usually die intestate; but in the sorts of situation where it did apply, it was fair. It was suspected in some circles that, at the time when it applied, many practitioners overlooked it. But it was not a good reason for abolishing the rule that practitioners dealing with

[69] It was much discussed in class—to the dismay of generations of succession students.

[70] This was because of the way in which s 49 referred across to s 47; the two sections were not entirely compatible.

[71] Administration of Estates Act 1925, s 47(1)(iii).

intestacies either do not know the law and/or cannot be bothered to make the relevant enquiries.

And there is an oddity in relation to the abolition of the main hotchpot rule. The rule was abolished for intestacies as from 1 January 1996, but its sister rule, the rule which applies to wills, still operates. The rule which applies to wills is not *called* 'hotchpot', but forms part of the 'equitable presumption of satisfaction'—the 'presumption against double portions' and the 'presumption that legacies are satisfied by portions'.[72] These are all different forms of the same rule, based on the maxim that 'equality is equity'. Suppose that a father, a widower, makes a will leaving his entire estate to his two children in equal shares and then makes a substantial lifetime gift to one of them; prima facie, the equitable presumption of satisfaction applies and the value of the gift is taken into account on the father's death. The same would have happened if the father had died intestate before 1996. But if the father dies *intestate* on or after 1 January 1996, the hotchpot rule will not apply—so there is an arbitrary distinction between the case of the testate and the intestate parent. The main hotchpot rule was not 'old fashioned' or arbitrary. It may have been a rule which did not apply very often, but when it did apply it was fair.

The second hotchpot rule—the one which was introduced in 1926 and covered benefits given by the will to issue—was badly drafted; but the cure for bad draftsmanship is redrafting, not abolition.

As to the third hotchpot rule—the one which dealt with benefits given by the will on a partial intestacy to the surviving spouse—the Law Commission's 1989 Report recommended abolition; but this recommendation was based on the supposition that the Commission's main recommendation, that the surviving spouse should inherit the whole of the intestate's estate, would be accepted and put into effect. If the main recommendation had been put into effect, this third hotchpot rule would have become redundant. This third rule was introduced in 1953 precisely to cover the significant increases then being made in the statutory legacy. If the system of sharing the estate between the spouse and any other members of the family (ie issue) is to be retained, and if the statutory legacy is to remain set at a generous level, which it certainly is, there was no logic in scrapping this provision in 1996.

And, given that the main recommendation from the 1989 Report was not enacted, it is arguable that, far from being repealed, the third hotchpot rule should have been extended: by enacting that it should cover not only property passing to the spouse under the will, but also the value of any property which vests in the surviving spouse as a surviving joint tenant under the *jus accrescendi*, the right of survivorship. This would be of particular significance in cases where the issue are

[72] See R Kerridge, *Hawkins on the Construction of Wills*, 5th edn (London, Sweet & Maxwell, 2000) 429–31. See also *Re Cameron* [1999] Ch 386 (Ch); *Re Clapham, Barraclough v Mell* [2005] EWHC 3387 (Ch), [2006] WTLR 203; *Evans v HSBC Trust Co* [2005] WTLR 1289 (Ch).

not the issue of the surviving spouse and would have extra relevance if, at some stage, the Farrer & Co/Uniform Probate Code proposal, whereby the surviving spouse who was not the parent of the deceased's children should receive a smaller statutory legacy than one who was,[73] were to be adopted. In such a case, if the survivor were to take any interest in property by way of the *jus accrescendi*, it would be totally consistent to deduct from the (smaller) statutory legacy the value of property so passing.[74] This reform will not be introduced for the time being, but it is hoped that it will be put on the table for further discussion at a later date.

9. Void Marriages—Manufactured Intestacy

Having considered a topic which is part of the law of intestacy and to which the Law Commission paid less attention than it deserved, it is now time to look at a topic to which the Commission paid no attention at all. This concerns what happens when someone who lacks mental capacity marries. It is an intestacy problem because the marriage revokes any existing will and, if the bride or bridegroom fails to make another will after the marriage (as, virtually certainly, she or he will), she or he will die intestate and her or his spouse will take the very generous provision made for a spouse under the intestacy rules.

The problem has arisen as follows. Until 1971, it was generally thought that a marriage without consent was void. This was assumed in *Re Park*,[75] though the position was not completely clear. Doubts were increased by the enactment of section 9(1)(b) of the Matrimonial Causes Act 1965, which made at least some cases of incapacity voidable. The section was discussed in *Bennett v Bennett*,[76] where Ormrod J took the view that there was substantial overlap between the test for a void marriage and the test under section 9 for one which was voidable. In addition to the doubts concerning the void/voidable question, there was also uncertainty as to the effect of a decree of annulment on a voidable marriage. Was it retrospective? It was generally thought that it was and that, once the decree had been granted, the marriage would be treated as never having existed. But, again, there were doubts.

In 1970, The Law Commission published its *Report on Nullity of Marriage*.[77] There were, unsurprisingly, no succession lawyers on the Commission. The Report suggested that incapacity should lead to a marriage's being voidable, rather than void, and, having described the consequences of a decree of annulment on a

[73] See the text accompanying nn 45–47 above.

[74] Where a couple are married and have children by earlier unions, they should not, of course, if properly advised, hold property as beneficial joint tenants. But they are not always properly advised.

[75] *Re Park* [1954] P 112 (CA).

[76] *Bennett v Bennett* [1969] 1 WLR 430 (PDA).

[77] Law Commission, *Family Law, Report on Nullity of Marriage* (Law Com No 33, 1970).

voidable marriage as being 'uncertain and inconvenient', the Commission went on to suggest that, when a voidable marriage was annulled, the decree should *not* be retrospective. The Commission's recommendations were then enacted by the Nullity of Marriage Act 1971. Nobody seems to have considered the succession implications of these changes to the law, but the problems they had created came to light, less than 10 years later in *Re Roberts*,[78] where the Court of Appeal upheld a decision of Walton J to the effect that a man who had lacked testamentary capacity at the time of his marriage, had (by it) revoked an earlier will, and so when he died 18 months later, he was intestate. As his receiver had taken no steps to annul the marriage while the man was alive, his widow took his estate. The Court of Appeal were not enthusiastic about the result, but the 1971 Act had made it inevitable.

The topic was then discussed in the Law Reform Committee's 22nd Report on *The Making and Revocation of Wills*,[79] which was completed two years after *Roberts*, in 1980. This Report suggested that those who would have benefited under a will revoked by the marriage of someone who, at the time of the marriage, lacked testamentary capacity should be given a remedy under the Family Provision legislation. Nothing then happened, and the whole matter seems to have been forgotten. It should not have been. The suggestion in the 22nd Report should have been discussed further and either enacted, or replaced by something better; the problem was serious.

The timing was unfortunate. The *Roberts* case demonstrated the problem, but the facts do not appear to have been particularly shocking. A case which showed how serious the position had now become was *Re Davey*,[80] where the first instance hearing took place one month after the 22nd Report had been completed. The deceased in *Davey* was a 92-year-old woman who went through a Register Office ceremony of marriage, at a time when she was not even capable of signing her own name. Her bridegroom was less than half her age and a friend of the matron in the nursing home where she was being looked after. The witnesses were linked to the matron. If anyone were to have any doubts about the wrongdoing in *Davey*, such doubts should be allayed by noting that this same nursing home also appeared in another succession case at almost the same time. In *Re Stott*,[81] Lady Stott, another guest in the same place, made a will in favour of the matron.[82] The characters were the same, though they played different roles. The matron arranged the marriage in *Davey*, but benefited in *Stott*. The husband in *Davey* acted as the go-between for the giving of the will instructions in *Stott*, and would have benefited in *Davey*. In fact, he failed to benefit in *Davey* because the 92-year-old woman's family

[78] *Re Roberts* [1978] 1 WLR 653 (CA).

[79] Law Reform Committee, *Twenty-Second Report: The Making and Revocation of Wills* (Cmnd 7902, 1980).

[80] *Re Davey* [1981] 1 WLR 164 (Ch).

[81] *Re Stott* [1980] 1 WLR 246 (Ch).

[82] That will was refused probate for lack of knowledge and approval—recent cases on this topic are addressed by Penelope Reed in Ch 7 of this volume. See also Brian Sloan's contribution in Ch 8 analysing the reversal of testamentary dispositions made in favour of informal carers.

discovered about the 'marriage' just before her death and were able, with days to spare, to arrange for the execution of a statutory will which undid the effects of the marriage. It is not clear exactly how the family of the victim in *Davey* discovered about her marriage. It seems likely that they found out about what had happened as a result of a falling out between the matron and the husband. Had that not happened, they would have known nothing until it was too late to take any action. The facts in the case are exceptional in a number of ways, not the least of which is that the 'nursing home' was actually a mansion flat in a fashionable part of West London.

Returning to the main point, given that the proposal put forward in the 22nd Report has not been enacted, and given that no other provision has been put in place to overcome the problem of what might be called the 'manufactured intestacy' which occurs whenever a person who lacks capacity goes through a ceremony of marriage, how many cases have there been during the period since the 1971 Act came into force where persons who would have benefited under wills have lost their entitlement because the testator, having lost capacity, has then married? The answer must be that nobody knows. Provided that those who arranged the marriage can prevent the victim's friends and family from discovering what has happened until after her or his death, it will be too late to take any action. There will, in the ordinary course of events, be no litigation, no case report—simply victims with no remedy. A recent case where litigation was begun, but too late to undo the mischief, was *Morley-Clarke v Brooks*.[83] Mr Morley-Clarke married his Russian 'carer' after he had had a stroke, and when he was suffering from dementia and cancer. The carer/wife then returned to Russia, where she remained. The husband's sons tried to annul the marriage, but Mr Morley-Clarke died before they obtained a decree: another pantomime with an unhappy ending. This area of the law deserves serious and urgent attention, and its being missed by two Law Commission Reports dealing with intestacy is symptomatic of the manner in which the law of succession is being neglected.[84]

10. The Inheritance and Trustees' Powers Act 2014

On 21 March 2013, the Government announced acceptance of the recommendations concerning intestacy[85] contained in the 2011 Law Commission Report, and the Inheritance and Trustees' Powers Bill 2013–14, a bill designed to implement the reforms suggested by Report other than those relating to cohabitants, was

[83] *Morley-Clarke v Brooks* [2011] WTLR 297 (Ch).

[84] And for a recent case on 'qualified' capacity, see *A v X* [2012] EWHC 2400 (COP), [2013] WTLR 187, where it was held that a man who was unable to manage his affairs had sufficient capacity to marry his carer (whom he had known for three months).

[85] Though not those concerning cohabitants.

introduced in the House of Lords on 30 July under the House of Lords procedure for Law Commission bills. It received the royal assent on 14 May 2014 and came into force on 1 October 2014. Those who are cynical about the recommendations, and who consider them too spouse-centred, may wonder to what extent there was a subconscious desire by government to ensure that property remains in, or is put into, the possession of the older generation.[86] The advantage of this, to government, is linked to the funding of pensions and care for the aged.[87]

10.1. The 2014 Act—The Major Change

Section 1(2) of the 2014 Act amends section 46 of the Administration of Estates Act 1925 by inserting a new Table in section 46(1)(i). This alters the spouse's entitlement by giving her or him the deceased's entire estate in all cases where there are no issue, and half the residue (after the spouse has taken the personal chattels and the statutory legacy) absolutely, rather than for life, if there are issue. This has been described in the heading above as 'The Major Change'. It does appear, at first glance, as a major change, but it has already been explained that only a relatively small percentage of intestates will be affected by it—about one per cent of the estates of those who die leaving spouses but no issue, and less than 10 per cent of the estates of those who die leaving both spouses and issue. It is suggested that the change, such as it is, is poorly directed. It is not the change which should have been made.

10.2. The 2014 Act—Minor Changes

Apart from the major change referred to above, the 2014 Act made five further relatively minor changes to the intestacy rules. These five minor changes do, at least, all have the merit of being changes for the better.

10.2.1. The Rate of Interest on the Statutory Legacy

Section 1 subsections (3) and (4) change the manner of calculating the rate of interest on the statutory legacy. Before the 2014 amendment, the rate was fixed periodically, though at irregular intervals, and from 1983 to 2014 it had remained

[86] For an English law reform project, this was high speed. When perpetuities were being reformed, it took 11 years for the recommendations of the relevant Law Commission Report (Law Com No 251, 1998) to be enacted.

[87] FR Burns, 'Surviving Spouses, Surviving Children and the Reform of Total Intestacy Law in England and Scotland: Past, Present and Future' (2013) 33 *Legal Studies* 85 at 117: 'While governments and law commissions may acknowledge the importance of family relationships, they will be concerned about how to fund pensions and aged care'. And more property in the hands of the aged also means higher revenues from taxes on death.

unchanged at six per cent. Under section 46(1) of the Administration of Estates Act 1925, as amended in 2014, the rate of interest will be the Bank of England rate effective on the day of the intestate's death.

10.2.2. The Manner of Determining the Statutory Legacy

Section 2 of and Schedule 1 to the 2014 Act amend the manner of determining the statutory legacy. Between 1966 and 2009, this sum was adjusted every few years by statutory instrument.[88] Under Schedule 1A to the 1925 Act, as inserted in 2014, the statutory legacy will be reviewed whenever the consumer prices index has risen by more than 15 per cent since the previous review and it must, in any case, be reviewed every five years.[89] Unless the Lord Chancellor otherwise determines, it will then be increased by reference to the increase in the consumer prices index.

What is surprising here is that the opportunity was not taken to raise the statutory legacy on 1 October 2014 to coincide with the coming into force of the principal provisions of the 2014 Act, as five years had then passed since it was last set, in 2009.[90] Where the intestate leaves issue, it remains set at £250,000. It is free of inheritance tax[91] and costs.[92]

10.2.3. A New Definition of 'Personal Chattels'

Section 3 of the 2014 Act gives a new definition of 'personal chattels'. Before 2014, section 55(1)(x) of the 1925 Act defined them as

> carriages, horses, stable furniture and effects (not used for business purposes), motor cars and accessories (not used for business purposes), garden effects, domestic animals, plate, plated articles, linen, china, glass, books, pictures, prints, furniture, jewellery, articles of household or personal use or ornament, musical and scientific instruments and apparatus, wines, liquors and consumable stores, but do not include any chattels used at the death of the intestate for business purposes nor money or securities for money.

[88] Family Provision Act 1966, s 1.

[89] The introduction of five yearly reviews is not a major change. Between 1966 and 2014, there was only one period when there was a gap of more than six years between revisions of the statutory legacy (see n 17 above). The addition of a review where the consumer prices index rises by 15% was a late amendment to the Schedule, inserted as the 2014 Bill was being debated in the House of Lords.

[90] The writer of this chapter is not in favour of any further increases in the statutory legacy, but he is not being hypocritical in pointing out that there should have been one in 2014. The statutory legacy was raised for those dying on or after 1 February 2009 by the Family Provision (Intestate Succession) Order 2009 (SI 2009/135). The failure to arrange a 2014 increase appears to have been an oversight.

[91] Transfers between spouses are, in any case, normally free of inheritance tax: Inheritance Tax Act 1984, s 18.

[92] The Second Schedule to the Intestates' Estates Act 1952 also gives the surviving spouse a special right to *require* the personal representatives to appropriate the intestate's interest in a dwelling-house in which the surviving spouse was resident at the intestate's death (the matrimonial home): *Re Collins* [1975] 1 WLR 309 (Ch).

The revised section 55(1)(x) now says:

> 'Personal chattels' means tangible movable property, other than any such property which—
>
> consists of money or securities for money, or
>
> was used at the death of the intestate solely or mainly for business purposes, or
>
> was held at the death of the intestate solely as an investment.

The revised section, instead of attempting to list what *are* personal chattels, includes all tangible movable property *other than* money, securities for money, and chattels used solely or mainly for business purposes, or solely as an investment. There are few reported cases on the original section, and this probably indicates that it worked satisfactorily, but the new section is slightly clearer and is certainly wider, in that it gives to the spouse property which is used for business purposes but which is *not mainly* so used.

10.2.4. Adoption and Contingent Interests

Section 4 of the 2014 Act covers adoption and contingent interests. It enacts that if, immediately before an adoption, a child has, in the estate of his or her parent, any contingent interest other than a contingent interest in remainder, that interest shall not be affected by the adoption.[93] This deals with the situation where an infant child is adopted after his parent's death. The statutory trusts[94] operate to make the child's interest in his parent's estate contingent on reaching majority and, before the enactment of this section that meant that the child, on adoption, lost his interest in the estate. He will now no longer do so.

10.2.5. Unmarried Fathers

Section 18 of the Family Law Reform Act 1987 operates where someone dies intestate and his or her parents were not married to one another at the time of his birth. It permits the deceased's administrators to presume that the intestate was predeceased by his father and anyone else related to him only through his father. The presumption operates 'unless the contrary is shown'. When the predecessor section to section 18 was first enacted, most births outside marriage were sole registrations, not naming the father. Many more births outside marriage are now registered and the large majority are now joint registrations which do identify the father. Section 5 of the 2014 Act disapplies the section 18 presumption where the intestate's father is named on the official record of the deceased's birth. This amendment will be relevant only if the deceased dies leaving no spouse and no

[93] The section amends the Adoption and Children Act 2002.
[94] For the 'statutory trusts', see Section 10.3 below.

descendants, because only then could the father, or anyone else related to the deceased through him, have an interest in the estate.

10.3. The Statutory Trusts

Since 1926, the issue, and the uncles and aunts if they become entitled on an intestacy, take the deceased intestate's estate on 'the statutory trusts'. Under 'the statutory trusts', such of the intestate's children[95] as are living[96] at his death are beneficially entitled—if more than one, in equal shares—subject to two qualifications. First, subject to representation, ie subject to the rule that such of the issue of a deceased child as are living at the intestate's death take that child's share—if more than one, in equal shares—*per stirpes*.[97] Secondly, subject to the rule that no child or other issue[98] is entitled to a vested interest until he or she attains the age of 18 years or marries under that age. The Law Commission's 2011 Report discussed whether to retain stirpital distribution, or to recommend a change to some form of *per capita* distribution. It recommended that there be no change to the existing rules. Had there been a change, the order of deaths would play a bigger part, and this could quite possibly have led to difficulties. The correct solution here was to leave well alone.

11. Provision for Cohabitants—More Unfinished Business

At the time of the last major revision of the family provision legislation in 1975, one change to the rules was the addition of dependants, as an additional class of applicant. When they were added, it seems generally to have been assumed that most dependants would have been cohabitants, and that almost all cohabitants would have been dependants.[99] After 1975, problems arose when cohabitants who had been dependants provided services, in particular when those with whom they were cohabiting fell seriously ill, and they then provided care for them. A cohabitant who cared for the man with whom she[100] was living could be alleged not to be a dependant, because by caring she would, so to speak, be earning her keep.

[95] Or uncles or aunts.

[96] This includes issue *en ventre leur mères* at the death: Administration of Estates Act 1925, s 55(2).

[97] *Per stirpes* means through each stock of descent, from the Latin *stirps*.

[98] Or uncle or aunt.

[99] At the time when dependants were introduced as a category of applicant, by the Inheritance (Provision for Family and Dependants) Act 1975 Act, a popular newspaper described the legislation as 'a mistress's charter'; see K Green, 'The Englishwoman's Castle—Inheritance and Private Property Today' (1988) 51 *MLR* 187 at 195.

[100] The carer would usually be the female cohabitant.

Adding cohabitants as a class in their own right would do away with problems of this sort.

The 1989 Law Commission Report considered whether cohabitants should be entitled to inherit on intestacy and it recommended that they should not. It went on to consider whether they should be entitled to make claims (as cohabitants, and even if they were not dependants) under the family provision legislation and it recommended that they should. This recommendation was accepted by the government and, since 1996, cohabitants have been able to make family provision claims. Under section 1 of the Inheritance (Provision for Family and Dependants) Act 1975, as amended by the Law Reform (Succession) Act 1995 and by the Civil Partnership Act 2004, a cohabitant is defined as a person who

> during the whole period of two years ending immediately before the date when the deceased died, ... was living ... in the same household ... and ... as the husband or wife of the deceased ... [or] as the civil partner of the deceased.

The 2011 Report again considered the position of cohabitants and this time it suggested that a cohabitant *should* be entitled to inherit from the estate of an intestate deceased partner. The definition of a cohabitant suggested in the 2011 Report is much the same as that used in the family provision legislation, except that the 2011 Report suggested that a cohabitant should be entitled to benefit on intestacy only if (i) the deceased was not married or in a civil partnership at the time of his death; and (ii) that the cohabitation should have lasted for five years, unless the deceased and the cohabitant had had a child together, in which case two years would suffice. If the cohabitant complied with the relevant conditions, he or she would obtain, on intestacy, an entitlement exactly equivalent to that of a spouse.

The Law Commission's 2011 Report was divided into nine Parts, starting with an Introduction and finishing with a Summary. Parts 2–4 were concerned with the reforms so far discussed in this chapter, Part 5 with administration, Parts 6 and 7 with family provision[101] and Part 8 with cohabitants. The Report then had attached to it two draft bills, first the draft Inheritance and Trustees' Powers Bill[102] and then the draft Inheritance (Cohabitants) Bill.[103] In March 2013 the Government announced acceptance of the recommendations concerning intestacy, other than those relating to cohabitants, and the first of the two draft bills became, in due course and with minor amendments, the Inheritance and Trustees' Powers Bill 2014. It seems clear that, when the Law Commission's 2011 Report was being drafted, it was assumed that its recommendations concerning cohabitants would receive less support than its other recommendations and that that is why there were attached to it not one draft bill, containing all its proposals, but two drafts, so that one could be enacted and the other left to one side at least for a while.

[101] For the impact of the 2014 Act on the family provision regime, see Rebecca Probert's contribution in Ch 2 of this volume.

[102] Appendix A to the Report.

[103] Appendix B to the Report.

When the first of the two draft bills was being discussed in the House of Commons Second Reading Committee on 3 March 2014, the Minister of State at the Ministry of Justice, when explaining why the Government had decided not to accept the Law Commission's recommendations relating to intestacy rights for cohabitants, made the following statement:[104]

> Legal rights for cohabiting couples are complex and potentially far reaching, and I am not trying to address them in the Bill. The family justice system is already in the middle of a comprehensive reform programme, so it would not be wise to consider further reform in this controversial area until we finish the reform of the much less controversial area that is the subject of the Bill.

There have, in fact, been a series of attempts to introduce private members' bills dealing with the rights of cohabitants in the House of Lords. Lord Lester sponsored such a bill in the 2008–09 parliamentary session, but it did not have government support and ran out of time. That is the probable fate of a private member's bill which lacks government support. In October 2013, Lord Marks sponsored another bill, but that ran out of time at the end of the 2013–14 parliamentary session. He then reintroduced it as the Cohabitation Rights Bill [HL] 2014–15, at the start of the new session, in June 2014, and he got as far as a second reading on 12 December. Again, he ran out of time, when the 2015 general election intervened. He has now sponsored the bill again, as the Cohabitation Rights Bill [HL] and it had its first post-election reading on 4 June 2015.

The problem with legislation which enacts the Law Commission's proposals in relation to inheritance on intestacy by cohabitants, is that it raises all the difficulties encountered in relation to spouses and issue, where the issue are not the issue of the surviving spouse, but in a more extreme form. And here there will be scope for disputes as what it means to be 'living … as the husband or wife … [or] civil partner of the deceased'. There have, in the period since cohabitants were inserted into the family provision code, been a number of cases where this wording has been discussed, but it is almost certainly going to cause more of a problem if an attempt is made to apply it to intestacy, especially if the deceased left issue who are not the issue of the cohabitant. The cases so far, all family provision cases, seem to show that a claim can succeed only if the relationship between the parties is 'openly and unequivocally displayed to the outside world',[105] but this is a negative condition—the claim will fail if the parties have, for whatever reason, attempted to disguise the link between them. The cases do not make it clear what amounts positively to living as someone's husband/wife or civil partner. Fifty years ago, 'living together as husband and wife' would generally have implied an economic link, with a breadwinner and a dependant, but it no longer implies that. What it does imply is not clear, and whatever it is, it is not obvious why it should form the basis for a claim to inheritance—particularly when such a claim, if successful,

[104] Second Reading Committee (n 58 above), Simon Hughes MP at col 4.

[105] *Baynes v Hedger* [2008] EWHC 1587 (Ch), [2008] 3 FCR 151.

will trump the deceased's children or other issue. There appears to have been only one case of a successful claim by a cohabitant for family provision since 1996[106] where the deceased also left children,[107] and the other successful claims appear, so far, to relate to persons to whose estates there were no strong moral claims.[108] What would a court be likely to make of a situation where (say) two middle-aged cousins, of different sexes, or of the same sex, shared a house and a part of their social life and the first to die did so, having survived his or her spouse, but leaving children and grandchildren?[109] It used to be said that the toast of the Chancery Bar was the layman who had drafted his own will. If legislation along these lines is ever enacted, the middle-aged, unmarried quasi-cohabitant who dies intestate leaving children will, quite possibly, end up as the toast of the Family Bar. Not everyone will welcome such an outcome.

Inserting cohabitants into the intestacy code might or might not work, but to insert them as equivalent to spouses, when spouses are already treated too generously in relation to issue who are not their issue, seems to be a recipe for trouble.

[106] When cohabitants first became entitled to make claims, see above.

[107] This was *Cattle v Evans* [2011] EWHC 945 (Ch), [2011] WTLR 947, but it was clear in this case that the deceased did not want his cohabitant to inherit his estate and that, had she been entitled to inherit on his intestacy, he would not have died intestate; he would instead have made a will in favour of his children. As it was, the cohabitant did succeed in her family provision application, but the costs probably exceeded the award, so the victory would have been Pyrrhic.

[108] See, for example, *Re Watson* [1999] 1 FLR 878 (Ch), where a middle-aged couple who lived together, but who slept in separate bedrooms, were held to have lived together as husband and wife. The deceased had never married and was childless. *Swetenham v Walkley* [2014] WTLR 845 (County Court, Central London) is very similar.

[109] A cousin might, of course, inherit on intestacy in any case, but whether he or she would so inherit, and what proportion of the estate, would—if there were no claim from a cohabitant—depend on who else survived. And the case of *Burden v UK* [2008] STC 1305, [2008] 2 FLR 787, (2008) EHRR 38, in which the European Court of Human Rights (Grand Chamber) held that there was no violation of the European Convention on Human Rights in denying to cohabiting sisters the tax privileges accorded to same sex cohabitants who had entered into a civil partnership, demonstrates the logical difficulties encountered in this field. The *Burden* sisters seem to have been quite as much of an economic unit as any childless cohabiting couple, and their economic status should, arguably, have been the most significant factor when trying to work out the fairness or otherwise of the application of the tax system to them.

2

Disquieting Thoughts: Who Will Benefit When We Are Gone?

REBECCA PROBERT*

1. Introduction

The Order of Service for the Burial of the Dead contains a stark reminder to the living that control over property is limited in both its temporal scope and spiritual importance: we are told that 'we brought nothing into this world, and it is certain we can carry nothing out' and that 'man walketh in a vain shadow, and disquieteth himself in vain; he heapeth up riches, and cannot tell who shall gather them'. In a pithy echo of this, the Law Commission noted in its recent Report, '[w]e all have to die, and we cannot take anything with us'.[1] Individuals may, however, have had very clear ideas about the persons or institutions they would wish to pass their assets to in the event of their death and many will have made a will setting out those wishes.[2] Such provision will usually be determinative, in that the majority of the 200,000-plus wills admitted to probate each year[3] are unchallenged. Yet the explicit wishes of the deceased are not the only factor to which the law accords importance. The rules on provision for family and dependants allow those who fall within a specified group of persons to challenge the provision that has been made

* The author is currently working as a specialist advisor with the Law Commission on a review of the law governing how and where people can marry in England and Wales.

[1] Law Commission, *Intestacy and Family Provision Claims on Death* (Law Com No 331, 2011) para 1.1 (hereinafter '2011 Report').

[2] But by no means all: A Humphrey, L Mills and others, *Inheritance and the Family: Attitudes to Will-Making and Intestacy* (Report published by the National Centre for Social Research, London, August 2010) 13, found that only one-third of the general population has made a will, although two-thirds of those aged over 65 have done so. On the differences between wills made at different stages of the life-course, see eg J Finch and L Wallis, 'Death, Inheritance and the Life Course' in D Clark (ed), *The Sociology of Death: Theory, Culture and Practice* (Oxford, Blackwell, 1993) 50.

[3] During the third reading of the Inheritance and Trustees' Powers Bill it was noted that '480,000 people died in England and Wales in 2011, with 220,000 of those deaths leading to the personal representatives obtaining a grant of probate in respect of a valid will and 40,000 leading to letters of administration being granted': *Hansard*, HC Deb 26 March 2014, vol 578, Simon Hughes MP at col 417.

for them by the will or the share to which they would be entitled on intestacy—or, indeed, the lack of any such provision or entitlement.[4]

These rules governing who can apply have recently been amended by the Inheritance and Trustees' Powers Act 2014. Based on the proposals advanced by the Law Commission in its 2009 Consultation Paper and recommended in its 2011 Report, the changes seem to have been broadly welcomed, albeit by a small number of consultees. They attracted relatively little discussion in Parliament, and the press coverage of the new legislation was largely neutral in tone.[5] However, given the significant increase in the number of claims for family provision coming before the courts—more than 400 per cent in less than a decade, according to comments in Parliament[6]—a careful review of the Act's provisions and likely effect is needed. The fact that most cases settle[7] does not detract from the importance of this; indeed, it could be seen as making it all the more important that there is certainty as to the basic underlying rationale.

This chapter will first sketch the background to the family provision rules and then go on to consider the key changes made by the 2014 Act in some depth.[8] It will conclude with an analysis of the current categories of who can claim.

2. From Testamentary Freedom to the Potential for Challenge

The last 80 years have seen a profound change in the range of individuals able to challenge the disposition of the estate and an equally important shift in attitude towards the legitimacy of such challenges. Although absolute freedom of testation was only established in the late nineteenth century,[9] Victorian testators were almost uniquely free from constraints as to how they could dispose of their

[4] The 1975 Act does not, however, apply to pension assets, on which see Alexandra Braun's contribution in Ch 10 of this volume.

[5] Many commentators focused on the importance of writing a will to ensure that the new intestacy rules would not apply: see eg L Barclay, 'After you've gone, ensure the inheritors are the chosen ones', *Independent on Sunday*, 19 October 2014; 'Warning over changing inheritance rules', *Lancashire Telegraph*, 9 October 2014.

[6] Second Reading Committee, 3 March 2014, Dan Jarvis MP at col 12. Minutes of the committee meeting are available online via: www.publications.parliament.uk/pa/cm201314/cmpublic/inheritance/140303/pm/140303s01.htm (last accessed 20 November 2015).

[7] See eg C Sawyer and M Spero, *Succession, Wills and Probate*, 3rd edn (London, Routledge, 2015) 315.

[8] For an overview of all of the changes, see N Pearce, 'The Inheritance and Trustees' Powers Act 2014: Changes to Intestacy Rules and Claims for Family Provision on Death' [2014] *Fam Law* 1591.

[9] AG Guest, 'Family Provision and the Legitima Portio' (1957) 73 *LQR* 74; G Douglas, 'Family Provision and Family Practices—The Discretionary Regime of the Inheritance Act of England and Wales' (2014) 4 *Oñati Socio-Legal Series* 222. For those with landed estates, the strict settlement acted as a sometimes unwelcome constraint on freedom of testation (as illustrated most famously by the Bennett Estate being entailed on the objectionable Mr Collins in Jane Austen's *Pride and Prejudice*).

property, and immune from later challenges to their wishes. As James LJ declared in one late-nineteenth-century case:[10]

> A testator's bounty is absolute and without control as to motive. A man may leave his virtuous wife and deserving children penniless, and bestow the whole of his fortune upon the vilest companions of his profligacy, the most worthless partners of his vices, the most wicked accomplices of his crimes, and the law cannot gainsay him, even if he should openly flaunt his shocking disregard of all ties human and divine on the very face of his will.

Such freedom of testation raised the possibility of a man leaving assets away from his legitimate family, and Victorian literature was full of examples of disinheritance.[11] The impact of such disinheritance is powerfully, if briefly, sketched in Rachel Ferguson's 1937 novel *Alas, Poor Lady*, which contains the following dialogue:[12]

> 'When my father died, it was found that he had left nearly all his money to another woman. She—he—they lived together …'
>
> 'But—your mother? She was his wife! She came first!' …
>
> 'They can do it, it seems. … In Scotland a man is compelled by law to leave a proportion of his estate to the widow. In England, no.'

But this was swiftly to change. The Inheritance (Family Provision) Act 1938 allowed a widow to challenge her deceased husband's will, along with the unmarried daughter and infant or incapacitated son of the deceased. The strikingly narrow range of those able to bring a claim reflected the sense that the new potential for challenge was an interference with a core principle of English law. The same idea informed the way in which the legislation was interpreted. Judges adopted a restrictive approach to allowing claims by family members who had been left unprovided for, claiming that the 1938 Act was the first interference with freedom of testation[13] and asserting that a testator was 'entitled to determine where his duty lies'.[14] In *Re Joslin*, for example, the court refused to order any extra provision for the legal widow despite the fact that she had been married to the deceased for 19 years. The estate went instead to the woman with whom the deceased had lived for the four years prior to his death, the court emphasising the moral obligations he owed to the children from this relationship, the fact that the woman with whom the deceased had been living would be dependent on the state if the estate

[10] *Occleston v Fullalove* (1874) LR 9 Ch App 147 at 161.

[11] See further R Probert, 'Freedom of Testation in Victorian England' in K Boehm, A Farkas and A Zwierlein (eds), *Interdisciplinary Perspectives on Ageing in Nineteenth-Century Culture* (Abingdon, Routledge, 2014) 115.

[12] R Ferguson, *Alas, Poor Lady* ([1937] London, Persephone Books, 2006) 197–98. It should be noted that the term 'lived together' needs to be read in its now less familiar meaning of a sexual relationship rather than in the modern sense of sharing a home—hence the family's surprise at being disinherited.

[13] *Re Inns* [1947] Ch 576 (Ch); *Re Makein (deceased)* [1955] Ch 194 (Ch).

[14] In this vein Farwell J in *Re Joslin* [1941] Ch 200 (Ch) 202.

were transferred to the legal widow, and the desire to discourage litigation over small estates.[15] It was clear, nonetheless, that the choices made by a testator could now be scrutinised,[16] and a generation after the Act was passed we find a rather different formulation of the principle of testamentary freedom being put forward by Harman LJ: 'of course a man is entitled by the law of England, *subject to making "reasonable provision" for his dependants*, to make what testamentary disposition he likes' (emphasis added).[17] At one level it might seem that the principle had remained unscathed, but the important *caveat* smuggled into the middle of the sentence made all the difference.

In the wake of this, the Inheritance (Provision for Family and Dependants) Act 1975 considerably expanded the list of persons who were entitled to apply to the court. The new additions included the former spouse of the deceased (at least if they had not formalised another relationship);[18] any children of the deceased, of whatever age;[19] those treated as a child of the family in relation to a marriage;[20] and a person who 'immediately before the death of the deceased was being maintained, either wholly or partly, by the deceased'.[21] The expansion in the scope of the court's power to award discretionary provision was part of the shift away from formal rules to the greater flexibility and increased focus on protection that were characteristic of the period. Just as characteristic was the expansion in the specific categories of those who could seek such provision. Marriages were becoming increasingly likely to end in divorce, but the divorced were also very likely to remarry, with more step-children being created as a result. There was increasing awareness of equality issues, and so the differential treatment of sons and daughters could no longer be justified. The 1970s also saw an increase in—and greater awareness of—cohabitation, and it was specifically intended that those who had been living with the deceased should be able to claim as 'dependants'. The Law Commission's 1974 Report[22] noted that one of the purposes of family provision law was to ensure that reasonable provision was made for those whom the deceased had been *legally* liable to maintain, but went on to argue that the law also recognised moral obligations. Since a failure to make provision may have been accidental, making an order for financial provision 'would be doing for the deceased what he might reasonably be assumed to have wished to do himself'.[23] This, it was thought, was a particularly compelling argument 'where the "dependant" is a person with

[15] ibid. See also *In re Charman (deceased)* (1951) 2 TLR 1095; *In Re Howell* [1953] 1 WLR 1034 (CA); *Re E* [1966] 1 WLR 709 (Ch).

[16] See eg *In Re Borthwick* [1949] 1 Ch 395 (Ch); *Whittle v Painter* (1973) 3 *Fam Law* 140.

[17] *In re Thornley (deceased)* [1969] 1 WLR 1037 (CA) 1041.

[18] Inheritance (Provision for Family and Dependants) Act 1975, s 1(1)(b).

[19] ibid s 1(1)(c).

[20] ibid s 1(1)(d).

[21] ibid s 1(1)(e), and see further s 1(3).

[22] Law Commission, *Second Report on Family Property: Family Provision on Death* (Law Com No 61, 1974) (hereinafter '1974 Report').

[23] ibid para 90.

whom the deceased has been cohabiting',[24] and the new provision was generally welcomed[25] and quickly invoked.[26]

The pace of change then began to speed up. The Law Reform (Succession) Act 1995 amended the 1975 Act by allowing a claim by a cohabitant who had been living with the deceased in the same household immediately before the date of the death, and for at least two years before that date, as the husband or wife of the deceased.[27] Claims by bereaved cohabitants have accounted for a significant proportion of the reported cases, raising difficult questions about the nature of the relationship,[28] when it had begun to be a cohabiting one,[29] and whether it had in fact ended prior to the death of the deceased.[30] (There is, it should be noted, no provision for a *former* cohabitant—as opposed to a former spouse or civil partner—to apply for provision). A decade later, the Civil Partnership Act 2004 put same-sex couples in the same position as their opposite-sex counterparts, whether they had formalised their relationship or were living together in a similar kind of relationship.[31] As Elizabeth Cooke, the Law Commissioner responsible for the recent proposals, has noted when writing in a personal capacity, 'this is an area of law that has to be sensitive to changing family structures and social mores, and so requires amendment from time to time'.[32]

While the Inheritance and Family Provision Act 2014 has added no new categories of claimants to the list, it has made some significant changes to the definition of who falls within those categories, in particular in relation to a 'child of the family' and a 'dependant'.

3. Child of the Family

One of the key changes made by the 2014 Act is to enable a person who was 'treated' as a child of the family to bring a claim. Previously, a claim could only be

[24] ibid.

[25] *Cosmopolitan*, February 1975, p 23; *The Times*, 18 September 1975, p 15; 'New rules for those cut off without 5p', *The Times*, 31 January 1976; *Hansard*, HC Deb 16 July 1975, vol 895, col 1686. Cf A Samuels, 'Inheritance (Provision for Family and Dependants) Act 1975' (1976) 120 *Solicitors' Journal* 123.

[26] See eg *In the estate of McC* (1978) 9 *Fam Law* 26 (Fam); *Malone v Harrison* [1979] 1 WLR 1353 (Fam); *Re Beaumont (deceased)* [1980] Ch 444 (Ch).

[27] Inheritance (Provision for Family and Dependants) Act 1975, s 1(3)(1A).

[28] See eg *Re Watson (deceased)* [1999] 1 FLR 878 (Ch); *Baynes v Hedger* [2008] EWHC 1587 (Ch), [2008] 2 FLR 1805; aff'd [2009] EWCA Civ 374, [2009] 2 FLR 767.

[29] See eg *Kaur v Dhaliwal* [2014] EWHC 1991 (Ch), [2015] 2 FCR 40. One change that was recommended by the Law Commission but not implemented in the 2014 Act was the removal of the current qualifying period of two years if the couple were living together at the date of death and had had a child together.

[30] See the generous decision in *Gully v Dix* [2004] EWCA Civ 139, [2004] 1 WLR 1399. See also *Witkowska v Kaminiski* [2006] EWHC 1940 (Ch), [2007] 1 FLR 1547.

[31] Inheritance (Provision for Family and Dependants) Act 1975, s 1(1)(a), (b) and (ba), as amended by the Civil Partnership Act 2004.

[32] E Cooke, 'The Law of Succession: Doing the Best We Can' in R Probert and C Barton (eds), *Fifty Years in Family Law: Essays for Stephen Cretney* (Antwerp, Intersentia, 2012) 175 at 176.

brought where the deceased was married to, or in a civil partnership with, the parent of the child in question; now, however, the definition has been broadened to include *any* person whom the deceased treated as a child. As the amended version of the 1975 Act now states, this may be in the context of 'any family in which the deceased at any time stood in the role of a parent',[33] and the family in question may have consisted of just the deceased and the claimant.[34]

The distinction between the children of one's spouse and the children of one's partner has long been criticised,[35] and its removal is to be welcomed. As the Law Commission noted when initially proposing the change in its Consultation Paper,[36]

> we do not think that it is right for a child to be treated differently depending on whether his or her legal parent happened to have married or formed a civil partnership with the deceased, or alternatively chosen to cohabit with him or her. The bond between the deceased and the child may be just as strong in either case.

It is clear from the overview of consultees' responses that the majority—whether professionals, individuals or charities—felt the same way.[37] During the second reading, meanwhile, it was specifically noted that the change would 'ensure that a claim by a deserving child for financial help will no longer be barred simply on the basis of the status of his or her parents'.[38] And it is interesting to note that in the two key reported cases on the interpretation of the subsection, the marriage between the claimant's parent and the person against whom the claim was eventually brought occurred at a relatively late stage in the relationship and did not mark any change in the way in which the claimant was treated.[39] In such cases, the fact of the marriage was essentially arbitrary in terms of the parties' relationship, albeit crucial in giving the 'child of the family' a claim.

The original proposal was, of course, linked to the Commission's suggestion that cohabitants should be included in the intestacy rules and, in appropriate cases, treated in the same way as spouses. It would have been a necessary concomitant of such change, since under the current intestacy rules the estate would pass to any children of the deceased, who might or might not also be children of

[33] Inheritance (Provision for Family and Dependants) Act 1975, s 1(1)(d), as amended by the Inheritance and Trustees' Powers Act 2014, Sch 2 para 2.

[34] Inheritance (Provision for Family and Dependants) Act 1975, s 1(2A), as inserted by the Inheritance and Trustees' Powers Act 2014, Sch 2 para 2.

[35] See eg S Cretney, 'Reform of Intestacy: The Best We Can Do?' (1995) 111 *LQR* 77 at 89; C Barton, 'Stepfathers, Mothers' Cohabitants and "Uncles"' [2009] *Fam Law* 327 at 332–33.

[36] Law Commission, *Intestacy and Family Provision Claims on Death: A Consultation Paper* (Law Com CP No 191, 2009) para 6.5 (hereinafter '2009 Consultation Paper').

[37] Law Commission, *Intestacy and Family Provision Claims on Death: Analysis of Consultation Responses* (14 December 2011) para 6.2, notes that 32 of the 40 responses on this point agreed with the provisional proposal (6 with some reservations or concerns) and 8 disagreed. The paper is available via: www.lawcom.gov.uk/wp-content/uploads/2015/03/cp191_intestacy_responses.pdf (last accessed 20 November 2015).

[38] Second Reading Committee (n 6 above), Simon Hughes MP at col 9.

[39] *Re Callaghan* [1985] Fam 1 (Fam); *Re Leach* [1986] Ch 226 (CA).

the surviving cohabitant. As the Commission noted, '[i]n assessing the claims of children of the family, the fact that a substantial part of the estate was inherited from the child's legal parent has often been relevant'.[40] The non-implementation of the Commission's recommendations relating to the rights of cohabitants did not, however, remove the need for reform on this point, since the child's parent might well have left the property to the surviving partner by will.[41]

While there has been less demand for the extension of the provision beyond the context of the couple family, it is in some ways a logical development of the existing case law. As the Court of Appeal held in *Re Leach*,[42] it was possible for children to be treated as a child of the family by a step-parent even after the death of their parent. It was pointed out that section 1(1)(d) only refers to a claimant having been treated as a child of the family by the deceased and that the phrase used was 'in relation to that marriage' not 'during the subsistence of that marriage'. Slade LJ commented that it would be 'too rigid and technical a construction' to regard the family unit as having come to an end with the death of the parent.[43]

It is also interesting to note that the new provision seems to echo the Law Commission's proposal from 1971—albeit one that was subsequently abandoned—to the effect that 'where the deceased had treated a child as a child of his family that child should be entitled to apply for family provision from the estate'.[44] The examples given to the Second Reading Committee of those who might fall within the expanded category included children who had been fostered on a long-term basis, or had been living with relatives without being formally adopted.[45]

Yet assessing the likely impact of the change is rather challenging. For one thing, despite a rather vague reference during the course of the Second Reading Committee to the aim of the change being 'to modernise the law of succession so that we better reflect the realities of modern family life',[46] there was no real discussion of the numbers affected. It might be a moot point as to whether fostering and informal adoption arrangements are more common now than in the past. And while it is certainly true, as the Commission noted, that '[c]ohabitation between people who have children from previous relationships is now common',[47] and certainly more common than it was in the 1970s when the original provision was enacted, it is interesting that the number of families with dependent step-children has in fact been falling in recent years. Data from the 2011 census showed that there were 544,000 families with dependent step-children in that year, as compared to 631,000 in 2001, a fall of 14 per cent. Within married couple families the fall was relatively modest, from 346,000 to 340,000, but within cohabiting couples

[40] 2009 Consultation Paper (n 36 above) para 6.6.
[41] As was the case in *Re Callaghan* (n 39 above) and in *Re Leach* (n 39 above).
[42] *Re Leach* (n 39 above).
[43] ibid 234.
[44] Law Commission, *Family Property Law* (WP No 42, 1971) para 3.38.
[45] Second Reading Committee (n 6 above), Simon Hughes MP at col 9.
[46] ibid.
[47] 2009 Consultation Paper (n 36 above) para. 6.5.

the fall was much more significant, from 285,000 in 2001 to 203,000 in 2011, a drop of just under 29 per cent. The fall was all the more significant when viewed against the overall increase in the number of cohabiting couples, and indeed the near doubling of cohabiting couples with dependent children of their own, from 457,000 in 2001 to 811,000 in 2011.[48]

This might reassure those concerned about the potential proliferation of claims under the 1975 Act, although other aspects of the relevant data might not. While the proportion of cohabiting couple stepfamilies with three or more children is no larger than that of married couple stepfamilies, at 28 per cent, cohabiting families do tend to be less stable than married families.[49] As a result, any individual may have been treated as a child of the family by a succession of partners of their parent, and those partners in turn may have treated a number of individuals as if they were their own child over the years. Unlike the provisions relating to those cohabiting with or being maintained by the deceased, there is no requirement that the claimant must have been treated by the deceased as a child of the family immediately prior to his or her death, and so an individual would at least be able to *apply* for provision on the basis of a relationship that had since come to an end.

The potential scope of the amended provision is broadened still further by the way it has already been interpreted in the context of claims against step-parents. The 'child of the family' need not be a minor; indeed, he or she may have been an adult at the time the relationship began. In *Re Callaghan*,[50] the claimant was 47 at the time of the litigation, although the deceased had moved into his mother's home when he was a teenager; while in *Re Leach*,[51] the claimant had been 32 when her father's relationship with his second wife began, and 55 when the latter died. While the Law Commission had indeed recommended in its 1974 Report that there should be no age limits on applications by either a child or a child of the family, it seems highly unlikely that it would have anticipated claims of this kind succeeding when it proposed this new category. Its Report placed great weight on the fact that the courts had the power to make financial provision for a 'child of the family' in the context of divorce, where very clear age limits operate.[52] The resulting legislation also seemed to anticipate that claimants would be relatively young, given that the courts were directed to have regard to 'the manner in which the applicant was being or in which he might expect to be educated or trained'.[53] Despite this, the Court of Appeal in *Re Leach* rejected as 'unfounded' the submission by counsel

[48] Office for National Statistics, *Stepfamilies in 2011* (8 May 2014), Table 1. The datasheet is available via: www.ons.gov.uk/ons/dcp171776_360784.pdf (last accessed 20 November 2015).

[49] B Wilson and R Stuchbury, 'Do Partnerships Last? Comparing Marriage and Cohabitation Using Longitudinal Census Data' (2010) 139 *Population Trends* 37.

[50] See *Re Callaghan* (n 39 above).

[51] See *Re Leach* (n 39 above).

[52] Matrimonial Causes Act 1973, s 24(1)(a) and s 29; although note that in *Re Leach* (n 39 above) Slade LJ drew attention to the fact that there were no age limits on orders for a settlement under s 24(1)(b).

[53] Inheritance (Provision for Family and Dependants) Act 1975, s 3(3).

that 'an adult person can only qualify if he has been treated by the deceased as an unfledged person, in the sense that there has been an assumption by the deceased of parental responsibility, care and control'.[54] It was, however, rather telling that the hypothetical example given by Slade LJ to illustrate the potential harshness of holding that a child could only be a child of the family in relation to a marriage that was still subsisting related to a young child rather than an adult one, implicitly acknowledging that it is easier to make a compelling case for their support.

So how might a parent–child relationship be established where both of the individuals concerned were adults? In the reported case law, considerable weight was placed on the confidence that the step-parent placed in the claimant and the care that the latter provided. As the court noted in *Re Callaghan*:[55]

> the confidences as to his property and financial affairs which he placed in the plaintiff and his dependence upon the plaintiff to care for him in his last illness are examples of the deceased's treatment of the plaintiff as a child, albeit an adult child, of the family.

Similarly, in *Re Leach* the court drew attention to the way in which the claimant's step-mother had become increasingly dependent on her after her husband's death; the claimant's frequent visits and the step-mother's personal confidences; and the 'continuous nature of the relationship of mutual affection and trust between the two parties'.[56] In both cases, reference was also made to the privileges and duties/responsibilities of the parent–child relationship, although in *Re Leach* Slade LJ did acknowledge that 'the privileges of the quasi-parent may well increase and the responsibilities may well diminish as the years go by'.[57]

This—albeit unintentionally—seems to get to the heart of why we instinctively regard these cases as deserving ones, ie the extent of the care that the claimant provided for the deceased, despite the fact that this is not recognised as grounding a claim against the estate. In fact, discussion of this category, by both policy-makers and judges, has tended to focus on the risk that kindness by the older party will generate a claim against the estate. In *Re Leach*, for example, the court made it clear that the mere existence of a step-relationship would not be sufficient to give rise to a claim:[58]

> the legislature cannot have contemplated that the mere display of affection, kindness or hospitality by a step-parent towards a step-child will by itself involve the treatment by the step-parent of the step-child as a child of the family in relation to the marriage, for the purpose of section 1(1)(d), so as to place the parent and his or her estate under a potential liability to provide for the step-child.

Similarly, one concern voiced in relation to the reforms proposed in 2011 was that 'people might be deterred from undertaking voluntary work in youth clubs

[54] *Re Leach* (n 39 above) 235.
[55] *Re Callaghan* (n 39 above) 6.
[56] *Re Leach* (n 39 above) 240.
[57] ibid 237.
[58] ibid 235.

or sponsoring a child in the developing world by the fear of a claim against their estate';[59] the Law Commission, however, felt that such assistance was unlikely to generate a claim unless 'the quality and intensity of that help could be characterised as parental'.[60]

The most interesting cases are likely to arise where the family in relation to which the claimant was a 'child' consisted of just the claimant and the deceased. It is, after all, relatively easy to classify a relationship as having a parental quality to it where one party was married to or living with the parent of the other. In such cases there will usually (although not invariably) be a generational gap and a certain family dynamic. Where there is no such link, interesting questions are likely to arise as to whether a relationship is a friendship or a quasi-parental one. The courts have, it should be noted, refused to recognise a number of cross-generational relationships as constituting a 'family' within the purposes of the Rent Acts, with even lengthy co-residence being insufficient.[61] The young woman who cared for the elderly tenant for over a decade in *Ross v Collins*[62] was described as an 'unpaid housekeeper' by the court, despite the fact that she wrote what were described as 'lively and affectionate' letters to him when she was on holiday. Russell LJ went so far as to state that:[63]

> two strangers cannot, it seems to me, ever establish artificially for the purposes of this section a familial nexus by acting as brothers or as sisters, even if they call each other such and consider their relationship to be tantamount to that. Nor, in my view, can an adult man and woman who establish a platonic relationship establish a familial nexus by acting as a devoted brother and sister or father and daughter would act, even if they address each other as such and even if they refer to each other as such and regard their association as tantamount to such.

The House of Lords confirmed in *Joram Developments v Sharratt*[64] that there was no familial nexus even when the individuals in question specifically called themselves 'aunt' and 'nephew'. It may be that the more liberal approach to the definition of 'family' in *Fitzpatrick v Sterling Housing Association Ltd*[65] would require these cases to be reconsidered, but it is telling that the key developments in family law in recent years have focused on those united by a sexual bond rather than a platonic relationship.

It is, of course, worth noting that despite the potentially broad scope of the category, even before the recent reforms, there have been very few reported cases

59 2011 Report (n 1 above) para 6.37, noting the concerns of the Society of Trust and Estate Practitioners.

60 ibid para 6.38.

61 See eg *Sefton Holdings Ltd v Cairns* [1988] 2 FLR 109 (CA).

62 *Ross v Collins* [1964] 1 WLR 425 (CA).

63 ibid 432.

64 *Joram Developments v Sharratt* [1979] 1 WLR 928 (HL).

65 *Fitzpatrick v Sterling Housing Association Ltd* [2001] 1 AC 27 (HL).

in which it has been invoked.[66] And even if it is possible to imagine individuals being eligible to claim in a wide range of situations, the further hurdle of showing that the disposition of the estate is not such as to make reasonable financial provision for the claimant will by its very nature act as a brake on claims. After all, the courts have not been particularly receptive to claims by the biological children of the deceased, at least once they have attained adulthood.[67] In the case law to date, the reasonableness of making provision (or not) has been reviewed in the light of the relationship as a whole.[68] It is also worthy of note that in the few cases involving a child of the family, the claimant's parent had previously left a substantial amount to the deceased, and those who stood to benefit from the estate had had a fairly limited relationship with the deceased.

Finally, the removal of the difference between marital and non-marital step-children in this context also throws into sharp relief the continuance of differences between these two groups where the relationship between the adults breaks down. While step-parents may be ordered to make provision for the children of their spouse or former spouse in the context of divorce proceedings or under Schedule 1 of the Children Act 1989, in this context the step-relationship is created by marriage alone.[69] As a result, a parent's cohabitant (if not themselves a biological parent) cannot be ordered to make provision for the parent's child, regardless of how long the parties have shared a home, or whether the child was born during the relationship.[70] The irony of the fact that their assumed obligations to such children may reduce the amount they are liable to pay by way of child support for their biological children has not gone unnoticed.[71]

4. Being Maintained

The second key change made by the 2014 Act to the categories of those eligible to claim financial provision from the estate of the deceased relates to the category of those 'being maintained' by the deceased. Initially introduced by the Inheritance

[66] The only other case on this particular provision cited in the Law Commission's Consultation Paper is the county court decision in *Gora v Treasury Solicitor* [2003] Fam 93.

[67] See eg *Re Coventry (deceased)* [1980] Ch 461 (CA); *Re Jennings (deceased)* [1994] Ch 286 (CA); *Garland v Morris* [2007] EWHC 2 (Ch), [2007] 2 FLR 528. See also the prioritising of the cohabitant's claim over that of the adult children in *Webster v Webster* [2008] EWHC 31 (Ch), [2009] 1 FLR 1240. For discussion of the claims of adult children, see G Miller, 'Provision for Adult Children under the Inheritance (Provision for Family and Dependants) Act 1975' (1995) 59 *Conv* 22.

[68] Most recently *Ilott v Mitson* [2011] EWCA Civ 346, [2012] 2 FLR 170 (and see also [2015] EWCA Civ 797, [2015] 2 FCR 547, on the quantum of the award).

[69] Children Act 1989, s 105.

[70] See eg *T v B (Parental Responsibility: Financial Provision)* [2010] EWHC 1444 (Fam), [2010] Fam 193.

[71] See eg C Barton, 'Stepfathers, Mothers' Cohabitants and "Uncles"' [2009] *Fam Law* 327.

(Provision for Family and Dependants) Act 1975, questions had arisen as to whether potential applicants could be regarded as 'dependent' if they themselves had provided support for the deceased.[72] In the first case to consider the point, *Re Wilkinson (deceased)*,[73] the housework, physical help and general support provided by the sister of the deceased was held not to amount to 'full valuable consideration' for the other's provision of a home and payment of the bills. Mutual financial support, by contrast, was held to negate any claim in *Re Beaumont (deceased)*,[74] the court describing the picture as being:[75]

> one of two people, each with their own earnings and, latterly, their own pensions, who chose to pool such of their individual resources as were needed for them to be able to live with each other without either undertaking any responsibility for maintaining the other. Each paid his or her own way.

Before long, however, the courts moved to adopt a 'balance sheet' approach: if the net flow of benefits was from the deceased to the applicant, then dependency could be established.[76]

The 2014 Act reiterated that a person is to be treated as being maintained by the deceased '*only* if the deceased was making a substantial contribution in money or money's worth towards the reasonable needs of that person' (emphasis added).[77] Contributions 'made for full valuable consideration' are excluded but only if they are made as part of an arrangement of a commercial nature. This means that a claim is no longer precluded where the 'dependent' was contributing more to the needs of the deceased than vice versa.[78]

At the same time, the matters to which the court is directed to have regard in section 3 were redrafted to make it clear that the claimant does not have to show that the deceased 'assumed' responsibility for his or her maintenance,[79] although the 'basis on which the deceased maintained the applicant', the extent of any contribution made by way of maintenance, and the extent to which the deceased did assume responsibility for the applicant's maintenance all remain factors to be taken into account.[80]

[72] See generally G Miller, 'Dependants, Cohabitants and Family Provision' [2000] *Private Client Business* 305.

[73] *Re Wilkinson (deceased)* [1978] Fam 22 (Fam).

[74] *Re Beaumont (deceased)* [1980] Ch 444 (Ch).

[75] ibid 457. See also *H v G and D* (1980) 10 *Fam Law* 98.

[76] See eg *Jelley v Iliffe* [1981] Fam 128 (CA); *Bishop v Plumley* [1991] 1 WLR 582, [1991] 1 FLR 121 (CA); *Churchill v Roach* [2002] EWHC 3230 (Ch), [2004] 2 FLR 989; *Lindop v Agus, Bass and Hedley* [2009] EWHC 1795 (Ch), [2010] 1 FLR 631.

[77] Inheritance and Trustees' Powers Act 2014, Sch 2 para 3. The highlighted word 'only' does not appear in the 1975 Act, but the rest of the phrase does.

[78] As recommended by Law Commission's 2011 Report (n 1 above) para 6.76.

[79] For cases where this proved problematic, see eg *Re B (deceased)* [1999] Ch 206 (Ch); rev'd [2000] Ch 662 (CA) (mother living in home purchased with damages paid to daughter on account of medical negligence).

[80] Inheritance (Provision for Family and Dependants) Act 1975, s 3(4)(a) and (b), as inserted by the Inheritance and Trustees' Powers Act 2014, Sch 2 para 5(4).

The changes in wording in the revised legislation are slight, since the problems being addressed had arisen as a result of judicial interpretation[81] rather than being inherent in the terms of the original Act. As the Commission noted, the courts had set up the need to show that the deceased had 'assumed responsibility' for the claimant as a threshold condition but had then found ways 'to circumvent it by presuming assumption of responsibility from the fact of maintenance'.[82]

As regards the way in which individuals can establish that they were being maintained by the deceased, it seems unlikely that the 2014 Act will make any significant difference. In *Lindop v Agus*,[83] for example, the court focused on the fact that the deceased had been 'making a substantial contribution'[84] towards the claimant's reasonable needs. His contributions—providing a roof over her head, paying the outgoings on the property, providing transport for her and paying for holidays and some of her clothes—were itemised; hers, by contrast, were not mentioned. The court was content to assume, on the basis of these contributions and the fact that the deceased 'had substantially more money' than the claimant, that it was 'inherently likely that he would have contributed substantially more towards the outgoings' than she did.[85]

One group for whom the revised provision may nonetheless be beneficial is those cohabitants who fail to satisfy the two-year qualifying period to bring a claim on the basis of their relationship. After all, cohabiting partners would seem to have been the intended beneficiaries of the original provision. While the Law Commission's 2011 Report placed less emphasis on the potential for cohabitants to rely on this provision—largely, of course, because of the alternative recommendations being put forward to ameliorate their position—the case law has demonstrated that it does have a useful role to play in this context. There have been some quite lengthy relationships in which the actual period of sharing a home was relatively short and where the surviving partner was perforce required to claim as a dependent rather than as a cohabitant.[86]

The provision has also been successfully invoked by dependent friends[87] and relatives,[88] and it was these types of relationships on which the Law Commission

[81] See eg *Re Beaumont* (n 74 above); *Jelley v Iliffe* (n 76 above).

[82] 2011 Report (n 1 above) para 6.56. For examples of such circumvention, see eg *Re B (deceased)* [2000] Ch 662 (CA) and the discussion in *Baynes v Hedger* (Ch) (n 28 above) [130].

[83] *Lindop v Agus* [2009] EWHC 1795 (Ch), [2010] 1 FLR 631.

[84] ibid [46].

[85] ibid [48].

[86] See eg *Churchill v Roach* (n 76 above), in which the couple lived together briefly, but then for the next five years had separate establishments and separate domestic economies, despite spending weekends and holidays together.

[87] See eg *Rees v Newbery and the Institute of Cancer Research* [1998] 1 FLR 1041 (Ch), in which the deceased had allowed a friend to occupy a flat he owned at a much-reduced rent.

[88] *King v Dubrey, King v Chiltern Dog Rescue* [2014] EWHC 2083 (Ch), [2014] WTLR 1411; rev'd (in part) [2015] EWCA Civ 581, [2015] WTLR 1225.

focused in its 2009 Consultation Paper. It is however interesting to note that the potential claim was couched in hypothetical terms:[89]

> Consider two siblings or friends who live together. They pool their incomes, contributing equally to the rent and the household bills, and share the domestic work. By combining their incomes they are able to sustain a comfortable lifestyle together. On the death of one, the survivor is not able to meet his or her reasonable needs alone, even though there is now only one person to keep.

Despite the claim of Simon Hughes MP that the amendment 'brings the legislation up to date with modern practices and family life',[90] the case for change rests more on broad ideas of fairness than on any demonstrated need on the part of such individuals.

The terms of the rephrased version mean that it is still unlikely that a claim would succeed where the deceased had explicitly repudiated any responsibility for ongoing maintenance. Such was the case in *Baynes v Hedger*, where the deceased had repeatedly disclaimed responsibility when providing her impecunious god-daughter with what she intended to be merely temporary assistance.[91] And the extent to which the deceased had assumed responsibility for the claimant will continue to be relevant to the extent of any order made. In *King v Dubrey (sub nom King v Chiltern Dog Rescue)*,[92] for example, it was held that if the nephew of the deceased did need to invoke section 1(1)(e),[93] then the sum awarded would have to be proportionate to the extent of the dependency; any greater sum would constitute a 'windfall'.[94]

5. The Standard of Provision

Should an applicant successfully show not only that is he or she entitled to claim, but also that the disposition of the deceased's estate was not such as to make financial provision for him or her, the final task of the court is to decide what provision should be made. For most categories of claimants, the level is set at such provision as is required for the applicant's 'maintenance'.[95] However, in the case of a surviving spouse or civil partner, it is simply such provision as it would be reasonable for such a person to receive, regardless of whether that provision is required for his or

[89] 2009 Consultation Paper (n 36 above) para 6.22.

[90] Second Reading Committee (n 6 above) Simon Hughes MP at col 9.

[91] *Baynes v Hedger* (CA) (n 28 above) [46].

[92] *King v Dubrey* (Ch) (n 88 above) especially [53]–[67].

[93] An alternative claim was based on a *donatio mortis causa*.

[94] *King v Dubrey* (Ch) (n 88 above) [67]. The Court of Appeal did not interfere with the judge's conclusions in respect of the nephew's claim for reasonable financial provision: *King v Dubrey* (CA) (n 88 above) [77]–[82].

[95] For some generous interpretations of 'maintenance' see eg *Negus v Bahouse* [2007] EWHC 2628 (Ch), [2008] 1 FLR 381; aff'd [2008] EWCA Civ 1002, [2012] WTLR 1117; *Churchill v Roach* (n 76 above); *Webster v Webster* (n 67 above).

her maintenance. The court is specifically directed to consider the provision that the applicant might reasonably have expected to receive if the relationship had been terminated by divorce or dissolution rather than by death.[96]

The Law Commission reviewed the current approach and recommended that it should be made explicit that the court is not required to treat the provision that the surviving spouse might have expected on divorce 'as setting an upper or lower limit on the provision which may be ordered'.[97] This has now been implemented by the 2014 Act.[98]

Of course, whether the provision suggests an upper or lower limit depends on one's perceptions of what provision would be available on divorce. At the time that the 1975 Act was passed, the relevant legislation governing division of assets on divorce contained what was known as the 'minimal loss' principle—the direction that the court should exercise its powers in such a way[99]

> as to place the parties, so far as it is practicable and, having regard to their conduct, just to do so, in the financial position in which they would have been if the marriage had not broken down and each had properly discharged his or her financial obligations and responsibilities towards the other.

Against this background, the Law Commission noted that 'the courts have the widest possible powers ... to effect an equitable sharing of the family assets' and took the view that 'the court's powers to order financial provision for a surviving spouse should be equally wide'.[100] It went on to reiterate that 'in the normal case a wife should be regarded as entitled to a share in the capital assets of the family'[101] and recommended that provision should no longer be limited to maintenance.

Developments in the law relating to financial provision on divorce meant that the intended generosity of the provision to be made on death may have been overlooked. In the context of divorce, the focus was on the 'reasonable needs' of the claimant spouse even before the formal abolition of the minimal loss principle in 1984. The landmark decision of the House of Lords in *White v White*,[102] in which it was made clear that the applicant spouse's needs were not to be regarded as a ceiling on a claim and that any award should be tested against the 'yardstick of equality', was thus seen as having significant implications for provision on death as well.[103] Given the continuing uncertainties as to how assets should be divided on divorce, it is just as well that the courts have decided that there is no need to engage in a separate assessment of what precisely the survivor would have received in this alternative scenario.[104] The case law shows that surviving spouses or civil

[96] Inheritance (Provision for Family and Dependants) Act 1975, s 3(2).
[97] 2011 Report (n 1 above) para 2.146.
[98] Inheritance and Trustees' Powers Act 2014, Sch 2 para 5(2).
[99] Matrimonial Causes Act 1973, s 25(1).
[100] 1974 Report (n 22 above) para 14.
[101] ibid para 26.
[102] *White v White* [2001] 1 AC 596 (HL).
[103] See the detailed discussion in *Fielden v Cunliffe* [2005] EWCA Civ 1508, [2006] Ch 361.
[104] *P v G (Family Provision: Relevance of Divorce Provision)* [2004] EWHC 2944 (Fam), [2006] 1 FLR 431.

partners may receive either more or less than they would have done upon divorce or dissolution, depending on the size of the estate, the number of other beneficiaries and the duration of the marriage. Each case will turn on its own facts, just as upon divorce.[105]

More fundamentally, it might be wondered whether a comparison with what the survivor would have obtained on divorce is appropriate, regardless of the generosity or otherwise of the provision. Should not the court be giving due regard to the fact that the couple were only parted by death? The case law does, however, suggest why it remains appropriate: since a current spouse stands in a privileged position under the intestacy rules, a claim only usually needs to be brought where the property was left to someone else, in whole or in part. In a number of cases the marriage had ceased to function by the time of the death and the court accordingly decided that the surviving spouse would have received nothing had the marriage ended in divorce.[106]

6. Evaluating the Categories of Claimants

Each of the reforms effected by the 2014 Act can be seen either as a logical extension of the existing law or a response to a specific difficulty that had arisen in interpreting the previous statutory provisions. With any reform, however, the risk is that the justifiability of individual developments may distract attention from the underlying logic of the system more generally, or the lack thereof, and so this final section turns to the question of whether there is anything that unites and underpins the various categories of claimant.

The possibility of making a claim for financial provision against the estate of the deceased might, at least at first sight, seem to sit somewhat uneasily between the freedom of choice offered by wills and the fixed social expectations of different family relationships evident in the strict hierarchy that applies on intestacy. In particular, the family provision rules are generally seen as revealing a rather different concept of 'family' to that evident in the intestacy rules. The latter are based on status and blood relationships, while the former reveals a much more modern concept of the family. Indeed, Douglas has recently suggested that the family provision jurisdiction 'is at the forefront of dealing with the problems the law faces in squaring the traditional conception of what constitutes a family and what constitute appropriate family rights and obligations'.[107]

105 See eg the contrasting results in *Moore v Holdsworth* [2010] EWHC 683 (Ch), [2010] 2 FLR 1501; *Iqbal v Ahmed* [2011] EWCA Civ 900, [2012] 1 FLR 31; and *Lilleyman v Lilleyman* [2012] EWHC 821 (Ch), [2013] Ch 225.

106 See eg *Re Gregory* [1970] 1 WLR 1455 (CA); *Parish v Sharman* (unreported, 15 December 2000).

107 G Douglas, 'Family Provision and Family Practices—The Discretionary Regime of the Inheritance Act of England and Wales' (2014) 4 *Oñati Socio-Legal Series* 222.

But while differences between the rules relating to intestacy rules and family provision can be rationalised,[108] the fact remains that the current list of potential claimants under the 1975 Act is not seen as having a clear rationale. Herring, for example, has argued that the current law 'lacks a clear theoretical basis',[109] and arguments for the extension of the existing categories tellingly focus on specific examples rather than any overarching principle.[110]

In order to understand the categories that are included within the scope of the family provision legislation, it may be useful to look at those who are *excluded*. It may seem odd, for example, that the legislation does not grant a claim to a person who was caring for another,[111] or who had made a substantial contribution to the other's welfare. This could be explained on the basis that the family provision legislation, in contrast to the intestacy rules, is largely about needs rather than rights. Yet needs alone do not justify a claim, or necessarily indicate that it was unreasonable for the deceased not to have made financial provision for the claimant.[112]

The one thing that does unite all of the disparate categories is that the deceased has *done* something in relation to them, whether in terms of having established a familial relationship (through marriage, civil partnership or cohabitation with an adult, or through having a child or establishing a parent-child relationship) or provided financial support.[113] In other words, the deceased has chosen to act in a certain way. On this basis, the exclusion of parents—unless they have been supported by their child and survive him or her—becomes logical, since that relationship was not established by the choice of the deceased. The idea of choice provides a stronger justification for the estate of the deceased meeting the claim: an individual's needs can be met from a variety of sources, but our own choices create responsibilities for ourselves and our successors.

This is also distinct from the concept of a 'moral obligation' that has been alluded to in a number of cases, but rejected as a prerequisite for a claim.[114] Moral obligations may of course be seen as being generated by any number of routes: exactly what gives rise to a moral obligation will depend in large part on one's sense of morality. One could, for example, argue that there is a moral obligation to leave money to charitable causes, but the law is unlikely to compel this. The idea of

[108] See further G Douglas, H Woodward, A Humphrey, L Mills and G Morrell, 'Enduring Love? Attitudes to Family and Inheritance Law in England and Wales' (2011) 38 *Journal of Law and Society* 245 at 254.

[109] J Herring, *Older People in Law and Society* (Oxford, Oxford University Press, 2009) 329.

[110] See eg J Eekelaar, *Family Law and Personal Life* (Oxford, Oxford University Press, 2006) 48; B Sloan, 'The Concept of Coupledom in Succession Law' (2011) 70 *CLJ* 623.

[111] Although the fact that an eligible claimant is providing such care may strengthen their claim, by making it unreasonable that no provision should have been made for them.

[112] See eg *Barrass v Harding* [2001] 1 FLR 138 (CA).

[113] See eg *Jelley v Iliffe* (n 76 above) 137–38, in which the object of the 1975 Act was identified as being 'to remedy, wherever reasonably possible, the injustice of one, *who has been put by a deceased person in a position of dependency on him*, being deprived of any financial support, either by accident or by design of the deceased, after his death' (emphasis added).

[114] See eg *Re Coventry (deceased)* (n 67 above); *Re Hancock* [1998] 2 FLR 346 (CA).

having chosen to act in a certain way, however, focuses attention on what exactly has created the responsibility in question.

The focus on choice may meet the concern of a number of commentators that the family provision legislation effectively compels obligations on death that would not exist during one's lifetime.[115] Framing the family provision legislation as a means of responding to the choices made by the deceased allows us to look at the matter differently: if the deceased had not died, he or she could indeed have decided to have discontinued such support as was being provided, but where such support was being provided up until such time as he or she died, it can be inferred that a choice was made that it should continue. This is implicit in the requirement that the claimant was being maintained 'immediately before the death of the deceased' and illustrated by the case of *Kourgky v Lusher*,[116] in which a woman with whom the deceased had had a long-standing relationship failed to satisfy the court that she was still being maintained by him at this point. It was found that although there had been a general arrangement for her maintenance at one point, the deceased 'had abandoned that responsibility'[117] after returning to his wife.[118]

At the same time, recent case law suggests that individuals cannot resile from certain choices. Children can be seen as being in a different category from the other potential claimants, since in their case the choice made was responsible for their very existence. The case law suggests that the relationship can be severed by the child, but not by the parent. In the recent high-profile case of *Ilott v Mitson*,[119] for example, there had been an estrangement between mother and daughter but Arden LJ held that this should not deprive the latter of an award; although the daughter was 'partially responsible for the failure of the attempts at reconciliation, there is no suggestion that she wanted to be estranged from [her mother]'.[120] By contrast, in *Wright v Waters*[121] it was clear that the daughter had repudiated any relationship with her mother, since she had sent her a letter 'disowning her, stating that she did not wish to communicate with her and wishing that she was dead'.[122]

The way in which that choice was exercised will also be taken into account in assessing what provision should be made: was the support made during the

[115] See eg Herring (n 109 above) 328; *Older People in Law and Society*; M Oldham, 'Financial Obligations within the Family—Aspects of Intergenerational Maintenance and Succession in England and France' (2001) 60 *CLJ* 128 at 162.

[116] *Kourgky v Lusher* (1983) 4 FLR 65 (Fam).

[117] ibid 76. See also *Gregory-Davies v Bradley* (unreported, 13 March 2001, CA), in which it was decided that the claimant had long ceased to be maintained by the deceased.

[118] Cf *Graham v Murphy* [1997] 1 FLR 860 (Ch), in which it was noted that the deceased had undertaken 'de facto maintenance' on the basis that they were cohabiting, 'that she was a good deal better off financially than he was; and that she wanted to share her financial advantages'.

[119] *Ilott v Mitson* [2015] EWCA Civ 797, [2015] 2 FCR 547.

[120] ibid [51].

[121] *Wright v Waters* [2014] EWHC 3614 (Ch), [2015] WTLR 353.

[122] ibid [10]. See also *Garland v Morris* (n 67 above).

lifetime of the deceased given willingly or grudgingly,[123] was it generous or kept to a bare subsistence level? Had the deceased chosen to make specific promises to the claimant?[124] For what, in other words, did the deceased choose to assume responsibility?[125] Where the claim arises because no will was made and the intestacy rules make either no provision or only inadequate provision for the claimant, the court has also shown itself willing to infer what the deceased would have chosen.[126]

From this perspective there are not different approaches to wills, intestacy and family provision, but rather different ways of assessing the choices of the deceased, depending on the circumstances. Those choices may be expressed explicitly in a will, inferred from his or her actions towards certain individuals, or attributed ex post facto on the basis of evidence about the wishes of the majority.[127] This, of course, raises the question as to why one type of choice is seen as trumping the other: why, in other words, should the express wishes in the will not have priority? The answer must be that the law in this context feels it appropriate to give more weight to actions than to words.[128]

To return to the Book of Common Prayer quoted at the outset: perhaps we should not worry too much that we 'cannot tell who shall gather' our riches when we are gone, since the potential claims that may be brought will be ones that we have generated by one means or another. And after all, the law of succession—like the burial service itself—is for the living as well as the dead.

[123] See eg *Re Viner (deceased)* [1978] CLY 3091, in which the fact that the deceased supported his elderly sister grudgingly and at a fairly minimal level led the court to conclude that 'reasonable financial provision would be restricted to that made by the testator'.

[124] See eg *Re Pearce (deceased)* [1998] 2 FLR 705 (CA); *Espinosa v Bourke* [1999] 1 FLR 747 (CA).

[125] See eg *Re the estate of Lazarus* (unreported, 19 April 1983, CA), in which the deceased husband had provided only limited support for his wife. See also *Rhodes v Dean* [1996] 2 CLY 5555 (CA), in which it was held that the deceased had only assumed responsibility for the claimant's accommodation, not for her day-to-day living expenses.

[126] *Harrington v Gill* [1983] 4 FLR 265 (CA).

[127] The 'choice' model also offers a conceptual approach that has the potential to fit with the approach of both the Chancery and Family Divisions (for an analysis of their different approaches, see F Cownie and A Bradney, 'Divided Justice, Different Voices: Inheritance and Family Provision' (2003) 23 *Legal Studies* 566).

[128] In a similar vein it might be noted that a claim in proprietary estoppel may also trump the express words of the will. On proprietary estoppel in the succession law context, see Ben McFarlane's contribution in Ch 4 of this volume.

3

How Does the Common Law Forfeiture Rule Work?

IAN WILLIAMS*

1. Introduction

The common law forfeiture rule prevents unlawful killers from benefiting from their crimes, ruling out a convenient plot device in crime fiction, but otherwise serving an important public purpose. The operation of the rule has been the subject of considerable interest in the wider common law world in the past two decades, perhaps more so than any other individual part of succession law. Law reform bodies in Australia,[1] England and Wales,[2] Ireland[3] and New Zealand[4] have all considered the rule. Only the Scottish Law Commission concluded that no reform of the law is required.[5] While this paper is concerned with the common law forfeiture rule, some common law jurisdictions have enacted statutory forfeiture rules.[6] These statutory rules tend to be very similar to the common law rule, but show greater precision in explaining the operation of the rule.

In 2012, legislation about the operation of the forfeiture rule came into effect in England and Wales.[7] The forfeiture rule now operates by deeming that an unlawful

* The author would like to thank David Alexander for research assistance and Ying Khai Liew, the editors and all the other contributors to this volume for their helpful comments on an earlier draft.

[1] Tasmania Law Reform Institute, *The Forfeiture Rule* (Issues Paper No 5, 2003); Victorian Law Reform Commission, *The Forfeiture Rule* (2014).

[2] Law Commission, *The Forfeiture Rule and the Law of Succession* (Law Com No 295, 2005) (hereinafter '2005 Report').

[3] Irish Law Reform Commission, *Issues Paper on Review of section 120 of the Succession Act 1965 and Admissibility of criminal convictions in civil proceedings* (LRC IP 7-2014, 2014).

[4] New Zealand Law Commission, *Succession Law: Homicidal Heirs* (Report 38, 1997).

[5] Scottish Law Commission, *Report on Succession* (Scot Law Com No 215, 2009) para 7.2.

[6] Ireland's forfeiture rule is contained in the Irish Succession Act 1965, s 120. Most US States have a legislated 'slayer rule': American Law Institute, *Restatement of the Law, Third, Property (Wills and Other Donative Transfers)* (St Paul MN, American Law Institute Publishers, 2003) § 8.4, Comment i, Reporter's Note 1.

[7] Estates of Deceased Persons (Forfeiture Rule and Law of Succession) Act 2011, inserting new sections into the Wills Act 1837 and Administration of Estates Act 1925.

killer has predeceased her victim. The killer will consequently be unable to inherit from the victim. However, the legislation was not comprehensive. It applies only to testate and intestate succession, ignoring other circumstances in which the forfeiture rule applies. The coverage of testate succession is also limited. According to the new section 33A which has been inserted into the Wills Act 1837, the statutory deemed predecease rule only applies 'for the purposes of this Act'.[8] As the Wills Act 1837 is not a statute which gives general force to wills, but merely sets out various rules in relation to wills, their validity and effect, this leaves gaps.[9]

Predecease is only relevant in the Wills Act 1837 in relation to the operation of section 33, a section which modifies the operation of the doctrine of lapse when gifts are made to children or other lineal descendants of the deceased, and so the new section 33A can only have effect in relation to section 33. In other circumstances where predecease may be relevant, such as the situation where a gift is made to anyone who is not a lineal descendant of the deceased, section 33A is irrelevant. Similarly, section 33A seems to have no effect in relation to 'gift overs' in a will, when property is left to a person with an explicit provision about what is to occur if that person predeceases the testator. As that gift over does not take effect through the Wills Act, it is not covered by section 33A. At common law, if the donee unlawfully kills the testator, the killer will not be deemed to have predeceased the testator, and the gift over will not take effect.[10] Section 33A does not change this. The common law of forfeiture therefore continues to be relevant for testate succession in England and Wales.

The forfeiture rule is one of public policy, concerned with criminals not benefiting from their crime. This may be directed to removing an incentive for criminal behaviour, but the common law rule applies regardless of motive. A better explanation for the policy is the broader moral intuition that it is simply inappropriate for unlawful killers to receive a benefit from killing.

Basing the rule on public policy means that it is different to the civilian model, which addresses the problem of a donee unlawfully killing a testator through rules about unworthiness to inherit.[11] The civilian model is based on presumptions about the intentions of the testator or about protecting freedom of testation, and it covers a wider range of situations than killings.[12] It is not based on the idea that criminals should not benefit from their crime.[13] The same approach has

[8] This point is also made in F Barlow, R Wallington and others (eds), *Williams on Wills, vol 1: The Law of Wills*, 10th edn (London, LexisNexis, 2014) [9-17] (hereinafter '*Williams on Wills*').

[9] Failing to appreciate this point seems to explain why the Law Commission believed that the new legislation provided comprehensively for forfeiture in relation to testate succession: 2005 Report (n 2 above) paras 4.11, 4.13 and 5.3.

[10] *Re Jones (deceased)* [1998] 1 FLR 246 (CA).

[11] J MacLeod and R Zimmermann, 'Unworthiness to Inherit, Public Policy, Forfeiture: The Scottish Story' (2012–13) 87 *Tulane Law Review* 741, especially 742–44. This is not to say that the civilian rule does not have clear policy undertones, but that the doctrinal principle (taken from Roman law) is one of 'unworthiness to inherit', an idea which can encompass behaviour which is not even criminal.

[12] MacLeod and Zimmermann (n 11 above) 742–43, summarising the Austrian, French and German positions.

[13] MacLeod and Zimmermann (n 11 above) 745.

been taken by some American scholars.[14] In contrast, English judges stress that the underlying basis for the forfeiture rule is the rule of public policy that criminals should not benefit from crime.[15]

In many respects, this difference in underlying explanation may not affect the operation of the rule. Ireland's statutory forfeiture rule is based upon civilian code provisions about unworthiness to inherit, albeit limited solely to killings of the testator, but it has raised similar questions in relation to joint tenancies as those encountered under the common law forfeiture rule.[16] However, this similarity will not always exist. For example, a rule based upon presumed intentions might allow a killer who was forgiven by a testator before her death to receive an inheritance, but the policy based common law rule would not.[17] In *Beresford v Royal Insurance Co Ltd*, a life insurance policy which was payable on the suicide of the insured was subject to the forfeiture rule.[18] The term of the policy covering payment on suicide was contrary to public policy (as suicide was a crime at the time). Hence a claim under the policy failed. If an explicit contract term cannot overcome the forfeiture rule, it seems unlikely that mere 'forgiveness' will do so.

As a principle of public policy, the forfeiture rule is not always concerned with the overall justice of the outcomes in particular cases. Forfeiture cases are almost always hard cases and so they almost always create a risk of producing what seems to be bad law.[19] Judges have been refreshingly candid about this possibility. In one of the early cases, Lord Esher MR noted that the rule 'ought not to be stretched beyond what is necessary for the protection of the public', suggesting that outcomes beyond the killer not benefiting were not of concern.[20] Ungoed-Thomas J commented that the rule is 'clumsy, crude … and … somewhat uncivilised' in its operation in some cases,[21] while Mummery LJ stated simply that the rule 'is not the statement of a principle of justice designed to produce a fair result', indeed that as a principle of public policy it 'may produce unfair consequences in some cases'.[22]

[14] I Ehrlich and RA Posner justify the slayer rule as a form of presumed revocation: 'An Economic Analysis of Legal Rulemaking' (1974) 3 *Journal of Legal Studies* 257, 259. Building on this, the Reporter for the American Law Institute has described the slayer rule as being based upon the 'wrongful prevention of revocation' by the killer: *Restatement 3rd (Wills)* (n 6 above), § 8.4, Reporter's Note 7.

[15] See eg *Cleaver v Mutual Reserve Fund Life Association* [1892] 1 QB 147 (CA) 156 (Fry LJ). This distinction between the common and civil law traditions is noted in J Chadwick, 'A Testator's Bounty to his Slayer' (1914) 30 *LQR* 211, 211–12.

[16] LRC IP 7-2014 (n 3 above) 2–6. The Irish case of *Re Celine Cawley* [2011] IEHC 515 contains an excellent discussion of the problems associated with forfeiture and the common law concept of joint tenancy, a problem not addressed by civilian code provisions.

[17] The New Zealand Law Commission rejected a forgiveness rule: NZLC Report 38 (n 4 above) para 14. Taschereau J seems to have thought that a forgiveness rule should operate in the forfeiture context: *Lundy v Lundy* (1895) 24 SCR 650 (SCC) 653. Taschereau J's dissent also included reference to the civilian tradition, which may explain his position.

[18] *Beresford v Royal Insurance Co Ltd* [1938] AC 586 (HL).

[19] Especially in the testate succession context; strangely, very few testators seem to consider the possibility of being killed by family and friends, and so wills rarely make provision for this event.

[20] *Cleaver v Mutual Reserve Fund Life Association* (n 15 above) 153.

[21] *Re Dellow's Will Trusts* [1964] 1 All ER 771 (Ch) 775.

[22] *Dunbar v Plant* [1998] Ch 412 (CA) 422.

Public policy has the potential to generate considerable uncertainty. As Burrough J observed, 'it is a very unruly horse, and when once you get astride it you never know where it will carry you'.[23] Nevertheless, analysing the forfeiture rule from a policy perspective can be helpful. For example, it can illuminate the differences between cases concerning the transmission of wealth on death and those concerning motor indemnity insurance in respect of fatal road traffic collisions. Simply put, in motor insurance cases, unlawful killers are entitled to payments from their insurers for causing death to their victims, that payment being used to pay compensation to the victims' families. Contrast traditional forfeiture cases and cases where the forfeiture rule prevents a killer from receiving a benefit under a life insurance policy, where the killer is prevented from receiving a benefit from the victim's death. Once the policy of the rule is taken into consideration, it become clear why there is a seeming exception to the forfeiture rule in cases of motor indemnity insurance. In such cases there are two public policy concerns: preventing the killer from benefiting and ensuring adequate compensation for the families of victims of traffic accidents. The policy of compensating victims' families outweighs that behind the forfeiture rule, perhaps because the compensation policy has been specifically endorsed, even mandated, by Parliament.[24]

However, the introduction of the forfeiture rule to implement a particular policy concern has caused problems. The public policy principle is a broadly (perhaps poorly) defined one which prescribes an outcome, but does not require any particular method for reaching it. As Kirby P observed, the forfeiture rule was developed judicially 'to solve the necessities of particular cases. It developed without a great deal of consideration, either of its scope, or of its exceptions, or of its fundamental underlying rationale'.[25] Much of the debate has been about the types of killings to which the rule applies, where there is a marked discrepancy between the American approach and the approach taken in the rest of the common law world.[26] However, there is also disagreement and uncertainty about how the rule works. It is this latter issue which is addressed in this chapter.

The forfeiture rule operates in a variety of circumstances, stretching beyond testate and intestate succession. The rule takes effect in relation to survivorship and joint tenancies,[27] and as homicide can cause the acceleration of life interests and trigger payments under life insurance policies or from pensions and state

[23] *Richardson v Mellish* (1824) 2 Bing 229 at 252, 130 ER 294 at 303.

[24] See *Charlton v Fisher* [2001] EWCA Civ 112, [2002] QB 578 at [33] (Laws LJ) and JG Fleming, 'Insurance of the Criminal' (1971) 34 *MLR* 176.

[25] *Troja v Troja* (1994) 33 NSWLR 269 (NSWCA) 278.

[26] The American slayer rule applies only to intentional killings: *Restatement 3rd (Wills)* (n 6 above) § 8.4(a); American Law Institute, *Restatement of the Law, Third, Restitution and Unjust Enrichment* (St Paul MN, American Law Institute Publishers, 2011), § 45(1); Uniform Law Commission, *Uniform Probate Code* (2010) § 2-803. The English and Australian courts have rejected the idea that the forfeiture rule distinguishes between types of homicide on the basis of culpability: *Dunbar v Plant* (n 22 above) and *Troja v Troja* (n 25 above).

[27] Although there is still no authoritative determination as to quite how the forfeiture rule works in this context. See text to nn 113–117 below.

benefits, the rule can also apply to all such situations.[28] Ideally, the forfeiture rule will work in a coherent fashion across this wide range of contexts, perhaps even with a single mechanism for its operation. This may not be possible, but finding a position which works well for most of them, with a cogent explanation for the exceptions, should be the ambition.[29]

There are divergent views about how the forfeiture rule does, and should, operate. *Parry and Kerridge* strongly assert that the rule operates by way of a constructive trust, albeit that the courts have not appreciated this.[30] As the leading English succession textbook, the constructive trust view appears as a starting point for discussions of the English rule.[31] In the field of restitution, Virgo admits that the rule generally operates as a bar to the killer receiving any benefit, but argues that the forfeiture rule should operate through a constructive trust.[32] Trusts scholars typically take the view that the forfeiture rule prevents the killer from acquiring title, but that a constructive trust may have a role in situations where this does not occur.[33]

The argument of this chapter is that, in general, the forfeiture rule operates as a bar to unlawful killers, or those claiming through them, obtaining property rights at all. By killing the victim, a killer simply acquires nothing on the death of the deceased. Contrary to various suggestions in the academic literature, a constructive trust is not normally imposed to achieve the outcome demanded by public policy. However, there are some difficult situations in which a constructive trust may be appropriate. This integrates the forfeiture rule neatly into the structure of private law more generally. Typically, the forfeiture rule operates as part of the law of property, of which succession law is a part. There are instances in which

[28] For life insurance: *Amicable Society for a Perpetual Life Assurance Office v Bolland* (1830) 4 Bli NS 194, 5 ER 70; for pensions: *Glover v Staffordshire Police Authority* [2006] EWHC 2414 (Admin), [2007] ICR 661; and for benefits: *R v Chief National Insurance Commissioner, ex parte Connor* [1981] QB 758 (QB).

[29] In this sense, the approach is somewhat American. Modern US succession law is often at least, if not more, concerned with non-probate methods of transmitting wealth across generations, at least in part due to deficiencies in the probate system. The classic article is JH Langbein, 'The Nonprobate Revolution and the Future of the Law of Succession' (1983–84) 97 *Harvard Law Review* 1108; see now MB Leslie and SE Sterk, 'Revisiting the Revolution: Reintegrating the Wealth Transmission System' (2015) 56 *Boston College Law Review* 61.

[30] R Kerridge (assisted by AHR Brierley), *Parry and Kerridge: The Law of Succession*, 12th edn (London, Sweet & Maxwell, 2009) [14-81]–[14-82] (hereinafter '*Parry and Kerridge*'), following R Kerridge, 'Visiting the Sins of the Fathers on their Children' (2001) 117 *LQR* 371.

[31] For example, in MacLeod and Zimmermann (n 11 above) 746, *Parry and Kerridge* (n 30 above) is cited for the proposition that the forfeiture rule 'operates by way of creating a constructive trust', which is at least contestable.

[32] G Virgo, *The Principles of the Law of Restitution*, 3rd edn (Oxford, Oxford University Press, 2015) 543–52. A similar position is taken in G Virgo, *The Principles of Equity and Trusts* (Oxford, Oxford University Press, 2012) 309.

[33] G Virgo and EH Burn, *Maudsley and Burn's, Trusts and Trustees: Cases and Materials*, 7th edn (Oxford, Oxford University Press, 2008) 303; AJ Oakley, *Parker and Mellows: The Modern Law of Trusts*, 9th edn (London, Sweet & Maxwell, 2008) 444 (although the discussion of *Re Sigsworth* is misleading, as there is no mention of a constructive trust in the case itself); J McGhee (ed), *Snell's Equity*, 33rd edn (London, Sweet & Maxwell, 2014) [26-007].

other branches of private law are involved when property law fails to achieve the prescribed policy outcome, with gains-based remedies concerned with restitution for the killer's wrongdoing playing a significant role in some situations. As a general principle, the forfeiture rule cuts across the traditional taxonomies of private law, but is adequately served within the existing structure.

2. The Constructive Trust Model

2.1. Introduction

Under the constructive trust model, an unlawful killer receives all of the benefits to which she is entitled upon the death of her victim. The killer holds any assets received on trust, to prevent the killer from benefiting from them. Supporters of this approach identify several justifications for the use of constructive trusts.

2.2. Flexibility

The constructive trust can be applied flexibly, and for many writers the key feature here is the culpability of the killer.[34] Even with the flexibility granted to the English courts by the Forfeiture Act 1982, this flexibility may still be considered desirable.[35] The Forfeiture Act 1982 has no application to cases of murder.[36] There may be some murders where it is considered inappropriate to deprive the killer of all benefits to be received from the deceased.[37] Similarly, the strict time limits under the Forfeiture Act 1982 could be avoided if the forfeiture rule did not operate in a uniform manner.[38]

Evidently a major difficulty with arguing that the constructive trust model represents current English law is that the law is not flexible, although there is a hint by Phillips LJ in *Dunbar v Plant* that, had the Forfeiture Act 1982 not been created, some flexibility would have been introduced.[39] However, even the suggestions of

[34] A good example is the dissent of Kirby P in *Troja v Troja* (n 25 above) 278–86. American law does not use a constructive trust to achieve flexibility in relation to culpability, presumably because the slayer rule applies only to intentional homicide (see n 26 above).

[35] The Law Commission was sceptical about the benefits of flexibility: 2005 Report (n 2 above) para 3.25.

[36] Forfeiture Act 1982, s 5.

[37] 'Mercy killings' seem to be the only obvious category, although it was observed by Lord Hope in *R (Purdy) v Director of Public Prosecutions* [2009] UKHL 45, [2010] 1 AC 345 at [25] that some acts which constitute assisting suicide might also amount to murder, although they are not prosecuted as such.

[38] For the problem with time limits, see *Re Land* [2006] EWHC 2069 (Ch), [2007] 1 All ER 324. This is certainly preferable to the constitutionally problematic suggestion in *Parry and Kerridge* (n 30 above) [14-68] that 'the court has an inherent power to override the draconian effects of section 2(3) of the 1982 Act'.

[39] *Dunbar v Plant* (n 22 above) 435.

flexibility in *Dunbar v Plant* and other cases are all limited to a single issue—how culpability would affect whether the forfeiture rule applied at all. The constructive trust model introduces flexibility beyond this issue, also affecting how the rule applies and assets are distributed.

2.3. Testamentary Intentions

The forfeiture rule can operate to produce results which seem unlikely to represent the wishes of the deceased. *Re DWS* is a good example: a son killed his parents, who were intestate, and the forfeiture rule operated to prevent the son from benefiting from their intestacy.[40] It consequently also prevented the killer's son from benefiting. Instead, the estate passed to siblings of the deceased, who were probably not the people the victims would have wished to benefit. Similarly, in *Re Callaway*, a daughter was the sole beneficiary of her mother's will. She killed her mother and the property passed to the victim's son on intestacy. As Vaisey J noted, the forfeiture rule here operated to the 'frustration of [the victim's] testamentary intentions'.[41] A constructive trust imposed over the estate requires the killer to hold the property on terms determined by the court. Kerridge has argued that the court is to 'arrive at an equitable solution which reflects the likely wishes of the [deceased] in circumstances which he would never have contemplated as occurring'.[42] In this, Kerridge echoes the approach taken in the American Law Institute's *Restatement (Third) of Restitution and Unjust Enrichment*.[43]

There are several difficulties with the Kerridge approach. Even if one accepts that it should be taken, ascertainment of the deceased's intention will often be at best an 'attempt to guess' what she would have wanted.[44] The same sort of problems which arise in imputing intention in the context of trusts of the family home are equally present here, but more acute. The difficulties are more pronounced, in that in the succession context there are less likely to be the kinds of activity and financial conduct which can provide some basis for imputation.[45] Succession in the common law is a matter of (potentially capricious) gifts freely given; ascertaining any intention will consequently be challenging.[46] American law on

[40] *Re DWS (deceased)* [2001] Ch 568 (CA).

[41] *Re Callaway* [1956] Ch 559 (Ch) 565.

[42] Kerridge, 'Sins' (n 30 above) 375.

[43] *Restatement 3rd (Restitution)* (n 26 above) § 45(3).

[44] *Parry and Kerridge* (n 30 above) [14-82].

[45] Limited evidence is still a problem, which can be seen in the common intention constructive trust context, where intention can be imputed on the basis of what is 'fair'. Behrens J observed that the intention imputed on the basis of fairness was 'somewhat arbitrary but it is the best I can do with the available material': *Aspden v Elvy* [2012] EWHC 1387 (Ch), [2012] *Fam Law* 1085 at [128].

[46] As Gardner and Davidson note in relation to common intention constructive trusts, 'The fact that some outcome is fair, *alias* that reasonable persons in the parties' circumstances would have considered and agreed upon it, does not mean that the parties actually did so, for all sort of reasons, or even none': S Gardner and K Davidson, 'The Supreme Court on Family Homes' (2012) 128 *LQR* 178 at 179.

the constructive trust in forfeiture addresses this issue, identifying a hierarchy of claims and making clear that the estate should only be given to the person intended to receive by the deceased '*if* such a person can be identified', rather than assuming that intention can always be found (emphasis added).[47] A comment in the *Restatement (Third) of Restitution and Unjust Enrichment* also acknowledges that whether or not the child of a killer should be permitted to take under such a trust involves questions of policy in addition to intention, with several States prohibiting benefits from passing to children of the killer.[48]

A more fundamental problem is that there is no inherent reason why a constructive trust model leads to a trust which follows the intention (real or otherwise) of the deceased.[49] There are types of constructive trust which are directed to fulfilling a person's intentions. Secret trusts and mutual wills are examples of such trusts which will be familiar to succession lawyers.[50] These trusts are not directed to depriving a wrongdoer of their illegitimate gains, unlike the trust which it is argued should be imposed in the forfeiture context.[51] There is no obvious reason why a constructive trust arising following an unlawful killing should be a trust directed to perfecting intentions. This is not normally the approach taken in trusts imposed to deprive a wrongdoer of their gains. From a succession law perspective, following the intention of a testator is not the approach taken in relation to failed gifts in wills, void wills or intestacy.[52] Some justification needs to be advanced as to why such a following of intention is particularly necessary in the forfeiture context, but not elsewhere in succession law. No such justification has been advanced. The forfeiture rule is concerned with preventing a killer benefiting from her crime. Once that has been achieved, the rule has nothing more to say. The rule and the underlying policy bar one particular outcome, but a wide range of alternative outcomes remain available.

2.4. Effects on Third Parties

Youdan raised the problem that if an unlawful killer were denied title due to her crime, this would cause considerable complications. If the killer acquired physical control of the property, she would have the appearance of title, and innocent third parties might then rely upon this to acquire property from the killer. However, if

47 *Restatement 3rd (Restitution)* (n 26 above) § 45(3)(b).

48 *Restatement 3rd (Restitution)* (n 26 above) § 45, Comment d.

49 A point made by the Law Commission's 2005 Report (n 2 above) para 3.23.

50 On mutual wills, see Ying Khai Liew's contribution in Ch 5 of this volume.

51 See R Chambers, 'Constructive Trusts in Canada' (1999) 37 *Alberta Law Review* 173, especially 182–83.

52 In the Scottish forfeiture case of *Tannock v Tannock* 2013 SLT (Sh Ct) 57 at [36], it was observed that it is not appropriate to look beyond the express terms of the will in relation to ascertaining the deceased's intention, indeed that it is only generally appropriate to do so where there is a particular rule or statute allowing the court to do so.

the killer in fact had no more than a possessory title, these third parties would not themselves be able to acquire anything more than a possessory right.[53] Were the killer to hold the property on trust, on the other hand, then the usual bona fide purchaser rule would apply to protect many, but not all, such third parties in a well-understood way.

It will be shown below that this concern is misplaced.[54] The bar on the killer receiving benefits from the killing does not work in the way Youdan supposed; third parties already benefit from the bona fide purchaser rule, and the *nemo dat* problem he identified does not arise.

2.5. Parliamentary Sovereignty

The most powerful argument in favour of the constructive trust solution is that the forfeiture rule preventing title from passing to the unlawful killer seems to be contrary to express provisions in statutes. This argument has been particularly powerful in the United States, where it was first propounded,[55] but it has also been adopted by various writers elsewhere.[56] The point was also acknowledged by Sedley LJ in *Re DWS*, who observed that the application of the forfeiture rule to intestacy is a 'judicial interpolation in a statute which says nothing whatever on the subject'.[57] If statutes such as the Administration of Estates Act 1925 are read literally in forfeiture cases, then they appear to require that the killer be given the property.[58] A rule which seems simply to ignore statutory requirements is a constitutionally improper rule. It is constitutionally more appropriate to follow the statutory rules, but then for equity to impose a trust over the property received.[59]

There are two principal problems with this argument. The first is the simple one that not all instances of forfeiture are grounded in statute, most obviously forfeiture in the context of testate succession, but also joint tenancy. This is not an especially powerful argument, as the constructive trust approach has the merit of applying to both statutory and non-statutory contexts.

The second, much stronger, challenge is that the insistence on literal interpretation is misplaced. Sedley LJ in *Re DWS* noted the possibility of a non-literal

[53] TG Youdan, 'Acquisition of Property by Killing' (1973) 89 *LQR* 235, 255.

[54] See the text accompanying n 94 below.

[55] Starting with JB Ames, 'Can a Murderer Acquire Title by His Crime and Keep It?' in JB Ames, *Lectures on Legal History and Miscellaneous Legal Essays* (Cambridge MA, Harvard University Press, 1913) especially 312.

[56] See eg N Peart, 'Reforming the Forfeiture Rule: Comparing New Zealand, England and Australia' (2002) 31 *Common Law World Review* 1 at 15; Virgo, *The Principles of the Law of Restitution* (n 32 above) 551–52; Youdan (n 53 above) 251–52.

[57] *Re DWS* (n 40 above) [35].

[58] Literal interpretation is stressed in Kerridge, 'Sins' (n 30 above) 375 and in G Virgo, 'The Law of Restitution and the Proceeds of Crime: a Survey of English Law' [1998] *Restitution Law Review* 34 at 57.

[59] Virgo also describes this approach as more 'honest': Virgo, *Restitution* (n 32 above) 551–52; 'formalistic' may be as good a description.

rectifying construction in relation to intestacy, but regarded it as too much of a stretch and so constitutionally improper to apply.[60] Nonetheless, there are plenty of other principles of statutory construction beyond the literal. As *Bennion* observes, one principle of statutory construction which seems to apply generally is that '[u]nless the contrary intention appears, an enactment by implication imports the principle of the maxim *nullus commodum capere potest de injuria sua propria* (no one should be allowed to profit from his own wrong)'.[61] Several of the examples cited by *Bennion* are forfeiture cases, but not all of them.

As Lord Hope observed, '[a]s a general rule Parliament must be taken to have legislated against the background of the general principles of the common law'. It is only if Parliament is found to have decided not to follow the common law, that the common law principles are abrogated.[62] Just such an approach was applied in the forfeiture context by Lord Lane CJ in *R v Chief National Insurance Commissioner, ex parte Connor*. A woman who killed her husband applied for a widow's allowance under the Social Security Act 1975, which included no provision barring killers from receiving such an allowance. Lord Lane CJ said:[63]

> The fact that there is no specific mention in the Act of disentitlement so far as the widow is concerned if she were to commit this sort of offence and so become a widow is merely an indication, as I see it, that the draftsman realised perfectly well that he was drawing this Act against the background of the law as it stood at the time.

This is a well-recognised principle of statutory construction; one which removes the constitutional justification for the constructive trust approach.

2.6. Absence of Authority

The arguments in favour of the constructive trust approach are therefore somewhat equivocal. A particularly telling argument against the constructive trust model, at least as an accurate description of the current law, is that it has no basis whatsoever in English authority. There are no English cases which have applied the constructive trust approach. There are cases which clearly show a model of forfeiture in operation which does not apply a constructive trust model. For example, in *Re Pollock* the victim left her estate to her killer, and her executor applied for directions. The executor was told to distribute as if on intestacy, clearly demonstrating that the killer's estate was not to obtain the assets which might then have been held on trust.[64]

[60] *Re DWS* (n 40 above) [35].

[61] O Jones (ed), *Bennion on Statutory Interpretation: A Code*, 6th edn (London, Lexis Nexis, 2013) s 349.

[62] *Wisely v John Fulton (Plumbers) Ltd, Wadey v Surrey County Council* [2000] 2 All ER 545 (HL) 548.

[63] *R v Chief National Insurance Commissioner, ex parte Connor* (n 28 above) 765. Similarly *Glover v Staffordshire Police Authority* (n 28 above).

[64] *Re Pollock* [1941] Ch 219 (Ch).

However, the point never seems to have been raised directly.[65] The only mention of the constructive trust approach in English courts is in *Re K*, where Vinelott J observed, obiter, that some jurisdictions use a constructive trust in relation to killings and joint tenancies, but that England does not, instead simply severing the joint tenancy, suggesting that the constructive trust is not used.[66] In other jurisdictions, the point has been made and rejected.[67] In the United States, the constructive trust model is a residuary one, applicable only where title has already passed to the killer, something which is usually prevented by other rules of law.[68]

It has been claimed that the nineteenth-century case of *Cleaver v Mutual Reserve Fund Life Association* demonstrates that the constructive trust approach to forfeiture is compatible with English law.[69] It does not. In *Cleaver*, the husband insured his own life, for the benefit of his wife. By virtue of section 11 of the Married Women's Property Act 1882, that policy had to be held on trust by the husband for the benefit of his wife. The wife then murdered her husband. The forfeiture rule prevented the wife from benefiting from the insurance policy, and in consequence the benefit of the property passed to the husband's estate. As Fry LJ observed, this is a simple application of standard equitable principles: 'Whenever there is property produced by the payments of A. which is held in trust for B., and that trust fails or is satisfied, a resulting trust arises for A. or his estate'.[70] A general rule that the killer obtains benefits to which they are entitled on the death of the deceased, but holds them on constructive trust, is markedly different.[71] Furthermore, a resulting trust does not lead to property being held for the benefit of the person whom the settlor would have liked to receive it.[72]

2.7. Coherence

A forfeiture rule operating through a constructive trust poses difficulties for the coherence of the law. The constructive trust model raises difficult questions about the place of that trust in wider trusts doctrine.[73] Even if it is accepted that the

[65] Hence the argument in *Parry and Kerridge* (n 30 above) 350 at fn 296, that the decision in *Re DWS* (n 40 above) was *per incuriam*.

[66] *Re K* [1985] Ch 85 (Ch) 100.

[67] *Troja v Troja* (n 25 above) is the most well-known example.

[68] *Restatement 3rd (Restitution)* (n 26 above) § 45, Comment c.

[69] *Cleaver v Mutual Reserve Fund Life Association* (n 15 above), used by Kerridge, 'Sins' (n 30 above) 374 and Peart (n 56 above) 15.

[70] *Cleaver v Mutual Reserve Fund Life Association* (n 15 above) 158.

[71] *cf* Kerridge, 'Sins' (n 30 above) 374 ('a slight distinction') and Peart (n 56 above) 15 (a constructive trust approach 'seems to be consistent with *Cleaver's Case*').

[72] Even if one accepts the view that resulting trusts such as that in *Cleaver* are responses to the settlor's intention, that intention is much more limited than in the suggested constructive trust model. It is a presumed intention allowing only one possible beneficiary, the settlor: see B McFarlane and C Mitchell, *Hayton and Mitchell: Text, Cases and Materials on the Law of Trusts and Equitable Remedies*, 14th edn (London, Sweet & Maxwell, 2015) [14-161]–[14-164].

[73] See the text accompanying n 53 above.

forfeiture rule operates by preventing killers from obtaining rights in testate and intestate succession (as argued below), problems remain in addressing other difficult situations. Some such situations are sensibly, and plausibly, addressed through a constructive trust.[74] However, others are addressed through contract law, and a constructive trust would only be possible if the existing rules of contract were to be displaced.[75]

3. 'Killer Obtains No Rights' Model

3.1. Introduction

The dominant view in England is that in some sense the unlawful killer does not obtain rights to assets. Quite what this means, and how this occurs, is much less clear. Judges refer to a killer not being able to 'obtain, or enforce, any rights resulting to him from his own crime'.[76] As Phillips LJ observed in *Dunbar v Plant*, there is a difference between obtaining rights and not being able to enforce rights that one does have, but this issue has not been further addressed by the courts.[77]

Evidence that the unlawful killer simply does not obtain any rights is found in various cases connected with the forfeiture rule. The simplest are the pensions and benefits cases. In all these cases, the killer is simply not entitled to receive payments which would otherwise be due to him or her. *R v Chief National Insurance Commissioner, ex parte Connor* is a good example. In that case, a woman who had killed her husband applied for judicial review of the National Insurance Commissioner's decision not to grant her a widow's allowance, seeking *certiorari*.[78] This was not a case in which the widow asked the court to enforce her rights, but merely one in which she asked that a decision (that she had no entitlement) be overturned. The Court of Appeal rejected her case, strongly suggesting that she had no right under the relevant legislation. A similar approach was taken in *Glover v Staffordshire Police Authority*, where a widow was held not to be entitled to a pension after she killed her husband.[79] Because of the context of these cases, the courts were required to address directly the question of entitlement—did the killer have a right to be paid the benefit or pension? In both cases, the court answered in the

[74] See the text accompanying nn 114–122 and 129–134 below.

[75] See the text accompanying nn 123–124 below.

[76] *Re Crippen* [1911] P 108 (PDA) 112 (Sir Samuel Evans P). Very similar language was used almost a century later by Blackburne J at first instance in *Re DWS* (n 40 above) 571.

[77] *Dunbar v Plant* (n 22 above) 429.

[78] *R v Chief National Insurance Commissioner, ex p Connor* (n 28 above). Although one should be wary of reading too much into the individual words used by judges, it is notable that the language used throughout *ex parte Connor* is of the widow's actions 'disentitling' her (at 765 and 766).

[79] *Glover v Staffordshire Police Authority* (n 28 above). As the pension here was one provided under legislation, the case seems to fall between pensions and benefits cases.

negative. The benefits and pension providers were therefore not required to transfer any property to the widows.

In relation to testate succession, the case of *Re Pollock* shows that the killer is simply not entitled to rights in the estate of the victim. Under her will a woman left her entire estate to her husband, by whom she was killed (and who then killed himself). The wife's executors applied for directions. In an unusually clear statement of the effects of forfeiture, Farwell J said that the 'estate of [the victim] did not in the events which happened pass under her will to [the killer]' and the wife therefore 'died intestate'.[80]

The view of the law which holds that the killer obtains no rights is reinforced by the seeming rule that the killer, or those claiming through her, cannot be the personal representatives of the victim. In *Re Crippen*, a man killed his wife and was executed for the offence. His personal representative (and mistress) was not permitted to be the personal representative of the deceased wife.[81] While the husband's personal representative would normally have been the person appointed to act as the wife's personal representative too, the circumstances were held to be 'special' under statute and the administration was granted to others.[82] Although linked with a particular statutory rule, the case bears out the point made by Fry LJ in *Cleaver v Mutual Reserve Fund Life Association*: that the forfeiture rule operates to the exclusion of the killer and those claiming through her.[83] Given that a personal representative is not entitled to the benefit of the estate, the *Crippen* case suggests that an unlawful killer, and those claiming through her, is excluded from obtaining any rights from the killing, even when the use of those rights is supervised by the court, for the benefit of others.

Re K also suggests that this is the correct analysis. That case raised an awkward question about when the forfeiture rule took effect, as the killing occurred a short time before the Forfeiture Act 1982 came into force. As the Act did not have retrospective effect, the key question was when interested parties acquired rights. Vinelott J noted that beneficiaries under a will do not acquire a right to particular assets, but only a right to due administration of the estate. He held that the right to have the estate duly administered was a chose in action for purposes of the Forfeiture Act 1982. In the victim's will, a life interest in most of the estate (including the residue) was left to the killer, and the remainder to various residuary legatees. According to Vinelott J, those residuary legatees acquired a right for the purposes of the Forfeiture Act 1982 as soon as the killing occurred, 'in consequence of the forfeiture rule'. This meant that 'a right of action was acquired by each residuary legatee by way of acceleration of his or her interests'.[84] *Re K* suggests that a killer never acquires any rights in relation to the estate, not even the right to its due

[80] *Re Pollock* (n 64 above) 224.
[81] *Re Crippen* (n 76 above).
[82] See the Court of Probate Act 1857, s 73 (now the Senior Courts Act 1981, s 116).
[83] *Cleaver v Mutual Reserve Fund Life Association* (n 15 above) 159.
[84] *Re K* (n 66 above) 98.

administration. The forfeiture rule operates at the moment of killing to deny the killer rights and to accelerate the rights of the residuary legatees in the remainder. The same approach could be applied on intestacy: the killer is denied from obtaining any rights under the intestacy.

If this is correct, then the forfeiture rule does not work by depriving an unlawful killer of legal title directly. Instead, the killer never obtains any rights at all, rights which would otherwise be enforceable against personal representatives, pension providers, or welfare agencies. If the killer has no rights in relation to the victim's estate then the killer will obtain no benefit because the executors or administrators will not give property to the killer. In the pensions and benefits cases, the relevant organisations will not pay money to the killer. The killer will consequently never be given title to assets.

3.2. Consequences

This analysis of the operation of the forfeiture rule clarifies the effect of the rule.

3.2.1. Testate and Intestate Succession

Personal representatives are owners of the assets of the deceased and have the power to dispose of the assets as they wish. They hold the property 'for the purpose of carrying out the functions and duties of administration'.[85] However, if an unlawful killer never obtains a right to receive property from the estate, then she is not entitled to receive anything from the administration. Personal representatives who distribute property to the killer will have committed a *devastavit*, just as if they distribute property to someone clearly not entitled under a will or on intestacy.[86]

The personal representatives would then have a remedy against the killer for a mistaken distribution. Furthermore, the personal representatives would be liable to account for their incorrect distribution to the killer and would be personally liable to the people otherwise entitled to the victim's estate. This would be less of a burden on the personal representatives than at first appears. First, many forfeiture cases arise before distribution has occurred, on applications to the court for directions.[87] If the personal representatives comply with the terms of the court

[85] *Commissioner of Stamp Duties (Queensland) v Livingston* [1965] AC 694 (PC) 707. Although the Administration of Estates Act 1925 refers to personal representatives holding on trust, this does not seem to be a true trust to which all the usual rules of trusts are incident: *Parry and Kerridge* (n 30 above) [24-63].

[86] This explains the remark of the Law Commission, that 'no legal title can vest in the killer unless the property has been distributed in ignorance of the facts and the killing is discovered at a later stage': 2005 Report (n 2 above) para 3.23(1). This point was repeated verbatim by the Victorian Law Reform Commission (n 1 above) para 4.19.

[87] Usually such applications are helpful, but seemingly exceptionally in *Re Sigsworth* [1935] Ch 89 (Ch) 91–92, Clauson J held that lack of evidence meant that he would only decide the question of law about the applicability of the forfeiture rule in that case, on the assumption that murder had been

order, they will not be personally liable.[88] Secondly, any personal representative who distributes in ignorance of the killing seems likely to be relieved of liability, under section 61 of the Trustee Act 1925.[89] Such a distribution would be both honest and reasonable, and it is difficult to envisage a court holding that it would not be fair for the personal representative to be excused from personal liability.

The actual beneficiaries of the estate are not without remedies, but those remedies are very unlikely to be against the personal representatives. Instead, the remedy will be against the recipient of the inappropriately distributed assets, the killer.[90] When personal representatives distribute estate assets to someone not entitled to them, beneficiaries of the estate are entitled to personal and proprietary remedies, including through tracing, against the recipient.[91] Such remedies will therefore be available if personal representatives distribute assets to an unlawful killer. In the forfeiture context, this may look like the imposition of a constructive trust on the proceeds of wrongdoing. However, in *Re Diplock* the Court of Appeal treated this liability as a *sui generis* form of liability in succession law, one which had historically been available in the Court of Chancery. It is now better to see this as part of the law of unjust enrichment, based not on the wrongdoing of the killer, but on the personal representative's lack of authority in distributing to the killer.[92]

This analysis addresses the concern about killers not receiving title and therefore not being able to transmit that title to innocent third parties who may believe that the killer is the owner.[93] The killer does obtain title if the personal representatives distribute to her, because the personal representatives as owners of the property have the power to transfer title to the killer. The killer acquires title not directly from the killing, but from the actions of the personal representatives.[94] This transfer of title is nonetheless subject to claims both by the personal representatives and, if necessary, the beneficiaries. *Ministry of Health v Simpson* establishes that these claims can be proprietary. Consequently, anyone who acquires title from the killer therefore also obtains title, but will equally be subject to the proprietary claims. However, these are claims in equity, and subject to the usual bona fide purchaser defence. There is consequently no difference in the effect of

committed. He warned that '[t]he administrator, if he acts on my decision, will take the risk that the assumption of fact may conceivably hereafter turn out to be erroneous'.

[88] *Parry and Kerridge* (n 30 above) [24-07]–[24-08].

[89] Despite not being trustees, this section applies to personal representatives due to the Trustee Act 1925, s 68(17).

[90] This would apply even if the personal representatives distributed pursuant to a court order: *Parry and Kerridge* (n 30 above) [24-07].

[91] *Ministry of Health v Simpson* [1951] AC 251 (HL), approving *Re Diplock* [1948] Ch 465 (CA). The House of Lords did not consider the tracing point, but fully approved the Court of Appeal judgment, which did.

[92] See Charles Mitchell, Paul Mitchell and Stephen Watterson, *Goff and Jones, The Law of Unjust Enrichment*, 8th edn (London, Sweet & Maxwell, 2011) [8-51]–[8-57] and [8-79].

[93] See the text accompanying n 54 above.

[94] For the personal representatives as owner, see *Commissioner of Stamp Duties (Queensland) v Livingston* (n 85 above) 707.

the forfeiture rule on third parties between the constructive trust model and the analysis proposed here.

The approach taken here shows why it is better to understand the forfeiture rule as one which leads to a killer obtaining no rights, rather than one that results in a killer having rights which are unenforceable.[95] If the killer does obtain rights from the victim's will or intestacy, the personal representatives will not commit a *devastavit* if they distribute to the killer. The available remedies will become much more limited. This conclusion can only be avoided by acknowledging that the killer obtains rights, but that public policy nonetheless prevents the personal representatives from distributing to the killer, such that any distribution would still amount to a *devastavit*. This is much more cumbersome.

3.2.2. Pensions and Benefits

On this model, the killer does not become entitled to any payments under pension policies or welfare benefits. If payments are made, pensions providers or welfare agencies would be entitled to bring restitutionary claims. Such payments are recoverable because they are made by mistake.[96]

3.3. Benefits of this Model

In addition to clarifying the position of personal representatives and third parties, there are intellectual and practical benefits to an understanding of the forfeiture rule based on the killer obtaining no rights.

3.3.1. Taxonomy

Traditionally, the law of succession has been understood to form part of the law of property.[97] Analysing the forfeiture rule as a rule that prevents unlawful killers from obtaining title is consistent with this. It also means that the forfeiture rule is located in the same part of the law as the rules about unworthiness to inherit in civilian systems, facilitating comparison. This is particularly important for Ireland, which has a forfeiture rule associated with civilian code provisions.[98] It is also useful in maintaining links in this area with Scots law. There has been continued interaction between the English and Scots law relating to forfeiture situations.[99] The two are not identical, but it is helpful to take a position in English law

[95] For this distinction, see *Dunbar v Plant* (n 22 above) 429 (Phillips LJ).

[96] As noted in *Re Sigsworth* [1935] Ch 89 (Ch) 91–92, the 'mistake' is an assumption that the recipient of the money was not the killer of the deceased. This is described as an 'assumption of fact'. It might be described as restitution for a mistake on the basis of an 'incorrect tacit assumption', to use the language of *Goff and Jones* (n 92 above) [9-35].

[97] For Roman law, see eg G.2.98–G.2.245 as well as J.2.10–J.2.23.

[98] See n 16 above and the accompanying text.

[99] MacLeod and Zimmermann (n 11 above) especially 764–69.

which does not cause too much tension in relation to the mixed nature of Scots law.[100] Such an analysis of the common law of forfeiture also fits with the dominant American approach. Although there is considerable support for the constructive trust approach in the United States, most States have legislated slayer rules which prevent killers from receiving property from the estate of their victim.[101]

Within succession law itself, identifying the forfeiture rule as a rule which prevents killers from obtaining any rights places the rule into a familiar category. The constructive trust model means that the gift in a will or on intestacy succeeds, but a trust is then imposed over the relevant assets. By contrast, denying the killer any rights places the operation of the forfeiture rule clearly within the familiar category of failed gifts. This is what writers on succession law already recognise, placing their discussion of the forfeiture rule into their chapters on failed gifts, even if the authors advocate the constructive trust model.[102]

The various discussions by courts and legal scholars about how the forfeiture rule operates in relation to testate and intestate succession also place the rule within property law, succession law and the rules on failed gifts. Discussion has centred around the forfeiture rule operating as a deemed predecease or a deemed disclaimer.[103] Either of these positions is possible, although they have different effects in some situations.[104] Importantly, both approaches analogise the forfeiture rule to existing, and better understood, doctrines within the broader category of failed gifts: to lapse and disclaimer respectively. In judicial and academic reasoning, these links are attempts to understand how the forfeiture rule operates, rather than statements that the forfeiture rule is a deemed predecease or disclaimer rule. It is better to understand the forfeiture rule as a distinct mode of gifts failing.

Judges have recognised the utility of analogies to other forms of failed gifts and appreciated that such analogies need to be applied carefully. This is clear in cases where judges applying the forfeiture rule reject arguments that the rule causes 'gift over' provisions in wills to come into effect, as would be the case if the rule operated like lapse.[105] The better analogy is to disclaimer, simply because this is

[100] One difference is that Scots law does not permit total exclusion of the forfeiture rule under the Forfeiture Act 1982 (see *Cross, Petitioner* 1987 SLT 384), while English law does (see *Re K* (n 66 above)).

[101] See n 6 above and *cf Restatement 3rd (Restitution)* (n 26 above) § 45, Reporter's Note c, observing that a different approach was taken in the first *Restatement of the Law of Restitution* (1937), which sought to impose a constructive trust in all forfeiture situations.

[102] *Parry and Kerridge* (n 30 above) [14-64]–[14-69] and [14-81]–[14-82]; CV Margrave-Jones, *Mellows: The Law of Succession*, 5th edn (London, Butterworths, 1993) [30-63]; *Williams on Wills* (n 8 above) [9-17]. *Theobald on Wills* is something of an exception, with the forfeiture rule placed within a chapter entitled 'Who may be devisees or legatees?': John G Ross Martyn, Charlotte Ford and others, *Theobald on Wills*, 17th edn (London, Sweet & Maxwell, 2010) [12-011].

[103] The *Restatement 3rd (Wills)* (n 6 above) § 8.4(j) and (k), for example, uses deemed predecease, while the *Uniform Probate Code*, § 2-803(b) uses deemed disclaimer. Interestingly, the *Uniform Probate Code*, § 2-803(c)(1) prevents killers from acting as personal representatives or trustees by means of a deemed revocation.

[104] The principal difference is the effect on children of the killer. At common law, the children will inherit through a deemed predecease rule, but not through a deemed disclaimer.

[105] See eg *Re Jones* (n 10 above).

the only other form of failed gift which can apply to both testate and intestate succession.[106] Just such an analogy was expressly used at first instance in *Re DWS*, precisely because it was the closest analogy to the legal issue in that case, namely a failed gift in intestacy.[107] There may be other situations where the analogy is inappropriate and the forfeiture rule has to be understood without the benefit of such analogies.[108] In such situations it will have to be recognised that the forfeiture rule is a *sui generis* form of failure of gift, albeit one which often raises similar problems to other forms of failure.

Legislative rules, such as the predecease rule in the Estates of Deceased Persons (Forfeiture Rule and Law of Succession) Act 2011, work differently. Such rules create a failure through a genuine lapse (or in some other systems, a genuine disclaimer). Although this is an important change, it should not be overstated. Both the common law rule and the legislative rule operate within the general category of failed gifts. The forfeiture rule's place in legal taxonomy has changed, but only at a low level within the structure of succession law and private law more generally. While it will affect the outcome on some facts, such as those in *Re DWS*,[109] the general categorisation of the forfeiture rule as one species of failure of gifts is maintained.

3.3.2. Compatibility with Other Areas of Law

As noted above, the proposed constructive trust in relation to forfeiture appears to be at least very unusual in comparison with other constructive trusts as understood in England and Wales. The model proposed here avoids this difficulty.

Usefully, an understanding of the forfeiture rule in accordance with which the killer obtains no rights also avoids difficult questions about the interaction of the forfeiture rule and the statutory regime for confiscation of assets under the Proceeds of Crime Act 2002. The 2002 Act can apply if a defendant is convicted of an offence and 'obtains property as a result of or in connection with' the offence.[110] That property can include choses in action, and there is nothing to suggest that this does not apply to rights arising in relation to the victim's estate.[111] It therefore appears that if a killer were to acquire any rights from the killing, there would be a risk of these being seized by the state.[112] A model which regards the killer as

[106] *Parry and Kerridge* (n 30 above) [14-70]. It was sensible of the Law Commission to consider reform of forfeiture and disclaimer simultaneously in its 2005 Report (n 2 above)—both raise issues which cannot arise in relation to other types of failed gift.

[107] *Re DWS* (n 40 above) 579–80.

[108] For example, disclaimer can occur following an action by the intended beneficiaries after the death of the deceased: *Smith v Smith* [2001] 1 WLR 1937 (Ch). The forfeiture rule operates earlier, and there may be situations where this time difference could be relevant.

[109] See the text accompanying n 40 above.

[110] Proceeds of Crime Act 2002, s 76(4).

[111] Proceeds of Crime Act 2002, s 84(1)(c).

[112] As occurred before the 2002 Act in *Halifax Building Society v Thomas* [1996] Ch 217 (CA) in the context of a fraud.

obtaining no rights prevents the Proceeds of Crime Act 2002 from applying, while still preventing the killer from benefiting from his wrongdoing. The constructive trust model would also achieve this result, as the value of the rights the killer obtains as trustee would be nothing, but any model based around personal restitutionary claims would be difficult to accommodate with the Act. In such a situation the killer does obtain rights, and the Act's concession to the claims of others in relation to the criminal's offence is limited to claims made by the 'victim', which are necessarily precluded in homicide cases.[113] Denying that the killer obtains any rights seems the better solution.

3.3.3. *Practicality*

By preventing the killer from acquiring any rights, even a right to due administration of the estate, the forfeiture rule excludes the killer from the administration of the estate. This will often be a relief to other family members, some of whom may be acting as personal representatives or might have to deal with the killer as the personal representative. It also makes administration of the estate easier if the killer has been detained. The constructive trust model is also problematic in this regard: family members would be required to deal with the killer in order to ensure that the trust is not breached and the trust assets transferred elsewhere. On a model where the killer obtains no rights, action of this kind would only require other beneficiaries of the estate to engage with the killer in an adversarial manner, to claim personal or proprietary remedies.

4. Problematic Situations

The argument so far has not addressed some situations in which issues arise that are difficult for the forfeiture rule to resolve, namely the operation of survivorship in joint tenancies, the acceleration of interests in remainder vested in the killer that results from the life tenant's death, and effects on class gifts. Also difficult are some situations involving life insurance and the 'extended' forfeiture rule. However, the analysis of the forfeiture rule as the killer obtaining no rights through the killing illuminates why these situations are so difficult to resolve. These are not situations concerning the acquisition of rights by a killer, and fall outside the notion of the forfeiture rule outlined above (and outside of the idea of the law of succession as concerning the acquisition of rights in things). These are instead situations where the killer's enjoyment of existing or future rights is enhanced, to her benefit.[114]

[113] Proceeds of Crime Act 2002, s 6(6).

[114] Such situations are therefore also generally outside the scope of the Proceeds of Crime Act 2002, as the killer does not 'obtain' property, as required by section 76(4). The killer already held the property rights.

The final difficult situation, that of the 'extended' forfeiture rule, covers situations where the killer acquires benefits from the killing, but only does so indirectly. In many of these situations, the appropriate remedy is one for the victim's estate. Should the person entitled to that estate be the killer, the forfeiture rule in relation to testate and intestate succession will apply as above.

4.1. Joint Tenancies and Survivorship

If the killer and victim are joint tenants, then the killer was already entitled to all of the jointly owned property before the victim's death.[115] Lord Nicholls has cautioned against undue stress being placed upon the idea of joint tenants each owning the whole, describing it as an 'esoteric concept remote from the realities of life' that 'should be handled with care'.[116] But in this context the point is central. It explains why a joint tenancy situation has to be treated differently to most other applications of the forfeiture rule.

The current English position seems to be that a joint tenancy is severed by the killing of one joint tenant by another. The point has not been authoritatively decided[117] and there remain considerable uncertainties[118] and a range of possibilities.[119] The severance solution may be the desirable one, not for conceptual reasons, but for the pragmatic reason that it is relatively simple to apply, without any need to determine the killer's enrichment. However, it should be acknowledged that this position lacks a firm intellectual foundation and does not provide guidance in other difficult situations.

4.2. Killer's Interest in Remainder

If a killer has an interest in remainder in property, and the victim has a life interest, the killing of the victim accelerates the killer's interest. The benefit the killer receives from her existing property right increases from the moment of the victim's death. There seem to be no English cases on this point. Actuarial calculations could be used either to determine the longevity of the victim, providing a means

[115] This point is more or less made in TK Earnshaw and PJ Pace, '"Let the Hand Receiving It Be Ever So Chaste ..."' (1974) 37 *MLR* 481 at 488–92, although the authors there refer to the surviving joint tenant's rights being 'enlarged', which is not strictly correct. As McFarlane, Hopkins and Nield put it, 'Title simply "survives" in the remaining joint tenants': B McFarlane, N Hopkins and S Nield, *Land Law: Texts, Cases and Materials*, 3rd edn (Oxford, Oxford University Press, 2015) 567. In legal terms, there is no increase in the rights of the remaining joint tenant(s).

[116] *Burton v Camden London Borough Council* [2000] 2 AC 399 (HL) 404.

[117] As Tarrant observes, all of the English cases involve concessions by counsel, so are of little precedential value: J Tarrant, 'Unlawful Killing of a Joint Tenant' (2008) 15 *Australian Property Law Journal* 224 at 236–37.

[118] The discussion by Laffoy J in the Irish case of *Re Celine Cawley* (n 16 above) is excellent and highlights the difficulties and uncertainties.

[119] The many possibilities in relation to joint tenancy and survivorship are discussed well in Tarrant (n 117 above).

of calculating the extent to which the killer has been enriched by the killing. A constructive trust could then be imposed over the killer's remainder interest, in effect recreating the life interest, but necessarily in favour of the victim's estate rather than the victim herself. Alternatively, the actuarial calculations could be used to place a financial value on the killer's enrichment for a monetary award, again for the victim's estate. Both cases are examples of restitution for wrongs, and the remedy is gains-based.[120]

4.3. Class Gifts

The New Zealand Law Commission identified situations in which a killer may benefit from a killing, without directly obtaining any assets from it.[121] A killing might eliminate the victim from a class of which both the killer and victim were members, enlarging the killer's share of a gift to which they were both otherwise entitled, as in the joint tenancy situation. Alternatively, it might limit the membership of a class which has not yet closed, to the killer's benefit. An example would be where a gift is made to the grandchildren of an individual, one of whom is the killer, and the killer kills her only remaining parent, uncle or aunt, preventing any more grandchildren from being born.

In both cases, the killer was definitely entitled to some share of the gift. In the first case, the killer will obtain more than she otherwise would and a restitutionary, gains-based, remedy for her wrongdoing seems plausible. In the second case, the killer may obtain more than she otherwise would, but it is possible that no more grandchildren would have been born before the class closed in any event. Devising a suitable remedy in such a situation is more difficult. Notably, the New Zealand Law Commission, despite drafting a statutory forfeiture rule which identified these problems, did not seek to provide guidance as to how such situations should be addressed, simply commenting that it will ultimately be for the courts 'to settle the detailed application of [the forfeiture rule] to the many and varied interests in property to which it can apply'.[122] For all such situations, it seems that the appropriate remedy would be gains-based. The killer has obtained an illegitimate benefit from an unlawful act, and should be deprived of that benefit.

4.4. Life Insurance

A simple life insurance situation is already addressed under the forfeiture rule. Any policy owned by the victim will be an asset in the victim's estate and pass according

[120] The *Restatement 3rd (Restitution)* (n 26 above) uses the constructive trust model here. A similar issue arises if the killer's interest is contingent on surviving the victim; here it is presumed that the killer would not have been the survivor: *Restatement 3rd (Restitution)* (n 26 above) § 45, Comment g.

[121] NZLC Report 38 (n 4 above) 32 and 33 (draft Bill, s 11).

[122] ibid 33.

to the rules of testate and intestate succession, with the forfeiture rule working in the usual way. The difficulties arise in more complicated situations: first, if the life insurance policy has been assigned to the killer before the victim's death; secondly, where the killer took out the life insurance policy on the victim's life, for the killer's benefit; and thirdly, where the victim's life insurance is held on trust for the killer. In all of these scenarios, the problem is that the killer has acquired a right in the life insurance before the victim's death and that right becomes more valuable on the victim's death. In all of these situations, the solution lies in ordinary principles of law outside succession.[123]

The first two situations are addressed by a remark of Lord Esher MR in *Cleaver v Mutual Reserve Fund Life Association*: 'No doubt there is a rule that … if the performance of a contract would be contrary to public policy, performance cannot be enforced'.[124] This is a rule about the performance of contracts and part of contract law. As a matter of contract, a killer cannot enforce a life insurance policy on the victim's life. This is not a deprivation of the killer's existing rights. The killer has contractual rights (which amount to a chose in action), but contractual rights are always subject to the risk that a combination of events and general principles of contract law will render them worthless, as in frustration of contract. A similar limitation on contractual rights applies here.

The third situation is different. The killer does not hold the contractual rights directly; instead those rights are held by the victim or someone else, on trust for the killer. This is a common situation, as it avoids the need to assign the policy, or to address the requirement of an 'insurable interest' when seeking to insure the life of a third party. In the trust situation, the killer has a vested beneficial interest in the policy from the moment the trust is created. However, performance of the contract by the insurer is not barred, as there is no policy bar to the trustee enforcing the policy. The result in this situation is clearly identified in *Cleaver*—the trust fails and the trust property (the policy-holder's contractual rights against the insurer and then the policy proceeds) go on resulting trust to the victim's estate.

What is much less clear from *Cleaver* is quite how the trust fails. Lord Esher MR expressed the matter as one where the rule of public policy meant that the trust became impossible to be performed, but his analogy was to a situation where the beneficiary had predeceased the settlor, which looks closer to a model of the beneficiary ceasing to have any rights.[125] Fry LJ was also ambiguous, observing that the trust 'cannot be enforced' by the killer,[126] but also explaining that if the trustee claims the money due on the policy, it cannot be for the killer's benefit, suggesting that the killer no longer has rights under the trust.[127]

[123] *cf Foskett v McKeown* [2001] 1 AC 102 (HL) 122 (Lord Hope) and 134 (Lord Millett), noting that a policyholder's choses in action under the policy amount to a property right.

[124] *Cleaver v Mutual Reserve Fund Life Association* (n 15 above) 151.

[125] ibid 154. The language of performance was probably influenced by that of the Married Women's Property Act 1882, s 11, which refers to an object of the trust remaining 'unperformed'.

[126] *Cleaver v Mutual Reserve Fund Life Association* (n 15 above) 158.

[127] ibid 156.

The better approach is to treat this as a situation where the forfeiture rule actually does operate as a forfeiture: the killer-beneficiary loses her rights under the trust. This would then be a situation where 'for some reason, such as the impact of a rule of the law of trusts ... the provisions of a particular trust fail to exhaust the income and capital of a trust fund', leading to a resulting trust.[128] Here the forfeiture rule is a rule of public policy applicable throughout the law, including the law of trusts, which prevents the disposition of a trust asset (the proceeds of the policy) to the express beneficiary. A resulting trust then arises.

4.5. The 'Extended' Forfeiture Rule

A situation that has been discussed in American scholarship, but to no great extent elsewhere, is what has been called the 'extended' forfeiture context. This arises when a killer obtains benefits indirectly from the victim. Writers about the English law of forfeiture have only considered this problem in relation to the South African case of *Ex parte Steenkamp and Steenkamp*.[129] A couple made wills leaving property to their daughter and grandchildren. Their son-in-law (the daughter's husband) killed the couple, whose estates were administered according to the terms of their wills. One of the grandchildren died in infancy, and the rules of intestacy meant that the son-in-law acquired a share of the grandchild's estate. That estate consisted of assets received from the administration of the couple's estate. The killer ultimately obtained a benefit from the victim's estate. It was held that the killer was entitled to benefit from his own child's estate, and the source of that estate was irrelevant.

Steyn J's judgment cites only authorities from the Roman-Dutch civilian tradition, but the analysis of the common law forfeiture rule presented here would lead to the same outcome. The son-in-law did not acquire any rights to due administration of the couple's estate, but did acquire such rights to the administration of the grandchild's estate. We might quite legitimately consider this to be the wrong outcome as a matter of policy; the killer appears to have received an inappropriate windfall. That does not necessarily mean the issue should be addressed through the forfeiture rule itself. The killer here has not benefited from the death of his victims. An inappropriate windfall might be expressed alternatively as an unjust enrichment, making this an issue not for the law of succession, but of the law of restitution for wrongdoing. Virgo adopts this position, but observes that on the facts of *Steenkamp*, it is likely that the initial killing will not be seen as an operating

[128] D Hayton, P Matthews and C Mitchell, *Underhill and Hayton, Law Relating to Trusts and Trustees*, 18th edn (London, Lexis Nexis, 2010) para 21.5. The alternative presents the same problem as regarding killers as having rights in succession law, but not being able to enforce them—if the trustees were to distribute trust assets to the killer, this would not be a breach of trust (see text to n 95 above).

[129] *Ex parte Steenkamp and Steenkamp* 1952 (1) SA 744 (T).

cause of the killer's enrichment, preventing any gains-based remedy for his wrongdoing too.[130]

There is one relevant English case which has been largely overlooked. It relates to a different factual scenario, but a judicial remark suggests that causation may not be an insuperable obstacle to a restitutionary approach to the extended forfeiture situation. *Davitt v Titcumb* concerned the proceeds of sale of a house originally co-owned by two tenants in common.[131] The house was purchased with a joint mortgage to be repaid using an endowment policy, payable at a set date in the future or on the death of one of the tenants in common. The endowment policy was assigned to the mortgagee (a building society). One co-owner murdered the other, triggering payment under the policy. The policy provider paid the proceeds of the policy to the mortgagee, discharging most of the outstanding mortgage. The killer was convicted of murder. The personal representatives of the victim sold the house and the killer applied for his share of the proceeds of sale.

As a tenant in common, the killer had a distinct share in the beneficial ownership of the house before the killing occurred. However, it was held that he was not entitled to any of the proceeds of sale. Scott J rejected the killer's claim, on the basis of 'the inescapable fact that if the defendant can claim [his share of the proceeds of sale], he will be claiming a fund that would not have come into existence *but for* his criminal act' (emphasis added).[132] Such an analysis of the situation suggests that 'but for' causation is not an insurmountable obstacle to restitutionary claims for wrongdoing.[133] The benefit to the killer, of a share in the beneficial ownership, almost unencumbered by a mortgage charge, followed inevitably from the killing, as the personal representatives were required to use the assets received from the policy to discharge the deceased's debts. That is different to the situation in *Steenkamp*, where the benefit followed from assets received on succession. While *Steenkamp* was an intestacy case, the general principle is of freedom of testation, and so the courts might view a testamentary gift as a free choice by a third person, unlike the situation in *Davitt v Titcumb*.[134]

[130] Virgo, *Restitution* (n 32 above) 548. The Law Commission observed that the forfeiture rule is not concerned with ensuring that no one is in a position to benefit the killer, but did not consider the precise facts in *Steenkamp*: Law Commission, *The Forfeiture Rule and the Law of Succession: A Consultation Paper* (Law Com CP No 172, 2003) paras 5.19–5.22.

[131] *Davitt v Titcumb* [1990] Ch 110 (Ch).

[132] ibid 116.

[133] Scott J did not treat the case as a restitution case, instead arguing that the mortgagee only held the policy as mortgagee, so that the victim and killer were co-owners of the equity of redemption in the policy. The killer was then barred from asserting any rights under the policy due to the forfeiture rule, and so the funds used to discharge the mortgage were treated as solely those of the victim. The killer's share of the proceeds of sale was then used in paying an equitable contribution to the estate of the victim, due to the benefit he would otherwise receive from the victim discharging their joint debt.

[134] Even intestacy can be regarded as a choice, in that some people may be happy with the outcomes the law of intestacy prescribes, a point noted by Sedley LJ in *Re DWS* (n 40 above) [33].

5. Conclusion

The forfeiture rule raises a number of difficult questions of both principle and policy. This paper has shown that the forfeiture rule is best understood in the succession context as one which prevents a killer from obtaining any rights as a consequence of the killing, including the right to due administration of an estate. This approach does not address all situations in which the forfeiture rule is relevant. Some difficult situations can be settled through principles of contract and trusts law, while others are more appropriately resolved through gains-based remedies concerned with restitution for the killer's wrongdoing. Seen from this perspective, it may be better to describe the forfeiture rule more generally as a principle, with particular applications in various branches of the law.

4

Proprietary Estoppel: Undermining the Law of Succession?

BEN MCFARLANE*

1. Overview

The decision of the House of Lords in *Thorner v Major*[1] confirmed that the doctrine of proprietary estoppel may apply, and give rise to a cause of action, where a claimant (B) has acted in reliance neither on a mistaken belief as to her current legal rights,[2] nor on a representation of existing fact or law,[3] but instead on a promise made by another (A). That promise-based strand of proprietary estoppel has evolved very quickly over the last 50 or so years, and many of the cases crucial to its development, like *Thorner v Major* itself, involved an alleged testamentary promise.[4] By considering a number of specific points as to the operation of the promise-based proprietary estoppel doctrine (in Section 3),[5] this chapter examines the claim (set out in Section 2) that it undermines settled aspects of the law of succession.

The conclusion reached (in Section 4) is that the promise-based strand of proprietary estoppel does not, in itself, undermine the law of succession. On the

* I have benefitted from comments received at the conference which led to the book, and from discussions of the topic with Sarah Haren and with Professor John Mee. I am also grateful to John Williams for research assistance.

[1] *Thorner v Major* [2009] UKHL 18, [2009] 1 WLR 776.

[2] As in the 'classic case' (*Fisher v Brooker* [2009] UKHL 41, [2009] 1 WLR 1764 at [62] (Lord Neuberger)) of proprietary estoppel by acquiescence: see eg *The Earl of Oxford's Case* (1615) 1 Chan Rep 1, 21 ER 485; *Dann v Spurrier* (1802) 7 Ves 231, 32 ER 94.

[3] As in the case of proprietary estoppel by representation: see eg the analysis of Lord Evershed MR in *Hopgood v Brown* [1955] 1 WLR 213 (CA) 223.

[4] See eg *Re Basham* [1986] 1 WLR 1498 (Ch) and *Gillett v Holt* [2001] Ch 210 (CA).

[5] Lack of space precludes a discussion of all the concerns that may be raised as to the operation of the doctrine in the context of succession. For discussion, for example, of the application of inheritance tax rules where a proprietary estoppel is made out, see eg B McFarlane, *The Law of Proprietary Estoppel* (Oxford, Oxford University Press, 2014) [10.11]–[10.21].

contrary, it can instead be seen as performing a role characteristic of equitable doctrines: by preventing parties from unconscionably exploiting strict legal rules, it supports the continued existence of those rules by ensuring that they do not become a source of palpable injustice.[6]

This does not mean, however, that there is room for complacency. The point is that, to perform this role successfully, the doctrine must be carefully limited, so that intervention occurs only when the lack of it would lead to a result which would 'shock the conscience of the court'. The risk is that the courts may take too generous a view of the requirements, or effect, of the doctrine. The particular context of succession cases decided after the death of the alleged promisor (A) may heighten this risk: a court may consider that the parties who will lose out if B's claim succeeds, as objects of the bounty of A or of the intestacy rules, would have less cause for complaint than a living promisor deprived of her property by B's proprietary estoppel claim. Similarly, where A did in fact make a will in B's favour, but destroyed it for reasons unrelated to B, a court may consider that, by permitting a proprietary estoppel claim, it will in fact give effect to A's wishes.[7] It may even be the case that a court is tempted to respond to a defect in, for example, the scope of a statutory jurisdiction such as the Inheritance (Provision for Family and Dependants) Act 1975, by distorting the requirements of proprietary estoppel.[8]

It will be argued here that this risk has eventuated in a number of succession cases, with detrimental effects upon the clarity of the principles regulating when a promise-based proprietary estoppel claim arises and the proper response to such a claim. As those principles, of course, operate beyond testamentary promises, the problem can be seen as one of decisions made in the context of succession undermining the requirements and operation of proprietary estoppel more generally. So, just as the law of succession must be supplemented by a (carefully limited) doctrine of promise-based proprietary estoppel, so the proper functioning of the law of proprietary estoppel depends on a satisfactory law of succession.

[6] For a general discussion of this function of particular equitable rules, see eg H Smith, 'Property, Equity, and the Rule of Law' in L Austin and D Klimchuk (eds), *Private Law and the Rule of Law* (Oxford, Oxford University Press, 2014), referring to equity's ability to offer a limited 'safety valve' and thus to strengthen the force of more formal private law rules. See too M Harding, 'Equity and the Rule of Law' (2016) 132 *LQR* (forthcoming), arguing that 'equity's function of restraining unconscionable reliance on legal rights may serve the rule of law in a distinctive way, through contributing to conditions under which citizens are likely to form and maintain a disposition to engage with law'.

[7] Although note that in *Powell v Benney* [2007] EWCA Civ 1283, this temptation was (rightly) resisted: even though A had signed a piece of paper (unattested) purporting to leave property to B1 and B2, their successful proprietary estoppel claim led only to the award of a relatively small sum, which reflected the relatively small extent of the detriment suffered by B1 and B2.

[8] See the discussion in Section 3.6 below of *Wayling v Jones* (1993) 69 P & CR 170 (CA).

2. The Thesis to Be Examined

2.1. Some Concerns

Support can certainly be found, both amongst commentators and the judiciary, for the idea that, in some cases at least, judges have been tempted to reach for the 'portable palm tree'[9] and, in permitting a proprietary estoppel claim, have elected to 'dispense discretionary justice to the parties before the court [rather] than ... to apply, in a more mechanical way, the strict rules of property law and succession law'.[10] One case that has been subjected to such criticism is *Suggitt v Suggitt*.[11] A, a farmer, had made a valid will leaving his entire estate to his daughter, also expressing the wish, without imposing a trust, that the daughter should transfer the farmland to his son, B, if—in the daughter's opinion—B should 'show himself capable of working on and managing my farmland'. It was found that A had decided, before making that will, that B was not capable of running the farm: B had, for example, failed to complete his studies at agricultural college, and had previously left the farm for nine months for the bright lights of York. The Court of Appeal, however, confirmed the finding at first instance that A had promised B that the farmland, and the farmhouse on it, would unconditionally go to B on A's death; that B had 'positioned his whole life on the basis of the assurances given to him';[12] and that, notwithstanding countervailing advantages received by B, such as accommodation, B would suffer a detriment, as a result of that reliance, if no remedy were available to him. The Court of Appeal also upheld the decision that A's promises should be enforced, so that B would acquire the farmland and farmhouse, together worth 'some £3.3 million'.[13]

A case such as *Suggitt v Suggitt* can give rise to both conceptual and practical concerns. Conceptually, the essential question concerns the justification for giving at least some legal effect to an informal non-contractual promise: as discussed below,[14] this turns on identifying the requirements for, and consequences of, a successful proprietary estoppel claim. The question is raised most starkly in cases such as *Suggitt v Suggitt* and *Thorner v Major*, in which proprietary estoppel is used

[9] See *Taylor v Dickens* [1988] 1 FLR 806 (Ch) 820.

[10] See J Mee, 'Proprietary Estoppel and Inheritance: Enough is Enough' (2013) 77 *Conv* 280 at 297, criticising, in particular, *Suggitt v Suggitt* [2012] EWCA Civ 1140, [2012] WTLR 1607 and *Bradbury v Taylor* [2012] EWCA Civ 1208, [2013] WTLR 29. See too D Hayton, 'By-Passing Testamentary Formalities' (1987) 46 *CLJ* 215, criticising *Re Basham* [1986] 1 WLR 1498 (Ch), and M Dixon, 'Estoppel: A Panacea for All Wills' (1999) 63 *Conv* 46, defending the first instance decisions which denied proprietary estoppel claims in *Taylor v Dickens* [1988] 1 FLR 806 (Ch) and *Gillett v Holt* [1998] 3 All ER 917 (Ch) (the latter was reversed on appeal: *Gillett v Holt* (CA) (n 4 above)).

[11] *Suggitt v Suggitt* [2012] EWCA Civ 1140, [2012] WTLR 1607.

[12] ibid [38], quoting from the first instance judgment.

[13] ibid [50].

[14] See Section 3.1 below.

as a means to enforce A's promise to B[15] and thus leads to the same outcome as a contractual claim,[16] or even a valid will in favour of B.[17] Such cases, which might be seen to interfere with the 'basic and well understood feature of English law' that A has a 'right to decide, and change one's mind as to, the devolution of [A's] estate',[18] will be discussed below.[19] Practically, there may be doubts as to whether a first instance court has been sufficiently robust in applying those requirements: has 'careful, and sometimes sceptical, scrutiny'[20] been applied to the evidence as to A's promise[21] or B's reliance?[22] These two sets of concerns are of course linked: in each of *Suggitt v Suggitt* and *Thorner v Major*, for example, practical concerns as to whether a promise by A could be found[23] are linked to a conceptual question as to the certainty required of such a promise.[24]

Such concerns may also be magnified in the context of succession. First, as A's death will often seem, not least to A, to be some way in the future, A may be willing to make general assurances as to the disposition of her property on death, even if those promises are not seriously intended as capable of being relied on by B. This tendency is encouraged both by the fact that any problems created by the honouring or breaking of such a promise may not arise until after A's death and by the point noted by Robert Walker LJ in *Gillett v Holt*: 'it is notorious that some elderly persons of means derive enjoyment from the possession of testamentary power, and from dropping hints as to their intentions, without any question of an estoppel arising'.[25] Secondly, the assumed remoteness of A's death

[15] For the concern that the remedy awarded in *Suggitt v Suggitt* was excessive, see eg Mee (n 10 above) 283–87; for the same doubt as to *Thorner v Major* (HL) (n 1 above), see eg J Mee, 'The Limits of Proprietary Estoppel: *Thorner v Major*' (2009) 21 *Child and Family Law Quarterly* 367 at 381–82.

[16] See eg M Davey, 'Testamentary Promises' (1988) 8 *Legal Studies* 92 at 110 for the criticism that proprietary estoppel may be used to give binding effect to a non-contractual promise.

[17] For example, the earliest modern case applying proprietary estoppel to a testamentary promise, *Re Basham* [1986] 1 WLR 1498 (Ch), was criticised for allowing an informal promise to determine, in practice, the devolution of part of A's estate by D Hayton, 'By-Passing Testamentary Formalities' (1987) 46 *CLJ* 215.

[18] See *Gillett v Holt* (Ch) (n 10 above) 930 (Carnwath J), in a judgment overturned on appeal: *Gillett v Holt* (CA) (n 4 above).

[19] See Section 3.4 below.

[20] The phrase used by Lord Walker in *Thorner v Major* (HL) (n 1 above) [60]. See too *Creasey v Sole* [2013] EWHC 1410 (Ch), [2013] WTLR 931 at [105].

[21] See Section 3.3 below.

[22] See Section 3.6 below.

[23] In *Suggitt v Suggitt* [2011] EWHC 903 (Ch), [2011] 2 FLR 875, for example, the first instance judge, whilst finding in favour of B, noted that the evidence as to A's alleged assurances was 'opaque to say the least' and that B was not a 'very reliable witness'. In *Thorner v Major* [2008] EWCA Civ 732, [2008] 2 FCR 435, the Court of Appeal held that the evidence did not support the finding of a promise and, whilst the House of Lords restored the contrary finding at first instance, it was noted that A's remarks were 'oblique': see eg *Thorner v Major* (HL) (n 1 above) [2], [24], [50] and [80].

[24] In *Suggitt v Suggitt* (n 11 above), for example, there was a question as to whether A's assurances related to the farmhouse as well as the farmland; in *Thorner v Major* (n 1 above), there was a question as to whether a promise to leave the 'farm' to B was sufficiently clear to give rise to a claim. In each case, the question was resolved in favour of B.

[25] *Gillett v Holt* (CA) (n 4 above) 228.

may also make it more likely that A's promise is to be subject to implied but ill-defined qualifications, that the property to which it relates will not be specified,[26] and that the parties' circumstances may change significantly before the time when performance of the promise is due.[27]

2.2. Two Comparisons

Two comparisons, one contemporary and one historic, may also lend some support to criticisms of proprietary estoppel. First, the Court of Appeal has recently sought to restrict the doctrine of *donatio mortis causa*,[28] preferring to emphasise the importance of testamentary formality provisions 'intended to provide protection for the testator and his estate against abuse'[29] and noting that the doctrine 'paves the way for all of the abuses which those [statutory formality rules] are intended to prevent'.[30] The analogy between the doctrines of *donatio mortis causa* and proprietary estoppel is far from exact; nonetheless, a concern behind allowing post mortem claims based on an alleged oral statement of the deceased applies equally to the two doctrines.[31]

Secondly, a comparison can be made between proprietary estoppel and the defunct equitable doctrine of 'making representations good'.[32] The facts of *Loffus v Maw*,[33] for example, if repeated today, might well lead to a proprietary estoppel claim: A persuaded B to continue as his live-in carer by promising to give her, in his will, the right to take, for her life, the rents and profits on two of A's properties, and B continued to care for A until A's death three years later.[34] A's will did not

[26] There is also a particular problem as to whether a claim can be based on A's promise to leave B the whole of (or a specified proportion of) A's estate, or of A's residuary estate: see Section 3.2 below.

[27] Indeed, in *Thorner v Major* (HL) (n 1 above), Lord Scott at [19]–[20] thought those problems to be so acute that proprietary estoppel should be inapplicable to such promises and would have preferred to base a decision in B's favour on the finding of a remedial constructive trust.

[28] *King v Chiltern Dog Rescue* [2015] EWCA Civ 581, [2015] WTLR 1225, especially [54] (Jackson LJ): 'it is important to keep DMC within its proper bounds. The court should resist the temptation to extend the doctrine to an ever wider range of situations'. The specific restriction applied by the Court of Appeal to reverse the first instance finding of a *donatio mortis causa* was that the purported gift in question had not been made in contemplation of impending death.

[29] *King v Chiltern Dog Rescue* (n 28 above) [90] (Patten LJ).

[30] ibid [51] (Jackson LJ).

[31] In *Davies v Davies* [2015] EWHC 1384 (Ch), for example, in which a proprietary estoppel claim succeeded, it was noted at [9] that: 'It is easy to assert such oral promises when the person making the promises has passed away, when the only other witness is elderly and not available to give oral evidence, where there is little contemporaneous documentation and none that directly refers to such promises'.

[32] For full discussion of that doctrine and its demise, see eg F Dawson, 'Making Representations Good' (1982) 1 *Canterbury Law Review* 329; P Finn, 'Equitable Estoppel' in PD Finn (ed), *Essays in Equity* (Sydney, Law Book Co Ltd, 1985); and P Matthews, 'The Words Which Are Not There: A Partial History of the Constructive Trust' in C Mitchell (ed), *Constructive and Resulting Trusts* (Oxford, Hart Publishing, 2009) 25–44.

[33] *Loffus v Maw* (1862) 3 Giff 592, 66 ER 544 (Ch).

[34] A close modern parallel in which a proprietary estoppel claim succeeded might be eg *Ottey v Grundy* [2003] EWCA Civ 1176, [2003] WTLR 1253.

give B the promised right, but the Court of Chancery held that, as B had acted on a representation made by A with the purpose of influencing B's conduct, A was, at the time of his death, obliged to make that representation good. The decision in *Loffus v Maw* was, however, one of the final examples of the doctrine's application, as it was pushed out of the law by the hardening of the classical doctrine of consideration,[35] and the re-assertion of earlier authority[36] establishing the (surely correct) point that the law of estoppel by representation 'is applicable only to representations as to some state of facts alleged to be at the time actually in existence'[37] and so cannot apply to a promise to leave property to another. The fate of the doctrine of making representations good raises a key question: might a decision such as that in *Thorner v Major* one day be regarded, like that in *Loffus v Maw*, as the high-water mark of an ultimately unjustifiable equitable intrusion onto the solid territory of common law principles?

3. Specific Concerns

3.1. Giving Effect to Non-Contractual Testamentary Promises

At a conceptual level, there is no inconsistency between the operation of proprietary estoppel and the formality requirements for a valid testamentary disposition.[38] In a case such as *Suggitt v Suggitt*, for example, whilst B's successful claim could be seen as placing B in the same practical position as if A had indeed left the farmland and farmhouse to B, B did not arrive there as a result of A's having exercised a power to dispose of his property on death. Proprietary estoppel operated to impose a liability on A, arising during A's life,[39] and did not depend on any actual or assumed testamentary transfer.

This is why the concerns about the *donatio mortis causa* doctrine, noted above,[40] do not arise in the same way in connection with proprietary estoppel. The former doctrine runs the risk of undermining formal testamentary requirements, as it gives effect to a disposition of property taking effect on death and revocable until then; the latter instead recognises a liability imposed on A before A's death and which cannot simply be revoked by A. The point can also be seen

[35] See eg *Maddison v Alderson* (1883) 8 App Cas 467 (HL).

[36] See eg *Jorden v Money* (1854) 5 HLC 185 (PC).

[37] *Maddison v Alderson* (n 35 above) 473 (Earl of Selborne LC).

[38] See Wills Act 1837 (c 26 7 Will IV & 1 Vict), s 9.

[39] See eg *Gillett v Holt* (CA) (n 4 above): the parties' relationship broke down during A's lifetime, and a proprietary estoppel claim, based on A's testamentary promise, was available to B. For a more general discussion of the point at which a liability arises through proprietary estoppel, see eg B McFarlane, 'Proprietary Estoppel and Third Parties after the Land Registration Act 2002' (2003) 62 *CLJ* 661.

[40] See Section 2.2 above.

by comparing the position in relation to an *inter vivos* transfer of land. It cannot plausibly be argued that a promise-based proprietary estoppel claim is subject to section 53(1)(a) of the Law of Property Act 1925, which regulates A's power to create or dispose of an interest in land.[41] It has similarly been accepted, for example, that formal requirements imposed by section 53(1)(c) of the 1925 Act for the disposition of a subsisting equitable interest do not apply to a contract to make such a disposition.[42]

It may thus be argued that the suggestion of proprietary estoppel's undermining the law of succession in fact adds nothing to the broader argument that the promise-based strand of the doctrine undermines the law of contract.[43] It is therefore useful to see how that broader argument may be rebutted. There is a question, for example, as to the relevance of section 2 of the Law of Property (Miscellaneous Provisions) Act 1989 to promise-based proprietary estoppel claims: it has been judicially suggested[44] that the statute operates to render an *agreement* for the sale or other disposition of an interest in land void, and so can prevent a non-conforming promise from having *any* effect. The wording of the statute, however, makes clear that it applies only to deny *contractual* effect,[45] and the better view is that 'the fact that, if there was a contract it would be void is irrelevant: indeed, the very reason for mounting the proprietary estoppel claim is that there is no enforceable contract'.[46]

The crucial conceptual question, then, is whether proprietary estoppel is sufficiently distinct, in its requirements and operation, from contract law. In this connection it is helpful to consider the influential, but unreported, judgment of Hoffmann LJ in *Walton v Walton*,[47] which involved a testamentary promise. As in *Suggitt v Suggitt* and *Thorner v Major*, B had, over many years, worked for low pay and long hours on the farm of A, a relative. When B had complained as to his pay, the stock phrase of A, B's mother, was that 'You can't have more money and a farm one day'. The first instance judge found against B on the basis that, although promises had been made to B, they had not been intended by A to create a legal obligation, nor had they been treated as such by B. Hoffmann LJ accepted these findings of fact, and also, of course, that 'an intention to bring into existence an

[41] See *Kinane v Mackie-Conteh* [2005] EWCA Civ 45, [2005] WTLR 345 at [35].

[42] See eg *Neville v Wilson* [1997] Ch 144 (CA).

[43] This assumes that contracts to make testamentary dispositions do not raise any special conceptual concerns distinct from those of contract law in general: that seems to be the case, in England at least. For discussion see A Braun, 'Formal and Informal Testamentary Promises: A Historical and Comparative Perspective' (2012) 76 *Rabels Zeitschrift für ausländisches und internationales Privatrecht* 994.

[44] *Cobbe v Yeoman's Row* [2008] UKHL 55, [2008] 1 WLR 1752 at [29] (Lord Scott). This expressly obiter view was considered, and rejected, by Bean J in *Whittaker v Kinnear* [2011] EWHC 1479 (QB).

[45] See too Law Commission, *Transfer of Land—Formalities for Contracts for Sale Etc of Land* (Law Com No 164, 1985) para 5.2.

[46] Lord Neuberger, 'The Stuffing of Minerva's Owl? Taxonomy and Taxidermy in Equity' (2009) 68 *CLJ* 537 at 546.

[47] *Walton v Walton* (CA, 14 April 1994). See further B McFarlane, 'Proprietary Estoppel: The Importance of Looking Back' in J Pila and P Davies (eds), *The Jurisprudence of Lord Hoffmann* (Oxford, Hart Publishing, 2015).

immediately binding contract' is a requirement of a contractual claim. A's promise was likely to have been subject to 'unspoken and ill-defined qualifications', and so it could not have been reasonable for B to believe that A had intended to enter into a contract which 'subject to the narrow doctrine of frustration, must be performed come what may'. This uncertainty did not, however, prevent a claim based on proprietary estoppel, as, in contrast to contract law, the principle applied

> does not look forward into the future and guess what might happen. It looks backwards from the moment when the promise falls due to be performed and asks whether, in the circumstances which have actually happened, it would be unconscionable for the promise not to be kept.

Thus conceived, proprietary estoppel performs a different role to that of contract law, and no inconsistency is caused by its availability even where a contractual claim would fail.

The analysis of Hoffmann LJ in *Walton v Walton* was relied on by Lord Walker and Lord Neuberger in *Thorner v Major*,[48] and it plays a crucial role in addressing the concerns expressed in the same case by Lord Scott.[49] The 'backwards-looking' nature of proprietary estoppel requires a court to ask, at any given point,[50] whether it would be unconscionable for A to leave B to suffer a detriment as a result of B's reasonable reliance on A's promise. The doctrine does not impose an immediately binding duty on A to perform the promise, and so a relevant change in circumstances can be taken into account when applying that test.[51] The point here is not that B can succeed in a proprietary estoppel claim simply by showing that A's actual or threatened behaviour is unconscionable in a general sense.[52] Nor is it that a court can exploit the vagueness of unconscionability in order arbitrarily to reject B's claim even in a case where B has established the core elements of promise, reliance, and the prospect of detriment. It is rather that the broader notion of unconscionability can operate, as suggested by Lord Walker in *Cobbe v Yeoman's Row*,[53] as a form of check on A's liability and can thus provide a means by which a court can develop specific rules to address two key issues: first, when is a change of circumstances significant enough to have an effect;[54] and secondly, how should the

[48] *Thorner v Major* (HL) (n 1 above) [56]–[57], [62] and [101].

[49] See n 27 above.

[50] Where, for example, property was transferred by A to C, and B wishes to make a claim against C, the court needs to establish whether B had any rights in that property at the time of the transfer to C.

[51] This flexibility may offer an important advantage over, for example, the approach in German law, under which a contract to make a testamentary disposition is invalid (§ 2302 BGB), but a binding testamentary disposition can be made by means of an inheritance contract in notarised form (§§ 2274 ff BGB, especially § 2276).

[52] As rightly noted by Lord Scott in *Cobbe v Yeoman's Row* (HL) (n 44 above) [16]: 'unconscionability of conduct may well lead to a remedy but, in my opinion, proprietary estoppel cannot be the route to it unless the ingredients for a proprietary estoppel are present'.

[53] *Cobbe v Yeoman's Row* (HL) (n 44 above) [92]: 'If the other elements appear to be present but the result does not shock the conscience of the court, the analysis needs to be looked at again'.

[54] In *PW & Co v Milton Gate Investments Ltd* [2003] EWHC 1994 (Ch), [2004] Ch 142 at [201], for example, Neuberger J invoked the notion of unconscionability in explaining why events occurring after B's reliance may be taken into account in determining if an estoppel by convention has

effect of such circumstances be determined? The doctrine thus has the principled flexibility necessary to deal with the concerns raised by a testamentary promise intended to benefit B only many years after having been made by A.

This view of promise-based proprietary estoppel may be seen as linked to its function of supporting, rather than competing with, contract law and rules relating to the disposition of property. Whereas the latter two sets of rules can be seen as concerned with the exercise by A of a power, proprietary estoppel can play the secondary, and more limited role, of protecting parties from risks caused by the existence of that power. Whilst it is possible for Lord Walker's 'elderly persons of means'[55] to enjoy their testamentary power by dropping hints as to its exercise, proprietary estoppel recognises that there comes a point when an equitable line is crossed and the nature of A's conduct, and B's reliance on it, means that A comes under a liability to B. The possibility of such a liability not only reduces the risk of A's abuse of that power; it may also, somewhat paradoxically, assist A. It has been argued that, in a commercial context, it is useful to A to have the ability to make a form of pre-contractual commitment which, whilst not immediately binding, does have some legal effect:[56] by doing so, A can, for example, encourage B to undertake preparatory work which may well be of benefit to both parties. It could similarly be said that, if the law gives protection in at least some cases where B acts in reliance on a testamentary promise of A, it can benefit A by reinforcing B's motivation for acting in particular ways often requested by A. On this view, the existence of promise-based proprietary estoppel, far from undermining the law of succession, can be seen as a useful corollary to A's testamentary power. Perhaps more importantly, the existence of the equitable doctrine can help to support the strictness of the rules relating to testamentary dispositions, or to contracts to dispose of interests in land, by ensuring that such rules do not work a particular form of injustice upon B.

3.2. Promises in Relation to A's Estate or Residuary Estate

Even if it is accepted that it is not illegitimate to give effect to at least some non-contractual testamentary promises, a specific question arises as to whether a proprietary estoppel claim can be based on a promise that relates not to specific, identified property of A, but instead to all or part of A's residuary estate. Such a claim is supported by *Re Basham*,[57] but some doubt was cast on that decision

been established: 'Estoppel is a doctrine designed to do justice, and, at least normally, it seems scarcely consistent with doing justice to ignore facts, which have occurred since the date upon which an action was taken in reliance upon the estoppel, and which may well impinge significantly, or even determinatively, on the issue of unconscionability'.

[55] See *Gillett v Holt* (CA) (n 4 above), 228.

[56] See B McFarlane, 'The Protection of Pre-Contractual Reliance: A Way Forward?' (2010) 10 *Oxford University Commonwealth Law Journal* 95, drawing on eg A Schwartz and R Scott, 'Precontractual Liability and Preliminary Agreements' (2007) 120 *Harvard Law Review* 661.

[57] *Re Basham* [1986] 1 WLR 1498 (Ch).

by Lord Walker in *Thorner v Major*[58] and it has also been judicially described as 'mark[ing] the widest boundary of the application of the doctrine of proprietary estoppel thus far in [England] (and, so far as I have been able to ascertain, in any other common law jurisdiction)'.[59]

The resolution of this question turns on whether there is anything in the conceptual nature of a promise-based proprietary estoppel claim that prevents its application to such a promise. For example, Lord Walker's doubts as to the correctness of *Re Basham* are based on the judge's use in that case of authorities on mutual wills:[60] the implication then is that there is a relevant conceptual difference between the two doctrines which explains why a proprietary estoppel claim cannot be based on such a promise. Certainly, Lord Walker's discussion of the point is linked to his view that:[61]

> it is a necessary element of proprietary estoppel that the assurances given to the claimant (expressly or impliedly, or, in standing-by cases, tacitly) should relate to identified property owned (or, perhaps, about to be owned) by the defendant … It is the relation to identified land of the defendant that has enabled proprietary estoppel to develop as a sword, and not merely as a shield.

This raises a fundamental question as to the nature and scope of the principle underlying the promise-based strand of proprietary estoppel. As has been pointed out by commentators,[62] and judges in other jurisdictions,[63] it is difficult to see why the underlying notion of unconscionability should be triggered only where the detriment incurred by B arises as a result of reliance on a promise relating to A's property, as opposed to any other seriously intended promise. Lord Walker's suggested distinction is an even finer one, however, as it depends on the difference between identified property and A's general property. The difficulty with the suggestion is that it derives from the analysis of Lord Denning MR in *Moorgate Mercantile Co Ltd v Twitchings* that the effect of an estoppel on an owner of property may be that 'his own title to the property, be it land or goods, has been held to be limited or extinguished, and new rights and interests have been created therein'.[64]

58 *Thorner v Major* (HL) (n 1 above) [63].

59 *Macdonald v Frost* [2009] EWHC 2276 (Ch), [2009] WTLR 1815 at [13] (Geraldine Andrews QC).

60 *Thorner v Major* (HL) (n 1 above) [63]. See too D Hayton 'By-Passing Testamentary Formalities' (1987) 46 *CLJ* 215. For discussion of mutual wills, see Ying Khai Liew's contribution in Ch 5 of the present volume.

61 *Thorner v Major* (HL) (n 1 above) [61].

62 See eg D Jackson, 'Estoppel as a Sword' (1965) 81 *LQR* 223 at 241–42; D Nolan, 'Following in their Footsteps: Equitable Estoppel in Australia and the United States' (2000) 11 *King's College Law Journal* 202; B McFarlane and P Sales, 'Promises, Liability, and Detriment: Lessons from Proprietary Estoppel' (2015) 131 *LQR* 610.

63 See eg *Waltons Stores (Interstate) Ltd v Maher* (1988) 164 CLR 387 (HCA).

64 *Moorgate Mercantile Co Ltd v Twitchings* [1976] QB 225 (CA) 242, relied on by Lord Denning MR in *Crabb v Arun District Council* [1976] Ch 179 (CA) 187 (decided in the brief period before the Court of Appeal's decision in *Moorgate* was overturned in the House of Lords), which was in turn relied on by Lord Walker in *Thorner v Major* (HL) (n 1 above) [61].

Lord Denning's analysis, however, relates to the general doctrine of estoppel by representation, and merely depends on the fact that, if B can use such an estoppel to prevent A from asserting A's title to goods,[65] this may allow B, by relying on his or her own possessory title, to have a practically secure title to such goods.[66] The promise-based principle given effect to in a case such as *Thorner v Major*, however, is not subject to any such inherent limit: it does not operate simply to preclude A from denying A's title to goods, but can instead impose a liability on A.

The question then is whether there is any reason why such a liability can arise only if A's promise relates to specifically identified property. One concern is that if A's promise relates simply to her estate or residuary estate, it may be that A has reserved a power unilaterally to reduce the extent or the value of the rights to be acquired by B, and so has qualified the promise in such a way that it cannot be reasonably understood by B as seriously intended by A as capable of being relied on. In such a case, A's promise is 'likely to be regarded as too vague and imprecise'[67] to give rise to a proprietary estoppel claim. That result arises, however, by simply applying the general requirements of proprietary estoppel and so does not require any specific rule as to testamentary promises. A second possible concern is as to A's position in the period after B's claim arises (ie after B has relied in such a way as to raise the prospect of detriment) and before A's death: can A, for example, make a substantial contribution to charity? That concern can, however, be met without denying that A is under any liability to B. It has been accepted, for example, that A may make a valid contractual promise to leave B a share of A's estate.[68] Whilst Lord Walker in *Thorner v Major* described mutual wills as a 'special case',[69] it does prove that a way can be found to deal with A's position when subject to a liability that will crystallise only on A's death.[70] Indeed, as Lord Neuberger noted in *Thorner v Major*,[71] a further parallel can be drawn with the position of a debtor who has created a floating charge. It is therefore suggested that, Lord Walker's concerns notwithstanding, there is no reason for adopting a general rule that a proprietary estoppel claim can never arise from a promise to leave B all or a specified part of A's residuary estate.

[65] As was the case in eg *Pickard v Sears* (1837) 6 A & E 469, 112 ER 179.

[66] Lord Denning MR's analysis also drew on ostensible authority, which is again clearly distinct from promise-based proprietary estoppel and, as noted by Devlin J in *Eastern Distributors Ltd v Goldring* [1957] 2 QB 600 (CA) 607–11, may also differ from estoppel by representation.

[67] *Macdonald v Frost* (n 59 above) [20].

[68] See eg *Schaefer v Schumann* [1972] AC 572 (PC) 586 (Lord Cross) and 599 (Lord Simon).

[69] *Thorner v Major* (HL) (n 1 above) [63].

[70] *cf* the discussion of this point in Sections 4.1 and 4.2 of Ying Khai Liew's contribution in Ch 5 of this volume.

[71] *Thorner v Major* (HL) (n 1 above) [95]. An analogy may also be drawn to the 'ambulatory' nature of the common intention constructive trust (see *Stack v Dowden* [2007] UKHL 17, [2007] 2 AC 432 at [62]) and to the trust recognised in *Re Lehman Bros International Europe (in administration)* [2011] EWCA Civ 1544, [2012] 2 BCLC 151.

3.3. Establishing the Required Promise

A key objection to the outcome in a case such as *Suggitt v Suggitt* or *Thorner v Major* is that there was, on the facts, insufficient evidence from which a court could find that A had made a testamentary promise that B could reasonably understand as seriously intended by A as capable of being relied on by B. A linked objection is that it may be very difficult to predict whether, on the facts of any particular case, a court will find that such a promise was made. Doubts as to whether or not the required promise will be found can of course delay the administration of an estate, and give personal representatives an incentive to reach a settlement when a possibly dubious proprietary estoppel claim is made.[72] This uncertainty may be evidenced by the Court of Appeal's decision in *Cook v Thomas*.[73] It was accepted that the words used by A when discussing with B the fate of A's property on A's death were 'virtually identical' to those used in *Gillett v Holt*:[74] they were that A's farm was 'all going to be yours when I am gone' (or were substantially along those lines).[75] In *Cook v Thomas*, the Court of Appeal, whilst noting the 'coincidence between the words used',[76] distinguished *Gillett v Holt* and dismissed B's appeal against the finding at first instance that the required promise had not been made.

The objection that the courts are too liberal in finding a required promise may seem to be particularly relevant when considering the decision in *Bradbury v Taylor*.[77] The Court of Appeal[78] refused to interfere with the finding of the first instance judge that a promise had been made by A to leave his house to B1 and B2, and that B1 and B2 had relied on that promise by moving from Sheffield to live with A in Cornwall. That finding had been made even though the judge had inclined to the view that A had sent a letter to B1 and B2, setting out 'the terms of my offer to you to live here', which made no mention of the position after A's death and stated that 'there will be no contract, as this is a friendly arrangement'.

The result in *Bradbury v Taylor* may seem inconsistent with Lord Walker's exhortation to subject the evidence to 'careful, and sometimes sceptical, scrutiny':[79] this is of course particularly important in a case where A's death denies the court a first-hand account from the alleged promisor.[80] Whilst *Bradbury v Taylor* is, no

[72] For the concern that lack of clarity as to the application of proprietary estoppel will give rise to bitter and expensive litigation, see eg S Nield, 'If You Look After Me, I Will Leave You My Estate: The Enforcement of Testamentary Promises in England and New Zealand' (2000) 20 *Legal Studies* 85 at 103; B McFarlane, 'Proprietary Estoppel and Third Parties after the Land Registration Act 2002' (2003) 62 *CLJ* 661 at 686; Mee (n 10 above) 296–97.

[73] *Cook v Thomas* [2010] EWCA Civ 227 at [76].

[74] *Gillett v Holt* (CA) (n 4 above).

[75] *Cook v Thomas* (n 73 above) [72].

[76] ibid [76].

[77] *Bradbury v Taylor* [2012] EWCA Civ 1208, [2013] WTLR 29. For criticism of the finding of the required promise in this case, see Mee (n 10 above) 286–91.

[78] The leading judgment was given by Lloyd LJ and, as Mee (n 10 above) at 294 notes, 'Lloyd LJ may have been made more cautious by his experience in *Thorner*, when his judgment in the Court of Appeal, reversing the trial judge's decision, did not appear to be very well received in the House of Lords'.

[79] *Thorner v Major* (HL) (n 1 above) [60].

[80] See too *Davies v Davies* (n 31 above) [9].

doubt, a borderline case, it is possible to defend the Court of Appeal's approach in that case. The letter must be interpreted against the wider factual context of the parties' dealings. B1 and B2 had been reluctant to move away from their extended family in Sheffield, and to change the school of their elder child, and the judge had accepted their argument that A had 'wished to do enough to entice them'[81] to move, and that they had sought assurances from A before the letter was sent. As Lord Walker noted in *Thorner v Major*,[82] the three requirements of assurance, reliance, and detriment are often closely related, and an alleged promise will be easier to find if B, as in *Bradbury v Taylor*, embarked on a course of conduct which, in the absence of any promise from A, would be difficult to explain.[83]

This point may also be useful in explaining the apparent inconsistency between *Gillett v Holt*[84] and *Cook v Thomas*.[85] As Lord Neuberger noted in *Thorner v Major*:[86]

> Just as a sentence can have one meaning in one context and a very different meaning in another context, so can a sentence which would be ambiguous or unclear in one context, be a clear and unambiguous assurance in another context.

In *Gillett v Holt*, A's statements were found to be more than merely representations of A's current testamentary intention, because—like the assurances made in *Walton v Walton*—they were made when B raised concerns as to the future security of himself and his wife and could reasonably be understood as intended to be relied on, as they were used to dissuade B from pursuing opportunities elsewhere. More generally, as B had worked on A's farm for over 30 years, the extent of B's commitment to A was such as to suggest that A had assumed an obligation to B.[87] In contrast, in *Cook v Thomas*, B could not point to any substantial action that B would not have undertaken but for a promise by A. Lloyd LJ, for example, noted that an alleged promise by A in fact 'made no immediate difference to the position between the parties' whereas a commitment to leave A's property to B would have been a 'turning point in their relationship, after which everything would be seen differently'.[88]

Whilst recognising that, as in *Thorner v Major*, a promise may be implied from indirect statements and conduct,[89] the succession cases have generally emphasised the need for A to have made a promise or, synonymously, an assurance or

[81] Cited by Lloyd LJ: *Bradbury v Taylor* (n 77 above) [25].

[82] *Thorner v Major* (HL) (n 1 above) [29].

[83] For cases demonstrating this point outside the succession context, see eg *Eves v Eves* [1975] 1 WLR 1338 (CA); *Lloyd v Dugdale* [2001] EWCA Civ 1754, [2002] 2 P & CR 13.

[84] *Gillett v Holt* (CA) (n 4 above).

[85] *Cook v Thomas* (n 73 above).

[86] *Thorner v Major* (HL) (n 1) [84].

[87] See too *Davies v Davies* (n 31 above) [44]. In that case, the evidence of independent witnesses (not members of the family concerned) in support of promises having been made was also given particular weight: see at [18] and [21].

[88] *Cook v Thomas* (n 73 above) [79].

[89] This point has also been recognised outside the context of succession, as in eg *Bradley v Heslin* [2014] EWHC 3267 (Ch) [60], where it was acknowledged that a promise may be found as 'a matter of implication and inference from indirect statements and conduct'.

commitment.[90] This is significant, as courts have often stated that it suffices if A has simply *encouraged* a particular belief of B.[91] It is doubtful, however, that mere encouragement should suffice in a case where B has relied on a belief as to A's future conduct,[92] and the succession cases may therefore provide a valuable lesson for the wider law of proprietary estoppel.

3.4. Enforcing Non-Contractual Testamentary Promises

In cases such as *Suggitt v Suggitt* and *Thorner v Major*, the perception of a conflict between proprietary estoppel and the law of succession is strengthened by the fact that the effect of the former can be seen as equivalent to the writing, or rewriting, of a will, so as to dispose of particular property to B. An equivalence of outcomes, in any particular case, does not of course mean that any two doctrines necessarily overlap conceptually.[93] The distinction between the requirements of promise-based proprietary estoppel and of the law of contract nonetheless demands that a different approach be taken when determining the extent of the right acquired under either doctrine. In *Walton v Walton*, for example, Hoffmann LJ emphasised that in proprietary estoppel, '[t]he choice of remedy is flexible' and noted that, whilst a court might require A's promise to be kept, it might instead 'order [A] to pay compensation for the expense which has been incurred'. The variety of relief across particular cases cannot be explained simply as depending on the different content of A's promise, or on the practical difficulties in some cases of enforcing such a promise.[94] The point is rather the conceptual one that the doctrine of proprietary estoppel, unlike contract law, does not operate to impose a duty on A to put B in the position that B would have been in had A's promise been performed. It can instead be seen as imposing a basic liability on A to ensure that B suffers no detriment as a result of B's reasonable reliance on A's promise,[95] although it seems that A's liability should be reduced where A can show that, on the particular facts of the case, it would not be unconscionable for A to leave B to suffer some detriment.[96]

[90] See eg *Thorner v Major* (HL) (n 1 above) [2] (Lord Hoffmann): 'Such a claim, under the principle known as proprietary estoppel, requires the claimant to prove a promise or assurance'.

[91] For a recent example, see *Hoyl Group Ltd v Cromer Town Council* [2015] EWCA Civ 782.

[92] After all, in *Cobbe v Yeoman's Row*, it was found at first instance ([2005] EWHC 266 (Ch) [123]) that A had encouraged B to believe that the property would be sold to him, yet the House of Lords found that no proprietary estoppel arose.

[93] For example, a contractual claim based on a promise to repay a sum may have the same outcome as an unjust enrichment claim, but the two claims are clearly distinct.

[94] See eg *Ottey v Grundy* (n 34 above) for an example where A's promise was not enforced, even though it was very clear in its terms and there were no practical difficulties in its enforcement.

[95] See B McFarlane, *The Law of Proprietary Estoppel* (Oxford, Oxford University Press, 2014) [7.35]–[7.69].

[96] See eg *McGuane v Welch* [2008] EWCA Civ 785, [2008] 2 P & CR 24; *Uglow v Uglow* [2004] EWCA Civ 987, [2004] WTLR 1183.

The results in *Suggitt v Suggitt* and *Thorner v Major* notwithstanding, this difference in approach can also be seen in relation to testamentary promises. Two key cases[97] are *Jennings v Rice*[98] and *Henry v Henry*.[99] In the former, the Court of Appeal confirmed an order that A's administrators should pay B £200,000 from A's estate, even though B's claim was based on a promise of property worth (at least) £435,000. The Court of Appeal recognised that the extent of B's net detriment was crucial in assessing the extent of B's right: as Aldous LJ pointed out, it would be absurd if B were awarded the same sum even if B 'had been left £5 or £50,000 or £200,000 in [A's] will, or [A] had died one month, one year or twenty years after making the representation relied on'.[100] In *Henry v Henry*, the Privy Council similarly rejected the view, taken by the Court of Appeal of the Eastern Caribbean Supreme Court, that 'there is no power in the court to say that the promise (and the resulting benefit) is disproportionate to the detriment'. That statement was said to betray a 'fundamental misconception as to the nature and purpose of the doctrine of proprietary estoppel … Proportionality lies at the heart of the doctrine of proprietary estoppel and permeates its every application'.[101]

The language of proportionality has played an important role in emphasising that the promise-based strand of proprietary estoppel need not involve the enforcement of A's promise, but it is insufficiently precise. Parts of the judgments in *Jennings v Rice*, for example, can be seen as demanding that the extent of B's right be proportionate to each of B's expectation and B's detriment:[102] and such a test cannot possibly lead to predictable results. There is also uncertainty as to whether proportionality has a positive or merely a negative role. In *Suggitt v Suggitt*, for example, the Court of Appeal, adopting a view which has also found some support in Australia,[103] preferred to give the concept only a negative role, holding that A's promise would be enforced unless it is 'out of all proportion to the detriment which [B] suffered'.[104] As Mee has noted,[105] however, such an approach can lead to absurd results. Mee's argument is as follows. Consider a case identical in all other respects to *Jennings v Rice*, but in which the value of the property promised to B is £250,000. It might then be said that, given that lower value, the enforcement of A's promise would not be 'out of all proportion' to B's detriment.

97 See too *Ottey v Grundy* (n 34 above) and *Powell v Benney* (n 7 above).

98 *Jennings v Rice* [2002] EWCA Civ 159, [2003] 1 P & CR 8.

99 *Henry v Henry* [2010] UKPC 3, [2010] 1 All ER 988.

100 *Jennings v Rice* (n 98 above) [16].

101 *Henry v Henry* (n 99 above) [65].

102 See eg *Jennings v Rice* (n 98 above) [36] (Aldous LJ). See too *Davies v Davies* (n 31 above) [55]–[56], where Jarman QC considered the content of A's assurance in deciding if a particular response would be 'out of all proportion'.

103 See eg *Giumelli v Giumelli* [1999] HCA 10, (1999) 196 CLR 101 at [42], quoting from the judgment of Deane J in *Commonwealth of Australia v Verwayen* [1990] HCA 39, (1990) 170 CLR 394 at 443. See too *Delaforce v Simpson-Cook* [2010] NSWCA 84, (2010) 78 NSWLR 483 at [63] (Handley AJA).

104 *Suggitt v Suggitt* (n 11 above) [44]. See too *Davies v Davies* (n 31 above) [54].

105 J Mee, 'Expectation and Proprietary Estoppel Remedies' in M Dixon (ed), *Modern Studies in Property Law, Volume 5* (Oxford, Hart Publishing, 2009) 389 at 399–400.

This would mean, however, that if, as in *Jennings v Rice* itself, the value of the property increases to above, say, £400,000, then the extent of B's right is reduced, as the disparity between that value and the extent of B's detriment means that enforcing A's promise would be disproportionate. Moreover, if proportionality plays only a negative role, it can provide no specific guidance as to what should occur when the prima facie measure based on B's expectation is displaced.

The better view, it is submitted, is that proportionality should play a positive role,[106] and should be limited to ensuring that the right acquired by B does not exceed what is required to ensure that B suffers no detriment as a result of B's reasonable reliance on A's promise. It is also important that, in calculating that detriment, countervailing benefits acquired by B as a result of that reliance (such as rent-free accommodation) should be taken into account.[107] This does not mean, however, that it will never be appropriate for A's liability to be such as to ensure that B is put in the same position as B would have been in had A's promise been enforced. Such a result may be particularly appropriate where B's reliance is such that B has based his or her 'whole life' on A's promises, foregoing other valuable opportunities, so that B would suffer a very large detriment in the absence of any claim. Such cases may well arise in relation to testamentary promises, although it is unclear whether the first instance judge adopted the appropriate degree of scepticism in deciding that *Suggitt v Suggitt* was such a case.[108] That is primarily a practical question, however, and there is no conceptual inconsistency in allowing a proprietary estoppel claim, in an appropriate case, to place B in the same position as if a promised testamentary gift had been made to B. The important conceptual distinction between proprietary estoppel and the exercise of a power by A to give B a right, by means of a contract or a will, does however require greater emphasis to be put on the extent of B's detriment, rather than simply the content of A's promise, in assessing the extent of B's right.

3.5. Relationship with the Inheritance (Provision for Family and Dependants) Act 1975

A number of questions, yet to be considered by the courts, arise when considering the interaction of proprietary estoppel with a possible claim for financial provision under the Inheritance (Provision for Family and Dependants) Act 1975.

[106] As advocated by eg Hobhouse LJ in *Sledmore v Dalby* (1996) 72 P & CR 196 (CA) 208, drawing on the dissenting judgment of Mason CJ in *Commonwealth of Australia v Verwayen* (n 103 above).

[107] As was made clear in eg *Henry v Henry* (n 99 above). As confirmed in *Southwell v Blackburn* [2014] EWCA Civ 1347 at [17], just as the calculation of detriment is not 'purely an exercise in financial accounting', then '[t]he same is obviously true of benefit'.

[108] Note that the first instance judge accepted that B had based his 'whole life' on A's promises, despite also noting that the purported reliance by B was 'all in all nothing like the sort of work done in *Thorner v Major*': [2011] EWHC 903 (Ch) [59].

It is clear, of course, that the requirements and effect of such a claim differ from those of a claim under the 1975 Act, and so there is no inconsistency in a successful proprietary estoppel claim giving B benefits well in excess of any sum that might instead have been awarded under the 1975 Act.[109]

A question arises, however, when applying the detriment requirement of proprietary estoppel. It might be argued that the possibility of B's making a 1975 Act claim reduces, or even eliminates, B's detriment. It was suggested in Section 3.1 that proprietary estoppel has a secondary nature: this suggests that, in ascertaining whether or not B would suffer a detriment, any other rights or claims available to B must first be taken into account.[110] Certainly, if a valid contract exists between A and B, the existence of that right can be seen as a countervailing benefit that removes any detriment.[111]

Where a 1975 Act claim can be made, it is likely to be the case that A's failure to honour the testamentary promise is a pre-requisite of the statutory claim: it is then possible to argue that the existence of such a claim is a benefit that can be taken into account in assessing the extent of B's detriment. Of course, as far as A's personal representatives are concerned, any *pro tanto* diminution of a right arising through estoppel is irrelevant if matched by an award under the 1975 Act. The argument may however appeal to C, a third party who acquired property from A before A's death, and who has no defence against any right acquired by B in that property as a result of proprietary estoppel.

The complication in evaluating C's argument, however, is that a claim under the 1975 Act, like a proprietary estoppel claim, can also be seen as subordinate. The question of whether reasonable financial provision has been made, like the question of whether B faces the prospect of detriment, must depend on what other claims are available to B. It cannot, of course, be the case that the presence of each claim diminishes the other. As a result, a tie-break is needed. The better solution, it is submitted, is that, given the nature of the 1975 Act as a statutory last resort, a proprietary estoppel claim should be determined first, and without reference to possible claims under that Act. As a result, a court should reject C's argument that the extent of the right acquired by B can be reduced by the possibility of a 1975 Act claim.

A more finely balanced question arises when considering the effect on B's proprietary estoppel claim of a possible 1975 Act claim by X. In assessing X's claim, a court must have regard to the 'size and nature of the net estate of [A]'[112] and therefore A's personal representatives might well wish to point to B's proprietary

[109] As noted in eg *Ottey v Grundy* (n 34 above) [51].

[110] See eg the analysis of Deane J in *Waltons Stores (Interstate) Ltd v Maher* (n 63 above) 453–54.

[111] This seems to be the best explanation of *Lloyds Bank plc v Carrick* [1996] 4 All ER 630 (CA). Further, in assessing the detriment requirement in estoppel by representation, it seems that if B's reliance also gives B the benefit of a change of position defence to an unjust enrichment claim by A, that benefit can eliminate B's detriment and so prevent an estoppel arising: *Scottish Equitable v Derby plc* [2001] EWCA Civ 369, [2001] 3 All ER 818 at [47].

[112] Inheritance (Provision for Family and Dependants) Act 1975, s 3(1)(e).

estoppel claim as a means of limiting any financial provision made to X under the Act. The more difficult issue is whether a court, when assessing the extent of the right acquired by B through proprietary estoppel, should take account of X's possible statutory claim. This practical issue turns on the nature of the approach to be adopted when assessing the extent of A's liability to B in proprietary estoppel and so depends on the conceptual nature of B's claim. If, as courts have sometimes suggested, there is a large measure of discretion in calculating the extent of A's liability, then it would be no surprise if X's position were taken into account. For example, in *Jennings v Rice*, Robert Walker LJ stated that, in assessing the extent of a right arising through proprietary estoppel, a relevant factor would be '(to a limited degree) the other claims (legal or moral) on [A] or his or her estate'.[113] Similarly, in *Macdonald v Frost*, the estoppel claimants (A's daughters from a previous marriage) alleged that A had promised to leave his property to them, but also accepted that, even if their claim succeeded, 'the court would have to take into account the need to make some provision for [A's widow]'.[114]

It is nonetheless worth noting that, in *Jennings v Rice* itself, Robert Walker LJ emphasised that 'the court must take a principled approach, and cannot exercise a completely unfettered discretion'.[115] B might argue that, whilst the interests of third parties can affect the particular *remedy* awarded to protect B's right,[116] they should not, as a matter of principle, alter the *extent* of that right. Certainly, a right acquired as a result of a contract, or A's commission of a tort, will not be reduced simply because of another party's claim on A. It may be, however, that the 'backwards-looking' nature of a proprietary estoppel claim calls for a different approach, at least in a case such as *Macdonald v Frost*, where the potential 1975 Act claim is to be made by a party (A's future spouse) whose position was not taken into account at the time of A's alleged promise. A's legal and moral obligations to such a party might then be seen as a significant change of circumstances that can be taken into account in assessing the extent of B's right. To that extent, a court's likely desire to take into account a 1975 Act claim by a third party when assessing how to respond to B's proprietary estoppel claim can therefore be accommodated by adverting to the specific conceptual nature of B's claim.

[113] *Jennings v Rice* (n 98 above) [52]. See too *Campbell v Griffin* [2001] EWCA Civ 990, [2001] WTLR 981 at [34]–[35]. Such claims were considered in *Davies v Davies* (n 31 above) [57], without ultimately having any effect on the award made to B.

[114] *Macdonald v Frost* (n 59 above) [6]. A's widow, at the time of trial, was aged 86 and in poor health. B1 and B2 sought a declaration that the property and its proceeds of sale be held on trust 'in such shares as are found to be appropriate to achieve the minimum equity to do justice, with a power in the trustees to advance capital as and when required to meet [A's widow's] needs; the residue to go to [B1 and B2] when [A's widow] passed away'. Note, too, that in *Davies v Davies* (n 31 above) [58], it was noted that B was continuing to make a monthly payment to his mother, and it was held that: 'it is just as part of the equity which I have found that he should continue to do so for her life'.

[115] *Jennings v Rice* (n 98 above) [43].

[116] For example, *in specie* protection of B's right by means of an injunction or an order of specific performance might be inappropriate if this would cause harm to third parties: see eg *Giumelli v Guimelli* (n 103 above).

3.6. The Test for Reliance

The reasoning of the Court of Appeal in *Wayling v Jones*[117] provides an example of how the temptation for a court to make up for a perceived—but binding—deficiency in the law of succession may lead to a distortion in the principles of proprietary estoppel. As in *Thorner v Major*, there was a strong reason to believe that permitting B to acquire the property in question would be consistent with the wishes of A. There had been no falling out between the parties, and A's failure to honour his promise to leave a particular hotel to B seems to have been caused simply by A's failure to update an earlier will, which left the hotel then owned by A to B, rather than the hotel since acquired by A after selling the previous hotel. Further, although B had lived with A for over 15 years at the time of A's death, it was not possible for A's lack of reasonable financial provision for B to be addressed by a claim under the 1975 Act, as it then stood, as A and B were in a same-sex relationship and so B could not be said to have been living in the same household as A as the husband or wife of A.[118] This failing in the Act has now been remedied,[119] but it may well be that it motivated the court to press proprietary estoppel into service. Whilst this might be seen as having met the needs of justice in the specific case, to the extent that it served to disguise the flaw in the coverage of the Act by over-extending proprietary estoppel, it could be seen as having done a disservice to the law of succession as well as to proprietary estoppel.

The distortion in *Wayling v Jones* occurred because B had stated in cross-examination that he would have 'stayed with' A even if no testamentary promise had been made, and also that he would have stopped working for A if A had told him that the promise would not be honoured. To allow B to establish the reliance element of his claim, based on having worked for A for a long period for low pay, the Court of Appeal stated the test as being whether B would have acted in the same way had A told him that the promise would not be honoured. The *Wayling* test is certainly favourable to B: given the breach of trust that may well be involved in withdrawing a promise once made, it is likely to be simple for B to show that B would have acted differently if told by A that the promise would not be honoured. As a matter of principle, however, the test is impossible to defend.[120] The purpose of the reliance requirement is to establish a causal link between A's promise and the prospect of B's detriment. If B would have acted in exactly the

[117] *Wayling v Jones* (1993) 69 P & CR 170 (CA).

[118] Note that s 1(3) also prevented B from claiming as a party who had been maintained by A, as B had worked for A, and so A had thus received 'full valuable consideration' in return for maintaining B.

[119] Law Reform (Succession) Act 1995 added s 1(1A) to the Inheritance (Provision for Family and Dependants) Act 1975. As a result of the Civil Partnership Act 2004, s 1(1B) of the 1975 Act was added. For the effect of the Human Rights Act 1998 in a comparable case, see *Ghaidan v Godin-Mendoza* [2004] UKHL 30, [2004] 2 AC 557.

[120] For academic criticism of the *Wayling* test, see eg E Cooke, 'Reliance and Estoppel' (1995) 111 *LQR* 389 and J Mee, *The Property Rights of Co-Habitees* (Oxford, Hart Publishing, 1999). Note too that, when carefully analysing the reliance requirement in *Campbell v Griffin* (n 113 above), Robert Walker LJ made no mention of the *Wayling* test.

same way even in the absence of A's promise, responsibility for that detriment cannot be attributed to A, and so no proprietary estoppel should arise.[121] As with any causation test, its aim is to compare what has actually occurred with what would have happened in the absence of the events constituting the cause of action.[122] A's promise is one such event; A's failure to inform B of an intention not to perform the promise is not.[123] So, for example, in establishing whether B acted in reliance on a misrepresentation of A, the test is how B would have acted in the absence of such a misrepresentation, not how B would have acted if, having made the statement, A then told B that it was false.

It is also worth noting that, on the facts of *Wayling v Jones* itself, B may well have satisfied a standard causation test asking what B would have done had no testamentary promise had been made. B's admission was simply that he would have 'stayed with' A had A's promise not been made: it did not necessarily mean that B would have continued to work for A on the same terms, as A's promise had been made to B in response to B's complaints as to his low wages.[124] Nonetheless, there do seem to be some cases in which the application of the *Wayling* test was crucial to B's claim: in *Ottey v Grundy*,[125] for example, a claim was allowed based on a testamentary promise, even though it was far from clear that A's promise, not made in response to any complaint from B, caused B to change her behaviour. In such a case, then, criticisms of proprietary estoppel are well-founded. The problem is not, however, that the doctrine is undermining the law of succession; it is rather that it has been extended beyond its conceptual basis and so is unjustified even on its own terms. Indeed, given that the problem in *Wayling v Jones* could be seen to arise from gaps in the law of succession (either in relation to the rectification of wills or the scope of the 1975 Act), it could be said that the case provides an example of the law of succession undermining proprietary estoppel.

4. Final Thoughts

The principal conclusions of this chapter were set out in Section 1 and will not be repeated here. A further key point is that a proper understanding of the

[121] See eg *Jones v Watkins* (CA, 26 Nov 1987); *Western Fish Products Ltd v Penwith District Council* [1981] 2 All ER 204 (CA).

[122] It may also be noted that the so-called 'presumption of reliance' stemming from *Greasley v Cooke* [1980] 1 WLR 1306 (CA), if anything more than a statement that some facts will support an inference of reliance, is very difficult to justify, given that it is generally the task of the claimant to make out the elements of his or her claim: see eg *van Dyke v Sidhu* [2014] HCA 19, (2014) 251 CLR 505; *Steria Ltd v Hutchison* [2006] EWCA Civ 1551, [2007] ICR 445 at [129].

[123] Indeed, as shown by *Thorner v Major* (n 1 above), B's claim can be made out even if A never had such an intention not to perform the promise, but instead failed to do so as a result of inadvertence.

[124] Note that Balcombe LJ was minded to accept that submission as to the meaning of the admission that B would have 'stayed with' A: *Wayling v Jones* (n 117 above) 175. In *Walton v Walton* (n 47 above), A's promises—as in *Wayling v Jones*—were made in order to induce B to continue working for A for low pay, and it would seem that B could have passed a standard 'but-for' test of causation.

[125] *Ottey v Grundy* (n 34 above).

still-developing promise-based strand of proprietary estoppel must involve addressing the conceptual and practical concerns as to the potential of the doctrine to undermine the law of succession. This should occur, however, not as a result of a simple desire to protect the territory of the law of succession, but rather in order to secure the wider goal of ensuring that this form of proprietary estoppel is limited to addressing a specific form of unconscionable conduct and does not give the courts a general licence to adjust the rights of the parties. The approach taken by proprietary estoppel to testamentary promises will be a crucial test of whether the doctrine can be developed in that way: as demonstrated by decisions such as *Wayling v Jones*,[126] there may be significant practical reasons why a court might be tempted to depart from the specific requirements of proprietary estoppel in order to allow B some protection.

Even if it is motivated in part by a desire to protect the law of succession, the application of appropriate limits to proprietary estoppel will be of benefit to the general doctrine, which of course applies beyond the context of succession.[127] It would therefore be unfortunate if this jurisdiction were to follow New Zealand and instead adopt a context-specific statutory scheme in an attempt to meet some of the practical problems discussed in this chapter.[128] Whilst some support for enacting such legislation in England can be found,[129] it would have a clarifying effect only if it set up an exclusive regime, and there seems to be no good reason why the specific form of unconscionable conduct with which proprietary estoppel deals should go unchecked in the context of succession.[130]

To broaden matters further, it is possible to identify a tension which also informs the operation of other equitable doctrines.[131] On the one hand, an important justification for the very concept of promise-based proprietary estoppel is its ability to play a secondary role in mitigating some of the severity of the strict rules of contract law, property law, and of the law of succession. On the other hand, a role should not be mistaken for a rationale, and any such doctrine can only be called on when its specific requirements are met, and not whenever a failing is perceived in contract law, property law, or the law of succession. Some gaps, after all, are much needed.

[126] See also *Ottey v Grundy* (n 34 above).

[127] See in particular the point noted at the end of Section 3.3 as to the emphasis placed in succession cases on the need for A to have made a promise or assurance to B, and to the desirability of such a requirement beyond the context of succession.

[128] For discussion of the Law Reform (Testamentary Promises) Act 1949 (NZ), see eg Nield (n 72 above); Braun (n 43 above) 1018–19. As Braun notes at 1006–7, a more limited German provision (§ 2057a I 2 BGB) also provides some specific protection in the case of gratuitous care provided by a descendant of A.

[129] See eg Nield (n 72 above); B Sloan, 'Proprietary Estoppel: Recent Developments in England and Wales' (2010) 22 *Singapore Academy of Law Journal* 110 at 131–35.

[130] Note, for example, that the New Zealand Act—in contrast to the law of proprietary estoppel—allows a claim only against A's estate.

[131] For discussion see Smith (n 6 above); L Alexander and E Sherwin, *The Rule of Rules: Morality, Rules and the Dilemmas of Law* (Durham NC, Duke University Press, 2001), especially chs 3 and 4; McFarlane and Sales (n 62 above).

5

Explaining the Mutual Wills Doctrine

YING KHAI LIEW*

1. Introduction

Although English courts have applied the mutual wills doctrine since the eighteenth century,[1] it remains difficult precisely to define its operation, the legal principles involved, and its underlying rationale(s). These difficulties have caused many to doubt the usefulness and coherence of the doctrine. Recently, the Law Commission announced its plan to review the law concerning wills, with one of the four key areas to be reviewed being mutual wills.[2] The review is said to 'aim to reduce the likelihood of wills being challenged after death, and the incidence of litigation. Such litigation is expensive, can divide families and is a cause of great stress for the bereaved'. This is reminiscent of Mummery LJ's comments in *Olins v Walters*,[3] that the doctrine 'continues to be a source of contention for the families of those who have invoked it. The likelihood is that in future even fewer people will opt for such an arrangement and even more will be warned against the risks involved'. These statements suggest that there is a real possibility that a move might be made to abolish the mutual wills doctrine completely.

This chapter proposes a new way of understanding the mutual wills doctrine which is consistent with orthodox principles. It distinguishes between what will be labelled 'qualified interest' and 'absolute interest' situations, each applying to a different type of mutual wills agreement. From this renewed understanding, it will be seen that the doctrine is underpinned by two distinct rationales, which also form the basis of equity's intervention in other areas. This indicates that the best way to understand the mutual wills doctrine is not to treat it in isolation, but

* The author would like to thank Ben McFarlane and Ian Williams for their helpful comments on an earlier draft.

[1] *Dufour v Pereira* (1769) Dick 419, 21 ER 332, reported more fully in F Hargrave, *Juridical Arguments and Collections*, vol II (London, GG & J Robinson, 1799) 304 and 309.

[2] See under www.lawcom.gov.uk/project/wills/ (last accessed 19 February 2016). The other areas the Law Commission proposes to review are testamentary capacity, formality requirements and rectification. For a discussion of capacity, see Penelope Reed's contribution in Ch 7 of this volume. Rectification of wills and its relationship with testamentary formality requirements is addressed by Birke Häcker in Ch 6.

[3] *Olins v Walters, sub nom Re Walters (Deceased)* [2008] EWCA Civ 782, [2009] Ch 212 at [3].

to pay proper regard to its commonalities with other doctrines which give rise to constructive trusts, such as the rule in *Rochefoucauld v Boustead*,[4] the doctrine of secret trusts, and the doctrine of proprietary estoppel.[5]

2. Difficulties in the Present Understanding

In a typical mutual wills case, two individuals come to an agreement that the first to die (A) will leave his property to the survivor (B), with B promising to leave whatever is left at her death to one or more ultimate beneficiaries, C.[6] In a rarer type of arrangement, A and B agree to make respective wills which benefit C directly. In both cases, B also promises not to revoke her will after A's death, this being indicated by an intention to create legally binding obligations.[7] When A dies while relying on B's promise, that is, by leaving property to B or C as the case may be, a constructive trust[8] binds B to carry out the agreement. Any subsequent volunteer recipient of B's property, such as her personal representative, executor, or heir,[9] is likewise bound to fulfil the mutual wills agreement. The constructive trust arises notwithstanding the informality of the agreement, that is to say, despite the fact that the arrangement may not appear in B's will as would normally be required by section 9 of the Wills Act 1837,[10] and despite non-compliance with section 53(1)(b) of the Law of Property Act 1925[11] where it affects interests in land. As Mummery LJ observed in *Fry v Densham-Smith*,[12] 'if and when [the doctrine] applies, absolute beneficial testamentary dispositions ... do not take effect in accordance with their terms'.

Mutual wills agreements are characterised by two distinctive features which make the doctrine unique. First, the constructive trust binds not only A's property

[4] *Rochefoucauld v Boustead* [1897] 1 Ch 196 (CA).

[5] For a discussion of proprietary estoppel in the succession law context, see Ben McFarlane's contribution in Ch 4 of this volume.

[6] For the sake of exposition, it will be assumed in the hypotheticals which follow that A is male and B is female.

[7] *Birmingham v Renfrew* (1936) 57 CLR 666 (HCA) 675; *Re Cleaver (deceased)* [1981] 1 WLR 939 (Ch) 947; *Re Goodchild (deceased)* [1997] 1 WLR 1216 (CA) 1225; *Osborne v Estate of Osborne* [2001] VSCA 228 at [15]; *Birch v Curtis* [2002] EWHC 1158 (Ch), [2002] 2 FLR 847 at [60].

[8] *Birmingham v Renfrew* (n 7 above) 680 and 683; *Re Cleaver* (n 7 above) 947; *Re Newey (deceased)* [1994] 2 NZLR 590; *Re Dale (deceased)* [1994] Ch 31 (Ch) 46–47; *Manitoba University v Sanderman* (1998) 155 DLR (4th) 40; *Healey v Brown and Another* [2002] EWHC (Ch) 1405, [2002] WTLR 849, [8]; *Osenton v Osenton* [2004] EWHC 1055 (Ch) [33]; *Olins v Walters* (n 3 above) [39]; *Charles v Fraser* [2010] EWHC Civ 2154 (Ch) [59]; *Shovelar v Lane* [2011] EWCA Civ 802, [2012] 1 WLR 637 [37].

[9] *Dufour v Pereira* (in Hargrave) (n 1 above) 309, decided long before the Land Transfer Act 1897 made the concept of common law 'heir' obsolete.

[10] Among its requirements, a will must be put in writing and witnessed by two others to be valid.

[11] '[A] declaration of trust respecting any land ... must be manifested and proved by some writing signed by some person who is able to declare such a trust'.

[12] *Fry v Densham-Smith* [2010] EWCA Civ 1410, [2011] WTLR 387 at [31]. See also *Olins v Walters* (n 3 above) [40].

but also B's *own* property.[13] Secondly, B's promise is not to hold some property on trust immediately upon A's death, but to make a *testamentary* disposition in a particular form. These features pose tricky issues for a proper explanation of the mutual wills doctrine, in particular during B's lifetime after A's death. How is it possible to reconcile B's apparent freedom to make use of property in her hands with the fact that she has trust obligations in relation to the property?

Judges and commentators generally take one of three approaches, none of which appears satisfactory. The first views B's obligation as being 'floating', that is, suspended during her lifetime and 'crystallising' either upon B's death or when gifts or settlements are made during her lifetime that are 'calculated to defeat the intention of the [agreement]'.[14] This approach, however, does not explain the nature of B's duties and C's rights during B's lifetime. By virtue of what right can B deal with her estate? How does C have a right against a recipient to whom B has left her estate contrary to the mutual wills agreement? The 'floating trust' approach has also been criticised for the lack of certainty of subject-matter it entails,[15] which is required for the validity of any trust.[16] Others have suggested that the 'floating trust' should be given legal effect in the same way as the law recognises a floating charge.[17] However, it is difficult to reconcile this analysis with the policy underlying the Bills of Sale Act (1878) Amendment Act 1882, which prevents an individual from granting a floating charge over her personal chattels.[18] After all, 'there is all the difference between a trust and a charge, in their inception'.[19]

The second approach simply treats the doctrine as *sui generis* or anomalous.[20] Based on the view that the mutual wills doctrine is closely related to a contractual action,[21] its perceived anomaly lies in allowing C, a third party, to enforce

[13] See *Re Goodchild (deceased)* (n 7 above) 1224.

[14] *Birmingham v Renfrew* (n 7 above) 689. This analysis has been cited in many English cases, eg in *Re Goodchild* (n 7 above) 225; *Re Cleaver* (n 7 above) 947; *Healey v Brown* (n 8 above); *Birch v Curtis* (n 7 above).

[15] P Luxton, '*Walters v Olin*: Uncertainty of Subject Matter—An Insoluble Problem in Mutual Wills?' (2009) 73 *Conv* 498 at 503–4.

[16] *Knight v Knight* (1840) 3 Beav 148, 49 ER 58.

[17] *Barns v Barns* (2003) 214 CLR 169 (HCA) [152]. See too CJ Davis, 'Floating Rights' (2002) 61 *CLJ* 423 at 429.

[18] See L Gullifer, *Goode on Legal Problems of Credit and Security*, 5th edn (London, Sweet & Maxwell, 2013) [4-01].

[19] *Re Lehman Brothers* [2009] EWHC 3228 (Ch) [178].

[20] *Re Goodchild* (n 7 above) 1230; TG Youdan, 'The Mutual Wills Doctrine' (1979) 29 *University of Toronto Law Journal* 390 at 401; H Legge and A Norris, 'Contract and Conscience: The Decline of the Mutual Will' [1998] *Private Client Business* 332 at 336; R Croucher, 'Mutual Wills: Contemporary Reflections on an Old Doctrine' (2005) 19 *Melbourne University Law Review* 390; AJ Oakley, *Parker and Mellows: The Modern Law of Trusts*, 9th edn (London, Sweet & Maxwell, 2008) [10-331].

[21] The case of *Healey v Brown* (n 8 above) is often cited in support of this proposition. There David Donaldson QC, sitting as a deputy High Court judge, held that compliance with s 2(1) of the Law of Property (Miscellaneous Provisions) Act 1989 is a prerequisite for the mutual wills doctrine to apply. However, this cannot be sustained as a matter of principle and consistency. After all, it is indisputable that the mutual wills doctrine gives rise to constructive trusts, not merely contractual damages; and s 2(5) of the Act provides that 'nothing in this section affects the creation or operation of ... constructive trusts'.

a contract between A and B. However, the mutual wills doctrine is an equitable doctrine and, at least in the modern law, has nothing to do with a common law contractual action. Thus, it has been said that the doctrine does not involve making a claim for contractual relief such as specific performance because C is not a party to the 'contract';[22] that its principles are not precisely the same as those which apply to contractual disputes;[23] that it arises from the parties' course of conduct and not the contract itself;[24] and that the constructive trust is excepted from any otherwise relevant formality requirements.[25] Indeed, the doctrine has been applied to cases where the agreement is not even certain enough to amount to a contract enforceable at common law.[26] Moreover, to write off the doctrine as *sui generis* is an act of despair which should be avoided until and unless other alternative explanations have been explored and found wanting.

A third approach is to analyse the courts as imposing a remedial constructive trust, where judges are 'shaping the remedy to meet the circumstances'.[27] This approach immediately runs up against the oft-rehearsed view that English law recognises only 'institutional' and not 'remedial' constructive trusts.[28] There is also little to commend this approach. Remedial constructive trusts are said to reflect the 'crucial features' of judicial discretion and retrospectivity.[29] However, in the mutual wills context, constructive trusts do not appear to be imposed by way of discretion; and even if they were, an explanation for the pre-conditions for doing so is lacking. Furthermore, this approach does not identify the source and extent of B's and C's duties and rights; it merely addresses B's breach of the agreement. It therefore fails to explain why, for instance, C's interest does not lapse if she predeceases B but dies after A.[30]

In view of the inadequacies of the prevailing approaches, a fresh analysis is proposed, by which it is possible to explain B's duties and C's rights which arise upon A's death. This analysis explains not only how C obtains the right to the

[22] *Olins v Walters* (n 3 above) [36]. See also *Re Dale* (n 8 above) 38.

[23] *Re Hobley* (1997) [2006] WTLR 467 (Ch).

[24] *Lewis v Cotton* [2001] 2 NZLR 21 (CA Wellington) [44], [55].

[25] *Birmingham v Renfrew* (n 7 above) 680. Latham CJ was speaking in relation to the constructive trust exception to compliance with the formality requirement of s 53 of the Law of Property Act 1925, and the same exception would likewise apply to the Law of Property (Miscellaneous Provisions) Act 1989 by virtue of s 2(5).

[26] *Olins v Walters* (n 3 above); see especially counsel's submission reported at [24] which the Court of Appeal rejected.

[27] C Rickett, 'A Rare Case of Mutual Wills and its Implications' (1982) 8 *Adelaide Law Review* 178 at 196. See too eg *Healey v Brown* (n 8 above) [24]; *Re Newey* (n 8 above) 593; R Burgess, 'A Fresh Look at Mutual Wills' (1970) 34 *Conv* 230 at 246; AHR Brierley, 'Mutual Wills—Blackpool Illuminations' (1995) 58 *MLR* 95 at 99; Croucher (n 20 above) 409.

[28] *Westdeutsche Landesbank Girozentrale v Islington London Borough Council* [1996] AC 669 (HL) 714–15; *London Allied Holdings Ltd v Lee* [2007] EWHC 2061 (Ch) [273]; PJ Millett, 'Tracing the Proceeds of Fraud' (1991) 107 *LQR* 71 at 81; PJ Millett, 'Restitution and Constructive Trusts' (1998) 114 *LQR* 399 at 399.

[29] *London Allied Holdings Ltd v Lee* (n 28 above) [273].

[30] *Re Hagger* [1930] 2 Ch 190 (Ch).

agreed-upon interest when B dies, but also why C is allowed only to prevent certain dispositions by B during her lifetime.

3. The Qualified Interest (QI) and Absolute Interest (AI) Analyses

It is necessary first to note a crucial but rarely observed distinction. There are two different cases in which a promisor, B, may promise through an agreement to give an interest in property to another, and which may potentially attract a constructive trust.[31] The first is where B promises to give an interest in property she owns *absolutely*. The second is where B's promise relates to property that she does not yet own: B promises to take a *qualified* interest in the property, for instance, by an obligation to hold it on trust for the other. These cases will be referred to as 'absolute interest' (AI) and 'qualified interest' (QI) analyses.

In practice, these cases are treated differently. When B promises to give away property that is hers to begin with, courts exercise a measure of caution before depriving her of her interest. Consider proprietary estoppel cases where B promises or assures A that B will give A an interest in property B owns. For A to gain a right against B at all, A must act in detrimental reliance on B's promise; yet B is not invariably bound by a constructive trust to perform her promise. The court may choose from a wide range of remedial responses;[32] and being guided by the notion of the 'minimum equity to do justice to the plaintiff',[33] a remedy is imposed which achieves proportionality between A's detriment and B's promise.[34] Although a constructive trust is often imposed, compensatory damages (or 'equitable compensation') may also be awarded.[35] Since the property to which the promise relates is B's in her own right,[36] A's act of reliance does not confer an advantage on B in relation to the acquisition of the property: it does not increase B's chances of acquiring the property in question.

A markedly different approach is taken where B's promise relates to property she does not yet own. In the doctrine in *Rochefoucauld v Boustead*[37] and secret

[31] This precludes an outright gift, a declaration of an express trust, or contractually promising to transfer away property.

[32] See *Stack v Dowden* [2007] UKHL 17, [2002] 2 AC 432 at [37].

[33] *Crabb v Arun District Council* [1976] Ch 179 (CA) 198.

[34] *Henry v Henry* [2010] UKPC 3, [2010] 1 All ER 988 at [65].

[35] *Campbell v Griffin* [2001] EWCA Civ 990, [2001] WTLR 981; *Jennings v Rice* [2002] EWCA Civ 159, [2002] WTLR 367; *Ottey v Grundy* [2003] EWCA Civ 1176, [2003] WTLR 1253; *Henry v Henry* (n 34 above).

[36] *Paragon Finance plc v DB Thakerar & Co* [1999] 1 All ER 400 (CA) 409.

[37] *Rochefoucauld v Boustead* (n 4 above). In the typical case, B informally agrees to hold A's land on trust for A; and in reliance A transfers the legal title of the land to B. A constructive trust binds B to her promise.

trusts,[38] for instance, B informally promises A that she (B) will hold an interest in property yet to be acquired for the benefit of A or C. Where A acts in reliance on B's promise and confers an advantage on B in relation to the acquisition of the property,[39] that is, by transferring the property in question to B, courts bind B to carry out her promise without considering whether a lesser remedy would be more appropriate. As Millett LJ (as he then was) observed of such cases, B[40]

> does not receive the trust property in [her] own right but by a transaction by which both parties intend to create a trust from the outset … [Her] possession of the property is coloured from the first by the trust and confidence by means of which [she] obtained it.

It is suggested that the mutual wills doctrine can be analysed in the light of the distinction between the QI and AI analyses, which reveals what actually goes on in the decided cases. The following analysis makes a distinction between cases where B receives property from A pursuant to the parties' agreement, and cases where B does not do so.

3.1. B Receives Property from A

Mutual wills agreements typically involve B receiving property from A at A's death. It is clear that at this point B is subject to certain duties and C obtains certain corresponding rights. However, the specific assets in B's hands may well alter during the course of her lifetime. A conceptual distinction might therefore be made between property in B's hands at the time of A's death (which, by definition, includes property acquired from A), and property which B may amass afterwards.

3.1.1. At the Point of A's Death

At the time of A's death, it may be tempting to analyse B's obligations as relating to two distinct sets of property: one belonging to A and another to B. This would, however, misrepresent the true subject-matter of the parties' agreement, which is in fact a *fund*.

[38] In the typical case, B informally promises a testator, A, that she will hold any property B receives under A's will for C. A leaves property in her will to B absolutely, and this remains unchanged until his death, in reliance on B's agreement to fulfill A's intention. A constructive trust binds B to her promise.

[39] It may be that A's act of reliance on B's promise does not confer such an advantage, for instance where B promises to hold property yet to be acquired on trust for A and A's reliance consists of caring for B's aging mother or making a substantial donation. In such cases, when B acquires the property in question, she does so 'in her own right', and her promise is taken to relate to property she owns absolutely, as in cases reflecting the AI analysis.

[40] *Paragon Finance plc v DB Thakerar & Co* (n 36 above) 409. Incidentally, in *Paragon Finance*, Millett LJ did not comment on cases reflecting the AI analysis.

A fund is 'a set of properties, the identity of which fund or set continues despite a change in the items of property that it comprises'.[41] A fund exists only when certain assets are demarcated, for example, by a declaration of trust, by an executor, or to be treated as security.[42] In specific relation to an interest in a *trust* fund, Roy Goode writes:[43]

> The essential characteristic is that an asset or collection of assets is transferred to a trustee (or declared by a settlor to be held by himself as trustee on stated trusts) to manage on behalf of the beneficiaries, with power to change the assets within the limits, if any, set by the trust instrument or by law.

In the mutual wills context, this is the only explanation of the subject-matter of the trust which does full justice to, and avoids a distortion of, the parties' agreement, insofar as the property in B's hands at the point of A's death is concerned.[44] First, in contrast with other doctrines such as secret trusts, the doctrine in *Rochefoucauld v Boustead*, and even proprietary estoppel, B's promise in a mutual wills agreement usually relates not to specifically defined property; it is to leave 'whatever is left' at her death to C.[45] This indicates that the subject-matter of the agreement is a fund, since the parties do not intend to create rights and duties in relation to specific assets, but in relation to their combined assets *as a singular entity*. During B's lifetime, the assets are treated not as things, but as wealth,[46] since the parties are only concerned with specific assets as things at the time of B's death when the trust ends. Secondly, it follows that the parties do not intend C to obtain any interest in specific assets during B's lifetime, which reflects the nature of a beneficiary's interest in a trust fund.[47] When a breach occurs, a beneficiary may elect to enforce a proprietary interest in specific assets in the fund,[48] which is consistent with judicial statements in the mutual wills context that C may prevent certain

[41] JE Penner, 'Duty and Liability in Respect of Funds' in J Lowry and L Mistelis (eds), *Commercial Law: Perspectives and Practice* (London, LexisNexis Butterworths, 2006) [12.13], developing an idea propounded by Roy Goode: R Goode, 'The Right to Trace and its Impact in Commercial Transactions, Part I' (1976) 92 *LQR* 360 at 384; R Goode, *Commercial Law*, 2nd edn (London, Penguin, 1995) 66–67.

[42] Penner (n 41 above) [12.14].

[43] R Goode, 'The Right to Trace and its Impact in Commercial Transactions, Part II' (1976) 92 *LQR* 528, 529.

[44] Notably, Lord Camden observed in *Dufour v Pereira* (in Hargrave) (n 1 above) 308 that '[t]he property of both is put into a common fund, and every devise is the joint devise of both'.

[45] If the parties specifically identify the property or interest that B will leave to C at B's death, then there are three possibilities. If that property or interest was transferred from A to B upon A's death, then the case falls within the secret trusts doctrine, with the result that B obtains a life interest and C obtains an interest in remainder: see *Ottaway v Norman* [1972] Ch 698 (Ch). If the specified property or interest formerly belonged partly to A and partly to B, as in eg *Re Hagger* (n 30 above), then the specification relates to a 'fund' after all, and the analysis discussed in the text would be applicable. If the specified property or interest was not formerly A's at all, but was acquired by B of her own accord, then the appropriate analysis would be that discussed in Section 3.2 below.

[46] For the distinction between things as 'things' and as 'wealth', see B Rudden, 'Things as Thing and Things as Wealth' (1994) 14 *OJLS* 81.

[47] See eg Goode (n 43 above) 530; Penner (n 41 above) [12.16].

[48] Penner (n 41 above) [12.16].

dispositions from being made by B during her lifetime which are calculated to defeat the agreement.[49] Thirdly, like a beneficiary of a trust fund, C has a right to her due share in accretions to the fund,[50] which is expressly stipulated to be at B's death. Fourthly, the subject-matter of the mutual wills agreement reflects other features of a trust fund, namely that it does not comprise *merely* B's assets, and that it is clearly demarcated, that is, at A's death. Fifthly, as in the case of a trust fund, a power is imposed by law[51] which allows B to make changes to the specific assets comprising the fund.

Once the subject-matter of the parties' agreement is correctly identified as a fund, the QI analysis can be applied. On this understanding, B promises to qualify the interest she will take *in the fund*. This fund is acquired by B if and only if A completes his act of reliance, which confers an advantage on B in relation to the acquisition of the fund. The relevant advantage B obtains lies not merely in the acquisition of 'A's property' (although this is certainly so), leaving it necessary to find a separate explanation for the rights and duties arising over 'B's property'. Instead, it materialises in the form of a fund in B's hands. Stated in the reverse, without A's reliance, B would not only fail to acquire A's property, but would also never obtain the fund in question. Therefore, upon A's death, a fund is constituted in B's hands, over which a constructive trust attaches.

An objection to the fund analysis might be made by pointing out that a trust fund of an express trust always begins with capital provided by the settlor only, and does not include property belonging to the trustee. However, nothing prevents A and B *as settlors* from creating an express trust with B holding the trust fund on trust for C's benefit. The same can also be said in relation to mutual wills: B, in her capacity analogous to an express trustee, promises to hold the fund on trust, and A and B, in their capacity analogous to joint settlors of an express trust, together supply the assets which constitute the fund in B's hands.

3.1.2. *After A's Death*

It is more difficult to determine the appropriate analysis in relation to property B amasses on her own account after A's death, that is, any accretion to B's estate which is not a traceable proceed of the assets in B's hands at the time of A's death. One major difficulty is that no case specifically affirms that such 'after-acquired' property is capable of being bound.[52] It is often presumed that it is indeed so,[53]

[49] See the text following n 14 above.

[50] Goode (n 43 above) 530.

[51] See Section 4.1.2 below.

[52] See A Braun, 'Revocability of Mutual Wills' in KGC Reid, MJ de Waal, and R Zimmermann (eds), *Exploring the Law of Succession: Studies National, Historical and Comparative* (Edinburgh, Edinburgh University Press, 2007) fn 64. Note though, that in *Re Gillespie* (1968) 69 DLR (2d) 368 at [18], Stark J in the Ontario High Court construed the parties in that case as having agreed to *preclude* such after-acquired property from being subject to the trust.

[53] See eg LA Sheridan, 'The Floating Trust: Mutual Wills' (1977) 15 *Alberta Law Review* 211 at 235; J McGhee (ed), *Snell's Equity*, 32nd edn (London, Sweet & Maxwell, 2010) [24-036].

although this view is not unanimous.[54] If such 'after-acquired' property *is* bound, an explanation is required.

It might be thought that an explanation can be found in the equitable maxim 'equity considers as done that which ought to be done'.[55] This relies on the line of authorities which provides that, where valuable consideration is given, equity will enforce a declaration of trust over future property as a contract to assign the property,[56] and a constructive trust attaches to the property immediately when the property is acquired. However, this explanation attracts a number of insurmountable difficulties. First, the mutual wills doctrine is not based on a contractual analysis of the parties' agreement.[57] Secondly, this cannot account for any after-acquired property subject to the trust which is not land or a unique chattel, for instance B's salaries or pension pay-outs, since an order of specific performance is generally not available against such assets.[58] Finally, it is A, not C, who provides the consideration, therefore making it difficult to justify the imposition of a constructive trust in C's favour.[59]

One possibility is to extend the 'fund' analysis to cover after-acquired property, and to analyse such property by way of the QI analysis. This approach is plausible if we understand B's contribution to the trust fund as being 'her estate' instead of merely 'her assets at the time of A's death'. On this approach, B's promise is understood as relating to a fund which comprises properties received from A as well as B's own estate, the second of which includes after-acquired property. The great attraction of this explanation is the consistency it achieves in the law's approach to mutual wills arrangements which involve B receiving property from A.

Treating B's 'estate' as a proprietary entity in this manner is not free from controversy, however. In the first place, nowhere else in English law is one's estate treated as an entity of property capable of subjecting its owner to *inter vivos* obligations.[60] The closest idea to this conception can be found in the civilian 'patrimony', which is the sum total of one's assets minus liabilities.[61] Even so, this concept is neither here nor there for the purposes of the present discussion. It is most commonly employed for the purpose of explaining why each person is liable to her own

[54] See S Hudson and B Sloan, 'Testamentary Freedom: Mutual Wills Might Let You Down' in W Barr (ed), *Modern Studies in Property Law, Volume 8* (Oxford, Hart Publishing, 2015) 166.

[55] *Palette Shoes Pty Ltd v Krohn* (1937) 58 CLR 1 (HCA) 16.

[56] *Ellison v Ellison* (1802) 6 Ves Jun 656, 31 ER 1243; *Holroyd v Marshall* (1862) 10 HLC 191, 210; 11 ER 999, 1006; *Tailby v Official Receiver* (1888) 13 App Cas 523 (HL) 530; *Re Lind* [1915] 2 Ch 345 (CA). See also *Williams v Inland Revenue Commissioners* [1965] NZLR 395.

[57] See the text following n 21 above.

[58] *Sky Petroleum Ltd v VIP Petroleum Ltd* [1974] 1 WLR 576 (Ch) 578; *R Griggs Group Ltd v Evans* [2005] Ch 153 (Ch) [36].

[59] G Virgo, *The Principles of Equity and Trusts* (Oxford, Oxford University Press, 2012) 154–55.

[60] Penner (n 41 above) [12.14]; FH Lawson and B Rudden, *The Law of Property*, 3rd edn (Oxford, Oxford University Press, 2002) 171. Although, of course, one's estate can be made the subject-matter of a testamentary disposition.

[61] L Smith, 'Trust and Patrimony' (2008) 38 *Revue Générale de Droit* 379 at 383; although it has been suggested that this concept is helpful in an English law context: Lawson and Rudden (n 60 above) 46. In this regard, see the English case of *Mannox v Greener* (1872) LR 14 Eq 456 (Ct Ch), where the language of 'patrimony' was employed.

creditors,[62] and how a civilian 'trustee' administers and manages another's 'patrimony' and is therefore not liable to the latter's creditors.[63] It tends not to be used to the effect that one may subject oneself to *inter vivos* obligations in relation to one's own patrimony.[64]

Moreover, an objection might be made to the analysis on policy grounds. In the context of the law of assignment,[65] courts have suggested that the assignment by an individual of her entire estate, both real and personal, present and future, is unenforceable as being contrary to public policy, since it renders her destitute or a quasi-slave of the assignee.[66] The same might be said about the present analysis. However, those statements made in the assignment context are strictly obiter, and so the issue remains an open one. Moreover, the fact that B remains capable of making use of the capital assets of the mutual wills fund during her lifetime militates against that policy concern.

Ultimately, it seems plausible to extend the 'fund' analysis to cover B's entire 'estate', at least where the trust fund does not *merely* comprise B's estate *alone*, but includes contributions from A. The fact that A, too, contributes to the fund means that there is a clear demarcation[67] as to what properties make up the fund, as in the case of any ordinary trust fund.

Alternatively, the after-acquired property could be analysed by way of the AI analysis. On this approach, such property is not treated as being part of the trust fund; instead, as in a case of proprietary estoppel, B is treated as absolute owner of any after-acquired property, and C potentially gains a right to that property due to A's detrimental reliance on B's promise to leave the property to C. This places the analysis of B's after-acquired property within the discussion immediately below, concerning the situation where B does not receive property from A. It is argued there that, on the AI analysis, if a court deems that a constructive trust is not an award proportionate to A's detrimental reliance, then C would have no claim, since monetary compensation would be awarded in favour of A or A's estate. This is, however, not necessarily a cause for concern, since it would appear intuitive that B should be free to dispose of property she acquired on her own account if

[62] M Raczynska, 'Parallels between the Civilian Separate Patrimony, Real Subrogation and the Idea of Property in a Trust Fund' in L Smith (ed), *The Worlds of the Trust* (Cambridge, Cambridge University Press, 2013) 454, 456–57.

[63] G Gretton, 'Up There in the *Begriffshimmel*?' in L Smith (ed), *The Worlds of the Trust* (Cambridge, Cambridge University Press, 2013) 531ff; Raczynska (n 62 above) 454–55, fns 6 and 7, text to fn 8; RG Anderson, 'Words and Concepts: Trust and Patrimony' in A Burrows, D Johnston, and R Zimmermann (eds), *Judge and Jurist: Essays in Memory of Lord Rodger of Earlsferry* (Oxford, Oxford University Press, 2013) 347 at 351–58.

[64] As Raczynska (n 62 above) at 472 argues, a civilian patrimony is not an entity to which a proprietary interest can be asserted.

[65] See AG Guest and YK Liew, *Guest on the Law of Assignment*, 2nd edn (London, Sweet & Maxwell, 2015) [4-21].

[66] *Re Clarke* (1887) 36 Ch D 348 (CA) 354 and 355; *Tailby v Official Receiver* (n 56 above) 530 and 535; *King v Michael Faraday and Partners Ltd* [1939] 2 KB 753 (KB); *Syrett v Egerton* [1957] 1 WLR 1130 (Div Ct).

[67] Penner (n 41 above) [12.14].

A's detrimental reliance was relatively minor—for instance if A was destitute at the time of her death. The availability of judicial discretion to test the appropriateness of a constructive trust award in C's favour against the degree of A's detrimental reliance in relation to B's after-acquired property is therefore a plausible development of this area of law.

3.2. B Does Not Receive Property from A

In a less common category of mutual wills cases, B does not receive any property from A. The most well-known case of this sort is *Re Dale*,[68] where it was held that the doctrine can apply where A and B agree to make respective wills which benefit C *directly*.[69] A variation of this situation is where, pursuant to the supposition that B will be the first to die, B makes a will leaving her estate to A absolutely and A makes a will leaving her estate to C absolutely. A then dies first, leading to the creation of a substitutionary gift in B's will in C's (or another's) favour. So, too, if (i) A relies on B's promise by acting in a way other than transferring property to B; or (ii) the parties agree that A will make a testamentary disposition of Property 1 to B, and B will make a testamentary disposition of Property 2 to C, where Properties 1 and 2 are distinct assets which do not together make up a fund. In all these cases, B does not receive any property from A pursuant to the parties' mutual wills agreement.

It is clear that these cases can only be analysed by way of the AI analysis. B does not promise to take a qualified interest in property that will be acquired; B's promise relates to property which she already owns absolutely at the time the promise is made. Moreover, A's reliance consists of acts which do not confer any advantage on B in relation to the acquisition of the property to which B's promise relates. While it might not be immediately obvious, some support for the AI analysis of the relevant mutual wills cases can be gleaned from case law.

3.2.1. *The Case of* Re Dale

Re Dale appears to be the only reported case where the facts did not involve B receiving property from A. In that case, a husband (A) and wife (B) entered into a mutual wills agreement where each executed identical wills leaving their estate directly to their son and daughter (C1 and C2) equally. A died without revoking his will, but B made a fresh will altering the proportions that C1 and C2 were to obtain. A preliminary issue arose as to whether B should have had to receive a personal financial benefit for the mutual wills doctrine to operate. Morritt J held that 'such mutual benefit is a sufficient but not a necessary condition',[70] and B was compelled to perform her part of the agreement.

[68] *Re Dale* (n 8 above).

[69] And, to the same effect, if the agreement contemplates that A will make a testamentary disposition to C1, and B a testamentary disposition to C2: see *Olins v Walters* (n 3 above) [38].

[70] *Re Dale* (n 8 above) 43.

On close inspection, counsel framed the preliminary issue narrowly. It was assumed that B would incur no obligation at all if the mutual wills doctrine did not operate. Thus the only question was whether a personal financial benefit was required for B to be duty-bound.[71] In giving a negative answer, the judgment goes so far as to hold that B did in fact incur a duty. Notably, in the course of his judgment, Morritt J justified his conclusion by observing that 'certain cases of proprietary estoppel may be regarded as species of constructive trust, but in those cases the factor which gives rise to its imposition is not the receipt of property'.[72] Analytically, this is a crucial statement. It indicates that Morritt J recognised proprietary estoppel as the doctrine by which a constructive trust can be imposed where B's promise relates to property she owns absolutely. This exemplifies the AI analysis, and indicates that the case was treated differently from other typical mutual wills cases where B receives property from A.

It appears that Morritt J did not think it necessary to draw an explicit distinction between the QI and AI analyses because he thought that the overarching aim of the mutual wills doctrine was simply 'to prevent [A] from being defrauded'.[73] Such 'fraud' would occur if B were permitted to renege on the arrangement, because A had performed his part of the bargain 'on the faith of the promise of [B]'.[74] However, the idea of 'fraud' as a justification for the imposition of a constructive trust is confusing and imprecise.[75] In particular, it fails to explain why B should be bound to give effect to her promise when, in general, a promise does not necessarily give rise to a trust even if the promisee gives consideration or acts in reliance on the promise. It also fails fully to explain the significance of A's testamentary disposition. In contrast, the AI analysis explains the constructive trust which arises upon A's death as being a proportionate response to A's detrimental reliance on B's promise. In *Re Dale*, A left all his real and personal property—valued at £18,500—by will to C. There is no doubt that a proportionate response would have been to impose a constructive trust in order to give effect to A's expectation, thus explaining the decision in that case.

4. Explaining the Operation of the Analyses

The discussion thus far has identified two distinct analyses which make up the mutual wills doctrine. Where B does not receive property from A, B promises to give away property which she owns absolutely, and a court has the ability to

[71] ibid 33.

[72] ibid 47.

[73] ibid 49. Indeed, Morritt J (at 42) thought that the 'essence of the decision' in *Dufour v Pereira* (in Hargrave) (n 1 above) had to do with A's fraud. See further the text following n 162 below.

[74] *Re Dale* (n 8 above) 48–49.

[75] See discussion in YK Liew, 'Rochefoucauld v Boustead (1897)' in C Mitchell and P Mitchell (eds), *Landmark Cases in Equity* (Oxford, Hart Publishing, 2012).

award a remedy which is proportionate to the detriment A suffers in relying on B's promise. B will often, but will not necessarily, be bound to perform her promise though the imposition of a constructive trust. On the other hand, where B receives property from A, B promises to take a qualified interest in the trust fund yet to be acquired, and upon acquiring the fund a constructive trust is invariably imposed that binds B to carry out her promise. It was also seen that both analyses provide plausible explanations for B's obligations over property she acquires on her own account after A's death. This section explains how the QI and AI analyses operate within the mutual wills doctrine.

4.1. The Qualified Interest (QI) Analysis

4.1.1. An Orthodox Explanation

Unlike the 'floating trust' analysis which entails 'a floating obligation, suspended, so to speak, during the lifetime of the second testator [which] descend[s] upon the assets at [her] death and crystallize[s] into a trust',[76] the analysis of B as having acquired a fund implies that a constructive trust arises upon B's receipt of the fund, and that the rights and duties arising under the trust also arise at that point.[77] The existence of a fund means that there is a manager—a trustee—who holds the assets which constitute the fund.[78] Explained by way of orthodox principles, B immediately becomes a trustee under a constructive trust for the benefit of C upon acquiring the fund at A's death.

As for the content of B's obligations under the trust, this is determined by the parties' agreement. By promising to leave 'whatever is left' at B's death to C, B implicitly accepts that the traceable proceeds of any asset in the fund in her hands will be held upon the same trust. This is because the subject-matter in B's hands is treated as a fund, which entails that B has the power to sell and replace individual items in the fund.[79] Moreover, the parties also agree that (i) B will not have an absolute interest in the fund, (ii) B will have latitude to use the capital assets, and (iii) C will not have an absolute interest in the fund during B's lifetime. The first point is deduced from the fact that B has an obligation to make a testamentary disposition of the fund to C; the second is reflected by the fact that the parties are interested in determining the specific assets to be left to C only at the time of B's death; and the third follows from the fact that the parties' agreement is inconsistent with an intention to allow C to exercise her *Saunders v Vautier*[80]

[76] *Birmingham v Renfrew* (n 7 above) 689.

[77] *Olins v Walters* (n 3 above) [42]. As Lewison J observed in *Thomas and Agnes Carvel Foundation v Carvel* [2007] EWHC 1314 (Ch), [2008] Ch 395 at [27], the trust is brought into effect upon A's, and not B's, death.

[78] Lawson and Rudden (n 60 above) 171.

[79] ibid 171.

[80] *Saunders v Vautier* (1841) 4 Beav 115, 49 ER 282.

rights to collapse the trust for herself during B's lifetime.[81] The upshot is that, through interpretation[82] or by necessary implication[83] of the parties' agreement, they intend that B will obtain the life interest and C the remainder of the fund,[84] and that B should have a general, personal power by which she may appoint the capital assets in favour of anyone including herself.

4.1.2. Explaining 'Crystallisation'

This analysis accounts for the so-called 'crystallising' of C's rights, both when B makes dispositions calculated to defeat the agreement and when B dies, without attracting the conceptual difficulties inherent in the idea of a 'floating trust'. Writing in relation to rights under a trust fund, Roy Goode observes that[85]

> the beneficiaries … cannot bring an end to the management functions prescribed by the trust instrument, so as to have the fund distributed among themselves, except where so provided by the trust instrument or where all of them, being *sui juris* and collectively entitled to the fund, terminate the trust.

Because the 'trust instrument'—that is, the mutual wills agreement—provides that B will make a testamentary disposition to C, the prescribed event which brings the trust to an end is B's death, and this allows C to call for distribution of the trust assets. During B's lifetime, C may not unilaterally exercise her *Saunders v Vautier* rights to collapse the trust for herself because B has a life interest in the fund. Thus, in *Olins v Walters*,[86] where the dispute concerned C's interest during B's lifetime in what was formerly A's property, left to B pursuant to a mutual wills agreement, the Court of Appeal merely made a declaration[87] that the trust was immediately binding on B in relation to that property: there was no hint that C was able immediately to demand the transfer of the property.[88]

In relation to rights under a trust fund, James Penner has also written that 'when certain events occur—the most obvious example being a breach of trust—the beneficiary may elect to enforce a direct proprietary interest in individual items of the fund'.[89] This explains C's rights during B's lifetime. Because C is a beneficiary under the constructive trust, it is clear that B owes C and not any potential objects of the power a duty not to misuse her power.[90] One of the incidents of that duty

[81] *Gartside v Inland Revenue Commissioners* [1968] AC 553 (HL) 606.

[82] A technique used in *Barclays Bank Ltd v Quistclose Investments Ltd* [1970] AC 567 (HL) 580.

[83] See G Thomas, *Thomas on Powers*, 2nd edn (Oxford, Oxford University Press, 2012) [3.01] and [3.46].

[84] See Sheridan (n 53 above) 211; JE Penner, *The Law of Trusts*, 9th edn (Oxford, Oxford University Press, 2014) [7.52].

[85] Goode (n 43 above) 530.

[86] *Olins v Walters* (n 3 above).

[87] ibid [23].

[88] Admittedly, a declaration was the remedy C asked for: *Olins v Walters* (n 3 above) [16]. But if C had wanted to collapse the trust and claim the property before B's death, this would surely not have been allowed.

[89] Penner (n 41 above) [12.16].

[90] *Mettoy Pension Trustees Ltd v Evans* [1990] 1 WLR 1587 (Ch) 1613.

is that B must not exercise her power in such a way that would amount to a fraud on a power, as this would constitute a wrong against C.[91] The typical facts concerning the doctrine of a fraud on a power involve the donee of the power making what appears to be a prima facie legitimate appointment, but in fact doing so to allow the appointee to make use of the property in a way which runs counter to the terms on which the power was granted. However, judicial statements have not limited that doctrine to such facts, the focus instead being on B's motive or intention in exercising her power. Thus, in *Vatcher v Paull*,[92] Lord Parker famously observed that in this context 'fraud' 'merely means that the power has been exercised for a purpose, or with an intention, beyond the scope of or not justified by the instrument creating the power'. It is crucial that there is, 'at least, a deliberate defeating of what the donor of the power authorized and intended'[93]—an exercise of power with an 'ulterior object to be accomplished'.[94] An execution of a power for a corrupt purpose or a purpose foreign to the power is fraudulent and void.[95]

These statements explain why, in the mutual wills context, the courts have focused on B's motive or intention where she makes an *inter vivos* disposition out of the fund. For instance, in *Healey v Brown*,[96] the transfer of a flat by B to himself and his son as joint tenants was held to run 'directly and fully counter to the intention of the mutual will compact that the flat should pass to [C] on [B's] own death'.

It is important to stress that B's power is a 'bare' power conferred on B in her personal capacity, and not a 'fiduciary power' conferred on her by virtue of her status *qua* trustee.[97] This means that C cannot complain if B exercises the power for her own enjoyment. Thus, to the question some commentators have posed as to whether B may spend part of the trust fund on a world cruise, the analysis here entails an affirmative answer,[98] provided that B does so without any intention of defeating the mutual wills agreement. Indeed, it is immaterial that B might exhaust the entirety of the trust fund, provided that B's dispositions do not amount to a fraud on a power.[99] This ought not to be disconcerting, given that the exercise of any power of appointment necessarily diminishes the interest of the beneficiary of the gift over in default.[100] Nevertheless, it remains the case that B cannot make any appointment with the motive of defeating the mutual wills agreement, because the application of the fraud on a power doctrine does not depend on the donee of the power being a fiduciary.[101]

[91] ibid 1613.
[92] *Vatcher v Paull* [1915] AC 372 (PC) 378.
[93] *Re Dick, Knight v Dick* [1953] Ch 343 (CA) 360.
[94] *Duke of Portland v Topham* (1864) 11 HLC 32 at 55, 11 ER 1242 at 1251.
[95] *Cloutte v Storey* [1911] 1 Ch 18 (CA). See *Thomas on Powers* (n 83 above) [9.21]–[9.36].
[96] *Healey v Brown* (n 8 above) [14].
[97] *Thomas on Powers* (n 83 above) [1.50].
[98] As suggested by Davis (n 17 above) 425 and fn 25.
[99] *Barns v Barns* (n 17 above) [152].
[100] See eg *Re Ryder* [1914] 1 Ch 865 (Ch).
[101] See eg *Lane v Page* (1754) Amb 233, 27 ER 155; *Re Crawshay (deceased)* [1948] Ch 123 (CA); *Re Dick* (n 93 above).

4.1.3. Protecting B[102]

It might be thought to be unnecessary for B to have a life interest in the fund: B could hold the fund for C absolutely, subject to a general power in B's favour. However, the analysis set out above is to be preferred, as it provides adequate protection to B in at least two aspects. First, it remains possible for B and C collectively to collapse the trust by exercising their *Saunders v Vautier* rights.[103] In view of the fact that much could potentially change in B's and C's circumstances after A's death, this possibility is crucial. Suppose that C is comfortably well off, but B remarries and has another child (X). C may wish to allow B to reallocate her testamentary dispositions in order to make provision for X. The proposed analysis makes this possible. This does not mean, however, that C has an all-or-nothing choice, in that she must either choose to keep the trust intact *or* collapse the trust with B and C as joint tenants, no more and no less. Instead, C is free to secure an informal promise from B that B will dispose of the fund in a pre-determined form before agreeing to exercise their collective *Saunders v Vautier* rights in B's favour. For instance, C may make it a condition that B will make a testamentary disposition of the fund in favour of both C and X in equal shares. Because *this* promise by B is to the effect that B will qualify the interests she obtains in the fund after B's and C's *Saunders v Vautier* rights have been exercised in B's favour, a constructive trust would arise to compel B to hold the fund in favour of C and X.[104]

Secondly, the trust fund will very often include a family home, and the parties would normally intend for B to live in it during her lifetime. The Trusts of Land and Appointment of Trustees Act 1996, however, provides only for beneficiaries (as opposed to objects of a power) to have a right to occupy trust land, subject to certain conditions.[105] As a beneficiary under the trust, B's right to occupy the family home can easily be accounted for. As the 1996 Act provides, among the matters trustees are to consider when deciding upon which of two or more beneficiaries are entitled to occupy the land, they are to look to 'the intentions of the person or persons … who created the trust'.[106] In the mutual wills context, this compels B to give effect to A's and B's intentions when creating the mutual wills agreement.

4.1.4. Remedies

Mutual wills disputes characteristically come to light only after the death of both parties, and so it is largely a matter of speculation what remedies are available to C if B makes (or attempts to make) a disposition with an improper motive during her lifetime. In what is probably the only decided case where B was alive and

[102] I thank Ian Williams for the invaluable discussion which led to much of this subsection.

[103] *Stephenson v Barclays Bank* [1975] 1 WLR 88 (Ch).

[104] In a highly similar vein to the facts and decision in *De Bruyne v De Bruyne* [2010] EWCA Civ 519, [2010] 2 FLR 1240 and *Ottaway v Norman* (n 45 above).

[105] Trusts of Land and Appointment of Trustees Act 1996, ss 12, 13.

[106] Trusts of Land and Appointment of Trustees Act 1996, s 13(4)(a).

denying the mutual wills agreement,[107] C merely asked for and was granted a declaration that the arrangement amounted to an effective mutual wills agreement.[108] It remains unclear, therefore, whether remedies traditionally available to a beneficiary following an unauthorised disposition of trust property are available to C. It is submitted that C, as a beneficiary under the trust, is able to invoke the assistance of a court in order to ensure B's proper exercise of her powers,[109] for instance by requesting an injunction to prevent a purported disposition made with an improper motive. Of course, in practice C would rarely have the necessary foreknowledge to prevent such dispositions. Nevertheless, because a disposition amounting to a fraud on a power renders the transaction void, orthodox principles dictate that C may assert a proprietary claim against B or a third party recipient (D) pursuant to the evidentiary process of tracing and/or following, or may alternatively bring a personal claim for substitutive performance or reparation.

Consider first the possible claims against B. Where a trustee uses trust assets (money, for example) to purchase a new asset without authority, the beneficiary is normally able to trace into that new asset and either assert an equitable ownership over that asset or enforce an equitable charge or lien for the repayment of the value of the original trust asset dissipated.[110] In the mutual wills context, the analysis would depend on whether assets acquired by B after A's death are considered as part of the trust fund.[111] If they are, then all the property owned by B will constitute the trust fund. Therefore, there is no need to make a claim for equitable ownership against the new asset, since any traceable proceeds coming into B's hands immediately form part of that fund. Similarly, obtaining an equitable charge or lien would merely mean that the monetary value of the new asset is restored to the trust fund out of the trust fund itself, and the claim would be superfluous. If, however, B's after-acquired property is considered not to be part of the trust fund, then C might wish to enforce an equitable charge or lien against the traceable proceeds to compel B to repay the value of the original trust asset out of B's after-acquired property. The same analysis would apply in relation to a substitutive performance or reparation claim against B. If B's after-acquired property is analysed as part of the trust fund, then such claims are superfluous, since B would be restoring or compensating the trust fund with money from the trust fund; but if B's after-acquired property is deemed not to be part of the fund, then B may be compelled to restore the trust fund or compensate for losses out of B's after-acquired property.

Consider next the possible actions C could have against D, a volunteer recipient of dispositions made by B pursuant to a fraud on a power. In line with orthodox principles,[112] C would have no claim if D were a bona fide purchaser for value

[107] *Olins v Walters* (n 3 above) [4].
[108] ibid [16].
[109] Goode (n 43 above) 530.
[110] *Foskett v McKeown* [2001] 1 AC 102 (HL) 131.
[111] See discussion in Section 3.1.2 above.
[112] *Re Diplock* [1948] Ch 465 (CA).

without notice of B's fraud, but would be able to follow or trace, and then claim the trust property or its proceeds in D's hands if D were a volunteer. Alternatively, it may be that D is a purchaser for value but does not act in good faith. In such a case, whether D would be liable to a claim by C would depend on whether D had sufficient knowledge[113] of B's fraud on a power while the trust assets or traceable proceeds remained in her hands, and this would be determined according to the law concerning knowing receipt.[114] Finally, D would incur a personal liability if she dishonestly assisted in B's fraudulent exercise of his power.[115]

4.2. The Absolute Interest (AI) Analysis

4.2.1. An Orthodox Explanation

Since proprietary estoppel is the only orthodox doctrine by which B might be compelled to fulfil an informal promise to give away an interest in property which she owns absolutely, the enquiry is whether proprietary estoppel principles may explain mutual wills agreements reflecting the AI analysis.

It is first necessary to observe an interesting and important debate concerning whether proprietary estoppel remedies enforce a duty which B incurs from the moment A relies on B's promise, or whether they enforce a wrong-based duty which arises when B reneges on her promise which has been relied upon. The former analysis resembles an action for a debt due under a contract,[116] whereby the creditor can require the debtor to perform his primary payment obligation without asserting a breach of contract;[117] the latter analysis resembles an action for compensatory damages for a breach of contract,[118] where 'the remedy is calculated by reference to the claimant's loss', provided such loss is shown to have been factually caused by the defendant's breach.[119]

It appears that the latter analysis is the more compelling of the two. In the first place, there is little doubt that compensatory damages may be awarded in proprietary estoppel, and the availability of damages where B's breach causes a loss is a 'sure test'[120] or a 'powerful indicator'[121] that the remedy is wrong-based. Indeed, the notion of the 'minimum equity to do justice to the plaintiff' and the idea that the remedy should be proportionate reflects an approach of calculating the

[113] *Westdeutsche Landesbank Girozentrale v Islington LBC* (n 28 above) 707.

[114] See *Baden, Delvaux v Société Générale pour Favoriser le Développement du Commerce et de l'Industrie en France SA* [1993] 1 WLR 509 (Ch); *Bank of Credit & Commerce International (Overseas) Ltd v Akindele* [2001] Ch 437 (CA).

[115] See *Royal Brunei Airlines Sdn Bhd v Tan* [1995] 2 AC 378 (PC); *Barlow Clowes International Ltd (in liquidation) v Eurotrust International Ltd* [2005] UKPC 37, [2006] 1 WLR 1476.

[116] *White and Carter (Councils) Ltd v McGregor* [1962] AC 413 (HL).

[117] See C Mitchell, 'Stewardship of Property and Liability to Account' (2014) 78 *Conv* 215 at 223.

[118] *Photo Production Ltd v Securicor Transport Ltd* [1980] AC 827 (HL) 349.

[119] See Mitchell (n 117 above) 222–23.

[120] A Burrows, *The Law of Restitution*, 3rd edn (Oxford, Oxford University Press, 2010) 622.

[121] J Edelman, 'Equitable Torts' (2002) 10 *Torts Law Journal* 64, text between fns 56 and 57.

remedy by reference to A's loss. Moreover, it is difficult accurately to explain the law using the former analysis. Just as in the case of an action for a contractual debt, the former analysis would entail holding B to her promise (or, which amounts to the same thing, giving effect to A's expectations generated by B's assurance) in every successful proprietary estoppel case. However, this is clearly not what we find in the law, given that the cases—at least since 1999—have moved the law away from giving primacy to expectation relief.[122]

In support of the wrong-based analysis, Michael Spence defines the primary duty that B breaches as a 'duty to ensure the reliability of induced assumptions'.[123] This helpfully explains the cases which reflect the AI analysis. B's promise in a mutual wills agreement always induces A to assume that B will, at her death, leave property to C. When A relies on the mutual wills agreement, B incurs a primary duty to ensure that she acts reliably in order not to harm A. More specifically, A's reliance arises at some point while he is alive, because there will always be a point in time during A's lifetime at which it will be too late for A to change his will.[124] Thus, A obtains a substantive right[125] which corresponds to B's primary obligation during A's lifetime. At this point, however, A's act of reliance is just that—an act of reliance; it does not yet constitute a *detriment*,[126] since B will not yet have breached her duty by acting unreliably. If B ultimately fulfils her promise by leaving her estate as agreed, she would not have to account for any of her ordinary dealings with or dispositions of her property during her lifetime.

There are, however, two ways in which B may breach her duty to be reliable, which makes A's act of reliance a detriment. Most obviously, B may amend her testamentary disposition, for example, by executing[127] a new will which directs some or all of the property subject to her promise to a different recipient. Alternatively, B may deal directly with the property subject to the mutual wills agreement in a way which constitutes a breach, such as by making a disposition contrary to the agreement, or executing a charge over the property which undermines the reliability of her induced assumption.

Where a breach occurs, all the ingredients of a proprietary estoppel claim—promise or assurance, reliance, and detriment—are fulfilled. Although A has now died, the content and nature of B's promise indicate that A's substantive right is not one which is personal to A,[128] and therefore any potential proprietary

122 S Gardner, 'The Remedial Discretion in Proprietary Estoppel—Again' (2006) 122 *LQR* 492.

123 M Spence, *Protecting Reliance: The Emergent Doctrine of Equitable Estoppel* (Oxford, Hart Publishing, 1999) 2.

124 S Gardner, 'Reliance-Based Constructive Trusts' in C Mitchell (ed), *Constructive and Resulting Trusts* (Oxford, Hart Publishing, 2010) 66–67. On making out reliance for the purposes of proprietary estoppel, see also Section 3.6 of Ben McFarlane's contribution in Ch 4 of the present volume.

125 See B McFarlane, *The Law of Proprietary Estoppel* (Oxford, Oxford University Press, 2014) [8.165].

126 Or, as Spence (n 123 above) at 2 calls it, 'harm'.

127 It is sufficient for B to indicate that she will carry out a transaction in the future which is tantamount to a breach: *Bradbury v Taylor* [2012] EWCA Civ 1208, [2013] WTLR 29.

128 McFarlane (n 125 above) [8.162] ff.

estoppel claim against B does not disappear with A's death.[129] And because B's promise was to the effect that C would obtain the benefit of B's testamentary disposition, there is good reason to think that, when B commits a breach of his primary duty, C obtains an 'equity by estoppel' against B. This 'equity' requires liquidation by a court. Pursuant to this, a proprietary or personal remedy may be awarded. It is thus open to C to argue that it would be a proportionate response to A's detriment to enforce B's promise. If the court agrees, then the promised interest in B's property would be subject to a constructive trust in favour of C, giving effect to A's expectation. Since the 'equity' is 'capable of binding B's successors in title',[130] the proprietary effect of such an award is backdated 'by virtue of some doctrine of relation back'[131] to the time of B's breach. So, for example, if in breach of the mutual wills agreement B executes a new will in favour of D and then dies, D as a volunteer will similarly be bound by the constructive trust in favour of C. If, however, the court deems that a proportionate response to A's detriment would be to award compensatory damages, then these would be awarded for the benefit only of A's estate, since it was A who personally incurred detrimental reliance.

4.2.2. Potential Objections

The AI analysis of mutual wills cases where B does not receive property from A is not entirely free from difficulties. Four potential objections might be raised, which require close examination.

First, it may be objected that there is no proprietary estoppel case which allows one party (C) to succeed based on another's (A's) detrimental reliance. In the vast majority of cases, the claimant is A who *personally* incurs detrimental reliance. However, no judicial statement has conclusively ruled out the possibility that C might bring such a claim. In particular, there seems nothing to prevent C (as opposed to A where, for instance, A has died) from attempting to establish that A's detrimental reliance on B's *promise to grant C an interest* was so substantial that a proportionate remedy to A's loss would be an award of a proprietary remedy in

[129] The contractual parallel is that any contract (which does not contain 'an implied condition of the continued existence of the life of the contractor': *Taylor v Caldwell* (1863) 3 B & S 826 at 836, 122 ER 309 at 313) may be breached by one party after the death of the other, which gives the latter's executors or estate the right to pursue a claim for breach against the former. See, too, the observation in Gardner (n 124 above) 66. Moreover, the maxim *action personalis moritur cum persona* 'never extend[s] to personal actions founded on any obligation, debt, covenant, or other duty to be performed' (*Wheatley v Lane* (1668) 1 Wms Saund 216a, 85 ER 228), but is instead 'always understood of a tort' only (*Sollers v Lawrence* (1743) Willes 413 at 421, 125 ER 1243 at 1247).

[130] Section 116(a) of the Land Registration Act 2002 provides that an 'equity by estoppel … has effect from the time the equity arises as an interest capable of binding successors in title'. This section did not aim to create a new rule, but meant merely to confirm the existing state of the law: Law Commission, *Land Registration for the Twenty-First Century: A Conveyancing Revolution* (Law Com No 271, 2001) paras 5.30–5.31.

[131] K Gray and SF Gray, *Elements of Land Law*, 5th edn (Oxford, Oxford University Press, 2009) [9.2.89].

C's favour. In reply, one might cite *Lloyd v Dugdale*[132] as authority for the requirement that a claimant must have suffered personal detriment. One question which arose for consideration in that case was whether A had a proprietary estoppel claim where B's representation to A that A would personally acquire[133] B's property was detrimentally relied on, not by A, but by C.[134] The Court of Appeal held that 'it remained necessary for [A] to show some detriment incurred by him personally as a result of [B]'s representations'.[135] However, *Lloyd v Dugdale* is different because B did not promise to benefit C but *A*; and so the case indicates only that the *promisee*, A, must personally incur detrimental reliance. It says nothing about the possibility that *C* may rely on proprietary estoppel where B promises A to give *C* an interest in B's property, and where A, as promisee, has personally suffered detrimental reliance. Therefore, neither case law nor principle rules out this possibility where C is the object of B's promise or assurance. As Kevin Gray and Susan Francis Gray point out,[136] much can be said for allowing the benefit of an equity by estoppel to pass to a third party, and this possibility must be taken seriously.[137]

The second potential objection is that proprietary estoppel arises only where B's promise or assurance relates to an interest in land.[138] Although most decided cases have concerned land, it would be arbitrary if the success of a proprietary estoppel claim rose and fell with the subject-matter of B's promise. In fact, the decision in *Re Basham*[139] suggests that the claim is not so confined.[140] In that case, A made a successful proprietary estoppel claim where B promised to leave his residuary estate to A. Crucially, B's residuary estate included not only real property (a cottage),[141] but also cash, furniture and other chattels.[142] The applicability of proprietary estoppel to personalty was not held to be objectionable by the judge

[132] *Lloyd v Dugdale* [2001] EWCA Civ 1754, [2002] 2 P & CR 13 at [35]. See McFarlane (n 125 above) [4.107]–[4.112].

[133] *Lloyd v Dugdale*, [29]–[30].

[134] Although C was a company owned by A, it was held that C was a separate and distinct legal entity from A: ibid [48] and [58].

[135] ibid [35].

[136] Gray and Gray (n 131 above) [9.2.90].

[137] Alternatively, of course, one could say that C's right to enforce B's promise based on A's detrimental reliance gives rise to a *sui generis* claim that is akin, but not identical to proprietary estoppel. However, this seems unnecessary, given that the variable factors affecting such a case—B's assurance or promise, A's detrimental reliance and A's expectation—are identical to those affecting proprietary estoppel claims.

[138] See eg *Thorner v Major* [2009] UKHL 18, [2009] 1 WLR 776 at [61]. *cf* also the discussion of the question in Section 3.2 of Ben McFarlane's contribution in Ch 4 of the present volume.

[139] *Re Basham (deceased)* [1986] 1 WLR 1498 (Ch).

[140] See also S Wilken and K Ghaly, *Wilken and Ghaly: The Law of Waiver, Variation, and Estoppel*, 3rd edn (Oxford, Oxford University Press, 2012) [11.127] and cases cited therein; McFarlane (n 125 above) [10.61]. *cf* C Davis, 'Estoppel: An Adequate Substitute for Part Performance?' (1993) 13 *OJLS* 99 at 103–4, who suggests that proprietary estoppel can extend to property other than land, but not where the subject-matter is purely money.

[141] In fact, the cottage made up less than half the total value of the residuary estate which was granted to A by way of a trust pursuant to her proprietary estoppel claim.

[142] *Basham* (n 139 above) 1500. Similarly, see eg *Jennings v Rice* (n 35 above) [2] (land and furniture); *Thorner v Major* (n 138 above) [7], [13] and [48] (land, live and dead stock, chattels, and money).

in that case; and later cases[143] which have considered *Re Basham* have not taken issue with this aspect of the case. There have also been judicial suggestions that proprietary estoppel can apply to beneficial interests under a trust,[144] copyright interests,[145] and patents.[146] It is clear, therefore, that a proprietary estoppel claim may extend to personalty. This is particularly relevant in the mutual wills context, since it allows cases where B does not receive property from A to be considered by way of the AI analysis, even though B's promise may not relate exclusively to land.

A third potential objection is that B's promise may relate to after-acquired property, that is, property B acquires after reaching the agreement with A. This does not appear to be an issue, however, since if A has completed her acts of reliance (at A's death in the mutual wills context), a proprietary estoppel claim may be made against B as soon as B acquires the asset in question.[147] A related objection may be that proprietary estoppel requires A's expectation to relate to specific items of property;[148] and it is difficult to determine, at the time the agreement is made, what specific items of property B may acquire after A's death. However, in *Re Basham*,[149] where B promised to leave to A all of B's property in his will, A succeeded in a proprietary estoppel claim against B even though B's assets remained unspecified until B's death. Similarly, in *Thorner v Major*,[150] a proprietary estoppel claim was successful where the parties 'knew that the extent of the farm was liable to fluctuate'. It is therefore possible to say that, in principle, non-specification of items in a testamentary context is no bar to a proprietary estoppel claim.

Finally, it may be objected that the constructive trust which arises to bind B in the mutual wills context appears not to be awarded through an exercise of remedial discretion, but is awarded invariably, much like the QI cases. In reply, it can be said that the dearth of authorities dealing with cases where B does not receive any property from A provides no support for the proposition that no remedial discretion is exercised. But the AI analysis would remain plausible even if there were a high number of cases in which a constructive trust was awarded. Because in mutual wills cases A's reliance usually consists of the making of a testamentary disposition, it is difficult to conceive of a situation whereby a court might deem it disproportionate to bind B to his promise, since A's committing to a particular form of testamentary disposition is quite obviously a substantial detrimental reliance, thus justifying a constructive trust award. However, it is less obviously the

[143] See eg *Jiggins v Brisley* [2003] EWHC 841 (Ch), [2003] WTLR 1141 [80]; *Shovelar* (n 8 above) [38]; *Thorner* (n 138 above) [20] and [63]. The decision in *MacDonald v Frost* [2009] EWHC 2276 (Ch), [2009] WTLR 1815 [13]–[16], which doubted *Basham*, says nothing about the applicability of the claim to personalty.

[144] *Strover v Strover* [2005] EWHC 860 (Ch), [2005] WTLR 1245.

[145] *Fisher v Brooker* [2009] UKHL 41, [2009] 1 WLR 1764.

[146] *Yeda Research and Development Co Ltd v Rhone-Poulenc Rorer International Holdings Inc* [2007] UKHL 43, [2008] 1 All ER 425 at [22].

[147] *Watson v Goldsbrough* [1986] 1 EGLR 265 (CA). See *Wilken and Ghaly* (n 140 above) [11.130].

[148] *Layton v Martin* [1986] 2 FLR 227 (Ch) 238.

[149] *Re Basham* (n 139 above). See discussion in *Wilken and Ghaly* (n 140 above) [11.131]–[11.132].

[150] *Thorner v Major* (n 138 above) [62].

case where A's reliance consists of *inter vivos* actions, for example, where A sells property or makes a gift in reliance on B's promise to leave B's estate to C upon B's death. Remedial discretion in such a case is crucial, since a court would then be able to determine the appropriate level of remedy according to the degree of detriment A suffered. So, it would hardly be objectionable to deny C the benefit of a constructive trust where, for instance, A relied on B's promise by making an *inter vivos* donation of £100 to charity.

5. Two Distinct Rationales

The award of a constructive trust in all mutual wills cases creates a deceptive impression that the cases are united by a single principle. The reality is that different types of agreement give rise to different types of claim. In cases where B does not receive property from A, remedial discretion is exercised by way of the AI analysis where a breach of a primary obligation is shown to have caused compensable loss; in cases where B receives property from A, B is invariably bound to her promise through a constructive trust pursuant to the QI analysis. The paucity of cases reflecting the AI analysis means that courts have not found occasion to clarify what goes on in such cases and how they differ from the more common cases reflecting the QI analysis. Nevertheless, distinguishing the two classes of case enables us to understand them more clearly.

It also follows from the distinction between the QI and AI analyses that two distinct rationales underlie the mutual wills cases. The QI analysis concerns preventing the taking of an advantage; the AI analysis concerns compensating for harm caused.

5.1. The QI Analysis: An Advantage-Based Aim

In cases reflecting the QI analysis, the enforcement of B's promise can be understood as an application of the norm against taking an advantage for oneself of that which has been conferred by another, and which both parties have intended should not be taken. This is a specific application of a more general norm which dictates that one should not take for oneself an advantage that is not meant for one's absolute enjoyment. From this general norm, four cumulative elements can be deduced that lead to the conclusion that B ought *never* to take the advantage that she obtains from A for her own unqualified use, provided that all four elements are satisfied.[151] First, A must confer on B an advantage. This is because

[151] Most of these points are discussed in the context of the doctrine in *Rochefoucauld v Boustead* (n 4 above) in YK Liew, 'The Wider Ambit of the *Quistclose* Doctrine' (2015) 9 *Journal of Equity* 1 at 10–11.

the case for preventing B from taking an advantage for herself is strongest when that advantage is conferred by A rather than being obtained by B of her own accord. Secondly, both parties must agree that B should not take the advantage for herself, instead of this being A's purely unilateral intention. This is because the norm is more obviously applicable where B *herself* has promised to qualify her own use of the property. Thirdly, B's promise must have induced A to act. This ensures that B's promise is indeed the basis of A's actions. Finally, B's promise must be to the effect that she will qualify her interest in the advantage which she obtains from A. This ensures that B is never intended to take the unqualified use of that advantage. The last-mentioned point is found only in constructive trust doctrines reflecting the QI analysis: B is not meant to make use of the advantage for her unqualified use because B promises to qualify her interest *in the property she acquires with A's participation*. In the mutual wills context, B acquires the fund with A's participation, the fund being made up of assets originating from both A and B. Thus, it is indubitably clear that B ought never to take the absolute benefit of the property for herself.

Notably, the relevant norm is triggered by B's promise and A's reliance upon A's death, and not by B's receipt of A's property. The importance of A's reliance is reflected in the fact that if A makes a testamentary disposition to B, then B is bound to carry out her promise even if she elects to disclaim the benefits left to her by A.[152] On the other hand, the importance of B's promise in inducing A to act is reflected in the fact that the promise need not be a but-for cause of A's reliance. Although this point has never been explicitly considered in the mutual wills context,[153] it can be deduced from other constructive trust doctrines which reflect the QI analysis.[154] All that is required is for B's promise to 'form part of the basis on which [B] receives the property'.[155]

A question might arise as to why B is always compelled to perform her promise instead of equity merely reversing the transaction. One might reason that returning the property to A's estate would cause a *dis*advantage to A since A will already have died and so will no longer be able to exercise his testamentary freedom to give the property to the person he wished to be the ultimate recipient.[156] However, a more compelling explanation lies in the courts' consistent emphasis on the parties' agreement as the source of their legal obligations. This provides good reason to suppose that the parties' respective rights and liabilities are determined by their agreement and not by the fact of whether A is alive or dead. Indeed, the importance of B's promise in the parties' agreement is reflected in the 'qualified interest' label: the parties intend that B should not take the fund for her own unqualified

[152] *Re Hagger* (n 30 above) 195, which can be read as overruling the contradictory dicta in *Lord Walpole v Lord Orford* (1797) 3 Ves Jun 402 at 417–18, 30 ER 1076 at 1084.

[153] *cf* the passing remark in *Dufour v Pereira* (in Hargrave) (n 1 above) 308.

[154] B McFarlane, 'Constructive Trusts Arising on a Receipt of Property *Sub Conditione*' (2004) 120 *LQR* 667 at 686–87; Liew (n 151 above) 10.

[155] McFarlane (n 154 above) 687.

[156] JD Feltham, 'Informal Trusts and Third Parties' (1987) 51 *Conv* 246 at 248.

enjoyment *precisely* because B promises to qualify her interest in the fund; and when A confers the relevant advantage on B, which leads B to acquire the fund in question, B is bound to fulfil her promise in order that she does not have the unqualified use of the fund.

5.2. The AI Analysis: A Loss-Based Aim

In cases reflecting the AI analysis, B incurs a primary obligation when A acts in reliance on an assumption induced by B. Because the inducement of A's assumptions is an intentional act of will by B through the making of a promise, it is hardly objectionable to say that, once the inducement is relied upon, B has a primary duty to *ensure* that A is not harmed. No harm will befall A if B does act reliably by carrying out her promise; otherwise, equity may step in to compensate A through a remedy which achieves proportionality between A's detriment and B's promise. In Spence's words:[157]

> The primary obligation is that the inducing party must, in so far as he is reasonably able, prevent harm to the relying party. 'Harm' consists in the extent to which the relying party is worse off because the assumption has proved unjustified than he would have been had it never been induced. The secondary obligation is that, if the relying party does suffer harm of the relevant type, and the inducing party might reasonably have prevented it, then the inducing party must compensate the relying party for the harm he has suffered.

In the AI analysis, the focus is on the detriment A suffers in reliance on B's promise because B's promise relates to her own property. Such cases reflect the norm that 'the law ought to correct reliance losses'.[158] Unlike cases relating to the QI analysis, where B ought *never* to make unqualified use of the property she acquires, here it is less obvious that B should be compelled to part with the promised interest whenever A suffers a reliance loss. This is particularly so given that there can be various degrees of detriment that A may suffer and different kinds of expectation that he may form. By 'seek[ing] to react to multiple considerations',[159] therefore, it is unsurprising that the AI analysis allows for the exercise of remedial discretion in order to compensate A's reliance loss by way of a remedy proportionate to A's detriment.[160] In the mutual wills context, a constructive trust will almost always be the appropriate award which reflects the 'minimum equity to do justice to [A]', given that A's detrimental reliance is often undoubtedly substantial. This should not, however, obscure the fact that the constructive trust award is compensatory in nature.

157 Spence (n 123 above) 2.

158 Gardner (n 124 above) 79. See also *Wilken and Ghaly* (n 140 above) [11.94]: 'The prime aim of the discretion [in proprietary estoppel] should be to prevent detriment'.

159 Gardner (n 122 above) 507.

160 S Bright and B McFarlane, 'Proprietary Estoppel and Property Rights' (2005) 64 *CLJ* 449 at 453–54; *Wilken and Ghaly* (n 140 above) [11.94].

5.3. Subsuming the QI Analysis within the AI Analysis?

The logic of the QI/AI dichotomy means that it is possible to treat cases which reflect the QI analysis by way of the AI analysis. If B purports to qualify her interest in property yet to be acquired, it is logically possible to treat B as the absolute owner of that property when it is acquired, thus engaging the AI analysis. The reverse, however, is not possible: if B's promise relates to property she already owns absolutely, B's promise cannot be treated as purporting to qualify an interest in property acquired with A's participation.

It follows that it might be asked whether *all* mutual wills cases should be analysed by way of the AI analysis. On this approach, even in cases where B receives property from A, the fund B obtains would be treated as being acquired of B's own accord, and A's act of transferring property to B would be considered an act of reliance which, if B does not perform her promise, will constitute a detriment for which B must compensate. In favour of this approach, it might be suggested that it is presently[161]

> normatively questionable ... that the parties are able *conclusively* to decide for themselves what property is subject to a mutual wills arrangement without judicial intervention, while the property forming the subject of an estoppel representation might ultimately be considered a disproportionate remedy when a claim is litigated.

It is submitted that this analysis should be resisted. In the first place, it cannot explain and justify the crucial role which the parties' agreement plays. If A transfers property to B pursuant to an agreement which leads B to acquire a trust fund to be held for C's benefit, enforcing the agreement entails holding B to her promise, no more and no less. An AI analysis would add an unnecessary, superficial layer of reasoning: that B will be held to her promise *provided that this proportionately compensates for A's detrimental reliance.* While this approach is not technically unsound, it would attribute too little importance to the parties' agreement. Such an approach is, however, necessary where A does not transfer property to B, as in such cases the compensatory aim of the AI analysis provides a justification for holding B to her promise in relation to property she owns absolutely, where a constructive trust award is deemed to be the appropriate response.

It can also be observed that the mutual wills doctrine, like many other constructive trust doctrines,[162] is concerned with identifying the true nature of the parties' dealings. This can be seen from the fact that 'fraud', which is often used to justify the imposition of a constructive trust in the mutual wills context,[163] is in fact merely a *description* of the state of affairs which the constructive trust prevents.[164] The true nature of B's promise in the case where A transfers property

[161] Hudson and Sloan (n 54 above) 170.

[162] See eg discussion in Liew (n 75 above) 447 in relation to the doctrine in *Rochefoucauld v Boustead* (n 4 above).

[163] See eg *Dufour v Pereira* (in Hargrave) (n 1 above) 310; *Re Dale* (n 8 above) 42; *Olins v Walters* (n 3 above) [38].

[164] Liew (n 75 above) 448.

to B is precisely to qualify the interest in the trust fund that B obtains, according to the parties' agreement. If B's promise is then treated as relating to property she owns absolutely, this introduces an element of fiction into what has hitherto been recognised as an agreement-based doctrine. This is not to deny that there could be advantages in treating all mutual wills case by way of the AI analysis;[165] however, to do so would be tantamount to overhauling most of what presently constitutes the mutual wills doctrine, which seems uncalled for.

6. Mutual Wills and Other Constructive Trusts Doctrines

Apart from the mutual wills doctrine, there are also other constructive trust doctrines which reflect either the QI or the AI analysis.[166] It is therefore important to appreciate how the mutual wills doctrine relates to these other doctrines. Two particular issues will be evaluated: whether the doctrine of secret trusts provides a fall-back for an unsuccessful mutual wills claim; and, in the light of the doubts which have recently been expressed about the usefulness of the mutual wills doctrine, whether it is desirable to abolish the doctrine in view of its relationship with other closely related constructive trust doctrines.

6.1. Secret Trusts as a Fall-Back?

On a number of occasions it has been suggested that the secret trusts doctrine may provide a fall-back where a mutual wills claim is unsuccessful. Thus, in *Healey v Brown*,[167] David Donaldson QC said that, in cases where a mutual wills claim fails, an award may nevertheless be justified 'by reference to the separate case-law on so-called secret trusts'. This suggestion relates only to cases reflecting the QI analysis, since A must transfer property to B for it to be possible to say that B is a secret trustee of A's property. The question arises whether in such cases the secret trusts doctrine can be relied upon to compel B to hold (only) A's property on trust for C if the attempted mutual wills agreement does not evince the necessary intention to create legally binding and irrevocable obligations with respect to the fund.[168]

The QI analysis suggests a negative answer to that question. Consider the fact that the parties' intentions are solely determined with reference to their agreement. Apart from that agreement, there are no enforceable intentions, since the mutual wills agreement indicates that the parties' intentions are interdependent. That is to say, they do not have individual, independent intentions which merely happen

[165] Hudson and Sloan (n 54 above) 171.
[166] See Section 3 above, text accompanying nn 31 to 40.
[167] *Healey v Brown* (n 8 above) [28].
[168] See n 8 and the accompanying text above.

to coincide at a point in time. Because B's intention is formed with the knowledge that *both* parties' estates will be affected, the agreement is wholly irrelevant to a consideration of what she *might* have promised if only A's estate comprised the subject-matter of the agreement. Similarly, the transfer of A's property to B is done in reliance on B's promise, and so it is impossible to conclude that A would have dealt with his property in the same way if the intended agreement could not be given legal effect. Therefore, an intention in relation to *A's property alone* cannot be derived from the parties' agreement, which is reached in relation to what B will do with 'whatever is left' at her death.

This conclusion is fortified by the fact that B's promise relates to a fund and not to specific property. B's promise to qualify her interest in a fund is different from, and unrelated to, a promise to qualify her interest in specific assets which constitute the fund. Because in the mutual wills doctrine there is no requirement of segregation or separate accounting in relation to what was formerly A's property, it seems wrong even to speak of B's obligations as relating to 'A's property'; at most, it is an historical observation that A contributed to the fund. Thus, it cannot be suggested that B's acquisition of 'A's property' is qualified by a promise to hold it on trust for C. This would not only fail to take into account the true nature of B's promise, but would also fail to reflect the fact that B's obligation in the mutual wills doctrine differs from the obligation that arises in the secret trusts context.

All these considerations point to the fact that the distinction between mutual wills and secret trusts lies in the different *types* of agreement they enforce, and not in the different *degrees* of their reach—whether they cover 'A's property' only or 'A's and B's property'. The parties are, of course, free to choose one type of agreement or another; but a different type of agreement cannot be inferred from the agreement which they actually attempted to make.[169]

6.2. Abolishing the Mutual Wills Doctrine?

In recent times, many commentators have concluded that mutual wills agreements are not 'sensible',[170] and thus should be 'avoided'[171] or even 'abolished'.[172] In view

[169] Although certain obiter statements in *Re Goodchild* (n 7 above), namely at 1224 and 1229–30, might seem to suggest that a secret trusts agreement can indeed be derived from a failed mutual wills agreement, the ultimate result in that case is consistent with the point made in the text. The finding that there was lacking a sufficiently firm agreement between the parties to engage the mutual wills doctrine led to the result that B (and hence his 'heir' as his successor in title) was not bound by *any* constructive trust. This can be explained on the basis that the Court of Appeal was looking for a particular *type* of agreement; its absence meant that only one conclusion was appropriate—that B was free to dispose all of the property she owned.

[170] R Kerridge (assisted by AHR Brierley), *Parry and Kerridge: The Law of Succession*, 12th edn (London, Sweet & Maxwell, 2009) [6-41].

[171] R Hughes, 'Mutual Wills' [2011] *Private Client Business* 131 at 136. See too Braun (n 52 above) 221, fn 65.

[172] N Richardson, 'Legislation for Mutual Wills in New Zealand' (2010) 24 *Trust Law International* 99 at 109.

of the Law Commission's impending review of the mutual wills doctrine, it is not implausible that a recommendation might be made to abolish the mutual wills doctrine completely.

It is submitted, however, that such a move would be undesirable. It is impossible to make a principled distinction between the mutual wills doctrine and other related constructive trust doctrines. This point is best made by observing that many situations which fall within the mutual wills doctrine can also be analysed in terms of other QI or AI constructive trust doctrines, and therefore it would be a messy—and certainly arbitrary—task to refuse to give legal effect only to mutual wills agreements.

Consider first the following three cases which fall to be analysed by way of the QI analysis. In the first case, A and B come to an informal *inter vivos* agreement that A will transfer land to B, with B promising to leave 'whatever is left' at her death to C. In the second case, the *inter vivos* agreement is that A will transfer land to B, with B promising to hold all the property at A's time of death for herself for life and for C in remainder, with B having a general power of appointment during her lifetime. In the third case, A (a testator) comes to an informal agreement with B that, if A leaves a specific property to B absolutely in A's will, B will leave 'whatever is left' of that property at B's death to C. The first two cases can be analysed as falling within the ambit of the rule in *Rochefoucauld v Boustead*,[173] and the third as falling within the ambit of the doctrine of secret trusts.[174] At the same time, they arguably also fall within the ambit of the mutual wills doctrine. In relation to the first two cases, it has been recognised that the mutual wills doctrine is applicable if the agreement entails an *inter vivos* transfer of property from A to B, with B promising to make a particular testamentary disposition.[175] Moreover, all three cases reflect one of the two distinctive features of mutual wills agreements,[176] viz a promise by B to make a testamentary disposition in a particular form, as opposed to holding property on trust immediately upon receiving A's property. So even if the mutual wills doctrine were abolished, relief in these cases could still be obtained by application of the other QI constructive trust doctrines. Indeed, because QI constructive trust doctrines aim to prevent an advantage from being taken by B in specific situations, a principled distinction cannot be drawn between an advantage conferred by A in an *inter vivos* context and an advantage conferred by A in a testamentary context, nor between cases where B's promise relates only to A's property and those where it relates to a fund consisting of A's and B's property. Like cases should be treated alike.

Consider next cases falling within the AI analysis. A striking similarity exists between mutual wills cases where B does not receive property from A, and many

[173] *De Bruyne v Dr Bruyne* (n 104 above) indicates that the doctrine can apply to three-party cases.
[174] Specifically, *Ottaway n Norman* (n 45 above).
[175] *Lewis v Cotton* (n 24 above) [45]–[46].
[176] Noted in the text following n 12 above.

proprietary estoppel cases:[177] they all involve B promising to make a particular form of testamentary disposition of property she owns absolutely. Abolishing the mutual wills doctrine would therefore not prevent the law from providing compensation for detrimental reliance incurred by A as a result of such a promise by B. It would also be impossible to draw a principled distinction in terms of the nature of A's reliance. Why should the law refuse to provide compensation if A's reliance takes the form of a testamentary or *inter vivos*[178] disposition to C, as opposed to the more common proprietary estoppel cases where A provides services to B? If anything, there would be a stronger argument for compensating A in the former case, since A would no longer be alive to undo what has been done.[179]

The upshot is that the mutual wills doctrine cannot cleanly be hived off from other doctrines such as the rule in *Rochefoucauld v Boustead*, the doctrine of secret trusts, and the doctrine of proprietary estoppel, in order to justify abolishing the mutual wills doctrine. Instead, it is submitted that it would be better for the Law Commission to clarify that the doctrine reflects an amalgamation of the QI and AI analyses, as set out in this chapter. Recognising this renewed understanding not only allays the concerns which judges and commentators have expressed about the doctrine, but also indicates how the doctrine works alongside and consistently with other equitable doctrines in order to provide compensation for reliance losses or to prevent an undue advantage from being taken. So long as it continues to be possible to make wills without legal advice, there will be a variety of arrangements testators might attempt to enter, and these will need to be addressed in a way that is consistent with the courts' approach to the situations that fall within the ambit of the other, related doctrines.

7. Conclusion

On a proper understanding, the broad label of 'mutual wills' encompasses two distinct analyses which apply to different facts. On the one hand, where the mutual wills agreement entails A transferring property to B, B's promise to make a testamentary disposition to C qualifies the interest in the trust fund which consists of both A's and B's assets. A constructive trust always binds B to fulfil her promise; but B also obtains a power to make use of the assets which constitute the trust fund during her lifetime, which may not be used with the intention of defeating the agreement. On the other hand, where the agreement does not entail B receiving

[177] See eg *Wayling v Jones* (1993) 69 P & CR 170 (CA); *Gillett v Holt* [2001] Ch 210 (CA); *Jennings v Rice* (n 35 above).

[178] *Lewis v Cotton* (n 24 above) [45]–[46].

[179] On this point, *cf Thorner v Major* (n 138 above) [63], where Lord Walker suggested that it is inappropriate to rely on mutual wills authorities in relation to proprietary estoppel because mutual wills 'are arguably a special case'. This chapter suggests the contrary insofar as mutual wills cases reflecting the AI analysis are concerned.

A's property, B's promise to make a testamentary disposition to C relates to property that B owns absolutely. Where a constructive trust is awarded, it compensates A for the detriment he suffers in reliance on B's promise. B is able to make use of any assets which constitute the trust fund, provided that she does not breach her duty to ensure that she acts reliably in order not to harm A.

That the 'mutual wills' doctrine reflects an amalgamation of two analyses is not surprising at all. Because both QI and AI cases commonly involve a mutuality of wills, they obviously fall within the 'mutual wills' label.[180] Moreover, the constructive trust response is usually the appropriate remedy even by way of the AI analysis. Indeed, the courts have not found it necessary to distinguish the two cases because they can both loosely be described as preventing A from being 'defrauded'. Nevertheless, analytical clarity requires a distinction to be drawn between the QI and AI analyses. Accepting this distinction not only allays the common concerns that judges and commentators have about the mutual wills doctrine, but also encourages a proper appreciation of its relationship with other constructive trust doctrines.

[180] See eg the loose definition of 'the doctrine of mutual wills' in *Re Dale* (n 8 above) 37.

6

What's in a Will?—Examining the Modern Approach Towards the Interpretation and Rectification of Testamentary Instruments

BIRKE HÄCKER*

1. Introduction

On 17 January 1768, Horace Walpole, Fourth Earl of Orford, wrote a letter to Sir Horace Mann, a British diplomat in Florence with whom he regularly corresponded. In the context of reporting that the recently deceased Royal Navy Officer Sir William Rowley had all but disinherited his son and grandson, Walpole remarks:[1]

> It is rather leaving an opportunity to the Chancery, to do a right thing, and set such an absurd will aside. Do not doubt it. *The law makes no bones of wills. I have heard of a man who began his will thus: 'This is my will, and I desire the Chancery will not make another for me.' Oh! but it did.* (emphasis added)

The problem, of course, is that very often we simply do not know what a testator in his innermost mind really wanted, and we have to establish his intentions as best we can from the 'last will and testament' he has left behind. This formal instrument—it has aptly been observed—'carries the burden of communicating [to us his] last wishes'.[2] Our making sense of them occurs within the confines of what we might call a 'magic triangle' of testate succession law. This consists of,

* An earlier version of this chapter was presented to the Annual Conference of the Chancery Bar Association in London on 17 January 2015. The author would like to thank all those who commented on the paper as it evolved, especially Dr Ian Williams and the other participants of the 'Current Issues in Succession Law' conference as well as Professor Robert Stevens. All errors are my own.

[1] *Letters of Horace Walpole, Earl of Orford, to Sir Horace Mann, His Britannic Majesty's Resident at the Court of Florence, from 1760 to 1785, now first published from the original mss.*, concluding series, vol 1 (London, Richard Bentley, 1843) 376 (letter CXVI).

[2] E Drummond, 'Whose Will is it Anyway?' [2014] *Conv* 357 at 357.

firstly, the statutory formality requirements, secondly, the principles of interpretation, and thirdly, the rules on the rectification of wills.

The recent landmark case of *Marley v Rawlings*[3] was by comparison rather unusual, in that everybody involved knew *exactly* what the testator wanted, both in terms of the wording of his will and in terms of the substantive dispositions he wished to enshrine in it. The testator, Mr Rawlings, wanted everything to go to his wife, or if she predeceased him[4] (which in fact she did) to the man whom the couple treated as their son, Mr Marley. The obstacle that looked for a while as though it might frustrate the testator's wishes and lead to an intestacy[5] was that the solicitor who had prepared Mr and Mrs Rawlings' mirror wills got them mixed up, so that each spouse mistakenly executed the draft document intended for the other.

In allowing the intended beneficiary's appeal against the rejection of his rectification claim at first instance and in the Court of Appeal,[6] the Supreme Court ruled that the term 'clerical error' in section 20(1)(a) of the Administration of Justice Act 1982[7] should be given a wide meaning, effectively encompassing any 'mistake arising out of office work of a relatively routine nature'.[8]

That specific point of statutory construction, which lay at the heart of *Marley v Rawlings*, must now be regarded as settled, at least under the current regime.[9] But there is a great deal more to the decision. Lord Neuberger PSC, with whom the entire panel of Justices of the Supreme Court agreed, took the opportunity to address a number of other issues pertaining to the 'magic triangle' of testate succession law. His judgment sets out the modern approach towards the interpretation and rectification of testamentary instruments, and it does so against the backdrop of the formality requirements imposed by section 9 of the Wills Act 1837.[10] There is so much in it about each of these basic tenets and about their relationship with one another that *Marley v Rawlings* has been described as a veritable 'treasure chest for the probate practitioner'.[11] And because probate cases so rarely reach the

[3] *Marley v Rawlings* [2014] UKSC 2, [2015] 1 AC 129, [2014] 2 WLR 213.

[4] Or survived him for less than a calendar month, a stipulation probably inserted to avoid the estate effectively passing twice in close temporal proximity, with the concomitant (potential) inheritance tax implications.

[5] From which the couple's disinherited biological sons—the respondents—would have profited.

[6] *Marley v Rawlings* [2011] EWHC 161 (Ch), [2011] 1 WLR 2146; aff'd [2012] EWCA Civ 161, [2013] Ch 271.

[7] The provision is set out in the text following n 63 below.

[8] *Marley v Rawlings* (SC) (n 3 above) [75]. Critical: A Learmonth, '*Marley v Rawlings* in the Supreme Court' (2014) 20 *Trusts & Trustees* 725 at 730: '"Clerical error" is not just a phrase that popped into the Parliamentary draftsman's head. It is a phrase with an ancient legal pedigree. It dates from the time before photocopiers, when clerks wrote out and copied legal documents in copperplate script. It had always been used to mean a slip of the pen, and by extension, of the word processor: an inadvertent drafting error, and never anything else'.

[9] The Law Commission is planning to review the relevant legislation: see the text accompanying n 13 below.

[10] That provision is set out in the text accompanying n 58 below.

[11] See the case note by L Harris, '*Marley v Rawlings*: A Treasure Chest for the Probate Practitioner' [2014] *Private Client Business* 280.

highest judicial level,[12] we may expect this treasure chest to be exploited for quite some time to come.

A further aspect making the 'magic triangle' particularly topical is that the Law Commission in the summer of 2014 announced that its Twelfth Programme of Law Reform would include a project on wills. Two of the four key areas identified by the Law Commission as being most in need of review and potential reform are formality requirements and the rules on rectification.[13] The project was originally scheduled to commence early in 2015 and to take approximately three years, but has now been postponed, with a revised timetable expected to be published soon.[14]

Against this background, it is the purpose of the present chapter to explore five questions emerging from *Marley v Rawlings*. They are thrown up, but not fully resolved by the decision. On some of these, it will be necessary to take issue with the answers given or implied by the Supreme Court. The five questions, addressed in the following sections in this order, are:

- How are wills to be construed?
- Is rectification dispensable in the light of the modern canon of construction?
- Which comes first: interpretation or rectification?
- Does rectification presuppose the existence of a formally valid testamentary instrument, and what is the role of the testator's knowledge and approval?
- Do English courts have an innate power to rectify wills?

2. How Are Wills to Be Construed?

Given the order in which the Supreme Court decided to tackle the issues arising in *Marley v Rawlings*,[15] it is appropriate to begin by asking how wills are to be construed. This is a question which has vexed lawyers for a long time,[16] and much ink has been spilt on it over the years, simply because it is of such immense practical relevance. Except for a few very specific provisions in the Wills Act 1837 (to which the Supreme Court did not advert),[17] there is little legislative guidance

[12] R Ham, 'Thy Will Be Done: Construction and Rectification of Wills in the Supreme Court' (2014) 20 *Trusts & Trustees* 966, at 966, points out that the last time was in 1958 in *Wintle v Nye* [1959] 1 WLR 284 (HL).

[13] Law Commission, *Twelfth Programme of Law Reform* (Law Com No 354, London, 2014) paras 2.30–2.33. The other areas under review are 'testamentary capacity' and 'mutual wills', addressed by Penelope Reed and Ying Khai Liew in Chs 7 and 5 (respectively) of this volume.

[14] For the current project status, see www.lawcom.gov.uk/project/wills/ (last accessed 20 November 2015).

[15] See the text accompanying and following n 67 below.

[16] As Coke CJ famously stated in *Roberts v Roberts* (1611) 2 Bulstr 123 at 130, 80 ER 1002 at 1008, 'wills and the construction of them do more perplex a man, than any other learning, and to make a certain construction of them, this *excedit iuris prudentum artem*'.

[17] See ss 24–33 of the Wills Act 1837.

on it.[18] Although Lord Neuberger's comments on construction are—strictly speaking—obiter dicta,[19] courts, practitioners and academics are lapping them up eagerly.[20]

Endorsing a more general trend closely associated with the jurisprudence of Lord Hoffmann[21] and already supported by Lord Neuberger himself when he was Master of the Rolls,[22] Lord Neuberger held that the approach towards interpreting wills ought in principle to be the same as applies to any other document:[23]

> [17] Until relatively recently, there were no statutory provisions relating to the proper approach to the interpretation of wills.[24] The interpretation of wills was a matter for the courts, who, as is so often the way, tended (at least until very recently) to approach the issue detached from, and potentially differently from the approach adopted to the interpretation of other documents.
>
> [18] During the past 40 years, the House of Lords and Supreme Court have laid down the correct approach to the interpretation, or construction, of commercial contracts in a number of cases starting with *Prenn v Simmonds* [1971] 1 WLR 1381 and culminating in *Rainy Sky SA v Kookmin Bank* [2011] 1 WLR 2900.
>
> [19] When interpreting a contract, the court is concerned to find the intention of the party or parties, and it does this by identifying the meaning of the relevant words,

[18] For the guidance that Lord Neuberger sought to extract (indirectly) from section 21 of the Administration of Justice Act 1982, see the text accompanying n 38 below.

[19] *Marley v Rawlings* was in the end decided on the basis of rectification alone, and it seems that the general 'modern' approach towards construction was conceded by counsel for the respondents: Learmonth (n 8 above) 728.

[20] From the case law, see especially *Burnard v Burnard* [2014] EWHC 340 (Ch) [61]–[66]; *Re Huntley (Brooke v Purton)* [2014] EWHC 547 (Ch), [2014] WTLR 745 at [11]–[15]; *Re Freud (Rawstron v Freud)* [2014] EWHC 2577 (Ch), [2014] WTLR 1453 at [11]–[13]; *Reading v Reading* [2015] EWHC 946 (Ch) [23]–[27], [40]–[47]; *Royal Society v Robinson* (17.11.2015, ChD, unreported). In the context of an *inter vivos* declaration of trust, *cf* the reference to *Marley v Rawlings* in *Richards v Wood* [2014] EWCA Civ 1314, [2015] 1 WLR 3238 at [14].

[21] See especially Lord Hoffmann's landmark restatement of the modern canon of contractual construction in *Investors Compensation Scheme Ltd v West Bromwich Building Society (No 1)* [1998] 1 WLR 896 (HL) 912–13. For the wills context in particular, see his observations in *Charles v Barzey* [2002] UKPC 68, [2003] 1 WLR 437 at [6]: 'The interpretation of a will is in principle no different from that of any other communication. The question is what a reasonable person, possessed of all the background knowledge which the testatrix might reasonably have been expected to have, would have understood the testatrix to have meant by the words which she used'. *cf* already Lord Denning's (minority) view in *Re Allsop (Cardinal v Warr)* [1968] Ch 39 (CA) 47, rejecting literalism and insisting that one 'must look at the will in the light of the surrounding circumstances'.

[22] *RSPCA v Sharp* [2010] EWCA Civ 1474, [2011] 1 WLR 980 at [31].

[23] *Marley v Rawlings* (SC) (n 3 above) [17]–[20].

[24] That is not quite accurate: see n 17 above and text thereto, and especially s 24 of the Wills Act 1837, stipulating that '[e]very will shall be construed, with reference to the real estate and personal estate comprised in it, to speak and take effect as if it had been executed immediately before the death of the testator, unless a contrary intention shall appear by the will'. I have argued elsewhere that this provision—if taken at face value—is apt to mislead: B Häcker, 'A Case Note on *All Souls College* v. *Cod[d]rington* (1720)' (2012) 76 *Rabels Zeitschrift für ausländisches und internationales Privatrecht* 1051 at 1068, 1069–70, 1072.

(a) in the light of (i) the natural and ordinary meaning of those words, (ii) the overall purpose of the document, (iii) any other provisions of the document, (iv) the facts known or assumed by the parties at the time that the document was executed, and (v) common sense, but (b) ignoring subjective evidence of any party's intentions …

[20] *When it comes to interpreting wills, it seems to me that the approach should be the same. Whether the document in question is a commercial contract or a will, the aim is to identify the intention of the party or parties to the document by interpreting the words used in their documentary, factual and commercial context* … (emphasis added)

According to this approach, the fact that a will actually *differs* from a commercial contract in being made by only a single party is 'merely one of the contextual circumstances which has to be borne in mind when interpreting the document concerned', just as it would be if one were interpreting a unilateral notice or a patent.[25]

The law has therefore come a long way indeed from the literalism of the so-called *Wigram* rules.[26] It now subscribes to an avowedly intention-based approach.[27] Though it would be wrong to exaggerate the degree of assimilation,[28] one might say that the construction of wills has become much more continental or civilian

[25] *Marley v Rawlings* (SC) (n 3 above) [21]–[22], referring to *Mannai Investment Co Ltd v Eagle Star Life Assurance Co Ltd* [1997] AC 749 at 770–71 and 779–80; *Catnic Components Ltd v Hill & Smith Ltd (No 1)* [1982] RPC 183 (HL) 243; *Kirin-Amgen Inc v Hoechst Marion Roussel Ltd (No 2)* [2004] UKHL 46, [2005] 1 All ER 667 at [27]–[32]. His Lordship did not say anything about statutory construction, but it has been suggested that the 'unified approach' to interpretation might actually extend that far: Goh Y and Yip M, '*Marley v Rawlings*: Reflections from Singapore' [2014] *Singapore Journal of Legal Studies* 218 at 221–24, arguing that such a unified approach (supplemented by specific guidelines for particular types of documents) has several merits and should not be dismissed out of hand.

[26] See J Wigram, *An Examination of the Rules of Law, Respecting the Admission of Extrinsic Evidence in the Aid of the Interpretation of Wills* (London, Charles Hunter, 1831). The book was considered an authoritative manual and ran to four editions. A convenient summary of the propositions contained therein is provided by R Kerridge, *Hawkins on the Construction of Wills*, 5th edn (London, Sweet & Maxwell, 2000) (hereinafter '*Hawkins*') [2-17]–[2-27].

[27] The whole development, especially the abandonment of literalism by the House of Lords, is traced by *Hawkins* (n 26 above) [2-39]–[2-54]. As this treatment also indicates (at [2-02]), the 'intentional approach' had already been a serious rival to literalism well before the 19th century. Consider, for example, the following statement by Sir Joseph Jekyll MR in *Cowper v Cowper* (1734) 2 P Wms 720 at 741, 24 ER 930 at 937: 'I am sensible there is a diversity of opinions among the learned judges of the present time, whether the legal operation of words in a will, or the intent of the testator, shall govern? for my part, I shall always contend for the intention where it is plain, and I think the strongest authorities are on that side; for if the intention is sometimes to govern as it is admitted it must, and not always give way to the legal construction, and yet at other times shall not govern, there will then be no rule to judge by, nor will any lawyer know how to advise his client; a mischief which judges ought to prevent'.

[28] In particular, against the background of s 21 of the Administration of Justice Act 1982 (on which see the text accompanying and following nn 36–38 below), it would be rash to assert that English law now adopts the *same* approach towards the construction of wills as, for instance, German law (on which see the text accompanying nn 33–34 below). Though much of the detail is contentious in both legal systems, there would appear to remain substantial differences as regards what exactly is meant by the testator's 'intention' and how it is established in practice.

in spirit.[29] However, such an observation calls for an immediate caveat. If one looks at the modern English approach through civilian—in my case German—spectacles, then the suggestion that wills should in principle be interpreted in the *same* way as any other document is, as a matter of fact, rather surprising.

German lawyers construe contracts (as well as all types of legally relevant declarations by one party to another, such as unilateral notices) by reference to the declaring party's intention *as it would appear from the recipient perspective*.[30] This makes for an element of objectivity in their interpretation, not unlike the objective contextual circumstances Lord Neuberger mentions. The same is true of patents, which are construed as the notional 'person skilled in the art' would understand them.[31]

But wills, to a German lawyer, are different. They are different because they are not dependent for their legal validity on anybody receiving them or on their being published to the world at large in some official journal. Conceptually (though of course not practically), they take effect on death simply because they are there, whether or not they are actually found. People are said not to rely on them in the same way as they do on unilateral notices or patent claims.[32] This conceptual

[29] It is worth noting that the Law Reform Committee, whose 1973 Report on the interpretation of wills substantially promoted the intention-based approach, expressly drew on comparative work by the German émigré lawyer Ernst Joseph Cohn (1904–76): Law Reform Committee, *Nineteenth Report: Interpretation of Wills* (Cmnd 5301, London, 1973) para 56. See also n 61 and the accompanying text below.

[30] This is the combined effect of §§ 133, 157 BGB. The former provides: 'In interpreting a declaration of intention, the true intention is to be ascertained rather than adhering to the literal meaning of the expression'. Where, however, a declaration of intention needs to be communicated to the other party, § 133 is read in conjunction with § 157 BGB, which stipulates that '[c]ontracts are to be interpreted in accordance with the requirements of good faith and taking account of common usage'. In its generalised form, this approach is known as the 'objective recipient perspective' (*objektiver Empängerhorizont*).

[31] See eg BGH (7.11.2000) GRUR 2001, 232 at 233; OLG Düsseldorf (28.6.2007) case ref I-2 U 22/06 (available via juris); BGH (22.12.2009) BGHZ 184, 49 at 57–58. For the UK, see *Kirin-Amgen Inc v Hoechst Marion Roussel Ltd (No 2)* (n 25 above) [32]–[33], where Lord Hoffmann said: 'Construction, whether of a patent or any other document, is … not directly concerned with what the author meant to say. There is no window into the mind of the patentee or the author of any other document. Construction is objective in the sense that it is concerned with what a reasonable person to whom the utterance was addressed would have understood the author to be using the words to mean. Notice, however, that it is not, as is sometimes said, "the meaning of the words the author used", but rather what the notional addressee would have understood the author to mean by using those words. … In the case of a patent specification, the notional addressee is the person skilled in the art'.

[32] Since provisions in a will remain revocable (in most cases) until the testator's death, there can be no question of reliance before then. Afterwards, German law caters for reliance issues by means of generous rules protecting innocent parties' good faith, such as their reliance on a 'certificate of heirship' (*Erbschein*, roughly equivalent to a grant of probate) if this document fails to reflect the true legal position. As far as English law is concerned, Ham (n 12 above) 968 notes that '[i]n the context of wills … there is no question of one party relying on an objective understanding of the meaning of the will'. But contrast the Law Reform Committee's *Nineteenth Report* (n 29 above) para 3 ('In formulating rules for disputes about the meaning of a will, the law must hold the balance between giving effect to the

difference leads German lawyers to hold that wills—and wills alone—have to be interpreted solely in accordance with the testator's innermost subjective intent so far as we can establish it,[33] and there are no restrictions on the admissible evidence. The classic example used to illustrate this proposition is the case of a testator who leaves his 'library' to a particular legatee. If it can be shown that the testator habitually (or arguably even, for some reason, just on this one occasion) referred to his wine cellar as his 'library', then the bequest will be one of wine and not of books.[34]

In English law, we would hopefully arrive at the same result,[35] but it is questionable whether context alone can get us there. Unless it is clear from the will itself that the testator used the term 'library' in a peculiar idiosyncratic sense, we need extrinsic evidence to establish what he meant. Such evidence is let in through section 21 of the Administration of Justice Act 1982,[36] which is a product of recommendations made by the Law Reform Committee in 1973.[37] It reads:

21 Interpretation of wills—general rules as to evidence

(1) This section applies to a will—
  (a) in so far as any part of it is meaningless;
  (b) in so far as the language used in any part of it is ambiguous on the face of it;
  (c) in so far as evidence, other than evidence of the testator's intention, shows that the language used in any part of it is ambiguous in the light of surrounding circumstances.

(2) In so far as this section applies to a will extrinsic evidence, including evidence of the testator's intention, may be admitted to assist in its interpretation.

testator's "true" intentions on the one hand and enabling those concerned to rely on the words actually used in it on the other'.); Drummond (n 2 above) 364 ('Testators should expect their wills to be made public after death on grant of probate, and a will is a document prepared precisely in order to affect the rights of third parties'.). See also s 20(3) of the Administration of Justice Act 1982, seeking to protect the personal representative from liability after the initial six-month period during which applications for rectification orders are to be expected.

[33] Wills are construed in accordance with §§ 133, 2084 BGB. The wording of the former provision is set out in n 30 above. The latter provides: 'If the content of a testamentary disposition admits of different interpretations, then that interpretation is to be preferred in the case of doubt which allows the disposition to be effective' (*favor testamenti*).

[34] See eg G Otte, *Erbrecht: Eine Darstellung der Grundzüge in programmierter Form* (Berlin, Walter de Gruyter, 1974) 34; KH Gursky, *Erbrecht*, 6th edn (Heidelberg, CF Müller, 2010) 29; B Boemke and B Ulrici, *BGB Allgemeiner Teil*, 2nd edn (Heidelberg, Springer, 2014) 146. More nuanced: D Leipold in *Münchener Kommentar zum Bürgerlichen Gesetzbuch*, vol 9 (*Erbrecht*), 6th edn (München, CH Beck, 2013) § 2084 [18].

[35] See eg R Kerridge (assisted by AHR Brierley), *Parry and Kerridge: The Law of Succession*, 12th edn (London, Sweet & Maxwell, 2009) (hereinafter '*Parry and Kerridge*') [10-16] and [10-29].

[36] Our case would probably fall under subsection (1)(c): see *Parry and Kerridge* (n 35 above) [10-28].

[37] See Law Reform Committee, *Nineteenth Report* (n 29 above) especially paras 1–8 and 34–59; *Hawkins* (n 26 above) [2-47]–[2-65].

In *Marley v Rawlings*, Lord Neuberger adverted to this provision and in the light of it qualified his earlier statement somewhat. He said:[38]

> [25] In my view, section 21(1) confirms that a will should be interpreted in the same way as a contract, a notice or a patent, namely as summarised in para 19 above. In particular, section 21(1)(c) shows that 'evidence' is admissible when construing a will, and that that includes the 'surrounding circumstances'. However, section 21(2) goes rather further. It indicates that, if one or more of the three requirements set out in section 21(1) is satisfied, then direct evidence of the testator's intention is admissible, in order to interpret the will in question.
>
> [26] Accordingly, as I see it, *save where section 21(1) applies, a will is to be interpreted in the same way as any other document, but, in addition, in relation to a will, or a provision in a will, to which section 21(1) applies, it is possible to assist its interpretation by reference to evidence of the testator's actual intention* (eg by reference to what he told the drafter of the will, or another person, or by what was in any notes he made or earlier drafts of the will which he may have approved or caused to be prepared). (emphasis added)

This clarifies how the Supreme Court wants to resolve the conceptual tension between the necessarily objective contextual approach of contract interpretation and the more subjective approach (sometimes) appropriate for wills, but at the same time it puts rather a lot of pressure on section 21. The question is: *how much* evidence is admissible as a matter of ordinary 'context', and *how much* can come in via section 21? More of the former will probably entail less of the latter. Conversely, a restrictive take on the former is bound to put into sharp focus the question of when the language used in a will is 'meaningless' or 'ambiguous'. All in all, the broader the remit of section 21(1), the greater the difference in approach between the construction of wills and the interpretation of other documents will tend to be.

Looking at the case law, there appears to be a great deal of uncertainty concerning the admissibility of extrinsic evidence and the way it fits with the modern contextual approach. For example, where there was a mis-description of a party mentioned in the will, some judges have felt able to correct this without recourse to section 21 by taking a 'practical and common sense view' of context-sensitive construction,[39] while others have found the will to be merely 'ambiguous in the light of surrounding circumstances' and then relied on section 21 to admit extrinsic evidence.[40] In *Reading v Reading*, Asplin J recently combined both approaches. She held that although the term 'issue' did not normally include stepchildren, when one considered the overall context and purpose of the will in question and 'appl[ied] common sense', the 'ordinary and natural meaning of the words "issue of mine" and "such of my issue" respectively include[d] both children and step-children and their children rather than descendants of all degrees'.[41] However, in

[38] *Marley v Rawlings* (SC) (n 3 above) [25]–[26].
[39] *Re Rogers* [2006] EWHC 753 (Ch), [2006] 1 WLR 1577 at [14]. Lightman J did not advert to s 21.
[40] *Burnard v Burnard* [2014] EWHC 340 (Ch) [64].
[41] *Reading v Reading* [2015] EWHC 946 (Ch), [2015] WTLR 1245 at [40]–[47], especially [47].

case she was wrong about this, she added that the admission of extrinsic evidence under section 21(1)(c) would have led to the same conclusion.[42]

As far as the width of the statutory gateway for extrinsic evidence is concerned, one recent decision maintained that 'the concept of ambiguity in section 21 of the 1982 Act should be broadly interpreted' and concluded that this allowed the relevant will to be treated as if one of its clauses was in fact omitted,[43] while in the litigation concerning the will of the late Lucian Freud, the parties took a much narrower view of the provision: it was common ground between them that extrinsic evidence (such as the instructions given to the solicitors who drafted the instrument) could *not* be admitted as an aid to interpretation.[44] This chimes with the statement of Proudman J in *Gledhill v Arnold* that, when construing a will, 'the court is not engaged in an exercise in order to avoid an obviously absurd or unintended result'.[45] Nevertheless, as Richard Spearman QC observed, sitting as a Deputy Judge of the Chancery Division in *Re Freud*:[46]

> To lay people involved in a single piece of litigation, this may seem surprising. Suppose a testator gives clear and unequivocal instructions in writing as to what he wants to achieve by his will, his solicitor sends him a draft will with a covering letter explaining how the solicitor has sought to reflect those intentions in the draft will, and the testator signs the will and returns it to the solicitor with a letter saying that he is happy that his intentions have been achieved? Some might think all that a good aid to interpretation.

The line becomes even harder to hold when one considers that extrinsic evidence is admissible without restrictions when it comes to rectifying (rather than merely construing) a will, bearing in mind that a rectification claim is often run alongside the interpretation argument. This leads us straight to the next question.

3. Is Rectification Dispensable in the Light of the Modern Canon of Construction?

Whether and to what extent rectification is now dispensable in light of the modern canon of construction is a question which has often been asked, but which is still

[42] ibid [48]–[49]. In the case of *Re Harte* [2015] EWHC 2351 (Ch), decided shortly after the 'Current Issues in Succession Law' conference, David Hodge QC, in his capacity as a judge of the High Court, relied on a combination of intention-orientated construction with the aid of evidence admitted via s 21 (in respect of some clauses of a will) and rectification under s 20 (in respect of other dispositions) to resolve the case at hand.

[43] *Re Huntley (Brooke v Purton)* [2014] EWHC 547 (Ch), [2014] WTLR 745, especially [14]–[15].

[44] *Re Freud (Rawstron v Freud)* [2014] EWHC 2577 (Ch), [2014] WTLR 1453, especially [13]–[15].

[45] *Gledhill v Arnold* [2015] EWHC 2939 (Ch) [23]. Although her Ladyship refused to construe the relevant will as contended for by the claimants (because there was 'nothing odd about the Will as it stands': at [23]), she did allow the alternative claim for rectification to succeed, observing by way of justification merely that, '[g]iven the width of the expression "clerical error" as explained in *Marley* [*v Rawlings*,] a failure correctly to record the instructions was the result of a clerical error' (at [26]).

[46] *Re Freud* (n 44 above) [15].

not finally answered, in the realm of contract law.[47] *Marley v Rawlings* highlights that it is also a live issue in the realm of wills.[48]

Two of their Lordships, it seems, were at one point inclined to solve the case on the basis of construction,[49] but Lord Neuberger preferred the rectification route and left the matter of construction open,[50] although he did indicate that he saw some problems about simply 'reading' the document signed by Mr Rawlings as though it contained the words set out in the instrument signed by his wife.[51]

In *practice*, it is of course advisable to pursue both a rectification claim and the argument based on interpretation whenever possible, and it may not matter

[47] See eg J McGhee, *Snell's Equity*, 33rd edn (London, Sweet & Maxwell, 2014) at [16-008]: 'That an instrument can be interpreted broadly to correct a mistake clearly restricts the range of circumstances in which rectification will be necessary. However, in some situations the parties will still need to seek rectification rather than interpretation'. Compare and contrast A Burrows, 'Construction and Rectification' in A Burrows and E Peel (eds), *Contract Terms* (Oxford, Oxford University Press, 2007) 77 at 99, who predicted some years ago that at least 'in the context of the rectification of *contracts* for mistakes of *fact*, rectification has not merely been rendered less important by modern developments in the law of construction but is on the point of being rendered largely superfluous'. Following *Chartbrook Ltd v Persimmon Homes Ltd* [2009] UKHL 38, [2009] 1 AC 1101, where the House of Lords refused to jettison the exclusionary rule (under which evidence of pre-contractual negotiations cannot be used as an aid to interpretation), R Buxton, '"Construction" and Rectification after *Chartbrook*' [2010] *CLJ* 253 at 262 argued that 'on any view of its reach rectification should in practice transcend its present status as a safety net in cases where the inadmissibility of prior negotiations in issues of construction produces a conclusion that those negotiations show to be plainly wrong. Rectification should in future occupy the whole of the field when it is necessary to correct errors in the formal expression of a contractual consensus' (footnotes omitted).

[48] Various commentators specifically address the point, eg Drummond (n 2 above) 362–64; J Goodwin and E Granger, 'Where There's a Will There's a Way: *Marley v Rawlings and Another*' (2015) 78 *MLR* 140 at 145–46; M Thomas, 'Where There's a Will There's a (Wrong) Way: Marley v Rawlings and another' (2014) 28 *Trust Law International* 38 at 40–41.

[49] Robert Ham QC, who was counsel for the successful appellant in *Marley v Rawlings*, notes that '[d]uring the course of argument, at least two of the justices seemed strongly attracted by the construction argument': Ham (n 12 above) 967.

[50] *Marley v Rawlings* (SC) (n 3 above) at [41]: 'In my judgment, unless it is necessary to decide this difficult point, we should not do so on this appeal. Interpretation was not the basis on which the courts below decided this case and it was not the ground on which Mr Ham primarily relied. Furthermore, and no doubt because of those points, only limited argument was directed to the issue of whether the issue was one of interpretation or of rectification. For the reasons developed below, I consider that this appeal succeeds on the ground of rectification, so I shall proceed on the basis that it fails on interpretation'.

[51] ibid [42]. See also Drummond (n 2 above) 363: 'This was the better course, since it is difficult to see *Marley* as a case of construction at all. The words "if my husband Alfred Thomas Rawlings … survives me … then … I leave to him my entire estate" in the document signed by Mr Rawlings do not state that his estate was to be left to his wife Maureen Catherine Rawlings if she survived him. Looking outside the will for an explanation does not show us what he intended by those words; it tells us that he intended to use different words. No wonder that they appeared ambiguous or meaningless, in the language of s.21'.; Learmonth (n 8 above) at 728: '[W]e [ie counsel for the respondents in *Marley v Rawlings*] pointed out that, as consistently held by the Supreme Court and the House of Lords before it, interpretation is an exercise in discovering *what the party or parties meant by the language* used in the document. The facts of the case showed that there was nothing wrong with the language of the will requiring any unusual construction. Where the document in question was never intended by its draftsman or its signatory for that party, that was a futile exercise; the words meant exactly what they said, and though they were meaningless in the mouth of the person who signed the document, there was no basis for construing them to mean what someone else would have meant' (footnotes omitted).

much whether the claimant in the end wins on one or the other. But it is nevertheless worth considering, in *theory*, to what extent the modern canon of construction makes the rectification exercise superfluous, not least because rectification is normally subject to a six-month time limit,[52] while interpretation is not similarly confined. Lord Neuberger in *Marley v Rawlings* rightly emphasised that the demarcation line was not of purely academic interest:[53]

> At first sight, it might seem to be a rather dry question whether a particular approach is one of interpretation or rectification. However, it is by no means simply an academic issue of categorisation. If it is a question of interpretation, then the document in question has, and has always had, the meaning and effect as determined by the court, and that is the end of the matter. On the other hand, if it is a question of rectification, then the document, as rectified, has a different meaning from that which it appears to have on its face, and the court would have jurisdiction to refuse rectification or to grant it on terms (eg if there had been delay, change of position, or third party reliance).

It is submitted that there are *at least two* reasons why rectification of wills still has important roles to play and cannot simply be replaced by a liberal approach to construction. The first is somewhat contingent on what was said above about the uncertainties of interpretation. So long as there are cases where extrinsic evidence of the testator's subjective dispositive intention is not admitted as an aid to construction,[54] rectification will remain the vehicle of choice for bringing it to bear.

But even if the contextual approach, coupled with an extremely broad reading of section 21(1) of the Administration of Justice Act 1982, were to bring the intention-based interpretative method to perfection,[55] there would still be situations where rectification is indispensable. The reason is the following: While it may be possible in an appropriate case to construe 'library' to mean 'wine cellar',[56] one cannot read something into a will which is not there at all. Assume that the testator had intended to leave his wine cellar to another member of his gentlemen's club, but that amongst a whole long list of various bequests to individuals which he wanted to include in his will, this one for some inexplicable reason went missing from the final draft. There is just a plain gap in the will, a gap that one would not notice just from looking at the document, and one that no amount of interpretation can fill.[57] Formality requirements are the essential crux of the matter. A testator's wishes are only legally relevant in so far as they have been expressed in a way which complies with section 9 of the Wills Act 1837:[58]

[52] See Administration of Justice Act 1982, s 20(2), set out in the text following n 63 below. Note that courts have discretion to extend this period, which they appear to be making generous use of.

[53] *Marley v Rawlings* (SC) (n 3 above) [40].

[54] See the text accompanying nn 43–46 above.

[55] This is not to say that a completely subjective intention-based approach would necessarily be desirable under English law, particularly from the reliance point of view: *cf* the discussion in n 32 above.

[56] See the text accompanying and following n 34 above.

[57] If the gap is obvious on the face of the document, then interpretation could conceivably help.

[58] As substituted by the Administration of Justice Act 1982, s 17: see n 117 below.

9 Signing and attestation of wills

No will shall be valid unless—

(a) it is in writing, and signed by the testator, or by some other person in his presence and by his direction; and
(b) it appears that the testator intended by his signature to give effect to the will; and
(c) the signature is made or acknowledged by the testator in the presence of two or more witnesses present at the same time; and
(d) each witness either—
  (i) attests and signs the will; or
  (ii) acknowledges his signature, in the presence of the testator (but not necessarily in the presence of any other witness),

but no form of attestation shall be necessary.

If an intended bequest is simply missing from the draft which has been signed and attested, it cannot take effect, however genuine the testator's intention may be.[59]

This is a predicament faced by any legal system which subjects wills to strict formalities. German lawyers try to address the problem by a doctrine known as the *Andeutungstheorie*. It maintains that a testator's subjective dispositive intent has to be at least hinted at or in some way alluded to in the formal instrument if it is to be enforced.[60] If there is no 'peg' to hang a particular interpretation on, then it quite simply fails.[61] That would be the end of the matter for German testators who forget individual bequests when copying out their wills from preliminary drafts.[62]

[59] Drummond (n 2 above) 364 makes the same point: 'Suppose ... that a will fails—for no apparent reason—to make provision for someone who was close to the testator; investigation shows that the testator did intend to make provision, but that the wording never made it to the will. Adding wording for the testator's intention into the will, on the basis that the background shows that something went wrong with the language of the will, would surely contravene s.9 of the Wills Act 1837 unless carried out by way of rectification under s.20 of the 1982 Act'.

[60] See eg BGH (9.4.1981) BGHZ 80, 242; BGH (8.12.1982) BGHZ 86, 41; BGH (16.7.1997) NJWE-FER 1997, 252; Otte (n 34 above) 36–37; Leipold in *Münchener Kommentar* (n 34 above) § 2084 [14]–[16]; L Michalski, *BGB-Erbrecht*, 4th edn (Heidelberg, CF Müller, 2010) [336]–[340]; but *cf* U Foerste, 'Die Form des Testaments als Grenze seiner Auslegung' (1993) 44 *Deutsche Notar-Zeitschrift* 84.

[61] This is probably what Ernst Joseph Cohn had in mind when using the metaphor in his submission to the Law Reform Committee: see *Nineteenth Report* (n 29 above) para 56: 'There must be [under the proposed regime which was subsequently implemented in the Administration of Justice Act 1982, s 21] a legitimate dispute about the language of the will as a "peg" on which to hang the admission of the evidence—to borrow an idea expressed to us by Professor E.J. Cohn in a paper about the laws of the continental countries, for which all of us were particularly grateful. It appears that in those countries no exclusionary rules of evidence are in force today and the courts consider their task to be to give effect to the testator's intention, however proved, provided there is the necessary peg in the words of the will'.

[62] The German Civil Code recognises only holographic (ie handwritten) wills and those made in notarial form as 'regular testaments': §§ 2231–2247 BGB. It is worth mentioning, however, that in the specific circumstances of *Marley v Rawlings*, German law might have been able to treat Mr and Mrs Rawlings' mirror wills as a 'joint testament of spouses' (§ 2265 BGB), in which case the mix-up of drafts would not have been fatal. Indeed, such a mix-up is arguably far less likely to happen

But not all is lost for testators in England. The rules on rectification (for which there is no German equivalent)[63] ensure that the defect can be cured where the testator's wishes have accidentally not been committed to the correct form. Section 20 of the Administration of Justice Act 1982, which also goes back to the Law Reform Committee's 1973 recommendations, provides, so far as is relevant here:

20 Rectification

(1) If a court is satisfied that a will is so expressed that it fails to carry out the testator's intentions, in consequence—
  (a) of a clerical error; or
  (b) of a failure to understand his instructions,
  it may order that the will shall be rectified so as to carry out his intentions.
(2) An application for an order under this section shall not, except with the permission of the court, be made after the end of the period of six months from the date on which representation with respect to the estate of the deceased is first taken out.
(3) …
(4) …

Rectification is therefore possible if the reason why the testator's wishes have not found their way into the instrument is that the testator himself or a person aiding and advising him has made a 'clerical error' (a term given a very broad interpretation by *Marley v Rawlings*),[64] or if a person drawing up the will for the testator has failed properly to understand his instructions.[65] It may perhaps be that section 20 is drafted too narrowly as it stands,[66] but the provision is certainly not superfluous.

The clear answer to the second question (namely, whether rectification is dispensable in the light of the modern canon of construction) is thus 'no'—however generously one admits extrinsic evidence under section 21, and however intention-focused the interpretative exercise eventually becomes. Yet in order to understand exactly what role rectification can legitimately continue to play alongside the modern approach to construction, it is helpful to clarify the relationship between the two in another respect as well.

in the first place where testators have to write out their will by hand or where they undergo a fairly elaborate process of notarial attestation, including an obligatory reading-out of the entire document (§ 13 BeurkG). In England, it is standard practice for wills drafted by professionals to be read out to the testator before they are executed, but there are no comparable safeguards for home-made wills.

[63] German law does not allow for the rectification of wills, but a testamentary disposition which the testator did not intend, or in relation to the content or effect of which he was mistaken, is generally rescindable: § 2078 BGB. This means that individual provisions or whole wills may be struck out as ineffective, but nothing can be substituted or added.

[64] Section 20(1)(a). See the text accompanying n 8 above.

[65] Section 20(1)(b).

[66] See the text accompanying nn 215–216 below, but *cf* also the text following n 220 below.

4. Which Comes First: Interpretation or Rectification?

Are we first to construe the will and then rectify it as necessary to give effect to the testator's intention, or should rectification not rather *precede* interpretation proper?

Lord Neuberger in *Marley v Rawlings* was quite clear that he thought interpretation came first. He said:[67]

> Although Mr Ham [counsel for the appellant] primarily based his contention that the will was valid on the ground of rectification (which was the sole basis on which the case was considered in the courts below), he accepted that the interpretation argument ought to be considered first ...

This has an intuitive appeal. It is a pragmatic approach which is also expressly or impliedly adopted by a number of other recent cases (including non-wills cases).[68] Why bother with rectification when we can arrive at the desired result by interpretation? In *Re Huntley*, for example, David Donaldson QC held that there was 'no need, nor indeed logical scope, for rectification' where the will—on its proper construction—already reflected the testator's intention,[69] and he doubted whether it was even possible and proper to rectify for the sake of clarity alone.[70] The 'interpretation-first' approach can indeed draw some support from the wording of section 20, according to which rectification depends on a court finding that 'a will is so expressed that it fails to carry out the testator's intentions'.[71]

However, it is worth noting that the Law Reform Committee, in whose recommendation sections 20 and 21 are rooted, took a very different view in 1973.

[67] *Marley v Rawlings* (SC) (n 3 above) [33].

[68] Beside *Re Huntley* (n 43 above), quoted and discussed in the text accompanying n 69–70 immediately below, see *Kevern v Ayres* [2014] EWHC 165 (Ch), [2014] WTLR 441 at [15]; *Burnard v Burnard* (n 40 above) [66]; *Reading v Reading* (n 41 above) especially [40]; *Gledhill v Arnold* (n 45 above); *Re Harte* (n 42 above).

[69] *Re Huntley* (n 43 above) [19].

[70] ibid: 'The power to make [a rectification] order nonetheless *ex abundanti cautela* is supported, if somewhat tenuously, by a decision of the Privy Council (see *Standard Portland Cement Co Pty Ltd v Good* [1982] 57 ALJR 151). To that may be added a more extensive Australian jurisprudence (reviewed in *Frankins Pty Ltd v Metcash Trading Ltd* [2009] NSWCA 407), which has however not so far found any echo in English case law. For my own part, I find it difficult to understand what an order for rectification can contribute in such a case, and do not intend myself to take that course here, whether or not it is theoretically open to me'(footnotes omitted).

[71] *cf* Ham (n 12 above) 967–68, who draws attention to the opening words of section 20, but then asks—in the light of the 'sensible pragmatic conclusion' adopted in *Marley v Rawlings*, namely of leaving open whether the case could have been solved by interpretation—why parties should 'have to argue, and the court decide, a difficult point of construction, where there is clear evidence of intention upon which to grant rectification?'. Compare and contrast Learmonth (n 8 above) 728: 'Disappointingly, and rather illogically, Lord Neuberger ... did not actually decide the [construction] point. It was illogical to duck the question because the jurisdiction in section 20 of the 1982 Act to rectify a will arises only if it does not reflect the testator's intentions. Until one has determined the true construction of a will, therefore, one cannot say if it can be rectified'.

The Committee expressly considered the right order of doing things, identifying two diametrically opposed approaches,[72] and concluded that:[73]

> The procedure would be *first* to rectify the will (wherever appropriate) in order to make it contain the words it was intended to contain *and then* to admit all such evidence relevant to discovering what meaning those words would have conveyed to the testator. (emphasis added)

According to this approach, rectification and interpretation are quite distinct exercises, and rectification is not merely 'ancillary'[74] to interpretation. The first step is always to make sure that the document actually *says* what it was intended to say, ie that it contains the words the testator wanted to use. In a second step, one then considers what the testator *meant* by those words, ie what *sense* they bore for him.[75] That is the reason why the provision on rectification (section 20) actually precedes the rules as to the admissibility of evidence for the purposes of interpretation (in section 21).

This way of looking at things also explains why *Marley v Rawlings* was rightly solved by means of rectification. It was not a case where Mr Rawlings attributed to the words in the document he had signed some peculiar meaning. Rather, he thought he was putting his signature to a different set of words.[76] And that *intended* set of words conveyed to him exactly the same meaning as it would to anybody else. The problem therefore was not one of interpretation at all.[77]

[72] Law Reform Committee, *Nineteenth Report* (n 29 above) paras 15–16: '[15] Although interpretation and rectification merge indistinguishably into the fundamental problem of the proper extent of the court's power to decide on the effect of a will, as a matter of procedure they must to some extent be separated. Two main views have emerged in discussion about which ought to come first. One view is that interpretation is all, or nearly all, and that rectification is merely ancillary to it. This view is held by those who start from the proposition that the duty of the court is to find out what the testator meant by his will, or even (as some contend) what he meant its effect to be. When the primary task has been accomplished, it may in some cases be appropriate to make a consequential amendment to the words of the will as a matter of record; this is then the role of rectification. [16] The other view is that the process should be the reverse. The court should first ascertain precisely what words the testator meant, or must be taken to have meant, his will to contain; if necessary it should rectify the words admitted to probate so as to make them conform with that intention. Then, and only then, should it proceed to the task of ascertaining what those words mean, in accordance with the rules of interpretation. It is this second view which we are inclined to think is the right one'.

[73] ibid para 49.

[74] ibid para 15, quoted in n 72 above.

[75] The Law Reform Committee did not seek to deny that '[t]here is a certain artificiality in trying to distinguish between the words which the testator intended to use and the meaning which he intended them to have': ibid para 58.

[76] Drummond (n 2 above) 357 perceptively outlines the facts of the case by saying that '[u]nfortunately, the words [Mr Rawlings] had chosen were not those to which he put his signature'.

[77] Drummond (n 2 above) 363 makes essentially the same point in the passage already quoted in n 51 above: 'Looking outside the will for an explanation does not show us what [Mr Rawlings] intended by those words; it tells us that he intended to use different words'. See also Learmonth (n 8 above) 728: '[I]t would have been useful for practitioners to know whether one can interpret the language of a will that was never intended for the testator as if it was'.; Goodwin and Granger (n 48 above) 146: 'rectification, as opposed to interpretation, allows for the kind of wholesale changes to a document that were necessary in this case'.

Of course the initial act of appraising the will after the testator's death always involves an interpretation of sorts (if only to assess the testamentary character of the instrument and to determine who should apply for probate), but thereafter the Law Reform Committee's favoured approach is arguably still the best way of rationalising the relationship between rectification and interpretation in the narrower sense.

When section 20(1)(a) of the Administration of Justice Act 1982 speaks of a will which is 'so expressed that it fails to carry out the testator's intentions' in consequence of a 'clerical error', what this must refer to is his *intention of using a particular set of words.* Hence, if the testator wanted to leave a bequest of £1,000 to charity, but by some transcription error or slip of the pen the figure in the instrument ended up as £100 or £10,000, that is a clear case for rectification.[78] By contrast, if the testator was a baker by profession and left 'a dozen casks of wine' to a colleague, meaning thirteen casks, we should get there by interpretation on the modern contextual approach.[79]

Section 20(1)(b) is more difficult to rationalise than subsection 1(a) because here the testator will typically have left the exact choice of words to the draftsman. Here, therefore, the word 'intention' must bear a slightly wider meaning and refer to the dispositions the testator had in mind and asked his legal adviser to implement. Rectification—we are told—is possible if the draftsman failed to understand the testator's instructions, but not if he understood them correctly and mis-implemented them without any clerical error occurring.[80] The best explanation is probably the following: If the draftsman misunderstands what the testator wants and faithfully transposes his (supposed) wishes, then something has gone wrong in the transmission of information between the testator and the draftsman. Were one to regard the latter as a kind of 'drafting machine' helping to translate the testator's lay language into precise legal concepts and terminology, then one could say that the error has occurred in the process of feeding the relevant information into the machine. In some respects this resembles a clerical error.

Compare and contrast the case where the draftsman *correctly understands* what the testator wants[81] and deliberately chooses words which he *thinks* implement

[78] See Law Reform Committee, *Nineteenth Report* (n 29 above) para 18, example (a), and para 19.

[79] If context alone is insufficient to show that the testator had in mind a 'baker's dozen' (rather than an ordinary dozen), then the use of the word 'dozen' must at least be regarded as ambiguous in the specific professional context, so that extrinsic evidence about his actual dispositive intent will be admissible under s 21 of the Administration of Justice Act 1982 for the purposes of determining whether he meant 12 or 13 casks.

[80] If the draftsman makes a clerical error in the process of drafting the will, then s 20(1)(a) applies in the same way as if the testator had made the error.

[81] There is a question about how to handle cases where the draftsman fails to clarify what exactly the testator wants. In *Re Martin (Clarke v Brothwood)* [2006] EWHC 2939 (Ch), [2007] WTLR 329, for example, the solicitor apparently did not notice that the testatrix's instructions left a large part of the estate undisposed of. He pleaded clerical error, and the judge allowed rectification under s 20(1)(a), so that a 'one-twentieth' share of the estate became '20 per cent' thereof. However, there was hardly a clerical error on the facts. It has been suggested that rectification should—if at all—have been ordered

that intention, but where these words actually fail to achieve the desired end.[82] Given that the testator effectively adopts the draftsman's words as his own by means of his signature, the situation is no different from one where the testator executes a badly drafted home-made will.[83] The draftsman's mistake becomes—vicariously—the testator's.[84] Unlike in the case of a clerical error, the problem does not lie with the actual words in the will. It lies with the reasons behind choosing them. And that is simply bad estate planning.[85]

This kind of bad advice may of course give rise to a negligence liability on the part of the draftsman under the principle recognised in *White v Jones*,[86] just as a clerical error made by the solicitor or a failure to understand or clarify the client's instructions will also typically give rise to liability in the tort of negligence.[87] In the latter two situations, a potential claim in the tort of negligence will compete with a potential rectification claim. Let us briefly consider such a scenario and its implications for the question we are considering.

Where the draftsman of a will has been negligent, it is generally assumed that, in order to mitigate his loss, the claimant has to try to have the will rectified before pursuing his damages claim.[88] Behind this postulate stands the idea that the

under s 20(1)(b), on the basis that '[a]ny competent lawyer should have queried whether Miss Martin really had intended to dispose of only part of the residue' and that, since he had not done so, 'the solicitor had failed to understand his "instructions" in the wider sense of the term': R Kerridge and AHR Brierley, 'Re Martin: Rectification of a Will—The Right Result for the Wrong Reason?' [2007] *Conv* 558 at 562.

[82] *Reading v Reading* (n 41 above) would have been an example of such a situation, had Asplin J not felt able to read the word 'issue' as including stepchildren in the circumstances of the case. There was no question of the draftsman having misunderstood the testator's instructions, and Asplin J held that he had not made a clerical error either when overlooking the fact that the term 'issue' does not normally cover stepchildren: 'Instead, in carrying out his professional duty and judgment as a draftsman of the will, he failed to use an apposite term' (at [52]).

[83] The Law Reform Committee, *Nineteenth Report* (n 29 above) para 20, made a similar point when discussing the 'situation … where the testator (and possibly his solicitor as well) fails to understand the legal effect of the words actually used, and thus produces the wrong result, through using the intended expression. … All concerned may know what the testator wants, but fail to use the right technique to achieve it'.

[84] The idea of 'vicarious mistake' in the rectification context is one the present author first discussed in B Häcker, 'Mistakes in the Execution of Documents: Recent Cases on Rectification and Related Doctrines' (2008) 19 *King's Law Journal* 293 at 303.

[85] There is a question, which cannot be pursued further here, as to whether testamentary dispositions could—or should as a matter of principle—be treated as rescindable for 'sufficiently serious' motivational mistakes in the same way as voluntary *inter vivos* dispositions, by analogy with the ruling in *Pitt v Holt* [2013] UKSC 26, [2013] 2 AC 108.

[86] *White v Jones* [1995] 2 AC 207 (HL), establishing that a solicitor entrusted by the testator with the task of drawing up his will may under certain circumstances also owe a duty of care to prospective beneficiaries.

[87] *Parry and Kerridge* (n 35 above) [15-16] argue that whenever a professionally-drawn will can be rectified, it should always be possible to make out negligence on the part of the draftsman. There could thus never be a 'rectifiable but "non-negligent misunderstanding"'.

[88] *Walker v Medlicott* [1999] 1 WLR 727 (CA) 738–39, 742–44 (alternative ground). More critical *Hawkins* (n 26 above) [1-20]: 'Rectification is the best remedy in a case where negligence and rectification overlap, but it is surely the duty of the party who has been negligent to suggest it. It seems unfair to someone who appears to have suffered as a result of negligent will-drafting to be told that, even if

draftsman or his insurers will then 'merely' have to pay for the cost of the rectification suit which—if successful—puts everything right.[89] In *Marley v Rawlings*, that is in essence precisely what happened (except that the cost of the litigation there apparently *exceeded* the value of the estate).[90] Following a detailed discussion of the relevant allocation mechanisms, the Supreme Court eventually decided that the bulk of the cost should under the circumstances be borne by the insurers of the Rawlings' negligent solicitor.[91]

It is submitted that the proper allocation of costs is another reason for preferring the Law Reform Committee's 'rectification-first' approach to the 'interpretation-first' approach now apparently favoured by many judges. It better reflects the common law's traditional two-stage process, distinguishing between the grant of probate on the one hand and the construction of the will as admitted to probate on the other, even where both functions are nowadays performed by the same court.[92] Procedurally and notionally, there is still a difference between the two steps,[93] and that should be made as transparent as possible to everybody involved. If, in *Marley v Rawlings*, in addition to the problem that the wills were switched, there had been a question about what the words to which Mr Rawlings had intended to put his signature meant, surely it would have been proper for the costs connected with *this* aspect of the litigation to be borne by one of the parties or by the estate, but not (or at any rate not necessarily) by the solicitor's insurers.

5. Does Rectification Presuppose the Existence of a Valid Testamentary Instrument, and What Is the Role of the Testator's Knowledge and Approval?

Moving from the relationship between rectification and interpretation to the relationship between rectification and formalities, a question which has recently

the draftsman denies negligence and denies that rectification is applicable, he (he victim) should apply for rectification in order to mitigate the damage caused by the person who (i) appears to have been negligent and (ii) is refusing to co-operate in undoing the effects of his own negligence'.

[89] Where a will is rectified, this also avoids the 'windfall' problem entailed by *White v Jones*-type claims.

[90] In this respect—though fortunately not in terms of duration or complexity—*Marley v Rawlings* could be said to resemble the famous case of *Jarndyce v Jarndyce* around which the plot in Charles Dickens' novel *Bleak House* is spun.

[91] *Marley v Rawlings (No 2)* [2014] UKSC 51, [2015] 1 AC 157.

[92] It may be precisely because the (historically founded) distinction between a court's probate jurisdiction and its jurisdiction to interpret wills is less pronounced in the civilian tradition than in England (owing to a different evolution of jurisdictional competition and procedural competences) that German courts tend first to determine what disposition the testator really wanted to make and only then ask whether his intentions have been manifested in a way which complies with the testamentary formality requirements: see especially BGH (8.12.1982) BGHZ 86, 41 at 45–47.

[93] The point is forcefully made, albeit in the Canadian context, by M Cullity, 'Rectification of Wills—A Comment on the *Robinson* Case' (2012) 31 *Estates, Trusts & Pensions Journal* 127.

puzzled commentators is whether or not rectification under section 20 of the Administration of Justice Act 1982 presupposes the existence of a formally valid testamentary instrument. In other words: Does the document one is putting before the court have to comply with section 9 of the Wills Act 1837 (as amended by the Administration of Justice Act 1982) already before or only after rectification? And what is the role of the testator's knowledge and approval in all this?

Proudman J at first instance and the Court of Appeal in *Marley v Rawlings* thought that when section 20 spoke of a 'will' failing to carry out the testator's intentions, it meant a formally valid testamentary instrument,[94] and for various reasons they held that the document signed by Mr Rawlings did not comply with section 9.[95] The Supreme Court disagreed on both counts,[96] which makes it quite hard to determine the exact *ratio* of the decision for the purposes of precedent.

Lord Neuberger began by saying that although Mr Rawlings had been handed the draft prepared for his wife, the resulting 'will' was his—and not his wife's—simply because he had signed it.[97] Nor could there be any doubt that he intended by his signature to give effect to the will.[98] Section 9 of the Wills Act 1837 was not therefore a problem:[99]

> [W]hatever else may be said about the document, it is, on its face (and was in fact according to the evidence), unambiguously intended to be a formal will, and it was, on its face (and was in fact according to the evidence), signed by Mr Rawlings, in the presence of two witnesses, on the basis that it was indeed his will.

[94] However, it has been pointed out that, in the context of rectification, a 'will' is not actually the physical object on which the testator's testamentary wishes and dispositions are written down, but 'a set of words, put together in a particular order': R Kerridge, 'When a Husband Executes his Wife's Will' [2012] *Conv* 505 at 508.

[95] *Marley v Rawlings* (Ch) (n 6 above) [18]–[27], especially at [21], Proudman J ruling that 'section 9(b) of the 1837 Act provides a complete answer to the claim, namely that the testator did not intend by his signature to give effect to the will which he signed. If asked whether he did he would not have said, "yes, subject to correction of errors by substituting my wife's name for mine wherever it occurs". He would simply have responded, "no, of course not, that is my wife's will".'; *Marley v Rawlings* (CA) (n 6 above), especially at [39]–[52], [94]–[95], [99]–[102], where the Court of Appeal agreed that the document signed by Mr Rawlings fell foul of section 9(b) and Black LJ further suggested (at [46]) that there was also a problem about section 9(a): 'There is, to my mind, a real question as to whether this will was signed by "the testator". The will had been drawn up for Mrs Rawlings and said that it was "the last will of me Maureen Catherine Rawlings". The obvious person to describe as the testator in relation to this will was therefore Mrs Rawlings and she did not sign it. Mr Rawlings was intending to be a testator but not through the medium of this will'.

[96] See *Marley v Rawlings* (SC) (n 3 above) [55]–[59] and [60]–[67].

[97] ibid [59]: 'It is true that the will purports in its opening words to be the will of Mrs Rawlings, but there is no doubt that it cannot be hers, as she did not sign it; as it was Mr Rawlings who signed it, it can only have been his will, and it is he who is claimed in these proceedings to be the testator for the purposes of section 9. Accordingly, section 9(a) appears to me to be satisfied'.

[98] His Lordship continued (ibid): 'There can be no doubt … from the face of the will (as well as from the evidence) that it was Mr Rawlings's intention at the time he signed the will that it should have effect, and so it seems to me that section 9(b) was also satisfied in this case'. More precisely, one might say that Mr Rawlings was intending to give effect to the document *as a will* or rather perhaps as a testamentary instrument with the contents *as he supposed them to be*. For the rationale behind s 9(b), see the text accompanying nn 107–124 below.

[99] *Marley v Rawlings* (SC) (n 3 above) [57].

But then his Lordship added that, even if section 9 had not been satisfied by the original instrument, it would still have been possible to rectify. All that mattered was that the instrument should comply with section 9 *after* rectification.[100] On this view, section 20 of the Administration of Justice Act 1982 does not presuppose a formally valid will, but only a 'document which is on its face bona fide intended to be a will' or at any rate one 'which, once it is rectified, is a valid will'.[101] Speculation is rife over whether that would include or exclude cases where the testator mistakenly signs—instead of the draft will prepared for him—a gas bill,[102] a shopping list,[103] a laundry ticket,[104] or indeed just a series of 'loose blank sheets of paper' with nothing written on them.[105]

Although Lord Neuberger's judgment is thus somewhat ambiguous with respect to the correct interpretation of the word 'will' in section 20,[106] there are in fact two important lessons to be learnt from it. The first is that section 9 of the Wills Act 1837 should not be overstretched by reading too much into its requirements. Section 9(b) in particular is in danger of being turned from a purely formal into an essentially substantive hurdle if one takes it to mean that the testator must (apparently) have had more than a generic testamentary intention or *animus testandi*—more than a mere awareness that something is being signed and executed *as a will*.

There is a tendency to overcharge section 9(b) by insisting that 'the testator must intend to make *this will* and not another one'.[107] Indeed, at times the formal postulate that the testator must have 'intended by his signature to give effect to the will'[108] is even conflated with the need for him to know and approve the actual content of the document he has signed. Such an amalgamation of section 9 with the so-called doctrine of 'knowledge and approval' is evident in Proudman J's first instance decision. Under the heading 'Conformity with the Wills Act 1837', her Ladyship discussed the well-known crossed wills cases of *Re Hunt*[109] and *Re Meyer*[110] and quoted with express approval Sir James Hannen's statement to the

[100] His Lordship said that he 'saw the force' of insisting on a formally valid instrument in terms of 'academic linguistic logic', but gave five reasons why he thought the point was wrong: ibid at [61]–[67]. One of them was that 'it seems to me to be equally logical, but plainly more consistent with the evident purpose of the amendments made to the law of wills by sections 17 (which contains the new section 9) and 21 of the 1982 [Administration of Justice] Act, to deal with the validity and rectification issues together, at least in a case such as this, where the two issues are so closely related' (at [63]).

[101] ibid [65] and [66] respectively.

[102] Harris (n 11 above) 284.

[103] B Häcker, 'Thy Will Be Done' (2014) 130 *LQR* 360 at 362.

[104] See Learmonth (n 8 above) at 731, giving this example in order to throw doubt on the wide reading of 'clerical error' in s 21(1)(a) of the Administration of Justice Act 1982.

[105] H Cumber and C Kynaston, 'Where There's a Will There's a Way: *Marley v Rawlings*' (2014) 25 *King's Law Journal* 137 at 143 (case study 4).

[106] *cf* the view set out in n 94 above.

[107] See *Marley v Rawlings* (CA) (n 6 above) [29] (Black LJ outlining the defendants' submissions).

[108] See the wording of section 9(b), set out in the text accompanying n 58 above.

[109] *In the Goods of Hunt* (1875) LR 3 P & D 250.

[110] *In the Estate of Meyer* [1908] P 353.

effect that the deceased in *Hunt* 'did not in fact know and approve of any part of the contents of the [signed] paper as her will, for it is quite clear that if she had known of the contents she would not have signed it'.[111] From this, Proudman J concluded that 'section 9(b) of the 1837 Act provides a complete answer to the claim [in *Marley v Rawlings*], namely that the testator did not intend by his signature to give effect to the will which he signed'.[112]

Lord Neuberger in the Supreme Court, by contrast, emphasised that the requirement of knowledge and approval was separate from questions of formality under section 9.[113] He explained that a formally valid will may of course be invalid as a matter of substance.[114] As has variously been pointed out,[115] the current wording of section 9(b) is the product of amendments made in order to dispense with the original need for a will to be signed by the testator 'at the foot or end' thereof,[116] and was thus intended to lower rather than increase or expand formality hurdles.[117] That an instrument can be formally valid and yet be substantively invalid (in part or *in toto*) as far as its content goes is, moreover, evident from the case law on what is commonly termed 'rectification by omission'.[118] Prior to the enactment of section 20 of the Administration of Justice Act 1982, this was the only way in which courts could—in a very broad sense—'rectify' wills, namely by deleting and not admitting to probate passages which the testator had been shown not to know or approve of.[119]

Whether or to what extent the doctrine of 'knowledge and approval' has actually become superfluous in the light of various developments over the past few decades (such as the introduction of a statutory rectification mechanism,[120] the evolution of a more intention-based canon of construction,[121] and the refinement of the rules on testamentary capacity and undue influence) is a question which cannot

[111] *Marley v Rawlings* (Ch) (n 6 above) [19], quoting from *Re Hunt* (n 109 above) 252. Note that Sir James Hannen himself did not specifically advert to the formality requirements of section 9 of the Wills Act 1837 (as then in force).

[112] *Marley v Rawlings* (Ch) (n 6 above) [21].

[113] *Marley v Rawlings* (SC) (n 3 above) [55]–[56], [58], [60].

[114] ibid [55]: 'The fact that it is pretty clear from the provisions which it contains that a will may well face problems in terms of interpretation *or even validity* does not mean that it cannot satisfy the formality requirements' (emphasis added).

[115] See eg *Marley v Rawlings* (CA) (n 6 above) [12]–[15] (Black LJ); Ham (n 12 above) 966–67.

[116] The original section 9 of the Wills Act 1837 required the will to be 'signed at the Foot or End thereof by the Testator; by some other Person in his Presence or by his Direction'. The wording of the section was subsequently supplemented by various detailed provisos introduced through the Wills Act Amendment 1852 (Lord St Leonard's Act), s 1: 'if the signature shall be so placed at or after, or following, or under, or beside, or opposite to the end of the will, that it is apparent on the face of the will that the testator intended to give effect by such his signature to the writing signed as his will'.

[117] The current section 9 was substituted by the Administration of Justice Act 1982, s 17, implementing a recommendation by the Law Reform Committee, *Twenty-Second Report: The Making and Revocation of Wills* (Cmnd 7902, London, 1980) paras 2.7–2.8

[118] On the omission of words from probate, see eg *Parry and Kerridge* (n 35 above) [5-40]–[5-41].

[119] Such an argument was also run—unsuccessfully—in *Marley v Rawlings*: see *Marley v Rawlings* (SC) (n 3 above) [43]–[49].

[120] See Häcker (n 103 above) 362; Ham (n 12 above) 969.

[121] See Section 2 above, especially the text accompanying nn 26–29.

be pursued here.[122] What may be hoped, however, is that when the Law Commission comes to review statutory formality requirements it will bear in mind the dangers of intertwining form and substance and of requiring section 9 to do too much work.[123] The testator's signature—or a signature made on his behalf and by his direction—is no more than the physical manifestation (at the moment still an indispensable physical manifestation)[124] that he had the requisite *animus testandi* and intended to give effect to the wording of the will *as he believed it to be set out in the instrument* (irrespective of whether it was in fact so set out).

This leads us to the second lesson contained in Lord Neuberger's judgment. It relates to his observation that issues of formal validity and rectification may have to be considered together in appropriate cases.[125] Although his Lordship has been criticised for 'over-extend[ing] the scope of rectification' and for potentially 'opening ... the floodgates of litigation',[126] it is submitted that he was exactly right to make this connection *with respect to the testator's intended wording*.[127] As explained above, one of the main roles of rectification operating beside the modern principles of interpretation is to make up for a lack of form where the testator's intended wording has, for some reason, not found its way into the executed instrument, so that there is no 'peg' allowing us to treat his wishes as validly expressed.[128] Recall the example of a whole self-standing passage being inadvertently missed out from a draft prepared by or for the testator on account of some clerical error. Here rectification supplies the words to which the testator—by his signature—intended to give effect, so that the wording as he *believed* it to be becomes congruous with the *actual* physical manifestation of his testamentary intent.

From the foregoing, it will also have become obvious, however, that there has to be some material base for the rectification exercise. A court cannot rectify a nothing, whatever view of section 9(b) of the Wills Act 1837 one chooses to adopt. There needs to be some physical instrument into which any passage which may have been accidentally omitted before a draft was executed can be 'inserted'.

[122] The relationship between testamentary capacity and the doctrine of knowledge and approval is discussed in Penelope Reed's contribution in Ch 7 of this volume. And, as Brian Sloan notes in Ch 8 (text accompanying fn 75), in practice '[m]ost claims of undue influence appear to be accompanied by claims of want of knowledge and approval and testamentary incapacity'.

[123] The 1980 Law Reform Committee seems to have partly succumbed to this danger when it formulated as one of its starting points for the consideration of *formality requirements* the aim 'to prevent the admission to probate of wills which, because they are forged *or for any other reason*, do not represent the true wishes of the testator' (emphasis added): Law Reform Committee, *Twenty-Second Report* (n 117 above) para 2.2.

[124] *cf* the text accompanying nn 133–136 below.

[125] See the text accompanying nn 100–101 above, and especially the quote set out at the end of n 100 above.

[126] Cumber and Kynaston (n 105 above) 142 and 143 respectively. Contrast Goodwin and Granger (n 48 above) 149, maintaining that 'the floodgates argument, as is often the case, does not stand up to scrutiny'.

[127] But see Thomas (n 48 above) 42, who finds Lord Neuberger's argument (that 'there is a logic in dealing with rectification and validity issues together at least in cases where the two issues are closely linked': *cf* end of n 100 above) 'a little incongruous after his argument about the difference in the role of the Court of Probate and Court of Construction'.

[128] See the text accompanying nn 56–66 above.

Section 20 of the Administration of Justice Act 1982 thus surely requires as a minimum that there exists[129] some properly signed and attested document,[130] and that the testator should have had *animus testandi* when the signature was applied.[131] In an extreme (but also highly unlikely) case, this physical instrument may well be a shopping list or arguably even an otherwise blank sheet of paper.[132] Yet what would certainly not be possible under any circumstances is for the testator's missing *signature* to be supplied via rectification. On no reading of Lord Neuberger's judgment does *Marley v Rawlings* introduce anything like a full-blown 'judicial dispensing power'[133] or a 'substantial compliance'[134] doctrine.[135] A general dispensing power, which would allow a court to admit to probate wills failing to meet the formal requirements of section 9 (either before or after rectification), was at one point considered by the Law Reform Committee, but ultimately rejected on account of its uncertain remit and application.[136] If the current Law Commission were to come to a different conclusion and were to recommend the introduction of a judicial power to dispense with the core formalities for executing a will (ie the writing, the testator's signature and its witnessing), then such a step could only be taken by Parliament.

6. Do English Courts Have an Innate Power to Rectify Wills?

This takes us straight to the last question. If *Marley v Rawlings* does not introduce a fully-fledged judicial dispensing power, can we at least infer from the decision that the Supreme Court will in the future look favourably upon an argument that

[129] Or existed, in the case where a will (the contents of which are known) was properly executed and never revoked: *Sugden v Lord St Leonards* (1876) 1 PD 154 (CA).

[130] The physical writing need not necessarily be on paper, of course. In the case of *Hodson v Barnes* (1926) 43 TLR 71, for instance, an eggshell was used for a seaman's will.

[131] Whether or not one would regard this document as a formally valid will prior to rectification would, in some cases at least, depend on one's exact view of s 9.

[132] See the text accompanying nn 102–105 above.

[133] Full-blown dispensing powers exist in various Australian States and in New Zealand, being first introduced in South Australia in 1975. For a detailed discussion see N Peart, 'Testamentary Formalities in Australia and New Zealand' in KCG Reid, MJ de Waal and R Zimmermann (eds), *Comparative Succession Law, vol 1: Testamentary Formalities* (Oxford, Oxford University Press, 2011) 329 at 349–55.

[134] See JH Langbein, 'Substantial Compliance with the Wills Act' (1975) 88 *Harvard Law Review* 489. Comparing the South Australian 'dispensing power' with Queensland's 'substantial compliance' legislation, Langbein later preferred the former, describing it as a 'triumph of law reform', while he regarded the latter as a 'flop' on the basis that courts had treated 'substantial' to mean 'near perfect': JH Langbein, 'Excusing Harmless Errors in the Execution of Wills: A Report on Australia's Tranquil Revolution in Probate Law' (1987) 87 *Columbia Law Review* 1 at 1.

[135] But *cf* Drummond (n 2 above) 360, querying '[w]hether s 20 should *generally* enable a court "to rectify a document which was currently formally invalid into a formally valid will"' (footnote omitted).

[136] Law Reform Committee, *Twenty-Second Report* (n 117 above) paras 2.4–2.6, especially para 2.5: '[T]o attempt to cure the tiny minority of cases where things go wrong in this way might create more problems than it would solve'.

English courts have an innate power to rectify wills, and not merely in the form of 'rectification by omission'?

With regard to the latter,[137] Lord Neuberger's judgment clearly explains why the selective deletion exercise which it entails is, for obvious reasons, haphazard at best.[138] In another passage, however, his Lordship hinted at a more proactive role for probate judges. He suggested that courts should—as a matter of common law[139]—be able to rectify wills in the same way as they can rectify any other instrument if a relevant type of mistake is made out:[140]

> Rectification is a form of relief which involves 'correcting a written instrument which, by a mistake in verbal expression, does not accurately reflect the [parties'] true agreement'[141] ... It is available not only to correct a bilateral or multilateral arrangement, such as a contract, but also a unilateral document, such as a settlement[142] ... However, it has always been assumed that the courts had no such power to rectify a will[143] ... *As at present advised, I would none the less have been minded to hold that it was, as a matter of common law, open to a judge to rectify a will in the same way as any other document: no convincing reason for the absence of such a power has been advanced.* (emphasis added)

His Lordship stopped just short of holding that courts did in fact have such an innate power only because Parliament had in 1982 provided them with the statutory power to rectify wills under section 20. It was therefore 'unnecessary to consider [the] point further',[144] and 'it would be wrong for any court to hold, *at least in the absence of a compelling reason*, that it actually had an inherent power which was wider than that which the legislature conferred' (emphasis added).[145]

This obiter dictum is bound to invite argument in future cases (eg where a rectification claim cannot be fitted under either limb of section 20(1) of the Administration of Justice Act)[146] to the effect that Parliament in 1982 only legislated because it was advised at the time that courts lacked a power to rectify

[137] On which see n 118 above and the accompanying text.

[138] *Marley v Rawlings* (SC) (n 3 above) [43]–[49], especially [48]: 'The appellant's proposed exercise in deletion ... would involve converting what is a simple and beneficial principle of severance into what is almost a word game with haphazard outcomes'.

[139] In the sense of judge-made law, rectification being in origin an equitable (not a common law) remedy.

[140] *Marley v Rawlings* (SC) (n 3 above) [27]–[28]. Indeed, his broad reading of the term 'clerical error' seems to have been partly inspired by this consideration: ibid [76]–[77].

[141] His Lordship here referred to *Agip SpA v Navigazione v Alta Italia (The Nai Genova and The Nai Superba)* [1984] 1 Lloyd's Rep 353 at 359.

[142] His Lordship here referred to *In re Butlin's Settlement Trusts (Butlin v Butlin)* [1976] Ch 251.

[143] His Lordship here referred to *Harter v Harter* (1873) LR 3 P & D 11 (Sir James Hannen) and to *In re Reynette-James (Wightman v Reynette-James)* [1976] 1 WLR 161 (Templeman J). Quotes from these cases are set out in the text accompanying nn 152–153 below.

[144] *Marley v Rawlings* (SC) (n 3 above) [28].

[145] ibid [30].

[146] Or possibly even where a claim is out of time under s 20(2) and the court refuses to grant permission for an extension.

wills,[147] and that Parliament certainly did not thereby mean to restrict any inherent power which may have latently existed all along as a matter of common law. Such a jurisdiction has already been openly asserted in Jersey.[148] Furthermore, as indicated by Lord Neuberger himself, the argument fits very nicely with the Supreme Court's endeavours to put wills on a par with other instruments, such as commercial contracts and voluntary settlement deeds. If courts are to adopt the same approach to their interpretation, at least as a starting point,[149] why not also apply the same principles of rectification?[150]

Yet it is not all that simple. Although the Law Reform Committee in its 1973 Report tried to discredit the explanation provided by some nineteenth-century cases for why the equitable doctrine of rectification did not apply to wills,[151] there is in fact considerable force in what, for instance, Sir James Hannen said in 1873: 'I think it is not in the power of the Court to supply words accidentally omitted from a will. The Wills Act ... admits of no qualification'.[152] Or, as Templeman J put it roughly a century later:[153]

> Any document other than a will could be rectified by inserting the words which the secretary omitted, but in this respect the court is enslaved by the Wills Act 1834 [*sic*]. Words may be struck out but no fresh words may be inserted: see *In the Goods of Louis Schott* [1901] P. 190 and *In re Horrocks, Taylor v. Kershaw* [1939] P. 198, where Sir Wilfrid Greene M.R. delivering the judgment of the Court of Appeal said, at p. 216: 'The jurisdiction, where it exists, is admittedly confined to the exclusion of words and does not extend to the insertion of words, since the insertion of words would run counter to the provisions of the Wills Act.'

In an 1865 case concerning the will of a certain Peter Birks, Sir JP Wilde in the High Court of Admiralty had already observed:[154]

> The evidence in this case discloses that a blunder has been made, the effect of which is that certain portions of the intentions of the testator were not expressed in the paper which he last executed ... The question is, whether this blunder is one which it is within

[147] The absence of a judicial power to rectify wills was noted—with regret—by the Law Reform Committee, *Nineteenth Report* (n 29 above) paras 9–10: 'As the law stands, it is generally accepted that the equitable doctrine of rectification does not apply to wills ... It is not easy to perceive why ... In the end, we have been unable to discover any satisfactory reason for holding that the doctrine of rectification should not apply to wills'.

[148] *In Re Vautier (neé McBoyle)* [2000] JLR 351 (Royal Court), drawing on Canadian precedents.

[149] See Section 2 above, especially the text accompanying nn 21–25.

[150] Unfortunately, Lord Neuberger's observations (set out in the text accompanying n 140 above) fail to make sufficiently clear that there are actually significant differences between the principles governing rectification of bi- or multilateral bargain transactions, such as commercial contracts, and those governing the rectification of unilateral gratuitous transactions, such as voluntary settlements: see Häcker (n 84 above) 294–304. It is submitted that *if* the analogy is to be pursued further, the rectification of wills should follow the guidance of the latter.

[151] Law Reform Committee, *Nineteenth Report* (n 29 above) para 10, referring inter alia to the passage set out in the text accompanying n 182 below.

[152] *Harter v Harter* (n 143 above) 19.

[153] *In re Reynette-James* (n 143 above) 166.

[154] *Birks v Birks* (1865) 4 Sw & Tr 23 at 30, 164 ER 1423 at 1426.

the power of the Court to set right,[155] as the Court would, no doubt, desire to set it right if it has the power. I quite admit that it is beyond the power of the Court to interpolate anything in a will, or to supply an omission by parol evidence, for, by so doing, it would give the force of a testamentary act to parol evidence, contrary to the statute.

Interestingly, if one goes back to the time when the Wills Act 1837 was passed, one finds that probate courts *did* have a power to rectify wills (in certain situations)[156] before the statute came into force, and that they regularly used it.[157] In the late-eighteenth-century case of *Blackwood v Damer*, for example, the testator had written to his attorney with instructions for a will. The attorney, by a 'mere casual omission', forgot to insert the desired residuary clause when preparing the draft later executed. The High Court of Delegates nevertheless decreed that 'the residuary clause should stand as part of the will'.[158] In *Bayldon v Bayldon*, it appeared from the evidence that the testator had intended to leave a legacy of £5,000 to his nephew, but that[159]

this aged testator, in fair copying a draft will, occupying many sheets of paper, … omitted the legacy in question (an omission, too, occurring where and as it does, in a series of consecutive legacies to eleven persons, several of the same sir-name), casually and by accident …

Sir John Nicholl said that where it was proved that there was 'some casual error in the body of the will',[160]

the Court is at liberty, and is even bound, to pronounce for the will, not in its actual state, but with such error first reformed or corrected (either by the insertion, that is, of

[155] This language may, incidentally, have inspired Sir James Hannen in the crossed wills case of *Re Hunt* (n 109 above) to state famously (at 252): 'I regret the blunder, but I cannot repair it'. Note that Sir JP Wilde in the circumstances of *Birks v Birks* did eventually find a way of repairing the blunder. He held (at 4 Sw & Tr 31, 164 ER 1426) that since there was an earlier document ('paper A') which had been properly executed as a will and contained the passages that were missing in the final instrument ('paper B'), it was possible to read both together as containing Peter Birks' last will and testament: '[I]t would be monstrous for the Court to come to the conclusion that the testator intended to revoke those portions of paper A which were omitted from paper B by accident. Looking at all the circumstances, and the total absence of any language in paper B tending to revoke paper A, I think that paper A is still alive as far as is not inconsistent with paper B'.

[156] See the text accompanying and following n 171 below.

[157] Beside the examples listed in the text which follows, see also *Travers v Miller* (1826) 3 Add 226, 162 ER 462; rev'd *sub nom Miller v Travers* (1832) 8 Bing 224, 131 ER 395. Rectification was also acknowledged to be available in principle (subject to there being an 'ambiguity upon the face of the instrument', casting doubt on the *factum*: *cf* n 161 below), but ultimately denied on the facts of *Fawcett v Jones and Codrington* (1810) 3 Phil Ecc 434, 161 ER 1375; *Harrison v Stone* (1829) 2 Hag Ecc 537, 162 ER 949; *Shadbolt v Waugh* (1831) 3 Hag Ecc 570, 162 ER 1267.

[158] *Blackwood v Damer* (1783) 2 Add 239, 162 ER 467 (note attached to the case of *Bayldon v Bayldon*, cited in n 159 immediately below). *Blackwood v Damer* is also discussed at some length *sub nom Damer v Janssen* before and by the Prerogative Court of Canterbury in *Fawcett v Jones and Codrington* (n 157 above).

[159] *Bayldon v Bayldon* (1826) 3 Add 232 at 236–37, 162 ER 464 at 466 (Prerogative Court of Canterbury).

[160] ibid at 238. Sir John Nicholl suggested that, in order for the accidental omission or insertion to be pleaded and proved in evidence, there had to be 'some absurdity or ambiguity on the face of the will' (ibid), but that was later refuted: see n 161 immediately below.

something omitted, or by the omission of something inserted, or as the case may be, in the will, contrary to the true mind and intention of the testator) …

Shortly before the Wills Act 1837 was passed, the Prerogative Court of Canterbury came to decide *Castell v Tagg*, another case where it was alleged that a legacy had been inadvertently omitted from the executed copy of a will. Sir Herbert Jenner held 'that this is an allegation which ought to be admitted, and, if proved [as it subsequently was], that it will be sufficient to justify the Court in supplying the deficiency shewn in this will'.[161]

All this changed with the enactment of section 9. According to Edward Vaughan Williams, whose seminal *Treatise on the Law of Executors and Administrators* was at the time just between its second and third edition,[162] it was completely obvious that the statute had taken away the judges' ability to rectify wills:[163]

[W]ith respect to wills made on or after January 1, 1838, it is plain that, by reason of the provisions of the stat. 1 Vict. c. 26 [Wills Act 1837], the whole of every testamentary disposition must be in writing, and signed and attested pursuant to the Act: Whence it follows, that the Court has no power to correct omissions or mistakes by reference to the instructions in any case to which the statute extends.

The point is essentially one about the separation of powers. If Parliament says that 'no will shall be valid' unless it complies with a specified form,[164] meaning that only that which is expressed in the prescribed form may be admitted to probate and enforced, then to rectify the instrument so as to make it contain words which were not there (albeit that the testator intended them to be there) would be to confer judicial validity on testamentary dispositions failing to meet the correct form. This problem does not exist with most[165] other instruments that courts routinely rectify. Where the parties to a commercial contract, for example, have decided to put their agreement in writing, judicial rectification of the instrument purporting to contain their agreement amounts to no more than the court overriding a *self-imposed* formality requirement (on the basis that there is some problem with an express of implied entire agreement clause).[166] Nor do courts challenge Parliamentary supremacy where they rectify voluntary settlements which happen to

[161] *Castell v Tagg* (1936) 1 Curt 298 at 302, 163 ER 102 at 103. In so holding, Sir Herbert Jenner also disposed of the—supposed—requirement that there had to be some 'ambiguity on the face of the instrument' before a court could rectify the will. He said that the omission of the residuary clause in *Blackwood v Damer* (n 158 above) 'must be considered a deficiency, but no ambiguity', and that the forgotten legacy in *Bayldon v Bayldon* (n 159 above) 'was an omission, not an ambiguity'.

[162] Although the second edition was published early in 1838, it could not yet take account of the Wills Act 1837, since—as the preface states—'the greater part of [it] was printed before the passing of the … statute': EV Williams, *A Treatise on the Law of Executors and Administrators*, 2rd edn (London, Saunders and Benning, 1838) vol 1, vii (hereinafter '*Williams on Executors*, 2nd edn').

[163] EV Williams, *A Treatise on the Law of Executors and Administrators*, 3rd edn (London, Saunders and Benning, 1841) vol 1, 269 (hereinafter '*Williams on Executors*, 3rd edn').

[164] See the wording of s 9 of the Wills Act 1837, set out in the text accompanying n 58 above.

[165] Contracts for the sale of land and subsequent conveyances (where formalities are also an issue) are discussed in Section 6.2 below.

[166] For a more detailed exposition of this argument see Häcker (n 84 above) 318–20.

have been made by deed, if the relevant trust could just as well have been constituted informally.

There are two conceivable objections to the view advanced and defended here. They might be used to support an argument to the effect that the formalities introduced by the Wills Act *cannot in fact* justify the courts' abdication of their former power to rectify wills, whatever judges and commentators may have thought or said before *Marley v Rawlings*. It will be convenient to deal with them before concluding.

6.1. Rectification and Formalities Pre-1838

The first objection is that there were formality requirements for wills even before January 1838, namely at least since the Statute of Frauds 1677.[167] The Wills Act 1837 merely harmonised these after a Royal Commission had found that there were altogether 'ten different laws for regulating the execution of Wills under different circumstances'.[168] Broadly speaking, wills or testaments of personal property had to be in writing plain and simple,[169] while devises of real property had to be written, signed, witnessed and attested.[170] Yet far from undermining the argument made here, the pre-1838 law positively supports it on closer inspection. Leaving aside the additional complications caused by the division of competences between the ecclesiastical courts and the royal jurisdiction (especially that exercised by the common law courts),[171] it actually explains why judges in the early nineteenth century would insist that rectification was only possible where the testator's instructions related to personalty *and* where they had been committed to writing during his lifetime.

In *Rockell v Youde*, for instance, there was only oral evidence about some of the wishes regarding his personal estate which the testator had communicated to the

[167] With respect to realty, formalities had already been laid down in the Statute of Wills 1540 (32 Hen VIII, c 1) (see end of n 183 below).

[168] Real Property Commissioners, *Fourth Report Made to His Majesty by the Commissioners Appointed to Inquire Into the Law of England Respecting Real Property* (London, 1833) 12. R Kerridge, 'Testamentary Formalities in England and Wales' in KCG Reid, MJ de Waal and R Zimmermann (eds), *Comparative Succession Law, vol 1: Testamentary Formalities* (Oxford, Oxford University Press, 2011) 305 at 311 (fn 27), notes that if one takes deathbed wills into account, that number actually rises to eleven.

[169] Exceptionally, oral (nuncupative) wills were valid where the testator's personal estate was worth less than £30, in the case of deathbed wills, or if the testator was eligible to make a so-called 'soldier's will': see Statute of Frauds 1677 (29 Car II, c 3), ss 19–20 and 23.

[170] See Statute of Frauds 1677, s 5.

[171] Until the Court of Probate Act 1857, the ecclesiastical courts were responsible for the grant of probate and of letters of administration, which—at the time—related only to the testator's personal property. The subsequent interpretation of the will was for the most part left to the Court of Chancery (as a 'court of construction'). Devises of realty, by contrast, led to a direct transfer between the testator and the devisee and were under the jurisdiction of the common law courts, supplemented by Chancery. It was not until the Land Transfer Act 1897 that the testator's personal representative truly became his universal successor, through the estate administration mechanism being extended to realty.

solicitor before dying, while others had been taken down in writing. Although the solicitor had a 'perfect recollection' as to what the oral instructions were, Sir John Nicholl in the Prerogative Court of Canterbury held that to admit the claim 'would be to establish a precedent contrary to all the rules which have governed this Court subsequent to the passing of the Statute of Frauds',[172] justifying the decision as follows:[173]

> The Court has gone the greatest possible length when it has pronounced for instructions which have been reduced into writing during the lifetime of the deceased; but which have not been read over to him. The Court has always stopped short where the instrument has not been reduced into writing till after the death; and I cannot agree in the construction attempted to be put on the Statute of Frauds that this would be a will by word of mouth.[174] The Court is always anxious to carry into effect the intentions of a party; *but it must be when those intentions are shewn in a legal form*; it cannot act upon conjectures of its own. (emphasis added)

As the first edition of William's *Treatise*, published in 1832, explains:[175]

> Though the instrument be written in another man's hand, and has never been signed by the testator, yet in many cases it will operate as a good testament of personal estate.[176] Thus, if a person gives instructions for a will, and dies before the instrument can be formally executed, the instructions, though neither reduced into writing in his presence, nor ever read to him, will operate as fully as a will itself.[177] ... It is, however, essential that the instructions should be reduced into writing in the life time of the deceased; otherwise it would be a mere nuncupative will, and then of no effect under the statute.[178]

[172] *Rockell v Youde* (1819) 3 Phil Ecc 141 at 144, 161 ER 1281 at 1282.

[173] ibid 145. See also *Harrison v Stone* (n 157 above) 552, where Sir John Nicholl observed: 'Here is no written document suggested to be forthcoming which can in any degree lay a foundation for, and corroborate, the existence of any error. No fair copy, containing the words struck through, was engrossed for execution; no cotemporaneous evidence of that sort on which the Court can rely can be furnished. In *Blackwood* against *Damer* ([n 158 above]) the Court had evidence of that description: but still what it most relied upon were the written instructions. So again, in *Bayldon* against *Bayldon* ([n 159 above]), there were the instructions: the very draft of the will, in Baron Wood's own handwriting, had the names of the parties who were to be benefited. But upon mere parol declarations, without any thing in writing, after such a length of time, to hold that the words in the executed instrument were "erroneously and incautiously struck through;" and for the Court to reinstate them would be a most dangerous precedent'.

[174] It had apparently been argued that the testator had made an oral deathbed will which might have been valid under ss 19–20 of the Statute of Frauds: *cf* n 169 above.

[175] EV Williams, *A Treatise on the Law of Executors and Administrators*, vol 1 (London, Saunders and Benning, 1832) 51 (hereinafter '*Williams on Executors*, 1st edn'). The passage is preserved in *Williams on Executors*, 2nd edn (n 162 above) 54–55.

[176] Reference to T Wentworth, *The Office and Duty of Executors*, 14th edn (London, J & WT Clarke, 1829) 15.

[177] Reference to a plethora of cases, including *Wood v Wood* (1811) 161 ER 110, 1 Phil Ecc 357; *Huntington v Huntington* (1814) 2 Phil Ecc 213, 1616 ER 1123; *Sikes v Snaith* (1816) 2 Phil Ecc 351, 161 ER 1167; *Lewis v Lewis* (1818) 3 Phil Ecc 109, 161 ER 1272.

[178] Reference to *Sikes v Snaith* (n 177 above) 355 and *Rockell v Youde* (discussed in the text accompanying nn 172–173 above). Williams proceeds to illustrate this proposition by discussing at some length the case of *Nathan v Morse* (1821) 3 Phil Ecc 529, 161 ER 1405.

With regard to rectification, Williams consequently writes that[179]

> although it appears from [cases like *Blackwood v Damer*[180]] that … casual omissions in a will may be supplied by the instructions given for such will, yet it is clearly necessary that those instructions should have been reduced into writing in the lifetime of the testator: otherwise they cannot, by reason of the Statute of Frauds, under any circumstances, even of the plainest mistake, be admitted to probate as part of the will.[[181]]

A case dealing with real property is *Earl of Newburgh v Countess Dowager of Newburgh*, where the late Earl of Newburgh wanted to leave to his wife a life estate in his Sussex and Gloucestershire estates, but by a transcription error only the Sussex estate was included in the fair copy of the will. Before the will was executed, the solicitor attending the Earl read it over to him, but from the *original* abstract which included references to both estates. It was thus indisputable that the testator believed to be signing his name to (additional) words which were not in the instrument, though they had at one point been committed to writing. Sir John Leach VC nevertheless found that, realty being involved, 'the Court had no authority to correct the will according to the intention':[182]

> To assume such a jurisdiction would, in effect, be to repeal the Statute of Frauds in all cases where a devisor failed to comply with the statute by mistake or accident, and to operate this repeal, by admitting parol evidence of the intention of the devisor, which it was the very object of the statute to avoid …

He added that 'the difficulty was not that the will was a voluntary instrument, but that there could be no will without the forms of the Statute of Frauds, and the disappointed intention had not those forms'.[183]

In *Miller v Travers*, the testator in his will as executed left 'all his freehold and real estates whatsoever, situate in the county of Limerick, and in the city of Limerick' to certain trustees. Although he had a small estate in the city of Limerick, he owned nothing in county Limerick. The claimant alleged that the testator had meant his considerable real estate in the county of Clare and wanted to prove in evidence that the original draft referred properly to Clare county, but that, in making certain requested alterations to the will, the conveyancer mistakenly struck this out

179 *Williams on Executors*, 1st edn (n 175 above) 203–04; 2nd edn (n 162 above) 225.

180 See the text accompanying n 158 above.

181 Reference to *Rockell v Youde* (discussed in the text accompanying nn 172–173 above) and to the passage set out in the text accompanying n 175 above.

182 *Earl of Newburgh v Countess Dowager of Newburgh* (1820) 5 Madd 364 at 365–66, 56 ER 934 at 935. The decision was apparently affirmed by the House of Lords on 16 June 1825, but the only evidence we have for this is indirect: see *Miller v Travers* (n 157 above) 254–55. The report about the original proceedings only speaks of a later rehearing before the Vice-Chancellor, where the parties purported to change the allegations of fact, but the Court refused to entertain new evidence.

183 ibid 366. *cf* already *Towers v Moore* (1689) 2 Vern 98, 23 ER 673: 'Devise of land not to be explained by parol proof touching the declaration of the testator, or the instructions given by testator for the making his will' because '[d]evises concerning land must be in writing, and we cannot go against the act of parliament'. It is possible that the relevant devise in *Towers v Moor* dated from pre-1677. It would then have been governed by the Statute of Wills 1540, which required only simple writing.

and made unauthorised changes to the wording, which the testator subsequently failed to notice. Tindal CJ said:[184]

> [I]t may be taken, for the purpose of the argument, that if parol evidence was admissible by law, the evidence tendered in this case would be sufficient to establish, beyond contradiction, the intention of the testator to have been to include his estates in Clare in the devise to the trustees. Upon the fullest consideration, however, it appears to the Lord Chief Baron and myself, that admitting it may be shewn from the description of the property in the city of Limerick, that some mistake may have arisen, yet, still, as the devise in question has a certain operation and effect, namely, the effect of passing the estate in the city of Limerick, and as the intention of the testator to devise any estate in the county of Clare cannot be collected from the will itself, nor *without altering or adding to the words used in the will*, such intention cannot be supplied by the evidence proposed to be given. (emphasis added)

6.2. Comparison with Rectification of Contracts for the Sale of Land

The other possible objection to the argument advanced here against an innate judicial power to rectify wills is one which the Law Reform Committee had placed great weight on: '[I]n the case of other documents the doctrine of rectification applies even though statute requires them to be in a particular form, for example, under seal'.[185] It is impossible within the confines of the present chapter to subject this argument to a full scrutiny comprising instruments as varied as marriage settlements,[186] trusts of land,[187] dispositions of equitable interests,[188] and conveyances of all sorts, but it is worth following up the example of contracts for the sale of land, to which Lord Neuberger in *Marley v Rawlings* specifically referred.[189] Ever since the Statute of Frauds, such contracts have had to be written or at any rate evidenced in writing and signed by (or on behalf of) the parties,[190] and yet courts routinely rectify such contracts.[191]

[184] *Miller v Travers* (1832) 8 Bing 244 at 247, 131 ER 395 at 396.

[185] Law Reform Committee, *Nineteenth Report* (n 29 above) para 10, adding that 'evidence of what words a will was intended to contain may fall far short of general evidence of the testator's dispositive intention'. Against the concern that 'the testator may have read his will in the actual form and have been satisfied with it', the Law Reform Committee pointed out that 'similar contentions can be advanced in the case of other instruments, and however potent they might be as an argument for resisting rectification, there seems to be no ground for saying that they would exclude the jurisdiction to rectify'.

[186] There appears to have been an equitable jurisdiction to rectify marriage settlements in order to make them conform with the parties' intentions, despite the formalities imposed by the Statute of Frauds 1677: C MacMillan, *Mistakes in Contract Law* (Oxford, Hart Publishing, 2010) 46.

[187] See Law of Property Act 1925, s 53(1)(b).

[188] See Law of Property Act 1925, s 53(1)(c).

[189] *Marley v Rawlings* (SC) (n 3 above) [67].

[190] See Statute of Frauds 1677, s 4; Law of Property Act 1925, s 40; Law of Property (Miscellaneous Provisions) Act 1989, s 2. Starting out as a mere evidentiary requirement, the stipulation as to form has now become a condition of substantive validity: see the text accompanying nn 203–207 below.

[191] See eg *Joscelyne v Nissen* [1970] 2 QB 86 (CA); *Domb v Izoz* [1980] Ch 548 (CA).

There are two answers to this objection. First, it is by no means obvious that the line of cases on the sale of land is to be preferred to the old case law on wills. Judicial rectification of contracts for the sale of land and subsequent deeds of conveyance was, it seems, not finally recognised or beyond dispute until the 1923 decision by the Court of Appeal in *Craddock Brothers v Hunt*.[192] Prior to that case, courts often either refused to rectify such documents on the basis that to do so would infringe the Statute of Frauds 1677,[193] or alternatively they found ways around the Statute, such as by saying that it had not been pleaded, that it may not be used as an instrument of fraud, or by invoking the doctrine of part performance.[194] In particular, a number of judges had gratefully adopted an argument first made by Sir Edward Fry[195] and suggested that rectification in such circumstances had *become* possible through the procedural merger of law and equity in the Judicature Act 1873.[196]

Craddock Brothers v Hunt concerned two plots of land which at one point belonged to the same person. He had fenced them off in such a way that a part of one plot was occupied by a newly erected house, while the remainder of that plot and the whole of the second plot were given over to a yard. After the owner's death, his personal representatives sold the house and the yard to different purchasers, without anyone realising that the relevant contracts of sale and deeds of conveyance still referred to the measurements of the old plots. When the error came to light, a dispute arose between the claimant purchasers of the yard and the defendant who had bought the house, about the part of the yard which lay on the plot with the house. Given the state of authorities, it is not surprising that the Court of Appeal was divided on the question of whether rectification could be granted in favour of the claimants. Lord Sterndale MR and Warrington LJ held that it could, the former saying:[197]

[192] *Craddock Brothers v Hunt* [1923] 2 Ch 136 (CA), soon afterwards approved in *United States of America v Motor Trucks Ltd* [1924] AC 196 (PC).

[193] See eg *May v Platt* [1900] 1 Ch 616 at 621–63 (Farwell J); *Thompson v Hickman* [1907] 1 Ch 550 at 561–62 (though Neville J there adopted a more cautious approach); *cf* also *Woollam v Hearn* (1802) 7 Ves Jun 211 at 219–21, 32 ER 86 at 89–90 (Sir William Grant MR), and *Davies v Fitton* (1842) 2 D & War 225 at 232 (Sir Edward Sugden, later Lord St Leonards), both cases concerning leases of land.

[194] See eg *In re Boulter* (1876) 4 Ch D 241 (Bacon CJ); *Olley v Fisher* (1886) 34 Ch D 367 (North J); *Craddock Brothers v Hunt* [1922] 2 Ch 809 at 823 (PO Lawrence J); *cf* also *Garrard v Frankel* (1862) 30 Beav 445 at 457–59, 54 ER 961 at 966–67, and *Harris v Pepperell* (1867) LR 5 Eq 1, where Sir John (Lord) Romilly allowed rectification, but gave the opposing party an option to annul the contract.

[195] E Fry, *A Treatise on the Specific Performance of Contracts*, 2nd edn (London, Stevens & Sons, 1881) 346–55, especially § 779 and § 799. For a fuller account of Fry's influence see MacMillan (n 186 above) 54–60, 248–49.

[196] Supreme Court of Judicature Act 1873, s 24(7), invoked by *Olley v Fisher* (n 194 above) 369–70 (North J saying that: 'under [s 24(7)], the Court can now have no difficulty in entertaining an action for the reformation of a contract and for the specific performance of the reformed contract in every case in which the *Statute of Frauds* does not create a bar') and at first instance in *Craddock Brothers v Hunt* (n 194 above) 821–22. *Shrewsbury and Talbot Cab and Noiseless Tyre Co Ltd v Shaw* (1890) 89 *Law Times Journal* 274 is also often cited in this context, but note that the case actually concerned an agreement to purchase patents, where no statutory form was prescribed.

[197] *Craddock Brothers v Hunt* (CA) (n 192 above) 151–52, Warrington LJ agreeing (at 160).

> I think I am at liberty, at any rate since the Judicature Act, 1873, to express my opinion that rectification can be granted of a written agreement on parol evidence of mutual mistake, although that agreement is complete in itself, and has been carried out by a more formal document based upon it. I think the contrary view is based upon an insufficient consideration of the result of rectification. *After rectification the written agreement does not continue to exist with a parol variation; it is to be read as if it had been originally drawn in its rectified form,*[198] and it is that written document, and that alone, of which specific performance is decreed. (emphasis added)

There was, however, a strong dissent by Younger LJ, who observed that '[t]here can … be little doubt … that here we have in substance an attempt by the plaintiffs to obtain what in effect is specific performance of a written agreement with a parol variation'[199] and held that 'you can have no specific performance with a parol variation if thereby the Statute of Frauds would be infringed'.[200] His fundamental concern was the following:[201]

> [O]n principle, it seems to me to be necessary, if the statute is not pro tanto to be repealed altogether, that no defendant shall be required to convey land to a plaintiff under agreement unless there is a signed note or memorandum of that agreement forthcoming or unless the statute on the ground of part performance[202] or by reason of countervailing fraud or otherwise is inapplicable.

But even accepting that rectification of contracts for the sale of land is possible (and has been since at least 1873 or 1923), there is another reason why modern judges should shy away from asserting an innate power to rectify wills. This second answer to the argument based on the analogy between the two types of instruments is connected with the above-mentioned equitable doctrine of part performance. Part performance allowed courts to dispense with formalities[203] precisely—and only—because the Statute of Frauds, and later section 40 of the Law of Property Act 1925, provided that contracts for the sale of land which were not evidenced in writing were generally *unenforceable*.[204] They were not irredeemably void. By contrast, section 9 of the Wills Act 1837 has always treated

[198] Reference to *Johnson v Bragge* [1901] 1 Ch 28 (Ch) 37, a marriage settlement case decided by Cozens-Hardy J.

[199] *Craddock Brothers v Hunt* (CA) (n 192 above) 166.

[200] ibid 167.

[201] ibid 167–68. In support of this proposition, his Lordship cited with approval passages from the US case of *Glass v Hulbert* 102 Mass 24 at 35 (1869).

[202] See *Craddock Brothers v Hunt* (CA) (n 192 above) 169–70, where Younger LJ explained why he thought that there had been no part performance in the present case.

[203] The doctrine of part performance is not uncontentious in its origin and has variously been described as an act of 'judicial legislation'. It can be traced back to the decision of Jeffreys LC in *Butcher v Stapely* (1685) 1 Vern 363, 23 ER 524, ordering specific performance of a partly performed contract.

[204] The Statute of Frauds 1677, s 4, stipulated that '*no action shall be brought* … upon any Contract or Sale of Lands … unless the Agreement upon which such Action shall be brought, or some Memorandum or Note thereof, shall be in Writing, and signed by the Party to be charged therewith …' (emphasis added). The Law of Property Act 1925, s 40(1) was worded in similar terms, with s 40(2) expressly preserving the doctrine of part performance.

compliance with the prescribed formalities as an essential condition of *validity*.[205] Under these circumstances, no-one but Parliament is competent to dispense with them—neither private parties by their conduct, nor courts in the exercise of their inherent equitable jurisdiction.

Nowadays, of course, the doctrine of part performance is abrogated in respect of land, following a recommendation by the Law Commission.[206] A contract for the sale of land which does not incorporate all the agreed terms in the written form stipulated by section 2 of the Law of Property (Miscellaneous Provisions) Act 1989 is null and void.[207] It is therefore just worth highlighting that section 2(4) expressly envisages or preserves the possibility of rectification[208] and in this way gives legislative blessing to a judicial practice which could otherwise not be sustained.[209] For the very same reason, there can be no judicial power to rectify wills outside the statutory limits set by the Administration of Justice Act 1982.

7. The Way Forward

When the Law Commission comes to review the law of wills,[210] it has the unique opportunity to consider contemporaneously several key areas of testate succession law, among them two 'sides' of the 'magic triangle' outlined in the introduction.[211] It will form a view as to whether the formality requirements currently enshrined in section 9 of the Wills Act 1837 are still suited to fulfil their function,[212] and it

[205] 'No will shall be valid unless...'. Note that the Statute of Frauds 1677 had already contained similar wording in s 5, which declared devises of land to be 'utterly void and of none Effect' if they failed to comply with the stipulated formalities, *cf* the text accompanying n 170 above.

[206] See Law Commission, *Transfer of Land: Formalities for Contracts for Sale etc. of Land* (Law Com No 164, 1987) paras 4.13 and 6.4.

[207] Section 2(1) provides: 'A contract for the sale or other disposition of an interest in land *can only be made* in writing and only by incorporating all the terms which the parties have expressly agreed in one document or, where contracts are exchanged, in each' (emphasis added).

[208] Section 2(4) provides: 'Where a contract for the sale or other disposition of an interest in land satisfies the conditions of this section *by reason only of the rectification of one or more documents in pursuance of an order of a court*, the contract shall come into being, or be deemed to have come into being, at such time as may be specified in the order' (emphasis added). See also the recommendation by the Law Commission, *Transfer of Land* (n 206 above) para 5.6.

[209] But which it was crucial to maintain, given that the *entire contract* now fails if only one of the agreed terms is not properly recorded. Rectification therefore completes the contract and, in doing so, ensures its compliance with formalities. Yet note that rectification is not possible where the parties have deliberately decided not to record all of the agreed terms, even if they were under a misapprehension about the legal effect of the resulting document: *Oun v Ahmad* [2008] EWHC 545 (Ch).

[210] See n 13 above and the accompanying text.

[211] See the text following n 2 above.

[212] Kerridge (n 168 above) 327 has forcefully argued that their stringency is not the real problem: 'what troubles the present writer, more than the way in which some wills are refused probate because they do not comply with the strict formality rules, is that it is quite possible for a will to obtain probate in England when it ought to be clear to everyone that there are grave doubts as to whether it represents the freely expressed wishes of a competent and independent testator'.

may wish to think again about introducing a dispensing power modelled on the Australian paradigm.[213] It will also have a chance to scrutinise how the statutory power to rectify wills has fared since its introduction in 1982. However, in doing these things, it is essential that the Commission pay attention to the *interaction* between the various provisions and doctrines pertaining to testamentary matters. This is why it is a pity that the Commission's remit does not extend to the interpretation of wills. It would be helpful to know, for example, how the modern 'contextual' approach to construction and section 21 of the Administration of Justice Act 1982 sit with the statutory rules of construction in sections 24–33 of the Wills Act 1837, which apply 'unless a contrary intention shall appear *by the will*' (emphasis added).[214]

If the argument made here is correct, then the main role of rectification today is to supply missing formalities where the testator's words have not found their way into the executed instrument. Given the modern canon of construction and the possibility of admitting extrinsic evidence under section 21 of the Administration of Justice Act 1982, section 20 has little or no role to play when it comes to endowing the testator's words with the meaning he intended them to bear. 'Library' can sometimes mean 'wine cellar'—rectification does not come into it. All depends on the testator's habitual use of language. It is only when the provision about the 'library' or 'wine cellar' goes missing in the drafting process, or when the draftsman fails properly to understand the testator's instructions and as a result writes 'books' or designates X rather than Y as the recipient, that rectification is the appropriate remedy (under section 20(1)(a) or (b) respectively).

A lesson to learn from the Supreme Court's decision in *Marley v Rawlings*, however, is that the current confines of section 20 of the Administration of Justice Act 1982 ought to be carefully reviewed and clarified. There is otherwise a risk of future courts trespassing on Parliamentary terrain by invoking a (supposedly) innate judicial power to rectify wills, although no such power could have survived the coming into force of the Wills Act 1837.

What, therefore, should be done about section 20? Section 20(1)(a) in particular may need broadening. The point would have become more obvious if—instead of effectively leaving open the proper interpretation of section 9(b) of the Wills Act 1837—Lord Neuberger had been more explicit in explaining how rectification operates as a process of 'welding together' a formally valid instrument which is (in part or *in toto*) substantively invalid or at any rate incomplete, with the wording actually intended by the testator and supported by his *animus testandi*, but hitherto not couched in the correct form. Looked at in this light, rectification ought to be available whenever the testator believed the document he was signing to contain additional or different words from those which were actually there. In order to reduce the risk of such a scenario being falsely alleged, it may be prudent

[213] See n 133 above and the accompanying text.

[214] The Law Reform Committee's *Nineteenth Report* (n 29 above) makes only a passing footnote reference to s 24 (at para 3, fn 2) and does not otherwise address the question. There is a brief discussion in *Parry and Kerridge* (n 35 above) [10-57]–[10-58], arguing that '[t]he conflict between the sections in the Wills Act and section 21 is more apparent than real'.

to insist on a clerical error or the like (more generally: some objective circumstance lending extra plausibility to the allegation) being established in evidence. Yet there seems to be no good reason for refusing rectification where, for example, it is proved that the draftsman has deliberately altered the testator's desired wording without alerting him to this change.[215]

It *could* similarly be argued with respect to section 20(1)(b) that rectification should be made available where the draftsman correctly understood the testator's instructions, but then proceeded deliberately to mis-implement them.[216] There are examples of broader rectification provisions capable of encompassing such cases in other common law jurisdictions,[217] some even coupled with a dispensing power as regards the testator's signature.[218] However, a word of caution is apposite. Section 20(1)(b) is potentially a gateway for executors and draftsmen having a second bite at the estate planning cherry, unless the requirement of a 'failure to understand [the testator's] instructions' is kept in close check.[219] At the moment, it is just about possible to rationalise section 20(1)(b) by analogy with section 20(1)(a),[220] but if the requirement of a failure to understand instructions were dropped, without it being made clear at the same time that rectification is primarily about the *words* or the *terms* that the testator intends his will to contain (and not about his motives for including them or the ultimate aims behind his dispositions), then that would open the floodgates for a whole deluge of unwarranted rectification claims.

The language of a will 'fail[ing] to carry out the testator's intentions' and it being 'rectified so as to carry out his intentions' is apt to (mis)lead one into thinking about rectification as bringing the testator's underlying wishes to fruition and achieving his ultimate goals. Outside the wills context, we are already witnessing a broadening along these lines.[221] It is most notable in the Canadian jurisprudence following the landmark Ontario case of *Juliar*,[222] where it was held that the

[215] To cater for this (admittedly rather unrealistic) scenario, the 'vicarious mistake' explanation of rectification operating where documents have been prepared by a draftsman (see n 84 above) would have to be adjusted as follows: *if* the draftsman made a mistake when preparing the will, then rectification should only be granted where the mistake is one which would warrant rectification had the will been the draftsman's own.

[216] See also Learmonth (n 8 above) 731, describing the current legal position with its insistence on a mistake as 'rather anomalous'. Note that the case posited here differs from the one discussed in the text accompanying n 82 above in that the draftsman there *thinks* he is implementing the testator's instructions correctly and is merely mis-judging the legal consequences of his chosen words.

[217] See eg Wills Act 1997 (Victoria), s 31(1); Wills Amendment Act 2007 (Western Australia), s 50(1); Wills and Succession Act 2010 (Alberta), s 39(1). These provisions make rectification depend on a clerical error *or* the will simply not giving effect to the testator's instructions, for whatever reason.

[218] See eg Wills and Succession Act 2010 (Alberta), s 39(2).

[219] *cf* the discussion in n 81 above of the case where the draftsman fails to clarify the testator's instructions.

[220] As attempted in the text following n 79 above.

[221] Often going hand-in-hand with a concomitant encroachment on the area properly occupied by rescission or the doctrine of common mistake.

[222] *Attorney General of Canada v Juliar* (2000) 50 OR (3rd) 728 (Ontario CA). Leave to appeal to the Supreme Court of Canada was denied: [2000] SCCA No 621.

remedy of rectification was available to modify a transaction so as to implement certain tax-saving objectives:[223]

> (1) The court has a discretion to rectify where it is satisfied that the document does not carry out the intention of the parties. This is the basic principle. (2) Parties are entitled to enter into any transaction which is legal, and, in particular, are entitled to arrange their affairs to avoid payment of tax if they legitimately can … (3) If a mistake is made in a document legitimately designed to avoid the payment of tax, there is no reason why it should not be corrected …

Although the role of rectification in relieving parties from the (unintended) tax consequences of their transactions is nowhere as pronounced as in Canada,[224] there are occasional forays in the same direction in England and Wales.[225] But it is a trend which should be resisted both for *inter vivos* transactions and also for testamentary dispositions. Rectification is there—literally—to put the record straight, not to make for deceased testators the will which they would or should have made had they been properly advised.

The upshot is that *Marley v Rawlings* has sounded a warning bell. The rules governing the rectification of wills are ripe for a sensitive modern reassessment. They have not been rendered superfluous by the more contextual approach to construction, nor can their statutory enshrinement be legitimately regarded as superseded by a newly discovered innate judicial power. The rectification remedy concerns the actual (physical) content of a will. It channels the testator's intended words and terms into the executed instrument, imbuing them with the requisite formality. Echoing the man who began his will thus: 'This is my will, and I desire the Chancery will not make another for me',[226] we might say that the words and terms the testator knows and approves are the essence of his 'will', and that courts should not be encouraged to make another for him by a well-meaning—but less disciplined—appeal to his broader testamentary 'intentions'.

[223] ibid [33], drawing on *Re Slocock's Will Trusts* [1979] 1 All ER 358 (Ch) 363.

[224] See, most recently, *Fairmont Hotels Inc v Attorney General of Canada* 2015 ONCA 441, and *cf* the discussion of the post-*Juliar* world by L Smith, 'Can I Change My Mind? Undoing Trustee Decisions' (2008) 27 *Estates, Trusts & Pensions Journal* 284, especially 288–91; C Brown and AJ Cockfield, 'Rectification of Tax Mistakes Versus Retroactive Tax Laws: Reconciling Competing Visions of the Rule of Law' (2013) 61 *Canadian Tax Journal* 563.

[225] For recent examples, see *Lobler v Revenue and Customs Commissioners* [2015] UKUT 152 (TCC), [2015] STC 1893; *Vaughan-Jones v Vaughan-Jones* [2015] EWHC 1086 (Ch), [2015] WTLR 1287.

[226] See the text accompanying n 1 at the start of this chapter.

7

Capacity and Want of Knowledge and Approval

PENELOPE REED

1. Introduction

There is no shortage of probate disputes being fought out in the Chancery Division, and many more are started and settled. A significant number end up in the Court of Appeal. An ageing population, the increase in the incidence of dementia, and the rise in house prices making estates worth fighting over have all contributed to this.

There are, of course, a number of ways in which wills can be attacked: lack of due execution, undue influence,[1] forgery, lack of capacity and want of knowledge and approval. Those last two pleas often go hand in hand in practice. This chapter concentrates on recent cases in relation to them and on some of the problems to which they give rise.

2. Testamentary Capacity

2.1. The Test

It is notable, in an age when psychiatric medicine has become so sophisticated, that the test as to whether a testator has capacity or not is that set out in the appeal from a case decided by a jury in 1870. The test is that formulated eloquently by Cockburn CJ in *Banks v Goodfellow*.[2] In spite of suggestions by the Court of Appeal in recent years that it might be helpful to reformulate the test in modern language,[3]

[1] On which see Brian Sloan's contribution in Ch 8 of this volume.
[2] *Banks v Goodfellow* (1870) LR 5 QB 549, 565.
[3] *Sharp v Adam* [2006] EWCA Civ 449, [2006] WTLR 1059 at [82].

a suggestion abandoned after counsel attempted it overnight, it seems likely that the test will endure. Cockburn CJ formulated the test along the following lines:[4]

A testator—

(1) needs to have capacity to understand that he is making a will, and that it will have the effect of carrying out his wishes on death;
(2) must be able to understand the extent of the property he is disposing of;
(3) must recall those who have claims on him and understand the nature of those claims,[5] so that he can both include and exclude beneficiaries from the will;
(4) and, with a view to the latter object, no disorder of the mind should poison his affections, pervert his sense of right or prevent the exercise of his natural faculties, and no insane delusions should influence his will or poison his mind.

I will come in a moment to whether there are in fact three or four limbs to the test, but one factor which must never be forgotten is the fact that the court is looking for capacity to understand the above matters, not proof of actual understanding.[6] In that sense, the otherwise clear prose of Cockburn CJ is misleading insofar as it suggests otherwise.

2.2. Three or Four Limbs of the Test?

It is tempting to consider that the fourth limb set out in Cockburn's test simply explains the third, and that the inclusion of the words 'with a view to the latter object' suggests that ought to be the case. In other words, no disorder of the mind ought to affect the testator's recollection of those with claims on his bounty and his decision as to whom to benefit under his will.

However, that argument has been judicially rejected, at least at first instance in *Kostic v Chaplin*,[7] where it was argued that limbs three and four were a single requirement. Henderson J considered that the fourth limb had to be separately satisfied and referred to the then recent Court of Appeal decision in *Sharp v Adam*,[8] where the Court of Appeal had been satisfied that the testator was able to recall that he had daughters who had claims on him, but found that he was poisoned in his views against them by the illness from which he suffered.

[4] To quote Cockburn CJ in full: 'It is essential to the exercise of such a power that a testator shall understand the nature of the act and its effects; shall understand the extent of the property of which he is disposing; shall be able to comprehend and appreciate the claims to which he ought to give effect; and, with a view to the latter object, that no disorder of the mind shall poison his affections, pervert his sense of right, or prevent the exercise of his natural faculties—that no insane delusion shall influence his will in disposing of his property and bring about a disposal of it which, if the mind had been sound, would not have been made'.

[5] See *Boughton v Knight* (1873) LR 3 P & D 64 (Ct P).

[6] *Hoff v Atherton* [2004] EWCA Civ 1554, [2005] WTLR 99.

[7] *Kostic v Chaplin* [2007] EWHC 2298 (Ch), (2007) 10 ITELR 364.

[8] *Sharp v Adam* [2006] EWCA Civ 449, [2006] WTLR 1059.

Sharp v Adam was an unusual case. The testator suffered from progressive multiple sclerosis and had considerable difficulty communicating his wishes. The court praised the solicitor who took instructions for the will, but nevertheless held that the testator failed the fourth limb of *Banks v Goodfellow*. This was on the basis that the disease from which he suffered affected his personality, even if he retained the cognitive abilities to make a will, and that this had manifested itself in his exclusion of his daughters. In effect, the first instance judge looked at the exclusion of the daughters from the will and used this as evidence to support his finding (with which the Court of Appeal was not prepared to interfere) that the disease had poisoned the testator's mind.

2.3. The Impact of the Mental Capacity Act 2005

Since the coming into force of the Mental Capacity Act 2005,[9] the courts have grappled with its interaction with the common law test for capacity. Certainly, the Code of Practice accompanying the Act indicated that the new test would run alongside the common law test, and that courts dealing with issues of testamentary capacity could decide when it is was suitable to apply it. The Act provides in sections 1 to 3 as follows:

1. The principles

(1) The following principles apply for the purposes of this Act.
(2) A person must be assumed to have capacity unless it is established that he lacks capacity.
(3) A person is not to be treated as unable to make a decision unless all practicable steps to help him to do so have been taken without success.
(4) A person is not to be treated as unable to make a decision merely because he makes an unwise decision.
(5) An act done, or decision made, under this Act for or on behalf of a person who lacks capacity must be done, or made, in his best interests.
(6) Before the act is done, or the decision is made, regard must be had to whether the purpose for which it is needed can be as effectively achieved in a way that is less restrictive of the person's rights and freedom of action.

2. People who lack capacity

(1) For the purposes of this Act, a person lacks capacity in relation to a matter if at the material time he is unable to make a decision for himself in relation to the matter because of an impairment of, or a disturbance in the functioning of, the mind or brain.
(2) It does not matter whether the impairment or disturbance is permanent or temporary.

[9] The Act came into force in October 2007.

(3) A lack of capacity cannot be established merely by reference to—
   (a) a person's age or appearance, or
   (b) a condition of his, or an aspect of his behaviour, which might lead others to make unjustified assumptions about his capacity.

(4) In proceedings under this Act or any other enactment, any question whether a person lacks capacity within the meaning of this Act must be decided on the balance of probabilities.

(5) No power which a person ('D') may exercise under this Act—
   (a) in relation to a person who lacks capacity, or
   (b) where D reasonably thinks that a person lacks capacity,
   is exercisable in relation to a person under 16.

(6) Subsection (5) is subject to section 18(3).

3. Inability to make decisions

(1) For the purposes of section 2, a person is unable to make a decision for himself if he is unable—
   (a) to understand the information relevant to the decision,
   (b) to retain that information,
   (c) to use or weigh that information as part of the process of making the decision, or
   (d) to communicate his decision (whether by talking, using sign language or any other means).

(2) A person is not to be regarded as unable to understand the information relevant to a decision if he is able to understand an explanation of it given to him in a way that is appropriate to his circumstances (using simple language, visual aids or any other means).

(3) The fact that a person is able to retain the information relevant to a decision for a short period only does not prevent him from being regarded as able to make the decision.

(4) The information relevant to a decision includes information about the reasonably foreseeable consequences of—
   (a) deciding one way or another, or
   (b) failing to make the decision.

There is no doubt that there are differences between the statutory and the common law tests. The first and most obvious is that under the Act, there is an assumption that a person has capacity. This was a factor which was noted by the deputy judge in *Scammell v Farmer*,[10] who rejected the application of the Act to a will made and a death which occurred before it came into force. The position under the Act contrasts with the common law position as set out by Briggs J (as he then was) in *Key v Key*:[11]

> The burden of proof in relation to testamentary capacity is subject to the following rules:
>
> (i) While the burden starts with the propounder of a will to establish capacity, where the will is duly executed and appears rational on its face, then the court will presume capacity.

[10] *Scammell v Farmer* [2008] EHWC 1100 (Ch), [2008] WTLR 1261.

[11] *Key v Key* [2010] EWHC 408 (Ch), [2010] 1 WLR 2020 at [97].

(ii) In such a case the evidential burden then shifts to the objector to raise a real doubt about capacity.
(iii) If a real doubt is raised, the evidential burden shifts back to the propounder to establish capacity nonetheless.

In practice, the subtle distinction in the tests is unlikely to make a great deal of difference. As the courts have repeatedly emphasised, testamentary capacity cases are decided on the evidence, and only in exceptional cases will the burden of proof have an impact on the final decision.

The second distinction possibly arises from section 3(1), which requires a person to be able to understand all the information relevant to the making of a decision. This point impressed the deputy judge in *Re Walker*,[12] a case I will look at in more detail below.[13] However, it seems to me that the *Banks v Goodfellow* test also requires the testator to be able to understand all the information (as set out in that test) relevant to the making of a will.

A third, and in my view more significant, difference is found section 3(4), which requires the testator to be able to understand, use or weigh information as to the reasonably foreseeable consequences of the choices open to him. That does appear to be at odds with the common law test as it currently stands, as set out by the Court of Appeal in *Simon v Byford*.[14]

Simon v Byford involved a challenge to a will made in rather unusual circumstances, based on the third limb of *Banks v Goodfellow*. Mrs Simon had four children, one of whom predeceased her. The disputed will was prepared and executed at Mrs Simon's 88th birthday party, at which two of her children were present, but not her son Robert—who benefited more than his siblings under an earlier will of 1994 which left to him shares that would give him a controlling interest in the family company he ran. The will, excluding Robert as a beneficiary, was prepared and executed without the involvement of a solicitor and without any medical assessment of Mrs Simon's capacity to make a will, despite the fact that (as was common ground) she was by that stage suffering from mild to moderate dementia.

The court at first instance upheld the will,[15] as did the Court of Appeal. The High Court accepted that Mrs Simon was not capable of remembering why she had favoured one of her children in her earlier will by the time she made the disputed will. The Court of Appeal rejected the argument that this was a finding which meant that she could not fulfil the third *Banks v Goodfellow* limb because while she might be able to identify those with a claim on her bounty, she could not assess and weigh those claims properly. Lewison LJ stated:

> I do not believe that previous authority goes to the length of requiring an understanding of the collateral consequences of a disposition as opposed to its immediate consequences. Nor do I think it desirable that the law should go that far.[16]

[12] *Re Walker* [2014] EWHC 71 (Ch), [2015] WTLR 493.
[13] See the text accompanying n 20 below.
[14] *Simon v Byford* [2014] EWCA Civ 280, [2014] WTLR 1097.
[15] *Simon v Byford* [2013] EWHC 1490 (Ch), [2013] WTLR 1615.
[16] *Simon v Byford* (CA) (n 14 above) [45].

The will in *Simon v Byford* was made before the Mental Capacity Act 2005 came into force and Lewison LJ expressly did not apply the Act, but assuming that his analysis of the test at common law is correct, then it is at odds with the requirements of section 3(4).

A final difference arises because of the anomaly of the rule in *Parker v Felgate*.[17] That rule allows a testator who has lost capacity to execute a valid will, provided (i) that he had capacity at the time he gave instructions for the will and (ii) knows at its execution that he is making a will for which he has previously given instructions. This is looked at in more detail below,[18] but it sits very unhappily with the concepts under the Act which require the person to have capacity at the material time that the transaction is being carried through.

Clearly, there are some difficulties in the Act and the common law test sitting side by side. In *Scammell v Farmer*,[19] decided not long after the Act came into force, the deputy judge considered that the Act did not have retrospective effect and so did not apply to a will made before it came into force. That would seem to be uncontroversial, but he also considered that the Act would have not have applied in any event to the decision he had to make because the test set out in the Act applied only 'for the purposes of' the Act, which did not include the assessment of capacity.

Nicholas Strauss QC came to the same conclusion in the recent case of *Re Walker*.[20] He had the benefit of detailed and what appears to have been formidable argument before him, and his judgment is carefully reasoned. He identified the differences between the approach to the assessment of capacity under the Act and the common law test (although he did not focus on the timing point), and he agreed with Stephen Smith QC in *Scammell v Farmer* that the Act did not apply to the retrospective assessment of capacity. It applied for the purposes of the Act which, broadly speaking, involved decisions being made by the Court of Protection for those lacking capacity during their lifetimes, and not the retrospective assessment of capacity undertaken in contentious probate cases.

HHJ Dight came to a different conclusion in *Fischer v Diffley*.[21] He took the Mental Capacity Act 2005 as the starting point for the modern approach to the assessment of capacity, and his approach was followed in *Bray v Pearce*.[22]

It has to be acknowledged that there are differences between the statutory approach and the common law test, although in most cases those differences will not be decisive to the outcome of the case. However, the deputy judge in *Re Walker*

[17] *Parker v Felgate* (1883) 8 PD 171 (PDA).
[18] See Section 2.4 below.
[19] *Scammell v Farmer* (n 10 above).
[20] *Re Walker* [2014] EWHC 71 (Ch), [2015] WTLR 493.
[21] *Fischer v Diffley* [2013] EWHC 4567 (Ch), [2014] WTLR 757.
[22] *Bray v Pearce* (unreported, 6 March 2013, HC), a decision of Murray Rosen QC sitting as a deputy judge of the Chancery Division.

was particularly influenced by the fact that the test in the Mental Capacity Act 2005 was for the purposes of the Act only, and he regarded those purposes as involving quite different decisions from the question as to whether, retrospectively viewed, a testator had had capacity to make a will.

Yet the decisions which the Court of Protection can make on behalf of a person lacking capacity include making a will. It cannot be regarded as in any way satisfactory that the Court of Protection applies a different test to decide whether someone has testamentary capacity during their lifetime from the test applied by a court when looking back. Logically, the test ought to be the same.

Furthermore, the Court of Protection has power under section 15 of the 2005 Act to make declarations as to someone's capacity to do a particular act. It is fair to say that this is a power which is rarely used in practice, owing to reluctance on the part of the Court of Protection, but it nevertheless exists. It would seem quite extraordinary if the Court of Protection could make a declaration based on the statutory test that someone lacked capacity to make a will, but if he or she then went on to do so anyway, a court after the testator's death were to come to a different conclusion based on the common law test. This could have happened in *Simon v Byford*[23] because it appears to have been accepted that the testatrix, by the time the disputed will was made, did not have capacity to reason why she had previously left more shares to her son Robert.

Therefore, notwithstanding the respect that has to be accorded to *Re Walker* (it was perhaps the first time the point has been fully argued, and the very detailed and reasoned judgment ought to be acknowledged),[24] it ought not be the final decision on this particular debate. This is an issue which requires a case to be fully argued before the Court of Appeal.

2.4. Timing

As mentioned above, the Mental Capacity Act 2005 clearly requires a person to have capacity at the material time, and that must mean when the particular transaction in question is being effected. It is trite law that capacity is time- and issue-specific. However, the rule in *Parker v Felgate*[25] enables someone lacking testamentary capacity to make a will, which may seem somewhat surprising. An attack on the principle in the Court of Appeal failed in *Perrins v Holland*,[26] and the rule seems destined to remain as part of the law.

[23] See the text accompanying and following n 14 above.

[24] See n 20 and the accompanying text above.

[25] See n 17 and the accompanying text above.

[26] *Perrins v Holland* [2010] EWCA Civ 840, [2011] Ch 270, discussed in the text accompanying and following n 38 below.

Parker v Felgate involved a testatrix who had been in the process of giving instructions to her solicitor to prepare a will over a number of interviews, the last alterations being made on 24 July 1882 and 10 August 1882 before the will was engrossed.[27] On 26 August, the testatrix fell into a coma, but was roused sufficiently to execute the will on 29 August. These were the days when probate cases were heard by a jury. In his summing up to the jury, Sir James Hannen put forward three possible states of mind which would be sufficient to establish capacity. First,[28]

> If a person has given instructions to a solicitor to make a will, and the solicitor prepares it in accordance with those instructions, all that is necessary to make it a good will, if executed by the testator, is that he should be able to think thus far, 'I gave my solicitor instructions to prepare a will making a certain disposition of my property. I have no doubt that he has given effect to my intention, and I accept the document which is put before me as carrying it out'.

Secondly, even if she could not recollect all that had gone on between her and the solicitor,[29]

> [was she] in a condition, that if each clause of this will had been put to her, and she had been asked, 'Do you wish to leave So-and-So so much,' or do you wish to do this (as the case might be), she would have been able to answer intelligently 'Yes' to each question?

Thirdly,[30]

> A person might no longer have capacity to go over the whole transaction, and take up the thread of business from the beginning to the end, and think it all over again, but if he is able to say to himself, 'I have settled that business with my solicitor. I rely upon his having embodied it in proper words, and I accept the paper which is put before me as embodying it'.

The rule in *Parker v Felgate* was applied subsequently, albeit sporadically, in a number of cases. In *Re Wallace*,[31] the testator himself wrote out a 'Letter of Wish' which was used as the instructions for a formal will prepared the next day and executed by him the day after. In *Re Flynn*,[32] instructions were given on 21 October 1973. By letter of 5 January 1974, the deceased approved the same and asked the solicitor for it to be engrossed. On 8 January 1974, the engrossment of the codicil was sent by the solicitors to the deceased. Early in the morning of 9 January 1974, the deceased was admitted to West Middlesex Hospital. On the same day, the deceased executed the will only four days after he had approved it.

The doctrine then seemed to go to sleep for 20 years, but was resurrected in *Clancy v Clancy*,[33] where instructions for the will were given on 1 December 1999.

27 *Parker v Felgate* (n 17 above) 172
28 ibid 173.
29 ibid 174.
30 ibid.
31 *Re the Estate of Wallace* [1952] 2 TLR 925.
32 *Re Flynn* [1982] 1 WLR 310 (Ch).
33 *Clancy v Clancy* [2003] EWHC 1885 (Ch), [2003] WTLR 1097.

The testatrix herself, when in hospital on 24 March 2000, telephoned the solicitor to say that she wanted to make the will for which she had given instructions, and she executed it on 28 March at a time when she lacked testamentary capacity.

The rule was approved—albeit obiter—in *Perera v Perera*,[34] where the Privy Council observed that the first of Sir James Hannen's propositions was good law, but did not explain why.[35] The Privy Council also accepted that the rule existed in *Battan Singh v Amirchand*,[36] though they refused to apply it where instructions had come not from the testator, but from a third party.

The rule in *Parker v Felgate* provides an exception also to the general principle that the testator must know and approve the contents of the will at the date of execution. That point and how it impacts generally on the law of knowledge and approval is dealt with below.[37]

As stated above, there was a wholescale attack on the rule in *Perrins v Holland*.[38] The facts were quite startling. The testator suffered from severe multiple sclerosis. At the time he gave instructions for a will benefiting his carer and partner in April 2000, he was unable to read or write, had little or no control of his movements and was confined to a wheelchair. He had great difficulty in communicating. The court found nevertheless that he had capacity to give those instructions. A draft will was sent to him, but nothing of significance happened apart from his expressing doubts that it represented his wishes, until his carer contacted the solicitor over a year later saying that he wanted to execute the will. He did in fact execute it (in the car park of the solicitors who drew it up) in September 2001, 18 months after he had given instructions. By that time, it was found, he lacked testamentary capacity, but Lewison J held that the deceased fell within the second state of mind set out in *Parker v Felgate*.[39] In other words, the solicitor went over the will and Mr Perrins indicated his assent.

The argument before the Court of Appeal was that the rule had come out of nowhere, was based on a first instance decision (and a direction to the jury at that) and ought not to be followed. The Court of Appeal rejected this argument on the basis that the rule had been applied for 150 years and the Privy Council had approved it, albeit obiter.[40] However, the rule does appear anomalous. Undoubtedly it would have proved useful at the time when it was developed, because psychiatry was not so advanced and the Court of Protection did not exist to make statutory wills for those incapable of doing so. The then Chancellor of the High Court, Sir Andrew Morritt, said the rule had its rationale[41]

> in the freedom of testamentary disposition which the law favours, as explained by the court in *Banks v Goodfellow*, the usual preference of the court, if reasonably possible, to

[34] *Perera v Perera* [1901] AC 354 (PC).
[35] ibid 361. The Privy Council decided that the testator had capacity at execution.
[36] *Battan Singh v Amirchand* [1948] AC 161 (PC).
[37] See Section 3 of the present chapter.
[38] See n 26 above and the accompanying text.
[39] *Perrins v Holland* [2009] EWHC 1945 (Ch), [2009] WTLR 1387.
[40] *Perrins v Holland* (CA) (n 26 above).
[41] ibid [23].

> uphold transactions ... and the pragmatic recognition ... that the testator has no further opportunity to give expression to his wishes.

Lord Justice Moore-Bick set out the rule in this way:[42]

> Where the testator loses some of his faculties between giving instructions and executing the will, however, the position is different. One must then ask (i) whether at the time he gave the instructions he had the ability to understand and give proper consideration to the various matters which are called for, that is, whether he had testamentary capacity, (ii) whether the document gives effect to his instructions, (iii) whether those instructions continued to reflect his intentions and (iv) whether at the time he executed the will he knew what he was doing and thus had sufficient mental capacity to carry out the juristic act which that involves. If all those questions can be answered in the affirmative, one can be satisfied that the will accurately reflects the deceased's intentions formed at a time when he was capable of making fully informed decisions.

Attractive though that sounds, there is something both anomalous and uncomfortable about a testator who lacks capacity making a will. While the court should of course recognise that effect should be given to the wishes of a testator if at all possible, it is hard, if not impossible, for the court to be really sure that the will executed by a testator who lacks testamentary capacity reflects his wishes.

The Court of Appeal was particularly impressed in reaching its decision by the old case of *Harwood v Baker*,[43] which indicated (although it was not strictly part of the decision) that if a testator has come to a concluded decision about what he wishes to do when he *has* capacity, then 'less evidence of the capacity to weigh those claims during his illness might have been sufficient to show that the will propounded really did contain the expression of the mind and will of the deceased'.[44] However, that statement might be read simply as saying that if there is strong evidence that the testator had formed views as to what he wished to do, that itself would be strong evidence of his capacity if he then went on to give effect to them in a will. In a probate case, evidence of cogent and clear instructions will of course make it easier to prove capacity.

Further, while it is accepted that the rule in *Parker v Felgate* has withstood over 150 years, there are not a great number of reported cases in which it has been applied or recognised,[45] before *Perrins v Holland* none of them explained the rationale behind the doctrine, and the two Privy Council cases which refer to the rule do not apply it.[46] The attack on the principle did not come without

[42] ibid [55].

[43] *Harwood v Baker* (1840) 3 Moo PC 282, 13 ER 117 (PC).

[44] ibid 3 Moo PC 313 and 13 ER 129 respectively.

[45] In particular *Re Wallace* (n 31 above); *Re Flynn* (n 32 above); *Clancy v Clancy* (n 33 above); *Thomas v Jones* [1928] P 162 (PDA); *Otuka v Alozie* [2006] EWHC 3493 (Ch); *Battan Singh v Amirchand* (n 36 above); *Perera v Perera* (n 34 above).

[46] *Battan Singh v Amirchand* (n 36 above); *Perera v Perera* (n 34 above).

support,[47] but unless another case comes along which the Supreme Court is prepared to entertain, the rule appears to be here to stay.

Interestingly, the concern that there would be a flood of cases where reliance might be placed on the rule has not proved well founded. An unsuccessful attempt was made in *Markou v Goodwin*,[48] where the court was not convinced that capacity existed at the time that instructions for the will were given.

2.5. The Level of Capacity Required

Perrins v Holland is perhaps an example of the desire of the courts to uphold wills. How high the threshold for testamentary capacity is set is not entirely clear. It was said in the US case of *Den v Vancleve*:[49]

> By the term 'a sound and disposing mind and memory' it has not been understood that a testator must possess these qualities of the mind in the highest degree; otherwise, very few could make testaments at all; neither has it been understood that he must possess them in as great a degree as he may have formerly done; for even this would disable most men in the decline of life; the mind may have been in some degree debilitated, the memory may have become in some degree enfeebled; and yet there may be enough left clearly to discern and discreetly to judge, of all those things, and all those circumstances, which enter into the nature of a rational, fair, and just testament. But if they have so far failed as that these cannot be discerned and judged of, then he cannot be said to be of sound and disposing mind and memory.

On the other hand, this must not be misunderstood: perfect understanding is not required, but the level of understanding does have to be set reasonably high, so that the testator has the ability to satisfy the limbs of the *Banks v Goodfellow* test. This was made clear by Gibson LJ in *Hoff v Atherton*,[50] relying on the decision relating to lifetime gifts in *Re Beaney*.[51]

There was some suggestion in *Re Walker*[52] that the test under the Mental Capacity Act 2005 set a higher bar. That is not clear, and of course the Act introduces the concept of someone who has capacity (only) if assisted, which may suggest that in some cases the test might be easier to overcome.

At the end of the day, of course, the decision of the court as to whether a testator has capacity is a legal question, rather than a medical one, based on the facts as found. In most cases, those facts are built up from anecdotal evidence given by friends, family and professionals who dealt with the testator and who can give

[47] See F Barlow, C Sherrin and others (eds), *Williams on Wills*, 9th edn (London, LexisNexis Butterworths, 2008) [40.9]–[40.10].

[48] *Markou v Goodwin* [2013] EWHC 4570 (Ch), [2014] WTLR 605.

[49] *Den v Vancleve* (1819) 5 NJL 589, 2 Southard's Rep 589 (Supreme Court of Judicature of New Jersey) 660, as cited in *Banks v Goodfellow* (n 2 above) 567–68.

[50] *Hoff v Atherton* (n 6 above) [35].

[51] *Re Beaney* [1978] 1 WLR 770 (Ch).

[52] *Re Walker* (n 12 above), on which see also the text accompanying n 20 above.

evidence of understanding, confusion, forgetfulness and the like; evidence provided by the will draftsman, which is crucial and often decisive; and finally medical evidence. There is little doubt that expert evidence which might in theory be deployed has quite severe limitations, if what is involved is a retrospective assessment of capacity. Doctors who examined the testator, and particularly those who assessed capacity (even if it were not specifically testamentary capacity), have a much more important role to play. In *Key v Key*,[53] the evidence of the doctor who had had the advantage of examining the testator when he was alive was thus preferred to the august evidence of Professor Jacoby, a highly esteemed expert in the area. The issue of capacity is, of course, not one on which expert evidence will be determinative, and the experts themselves fully appreciate that.

The importance of the role of the will draftsman and the limitations of the medical evidence was brought out in the judgments of the Court of Appeal in *Burgess v Hawes*.[54] The judge at first instance found that Mrs Burgess lacked capacity at the time she made a will in the presence of her daughter, cutting out her son.[55] The Court of Appeal did not share the judge's view on the question of capacity, although it dismissed the appeal on the basis that the will should be set aside for lack of knowledge and approval. Mummery LJ went so far as to say that a judge should be slow to find that a testator lacked capacity where the will draftsman considered that he or she was capable:[56]

> [I]t is, in my opinion, a very strong thing for the judge to find that the Deceased was not mentally capable of making the 2007 Will, when it had been prepared by an experienced and independent solicitor following a meeting with her; when it was executed by her after the solicitor had read through it and explained it; and when the solicitor considered that she was capable of understanding the will, the terms of which were not, on their face, inexplicable or irrational.
>
> My concern is that the courts should not too readily upset, on the grounds of lack of mental capacity, a will that has been drafted by an experienced independent lawyer. If, as here, an experienced lawyer has been instructed and has formed the opinion from a meeting or meetings that the testatrix understands what she is doing, the will so drafted and executed should only be set aside on the clearest evidence of lack of mental capacity. The court should be cautious about acting on the basis of evidence of lack of capacity given by a medical expert after the event, particularly when that expert has neither met nor medically examined the testatrix, and particularly in circumstances when that expert accepts that the testatrix understood that she was making a will and also understood the extent of her property.

The above should not be taken as giving comfort to solicitors who do not do a good job, however experienced they might be. The Court of Appeal still found the

[53] *Key v Key* (n 11 above).
[54] *Burgess v Hawes* [2013] EWCA Civ 94, [2013] WTLR 453.
[55] *Burgess v Hawes* [2012] WTLR 423 (Walden-Smith J in the County Court, Central London).
[56] *Burgess v Hawes* (CA) (n 54 above) [57] and [60].

will to be invalid, albeit that it preferred to do so on the grounds of want of knowledge and approval. As was the case in *Key v Key*,[57] the solicitor had not followed what has become known as the golden rule; that is the judicial guidance given, in particular, by the late Lord Templeman when he was a judge at first instance in *Re Simpson*:[58]

> In the case of an aged testator or a testator who has suffered a serious illness, there is one golden rule which should always be observed, however straightforward matters may appear and however difficult or tactless it may be to suggest that precautions be taken: the making of a will by such a testator ought to be witnessed or approved by a medical practitioner who satisfies himself of the capacity and understanding of the testator, and records and preserves his examination and finding.

There are other precautions which should be taken. If the testator has made an earlier will this should be considered by the legal and medical advisers of the testator, and if appropriate, discussed with the testator. The instructions of the testator should be taken in the absence of anyone who may stand to benefit, or who may have influence over the testator. These are not counsels of perfection. If proper precautions are not taken injustice may result or be imagined, and great expense and misery may be unnecessarily caused.

Of course failing to follow the golden rule does not render a will invalid, although it may render the draftsman the subject of trenchant criticism as was the case in *Key v Key*. It is, at the end of the day, just good practice. It is also not always easy for solicitors to apply in practice: which clients are to be classed as aged? Do they also have to be infirm? What if the client refuses to be examined?

The Court of Appeal in *Burgess v Hawes* was also dismissive of the ability of an expert to assess capacity retrospectively. However, Mummery LJ's comments fail to acknowledge the practical difficulty that, without expert medical opinion, it is often difficult to understand the underlying medical conditions from which the testator has been suffering. A diagnosis of mental illness is not enough. There have been plenty of wills made by patients suffering from dementia which were upheld by the courts.[59] Further, in some cases, the court simply cannot come to a conclusion without such expert evidence.

Serious mental illness, including delusions, may not be an impediment to the ability to make a will, unless they have an effect on the testator's ability to fulfil the *Banks v Goodfellow* test, as was the case in *Kostic v Chaplin*.[60] In *Vegetarian Society v Scott*,[61] the fact that the testator was suffering from schizophrenia and logical thought disorder did not deprive him of testamentary capacity. Capacity

[57] *Key v Key* (n 11 above), discussed in the text accompanying n 53.

[58] *Re Simpson* (1977) 121 *Sol Jo* 224, better recorded at 127 *NLJ* 487.

[59] See eg *Hoff v Atherton* (n 6 above); *Man v Blackman* [2007] EWHC 3162 (Ch) [2008] WTLR 389; *Simon v Byford* (n 14 above).

[60] *Kostic v Chaplin* (n 7 above).

[61] *Vegetarian Society v Scott* [2013] EWHC 4097 (Ch), [2014] WLR 525.

is so 'time and task specific' that the court found the testator to have had capacity to make his will when he did make it, his thought processes being logical in this regard. The evidence of the expert in that case was crucial and decisive, just as it had been in *Kostic v Chaplin*.

2.6. Summary on Capacity

The interaction between the Mental Capacity Act 2005 and the common law test for testamentary capacity is an issue which requires resolution. The Act ought to create uniformity between the lifetime assessment of capacity and the retrospective assessment involved in a contentious probate case. If this issue could be resolved, then answers to questions such as whether the rule in *Parker v Felgate* ought still to apply should fall into place.

Further, the desire of the courts to uphold wills whenever they can is in most cases welcome, but there has been something of a tendency to uphold wills in circumstances where there must be very serious doubt as to the degree of understanding on the part of an elderly, perhaps vulnerable and demented testator.

3. Want of Knowledge and Approval

3.1. What Is Meant by Knowledge and Approval?

There appears to be some divergence of views among the judges as to what is meant by this requirement, which is essential to the validity of will. Traditionally, the matter has been dealt with rather formulaically. In the ordinary probate case, if the propounder of the will establishes testamentary capacity and due execution, knowledge and approval will be inferred. However, in cases where the circumstances are such as to arouse the suspicion of the court, the propounder must prove affirmatively knowledge and approval on the part of the testator, so as to satisfy the court that the will represents the wishes of the deceased. All the relevant circumstances will be scrutinised by the court, which will be 'vigilant and jealous' in examining the evidence in support of the will. In *Barry v Butlin* it was observed:[62]

> The rules of law according to which cases of this nature are to be decided, do not admit of any dispute, so far as they are necessary to the determination of the present Appeal: and they have been acquiesced in on both sides. These rules are two; the first that the *onus probandi* lies in every case upon the party propounding a Will; and he must satisfy the conscience of the Court that the instrument so propounded is the last Will of a free and capable Testator. The second is, that if a party writes or prepares a Will, under which he

[62] *Barry v Butlin* (1838) 2 Moore PC 480 at 483, 12 ER 1089 at 1090 (Parke B).

takes a benefit, that is a circumstance that ought generally to excite the suspicion of the Court, and calls upon it to be vigilant and jealous in examining the evidence in support of the instrument, in favour of which it ought not to pronounce unless the suspicion is removed, and it is judicially satisfied that the paper propounded does express the true Will of the deceased.

What suspicion-exciting circumstances the court can take into account was the subject of *Re R (deceased)*,[63] which confined them to the will-making process itself rather than other matters. This decision was followed in *Griffin v Wood*.[64] That narrow approach was the basis for many of the decisions in this area. A small extension could be seen to lie in *Tyrell v Painter*,[65] where execution of the will was procured by the major beneficiary's son. The case is authority for the proposition that it is not only wills actually prepared by the beneficiaries themselves which excite suspicion.

Succeeding on this ground of challenge used to be extremely difficult; the circumstances could be very suspicious, but the court would not reject the will. In *Fuller v Strum*,[66] for example, the claimant was the executor of and beneficiary under a will which, he claimed, the testator had dictated to him and read in his presence before signing in the presence of two other witnesses. It appeared that the testator benefited his adopted son, the defendant, only reluctantly, describing him (out of character—the judge found) as 'that Irish bastard'. The circumstances led the judge at first instance to hold that the testator had known and approved of only part of the will. The Court of Appeal disagreed with that approach and upheld the will on the basis that, on a balance of probabilities, the suspicion raised by the close involvement of the beneficiary in the drafting and execution of the will had been dispelled.

A particularly striking example of the courts refusing to hold wills invalid on this ground was to be found in *Hart v Dabbs*,[67] where the will had been prepared on the computer of the major beneficiary, the partner of the deceased. The testator was later found dead from exhaust fumes in his garage, and the beneficiary was implicated in his death, although not charged with murder.

A rare example of a successful challenge on this ground was *Franks v Sinclair*,[68] where the involvement of the testatrix's solicitor son in preparing his mother's will partially in his favour, marking an unexplained change in testamentary direction, was considered so suspicious that the will was not admitted to probate. Notably, the judge considered that the reading over of the will by the son was a mere formality designed to establish its validity, and that the testatrix would not have understood the technical language of the residuary gift.

[63] *Re R (deceased)* [1951] P 10 (PDA).
[64] *Griffin v Wood, Re Morgan (deceased)* [2008] WTLR 73 (Ch).
[65] *Tyrell v Painton* [1894] P 151 (CA).
[66] *Fuller v Strum* [2001] EWCA Civ 1879, [2002] 1 WLR 1097.
[67] *Hart v Dabbs* [2001] WTLR 527 (Ch).
[68] *Franks v Sinclair* [2006] EWHC 3365 (Ch), [2007] WTLR 439.

Finally, it might have been thought that the suspicions raised in *Simon v Byford*, discussed above,[69] would have proved more difficult to dispel: an 88-year-old demented testatrix, making a home-made will at her birthday party from which the son she was disadvantaging was absent, prepared on the computer of her son-in-law, whose wife stood to benefit. However, the judge at first instance considered those suspicions to be dispelled, and the Court of Appeal upheld that.

3.2. A Change of Approach?

There has been something of a change of emphasis in how this challenge is run, at least in some cases, as a result of the decision of the Court of Appeal in *Gill v Woodall and the RSPCA*.[70] That case involved a surprising will executed by Mrs Gill in favour of the RSPCA, for whom she had shown little respect during her lifetime, describing them as a 'bunch of townies'. The will was also surprising in that she cut out her only daughter, to whom she was close. Evidence was called that she was agoraphobic and suffered severe anxiety disorder. The judge at first instance had found against the will on the grounds of undue influence, but the Court of Appeal instead held that Mrs Gill had not known and approved its contents. Lord Neuberger MR (as he then was) stated that '[k]nowing and approving of the contents of one's will is traditional language for saying that the will "represented [one's] testamentary intentions"'.[71] He also held that the traditional two-stage approach to want of knowledge and approval was not correct, saying:[72]

> Where a judge has heard evidence of fact and expert opinion over a period of many days relating to the character and state of mind and likely desires of the testatrix and the circumstances in which the will was drafted and executed, and other relevant matters, the value of such a two-stage approach to deciding the issue of the testatrix's knowledge and approval appears to me to be questionable. In my view, the approach which it would, at least generally, be better to adopt is that summarised by Sachs J in the unreported cases of *Crerar v Crerar* [but see (1956) 106 LJ 694, 695], cited and followed by Latey J in *Morris* [1971] P 62, 78E–G, namely that the court should 'consider all the relevant evidence available and then, drawing such inferences as it can from the totality of that material, it has to come to a conclusion whether or not those propounding the will have discharged the burden of establishing that the testatrix knew and approved the contents of the document which is put forward as a valid testamentary disposition. The fact that the testatrix read the document, and the fact that she executed it, must be given the full weight apposite in the circumstances, but in law those facts are not conclusive, nor do they raise a presumption'.

[69] See nn 14–15 above and the accompanying text.
[70] *Gill v Woodall, Gill v Royal Society for the Prevention of Cruelty to Animals* [2010] EWCA Civ 1430, [2011] Ch 380.
[71] ibid [14].
[72] ibid [22].

The Court of Appeal therefore supported a more holistic approach than the rigid two-stage process. The case is factually an unusual one in terms of knowledge and approval cases. There was no involvement in the will-making process by the RSPCA to raise any suspicions. While Mrs Gill had capacity, her mental illness meant that she could not concentrate when the will was being explained to her. Further, there was involvement of a solicitor, which would normally result in the rejection of want of knowledge and approval as a plea. The Court of Appeal acknowledged that the facts of *Gill v Woodall* were unusual and re-emphasised that considerable weight had to be given to a will prepared by a solicitor.

The approach to the assessment of evidence advocated by Lord Neuberger has not been universally applied in subsequent cases. It was applied by Norris J in *Wharton v Bancroft*,[73] where a testator made a deathbed will in favour of his partner of 32 years, excluding his daughters. The will was made in contemplation of his marriage to his partner, which took place shortly after the will was executed. Norris J observed that the Court of Appeal in *Gill v Woodall* had stated that:[74]

> as a matter of common sense and authority, the fact that a will has been properly executed, after being prepared by a solicitor and read over to the testator, raises a very strong presumption that it represents the testator's intentions at the relevant time ... But proof of the reading over of a will does not *necessarily* establish 'knowledge and approval'. Whether more is required in a particular case depends upon the circumstances in which the vigilance of the Court is aroused and the terms (including the complexity) of the Will itself.

He did not find anything in the will-making process in that case to invalidate the will.

The *Gill v Woodall* approach was adopted by the judge in the case of *Burgess v Hawes*[75] (although approached in the old way by the Court of Appeal, which nevertheless upheld the judge's decision on this ground), where a daughter had been instrumental in getting her mother—who was found in any event to lack capacity[76]—to make a will excluding her brother, with whom the daughter had fallen out. The terms of the will made no sense in the factual context and contained a clause which stated that the reason for excluding the brother was that lifetime provision had been made for him, which was simply not true. The solicitor had not sent a copy of the draft will to Mrs Burgess (he stated in evidence that he felt it confused clients to do so), but had read it over to her before she executed it, and it was only afterwards that her daughter had spotted a mistake in it. The case is another example where the courts have been of late prepared to accept a plea of want of knowledge and approval, even where a solicitor has been involved.

While the Court of Appeal in *Gill v Woodall* emphasised that the facts of the case were exceptional, one is left with a feeling that the different approach will make is

[73] *Wharton v Bancroft and Others* [2011] EWHC 3250 (Ch), [2012] WTLR 693.

[74] ibid [28].

[75] *Burgess v Hawes* (CA) (n 54 above).

[76] See the text accompanying nn 54–56 above.

easier in the right cases to plead want of knowledge and approval successfully, and the number of cases where the plea has succeeded appear, indeed, to be increasing. It is clear that the involvement of the beneficiary in the will-making process is not a requirement for the challenge to be invoked. However, where the beneficiary is involved, this ground of attack provides a welcome alternative to pleading undue influence, since there is a costs-risk if the challenge fails and since positive evidence of the influence has to be forthcoming.

3.3. Conflation of Capacity and Want of Knowledge and Approval

In *Simon v Byford*,[77] Lewison LJ stated that testamentary capacity includes the ability to make choices, whereas knowledge and approval requires no more than the ability to understand and approve choices that have already been made. This was also very much reflected in his approach at first instance in *Perrins v Holland*,[78] namely that the requirement for knowledge and approval does not require the high level of ability which is needed to satisfy the test of capacity, and the Court of Appeal endorsed that.[79] The requirement that a testator know and approve the contents of his will is dispensed with in *Parker v Felgate* cases,[80] but interestingly in *Perrins v Holland*, Lewison J held that the testator, although lacking capacity when he executed the will, nevertheless knew and approved its contents.[81] On the basis of the test as narrowly formulated by Lewison J, that is indeed an acceptable finding.

The tests of capacity and want of knowledge and approval are, of course, conceptually different and must not be conflated. In response to a submission made to the Court of Appeal in *Hoff v Atherton*[82] to the effect that the judge should have considered whether it had been established that the testatrix had actual understanding, comprehension and appreciation of the claims to which she should give effect, proof of an ability to do so not sufficing, Chadwick LJ said:[83]

> That submission, as it seems to me, betrays a failure to appreciate that the requirements of testamentary capacity and knowledge and approval are conceptually distinct. A finding of capacity to understand is, of course, a prerequisite to a finding of knowledge and approval. A testator cannot be said to know and approve the contents of his will unless he is able to, and does, understand what he is doing and its effect. It is not enough that he knows what is written in the document which he signs.

77 *Simon v Byford* (CA) (n 14 above).
78 *Perrins v Holland* (Ch) (n 39 above).
79 *Perrins v Holland* (CA) (n 26 above).
80 See n 17 above and the accompanying text as well as the text accompanying nn 25–30.
81 *Perrins v Holland* (Ch) (n 39 above).
82 *Hoff v Atherton* (n 6 above).
83 ibid [62].

However, the Court of Appeal in *Perrins v Holland* rejected the submission that capacity was a precondition of knowledge and approval and that this paragraph supported it. Indeed, Sir Andrew Morritt CVO expressed the view that if that is what the passage meant, he was not prepared to follow it.[84] Support was found in the decision of the Privy Council in *Battan Singh v Amirchand*,[85] where the will was invalid because the testator lacked testamentary capacity, but the judge had rejected the allegation that the will was invalid for want of knowledge and approval, and that point was not raised in the appeal. The Privy Council recognised that:[86]

> A testator may have a clear apprehension of the meaning of a draft will submitted to him and may approve of it, and yet if he was at the time through infirmity or disease so deficient in memory that he was oblivious of the claims of his relations, and if that forgetfulness was an inducing cause of his choosing strangers to be his legatees, the will is invalid.

If the test of knowledge and approval is this narrow, requiring only the mechanical appreciation that the will contains certain matters (as suggested by the Privy Council), then it is perhaps hard to square it with the Court of Appeal's statement in *Gill v Woodall*[87] that knowledge and approval is shorthand for the will representing the testamentary intentions of the testator. If the testator is incapable at the time of execution of the will, can it really be said that simply being able to understand the words in the will is enough?

There is thus a very clear tension between the decision of the Court of Appeal in *Perrins v Holland* and the statements of Chadwick LJ in *Hoff v Atherton* set out above,[88] and also with his suggestion that, in the case of failing capacity, the court may need even more evidence that the testator knew and approved the contents of the will. As Chadwick LJ said,[89]

> it may well be that where there is evidence of a failing mind—and, *a fortiori*, where evidence of a failing mind is coupled with the fact that the beneficiary has been concerned in the instructions for the will—the court will require more than proof that the testator knew the contents of the document which he signed. If the court is to be satisfied that the testator did know and approve the contents of his will—that is to say, that he did understand what he was doing and its effect—it may require evidence that the effect of the document was explained, that the testator did know the extent of his property and that he did comprehend and appreciate the claims on his bounty to which he ought to give effect.

It is submitted that the approach by Chadwick LJ is to be preferred to the narrower approach adopted in *Perrins v Holland* and *Simon v Byford*. If the true approach

84 *Perrins v Holland* (CA) (n 26 above) [31].
85 *Battan Singh v Amirchand* (n 36 above).
86 ibid 170.
87 *Gill v Woodall* (n 70 above).
88 In the text accompanying n 83 above.
89 *Hoff v Atherton* (n 6 above) [64].

of the courts at this stage of the investigative process is to ascertain whether the will represents the testamentary intentions of the testator (and not, as in *Burgess v Hawes*, for example, the intentions of the daughter) it is difficult to see how the court can be satisfied of this if the testator lacked capacity at the date of execution.

3.4. Summary on Want of Knowledge and Approval

Gill v Woodall and *Burgess v Hawes* suggest that attacking wills on the basis of want of knowledge and approval may have a greater chance of success because the court has to be satisfied on the basis of the whole of the evidence that the will represents the testamentary intentions of the testator. However, this involves the court conducting a wider inquiry, which must involve some question as to the level of capacity enjoyed by the testator. On the other hand, if—as the Court of Appeal suggested in *Perrins v Holland* and *Simon v Byford* – the concept is a narrow one, relatively easy to fulfil and simply requires understanding on the part of the testator as to the contents of the document he is executing, this head of challenge has a much less important role to play.

4. Overall Conclusions

Probate cases frequently go to the Court of Appeal, but rarely do they reach the Supreme Court. As result, differing guidance on what is required for a capable testator and what knowledge and approval really mean has emerged. Many cases appear to be heavily driven by their merits: there can be a justifiable reluctance on the part of the appellate court to interfere with the findings of the trial judge, who has had the advantage of hearing the evidence in a highly fact-sensitive case, and there appears to be a strong desire to uphold wills.

While these may all be laudable aims, we nevertheless need well-defined principles underpinning this area of law. There ought not to be an anomalous exception enabling someone who lacks capacity to make a will. The test for assessment of capacity should be clear, whether it be statutory or at common law. Finally, the courts need to clarify what is required before a testator is regarded as knowing and approving the contents of his will.

8

Reversing Testamentary Dispositions in Favour of Informal Carers

BRIAN SLOAN*

1. Introduction

In previous work, the present author has considered the scope for and legitimacy of private law claims by informal carers.[1] Informal carers vitally provide support to elderly and disabled people in the absence of a contractual or other legal duty to do so,[2] and there have been a number of cases in which such individuals have sought provision out of the estates of care recipients where the carers have not been included in a will.[3] The concern of the present chapter, however, is different and to some extent the converse. It considers situations in which a testamentary disposition *has* purportedly been made, but some challenge to the gift is made with the aim of having it set aside.

The chapter begins by considering the context of such gifts and the range of possible challenges to them. It then focuses on the appropriateness and the efficacy of the testamentary undue influence doctrine as a means of reversing testamentary dispositions in favour of informal carers. In particular, it considers the relevance of informal care to normative debates about whether a presumption

* The author is very grateful for the comments of participants at the All Souls conference on an earlier draft of this chapter, but remains responsible for all errors.

[1] See especially B Sloan, *Informal Carers and Private Law* (Oxford, Hart Publishing, 2013) (hereinafter '*Informal Carers and Private Law*'), though *cf* ch 7 of that book.

[2] See J Herring, *Caring and the Law* (Oxford, Hart Publishing, 2013) ch 2 for a discussion of the difficulties relating to definitions in this context. In *Re Good (deceased)* [2002] EWHC 640 (Ch), [2002] WTLR 801, for example, one of the beneficiaries of a disputed will did have a contractual relationship concerning care-related matters with the testatrix, but in time the testatrix came to regard the carer's family as a surrogate family. *cf* C Sawyer and M Spero, *Succession, Wills and Probate*, 3rd edn (Abingdon, Routledge, 2015) para 4.8.3 for discussion of the suggestion that a presumption of testamentary undue influence should apply only where care *has* been provided pursuant to a contract.

[3] See eg *Jennings v Rice* [2002] EWCA Civ 159, [2003] 1 FCR 501.

of testamentary undue influence should be introduced to match the equivalent *inter vivos* presumption.[4]

2. Testamentary Gifts in Favour of Carers and the Range of Challenges to Them

There are around 5.8 million informal carers in England and Wales.[5] While the system of *formal* social care in England is in the process of being reformed via the Care Act 2014, there are several respects in which the Act is not intended to increase the overall level of care provision,[6] leading to serious doubts about the system's ability to cope with the increasing numbers of people who will require social care as the population ages.[7] It therefore seems likely that society will continue to rely upon informal carers in the decades to come.[8] Many such carers suffer financial and health disadvantages as a result of the responsibilities that they assume,[9] and although empirical evidence suggests a level of discomfort about the linking of inheritance and care,[10] some recipients of care may well choose to recognise a carer in their will due to a sense of gratitude or moral obligation.[11] Writing from a US perspective, Tate defends freedom of testation precisely on the basis that it enables care recipients to reward caring family members.[12] The Law Commission of England and Wales, moreover, has described a situation involving a carer as a 'conspicuous example of the need for testamentary disposition'.[13]

In the light of the fact that testamentary freedom remains the default principle of English succession law,[14] it is perhaps easier to argue that testamentary gifts

[4] See eg L Mason, 'Undue Influence and Testamentary Dispositions: An Equitable Jurisdiction in Probate Law?' (2011) 75 *Conv* 115; R Kerridge, 'Undue Influence and Testamentary Dispositions: A Response' (2012) 76 *Conv* 129.

[5] Office for National Statistics, 'More than 1 in 10 Providing Unpaid Care as Numbers Rise to 5.8 Million' (News Release, 15 February 2013).

[6] See eg Department of Health, *Care and Support Statutory Guidance: Issued under the Care Act 2014* (June 2014) para 23.16.

[7] See King's Fund, *A New Settlement for Health and Social Care: Final Report* (2014).

[8] See eg B Sloan, 'Informal Care and Private Law: Governance or a Failure Thereof?' (2015) 1 *Canadian Journal of Comparative and Contemporary Law* 275.

[9] See *Informal Carers and Private Law* (n 1 above) 16.

[10] See eg K Rowlingson, 'Attitudes to Inheritance: Focus Group Report' (Bath, University of Bath, 2004) 38, cited in M Izuhara, *Housing, Care and Inheritance* (Abingdon, Routledge, 2008) 110; G Douglas, HD Woodward and others, 'Inheritance and the Family: Public Attitudes' [2010] *Fam Law* 1308; *cf* DG Drake and JA Lawrence, 'Equality and Distributions of Inheritance in Families' (2000) 13 *Social Justice Research* 271.

[11] See *Informal Carers and Private Law* (n 1 above) 140.

[12] JC Tate, 'Caregiving and the Case for Testamentary Freedom' (2008) 42 *University of California Davis Law Review* 129

[13] Law Commission, *Intestacy and Family Provision Claims on Death* (Law Com No 331, 2011) para 6.93 (hereinafter '2011 Report').

[14] See eg *Re Coventry (deceased)* [1979] 2 WLR 852 (Ch) 864–65 (Oliver J), aff'd [1980] Ch 461 (CA).

in favour of carers should be upheld than to argue that carers should be able to bring a claim where they have not been included in a valid will.[15] For example, the Law Commission has said that scenarios involving carers 'cry out for discussion and planning [about making a testamentary disposition] before it is too late', and that 'neither the intestacy rules nor the law of family provision can be any substitute for that'.[16] That said, such gifts are not without their difficulties, and they may not be allowed to take effect for various reasons. At the most basic level, the property intended for the carer may simply fall outside of the care recipient's estate at the time of death. Leaving aside situations where legal title to property has been disposed of or has been the subject of an express declaration of trust before death, the size of estates can of course be reduced by inheritance tax.[17] The formal social care system can again interact with this topic. Unlike healthcare provided broadly free at the point of delivery by the National Health Service,[18] social care is subject to a means test that mandates that many elderly people make significant contributions.[19] Under the system pre-dating the Care Act 2014, those with assets above £23,250 could (subject to some exceptions) be expected to pay for all of their care unless and until their relevant assets are reduced to that threshold.[20] It is expected that the Act will broadly reduce the scope for a person's assets to be swallowed up in paying for care,[21] by imposing something of a cap on each person's eligible lifetime care costs[22] and increasing the capital limit below which means-tested help is available to £118,000 where a home is being taken into consideration.[23] Liability for social care nevertheless remains a significant potential fetter on the ability of testators to make provision for carers,[24] and while the Act makes it easier for a person to defer her liability to pay for care,[25] 'deferred payment agreements' take the form of secured loans prima facie repayable 90 days after the care recipient's death.[26]

Property earmarked for a carer in a will may also fall outside the estate by virtue of successful claims on the estate by non-carers, including those framed in terms

[15] See, by analogy, *Informal Carers and Private Law* (n 1 above) ch 7; B Sloan, 'Due Rewards or Undue Influence?—Property Transfers Benefitting Informal Carers' (2011) 19 *Restitution Law Review* 37.

[16] 2011 Report (n 13 above) para 6.93.

[17] See Inheritance Tax Act 1984.

[18] See National Health Service Act 2006, s 1(4).

[19] See eg Commission on Funding of Care and Support, *Fairer Care Funding* (July 2011).

[20] See National Assistance (Assessment of Resources) Regulations, SI 1992/2977.

[21] N Hopkins and E Laurie, 'Social Citizenship, Housing Wealth and the Cost of Social Care: Is the Care Act 2014 "Fair"?' (2015) 78 *MLR* 112; *cf* Department of Health, 'Letter from Rt Hon Alistair Burt MP: Delay in the Implementation of the Cap on Care Costs' (17 July 2015).

[22] Care Act 2014, s 15.

[23] Department of Health, *The Care Act 2014: Consultation on Draft Regulations and Guidance to Implement the Cap on Care Costs and Policy Proposals for a New Appeals System for Care and Support* (February 2015) para 9.7.

[24] See eg B Sloan, 'Adult Social Care and Property Rights' (2016) 36 *OJLS* (forthcoming); University of Cambridge Faculty of Law Research Paper No 24/2015, available via: papers.ssrn.com/sol3/papers.cfm?abstract_id=2600043 (last accessed 20 November 2015).

[25] Care Act 2014, ss 34–36.

[26] Department of Health, *Care and Support Statutory Guidance* (n 6 above) para 9.104; Care and Support (Deferred Payment) Regulations 2014 (SI 2014/2671), reg 7.

of proprietary estoppel[27] or the common intention constructive trust.[28] A gift to a carer might be thwarted by an earlier mutual wills arrangement.[29] In a fully orthodox manner, the doctrine of survivorship effectively operated (along with the loss of testamentary capacity by the survivor) to defeat a testamentary gift to the carer in *Campbell v Griffin*, and he was left to pursue a successful claim in proprietary estoppel instead.[30] Statute, namely the Inheritance (Provision for Family and Dependants) Act 1975, may also intervene,[31] and the present author has previously accepted that provision for carers should not be allowed to leave genuine dependants facing hardship.[32]

There is also the possibility of a challenge to the will itself, with reference to doctrines such as want of knowledge and approval or the absence of testamentary capacity.[33] A seemingly straightforward testamentary gift given in recognition of years of devoted service may therefore turn out to raise extremely difficult issues, particularly given the inevitability that care recipients will be vulnerable in some respects.

The remainder of this chapter will focus on the impact of one particular mode of challenge to a testamentary gift in favour of a carer, namely the doctrine of undue influence. It should nevertheless be noted that, as with the other methods of challenging a will, a carer might in principle also *invoke* that doctrine in order to challenge a will made in favour of someone else.[34]

3. Carers and Testamentary Undue Influence

This section summarises the English law of testamentary undue influence[35] as it might apply to dispositions made in favour of informal carers, before considering

[27] On proprietary estoppel and its interaction with the law of succession, see Ben McFarlane's contribution in Ch 4 of this volume.

[28] See eg *Palagiano v Mankarios* [2011] NSWSC 61.

[29] See eg *Charles v Fraser* [2010] EWHC 2154 (Ch), [2010] WTLR 1489, as well as S Hudson and B Sloan, 'Testamentary Freedom: Mutual Wills Might Let You Down' in W Barr (ed), *Modern Studies in Property Law, Volume 8* (Oxford, Hart Publishing, 2015) for a discussion. On mutual wills more generally, see also Ying Khai Liew's contribution in Ch 5 of the present volume.

[30] *Campbell v Griffin* [2001] EWCA Civ 990, [2001] WTLR 981 at [13].

[31] See eg *Perrins v Holland* [2009] EWHC 1945 (Ch), [2009] WTLR 1387.

[32] See *Informal Carers and Private Law* (n 1 above) 144.

[33] See eg *Perrins v Holland* [2010] EWCA Civ 840, [2011] Ch 270; *Abbott v Richardson* [2006] EWHC 1291 (Ch), [2006] WTLR 1567. For further discussion, see Penelope Reed's contribution in Ch 7 of this volume.

[34] In *Scammell v Farmer* [2008] EWHC 1100 (Ch), [2008] WTLR 1261, for example, a man described as the testatrix's carer supported the (unsuccessful) challenge by her granddaughters to a will made mainly in favour of her daughter.

[35] RJ Scalise, 'Undue Influence and the Law of Wills: A Comparative Analysis' (2008) 19 *Duke Journal of Comparative & International Law* 41 identifies mechanisms of dealing with what is now called testamentary undue influence in Roman law.

whether the context of informal care is relevant to normative debates about whether the *inter vivos* presumption of undue influence should be extended to testamentary cases.

3.1. The Doctrine of Testamentary Undue Influence

There have been a number of reported cases concerning undue influence in recent years, many involving carers. Nevertheless, it is significant that an undue influence claim pursued against a will made in favour of a testatrix's 'housekeeper, attendant, and companion' had already been considered by the Privy Council in 1906,[36] and HHJ Norris QC—as he then was—said in his 2004 judgment in *Cattermole v Prisk* that 'the enquiry starts (and frequently finishes) with a consideration of the principles set out' in the 1868 case of *Hall v Hall*.[37] Moreover, in the 2002 judgment in *Vaughan v Vaughan*, Behrens J opined that there had been 'no authority since 1970 where a court has sought to apply a different test from the test set out in the [earlier] authorities'.[38]

In *Hall v Hall*, Sir JP Wilde directed a jury to the effect that 'pressure of whatever character, whether acting on the fears or the hopes, if so exerted as to overpower the volition without convincing the judgment, is a species of restraint under which no valid will can be made'.[39] On his direction,[40]

> Importunity or threats, such as the testator has not the courage to resist, moral command asserted and yielded to for the sake of peace and quiet, or of escaping from distress of mind or social discomfort ... if carried to a degree in which the free play of the testator's judgment, discretion or wishes, is overborne, will constitute undue influence.

That said, '[p]ersuasion, appeals to the affections or ties of kindred, to a sentiment of gratitude for past services, or pity for future destitution, or the like ... are all legitimate, and may be fairly pressed on a testator'.[41] It had earlier been said that:[42]

> Undue influence, in order to render a will void, must be an influence which can justly be described, by a person looking at the matter judicially, to have caused the execution of a paper pretending to express a testator's mind, but which really did not express his mind, but expressed something else, something which he did not really mean.

[36] *Baudains v Richardson* [1906] AC 169 (PC) 173 (Lord Macnaghten).

[37] *Cattermole v Prisk* [2006] 1 FLR 693 (Ch) at [13(f)], referring to *Hall v Hall* (1868) 1 P & D 481 (Ct P).

[38] *Vaughan v Vaughan* [2002] EWHC 699 (Ch), [2005] WTLR 401 at [88]; *cf Cowderoy v Cranfield* [2011] EWHC 1616 (Ch), [2011] WTLR 1699 at [141] (Morgan J).

[39] *Hall v Hall* (n 37 above) 482.

[40] ibid.

[41] ibid.

[42] *Boyse v Rossborough* (1857) 6 HL Cas 2 at 34, 10 ER 1192 at 1205 (Lord Cranworth LC). See FR Burns, 'Reforming Testamentary Undue Influence in Canadian and English Law' (2006) 29 *Dalhousie Law Journal* 455 at 458–59 for an argument that the doctrine has since been applied more harshly than was intended in *Boyse v Rossborough*.

Almost 150 years after the judgment in *Hall v Hall*, Vos J opined that '[i]t is well known that it is extremely difficult to establish that a will is invalidated by undue influence',[43] and Evans has emphasised that '[s]evere risks ensue if it is pleaded but not actually established, in connection with costs'.[44] Undue influence requires a finding of 'coercion'.[45] At this point, it should be made clear that there is no

> suggestion that in circumstances [of alleged testamentary undue influence] there is any scope for a presumption that undue influence was brought to bear on [the putative testator], such that the burden is on [those seeking to uphold the impugned will] to rebut it,[46]

although this issue will be discussed in more depth in Section 3.2. By contrast, such a presumption can clearly exist in the context of presumed undue influence *inter vivos*.[47] This may mean that, as was clearly thought to be the case in *Cattermole v Prisk*, testamentary undue influence is equivalent to actual undue influence in the *inter vivos* context (in respect of which no presumption is invoked).[48] That said, the distinction between *inter vivos* and testamentary situations was emphasised in *Parfitt v Lawless*,[49] and Bell has said that 'it is not clear that the probate doctrine goes quite as far as its equitable counterpart in relation to improper pressure'.[50]

It has been said that there is 'an inherent improbability' about the events alleged in a claim of undue influence 'having happened or occurred'.[51] While the presence or absence of such influence is a question of fact[52] and '[t]he requisite standard is proof on the balance of probabilities',[53]

> as the allegation of undue influence is a serious one, the evidence required must be sufficiently cogent to persuade the court that the explanation for what has occurred is that the testator's will has been overborne by coercion rather than there being some other explanation.

[43] *Jeffrey v Jeffrey* [2013] EWHC 1942 (Ch), [2013] WTLR 1509 at [214]; and *cf Hansen v Barker-Benfield* [2006] EWHC 1119 (Ch), [2006] WTLR 1141 for consideration of an argument, inter alia, that a decision *not* to make a will was procured by undue influence.

[44] S Evans, 'A Correct Result, but an Instinctively Wrong One?' (2012) 76 *Conv* 255 at 259; *cf* Mason (n 4 above) 116.

[45] *Wingrove v Wingrove* (1885) 11 PD 81(PDA).

[46] *Re Good* (n 2 above) [121], cited eg in *Ark v Kaur* [2010] EWHC 2314 (Ch), (2010) 154(36) *Sol Jo LB* 34 at [18] (David Cooke J); *cf Ashwell v Lomi* (1869–72) LR 2 P & D 477 (Prerogative Court of Canterbury) and the position in Scotland: see eg *Horne v Whyte* [2005] CSOH 115, [2005] ScotCS CSOH 115.

[47] See eg *Hammond v Osborn* [2002] EWCA Civ 885, [2002] WTLR 1125 as well as *Informal Carers and Private Law* (n 1 above) ch 7 and Sloan, 'Due Rewards or Undue Influence' (n 15 above).

[48] See eg *Cattermole v Prisk* (n 37 above) [13]; *In the Estate of Wilkes* [2006] WTLR 1097 (Ch) 1107–11; *Hubbard v Scott* [2011] EWHC 2750 (Ch), [2012] WTLR 29 at [2] (Proudman J); and the much earlier Privy Council decision in *Craig v Lamoureux* [1920] AC 349 (PC).

[49] *Parfitt v Lawless* (1872) LR 2 P & D 462 (Ct P).

[50] AP Bell, 'Abuse of a Relationship: Undue Influence in English Law and French Law' (2007) 15 *European Review of Private Law* 555 at 564.

[51] *Schomberg v Taylor* [2013] EWHC 2269 (Ch), [2013] WTLR 1413 at [31] (Mark Cawson QC).

[52] *Re Edwards (decd)* [2007] EWHC 1119 (Ch), [2007] WTLR 1387 at [47 (ii)] (Lewison J).

[53] *Cowderoy v Cranfield* (n 38 above) at [141] (Morgan J).

The analysis of Lord Nicholls in *Re H (minors) (Sexual Abuse: Standard of Proof)*[54] in the context of child protection has been used to justify this approach,[55] although it is interesting that his Lordship's approach later had to be qualified in the former context.[56] Nevertheless, in the recent case of *Schrader v Schrader*, it was reiterated that '[t]he allegation is a serious one, so the evidence necessary to make out the case has to be commensurately stronger'.[57]

Where there is

> considerable evidence as to the circumstances in which the disputed will was prepared and executed … it is … appropriate … simply to ask whether the party asserting undue influence has satisfied [the judge] to the requisite standard that the will was executed as a result of undue influence.[58]

Nevertheless, 'a finding of undue influence can be made by a court drawing inferences from all the circumstances, even in the absence of direct evidence of undue influence',[59] although the undue influence must be in relation to the will itself and not only other matters.[60] In *Ark v Kaur*, David Cooke J put forward the view that undue influence 'is rarely capable of direct proof, and must usually be inferred from the surrounding circumstances'.[61] Similarly, in *Schrader v Schrader*, Mann J accepted that

> [i]t will be a common feature of a large number of undue influence cases that there is no direct evidence of the application of influence [because it] is of the nature of undue influence that it goes on when no-one is looking.[62]

That does not stop its being proved, albeit from 'more circumstantial' evidence.[63]

In *Cowderoy v Cranfield*, it was specifically held that the choice to benefit a Mr Cranfield via will was a free one,[64]

> influenced by [the testatatrix's] belief, or at any rate her hope, that if she made a will in favour of Mr Cranfield and told him that she had done so, that would help her because he would be more likely to continue to visit her and care for her.

Undue influence was nevertheless rejected because there was 'no evidence that Mr Cranfield ever tried to persuade, or otherwise influence, [the testator] to make a will in his favour'.[65] Even where 'persuasion but not coercion' is found, this is insufficient,[66] and 'persuasion and advice do not amount to undue influence so

[54] *Re H (minors) (Sexual Abuse: Standard of Proof)* [1996] AC 563 (HL).
[55] See eg *Killick v Pountney* [2000] WTLR 41 (Ch) 68.
[56] *Re B (children) (Sexual Abuse: Standard of Proof)* [2008] UKHL 35, [2009] 1 AC 11; *Re S-B (children) (Care Proceedings: Standard of Proof)* [2009] UKSC 17, [2010] 1 AC 678.
[57] *Schrader v Schrader* [2013] EWHC 466 (Ch), [2013] WTLR 701 at [96] (Mann J).
[58] *Cowderoy v Cranfield* (n 38 above) [141].
[59] ibid.
[60] *Killick v Pountney* (n 55 above).
[61] *Ark v Kaur* (n 46 above) [47].
[62] *Schrader v Schrader* (n 57 above) [96] (Mann J).
[63] ibid.
[64] *Cowderoy v Cranfield* (n 38 above) [147] (Morgan J).
[65] ibid.
[66] *Re Devillebichot (deceased)* [2013] EWHC 2867 (Ch), [2013] WTLR 1701 at [75] (Mark Herbert QC).

long as the free volition of the testator to accept or reject them is not invaded'.[67] Moreover,

> the fact that [the beneficiary of a disputed will] had the opportunity and the motive to attempt to persuade [the testator] to favour him does not necessarily mean that he made any such attempt or did anything for which he could be criticised.[68]

In fact, in *Abbott v Richardson*, the judge was 'sure' that the beneficiary 'did everything she could, in her own interests, to cause [the testator] to make a will', but this did not in the circumstances prevent him from concluding that 'its terms represented what [the testator] wanted to do' (albeit that the judge had already concluded that the testator lacked capacity in any event).[69] Similarly:[70]

> It is not sufficient to establish that a person has the power unduly to overbear the will of the testator, it must be proved that the power was exercised and it was by means of its exercise that the will has been produced against the wishes of the testator.

Even where a judge could not 'accept for one moment the evidence ... that everything [the testatrix] did was because ... that was what she wanted'[71] and the conduct of others was otherwise 'little short of disgraceful'[72] (or 'degrading and pernicious' in the language of an older authority),[73] there could be no finding of undue influence in the absence of specific complaints of undue pressure from a particular individual, although such cases inevitably turn on their facts and can thus appear inconsistent with each other.[74]

Most claims of undue influence appear to be accompanied by claims of want of knowledge and approval and testamentary incapacity, which in some respects have more generous evidential requirements for those seeking to challenge the will.[75] The Court of Appeal's judgment in *Gill v Woodall* did not consider undue influence in detail because it was held (reversing the judge below) that the testatrix had not in fact known and approved of the will's contents.[76] Lord Neuberger opined that[77]

> it seems ... rather unreal to consider arguments as to the nature and extent of the influence [the testatrix's husband] exerted on his wife to persuade her to leave the farm

[67] *Jeffrey v Jeffrey* (n 43 above) [238] (Vos J).

[68] *Cowderoy v Cranfield* (n 38 above) [16] (Morgan J).

[69] *Abbott v Richardson* (n 33 above) [200]; see, similarly, *Allen v Emery* [2005] EWHC 2389 (Ch), (2005) 8 ITELR 358.

[70] *Vaughan v Vaughan* (n 38 above) [87] (Behrens J); see also *Craig v Lamoureux* (n 48 above) and *Wingrove v Wingrove* (n 45 above) 83.

[71] *Vaughan v Vaughan* (n 38 above) [90] (Behrens J).

[72] ibid [91].

[73] *Baudains v Richardson* (n 36 above) 184 (Lord Macnaghten).

[74] See *Vaughan v Vaughan* (n 38 above).

[75] See eg P Ridge, 'Equitable Undue Influence and Wills' (2004) 120 *LQR* 617 at 622–23.

[76] *Gill v Woodall* [2010] EWCA Civ 1430, [2011] Ch 380, discussed further in Penelope Reed's contribution in Ch 7 of this volume.

[77] *Gill v Woodall* (n 76 above) [66]; *cf Ark v Kaur* (n 46 above) [19] (David Cooke J); *Walters v Smee* [2008] EWHC 2029 (Ch), [2009] WTLR 521 at [130].

> to the RSPCA, when I have just concluded that she did not know that she was doing that very thing.

Conversely, as Judge Hazel Williamson QC put it in *Tchilingirian v Ouzounian*,

> in relation to undue influence, the point is not that the testator did not actually know and understand what he was doing, but rather that he did know and understand this all too well, but was doing it against his will.[78]

She therefore found that undue influence could not be made out because the making of the will was consistent with hypotheses other than such influence, ie lack of testamentary capacity and want of knowledge and approval. Kerridge, however, has criticised this type of thinking with reference to *Wyniczenko v Plucinska-Surowka*,[79] on the basis that, where a will leaves the entire estate to a beneficiary who drafted it and the alleged testator did not know and approve of its contents, it must have been procured by either undue influence or fraud.[80]

The rigorous approach of the courts to undue influence means that, in the recent case of *Parker v Litchfield*, for example, where '[t]he picture generally was of an independent-minded woman who was keen to do things her way' and who 'proved capable of standing her ground when [the granddaughter alleging undue influence] complained about the new will', it was held that [t]here was 'no real evidence … to support the allegation of undue influence'.[81] In *Re Good (deceased)*, the testatrix 'was an elderly, vulnerable woman, who was substantially dependent on the Carapetos',[82] the 'adopted family' in whose favour she made a disputed will,[83] 'for her continued enjoyment of life at the house'.[84] Rimer J accepted that this 'no doubt provides a background against which there would or might have been scope for the exercise of some subtle, and undue, influence', and that there was a 'legitimate suspicion that this *may* have been what was happening'.[85] The facts were, however, 'also consistent with a perfectly innocent explanation', namely that 'the Carapeto family had … played a central and close role in Miss Good's life for some 20 years'.[86] The testatrix was 'genuinely very fond of them', they were 'on hand day and night', and it was not unlikely that she would discuss her testamentary affairs with them.[87] Ultimately, the judge was convinced that at the time of the disputed will, the testator 'was still a very intelligent, sensitive and independent-minded woman, who was capable of making her own decisions'.[88]

[78] *Tchilingirian v Ouzounian* [2003] EWHC 1220 (Ch), [2003] WTLR. 709 at [79]. See also Mason (n 4 above) 120.
[79] *Wyniczenko v Plucinska-Surowka* [2005] EWHC 2794 (Ch), [2006] WTLR 487.
[80] Kerridge (n 4 above) 132.
[81] *Parker v Litchfield* [2014] EWHC 1799 (Ch) [31] (Newey J); see, similarly, *Abbott v Richardson* (n 33 above).
[82] *Re Good (deceased)* (n 2 above) [127] (Rimer J).
[83] ibid [15].
[84] ibid [127].
[85] ibid.
[86] ibid.
[87] ibid. See, similarly, the much older case of *Baudains v Richardson* (n 36 above) 186.
[88] *Re Good (deceased)* (n 2 above) [127].

That said, and particularly significantly for cases involving carers, Lewison J stated in *Re Edwards (deceased)* that '[t]he will of a weak and ill person may be more easily overborne than that of a hale and hearty one'.[89] James Munby QC—as he then was—expressed the same view in *Killick v Pountney*, albeit that 'no amount of evidence of bodily or mental infirmity will of itself establish undue influence in the absence of some independent evidence tending to show the exercise of an improper influence'.[90] On the facts of that case, he found such undue influence on the bases, inter alia, that the defendant had extracted loans from the testator that were never repaid and exercised control over his possessions and papers, of the testator's increasing bitterness towards the defendant, and the defendant's treatment of the testator, rendering the will 'otherwise *almost* inexplicable' (emphasis added) but apparently completely inexplicable in the light of other factors,[91] the vulnerability of the testator's condition, the involvement of the defendant in executing the will, and his actual exercise of influence over the testator.

In spite of the fact that there is no presumption of testamentary influence, in which case the extent to which a gift 'calls for explanation' would assume prime importance, judges have given anxious consideration to the extent to which a testamentary gift might be explicable. Even where a testator changes his mind shortly after issuing instructions for a draft will, that course of action is not necessarily inconsistent and was not found to justify a finding of undue influence in *Wharton v Bancroft*.[92] Nor was

> evidence of a departure from imprecisely expressed intentions evidence … sufficiently cogent to persuade [Norris J] that the explanation for the departure is that [the testator's] volition was overborne by coercion, rather than that on his deathbed he saw things differently than he had in life.[93]

It was also recognised in that case that a 'deathbed marriage' with an understanding that it will revoke an existing will means that the making of a new will is not of itself suspicious.[94] On the other hand, undue influence was found in *Schomberg v Taylor*, on the basis of the testatrix's 'very fragile physical and mental state'[95] and 'cogent evidence' that the deceased's brother-in-law 'subjected [her] to unwanted pressure so far as the making of the new will [was] concerned … and of him doing so persistently',[96] which wore her down such that she was prepared to do what he wanted for a quiet life. In addition, there was 'no obvious reason why such a

89 *Re Edwards (decd)* (n 52 above) [47(vi)].
90 *Killick v Pountney* (n 55 above) 69.
91 ibid 76.
92 *Wharton v Bancroft* [2011] EWHC (Ch) 3250, [2012] WTLR 693 at [67] (Norris J).
93 ibid [112].
94 ibid [89].
95 *Schomberg v Taylor* (n 51 above) [107] (Mark Cawson QC).
96 ibid [108].

fundamental change [as] to virtually exclude [her two sons] from the [later] will should have been made at the time unless she had been pressured into making a change',[97] and conversely, there was no obvious reason why she would benefit the children of the undue influencer, whose own financial difficulties provided a motive for unduly influencing her.

The courts have, however, expressed an understanding of the motives of testators in leaving gifts to their carers, as demonstrated by *Re Good (deceased)*.[98] In *Bateman v Overy*, moreover, the deceased had made a will a few months before his death, leaving his whole estate to his son Stephen and cutting out his two other children.[99] He had become estranged from the others, and also wrote letters explaining his decision to omit them from the will. After his own wife's death, the deceased had moved to live with Stephen and his wife, Wendy. Stephen and Wendy built extensions to their property at that time (albeit partially financed by the deceased), one of which provided the deceased with his own ensuite room. His estate was very small at the time that the will was made because he had already made large gifts to Stephen and Wendy, despite their protestations. They also tried to discourage him from making the will. In rejecting the possibility of undue influence, the judge therefore held that:[100]

> [The deceased] wanted to thank Stephen and Wendy for the care which they had provided to him and the home which they welcomed him into. There was no question of him succumbing to pressure for the sake of a quiet life. The [last] will was what he wanted to do. In making it, he acted as a free agent.

Even where, as in the case of *In the Estate of Wilkes*,[101] there could be 'no doubt that [the substantial beneficiary of the disputed will] was capable of being aggressive, difficult and rude when seeking to put right some inadequacy in the care of the Testatrix or when seeking some benefit for his mother',[102] his care for her was 'outstanding' and there was 'no evidence of any real weight that he was ever aggressive towards the Testatrix, or sought to coerce her into dealing with her affairs against her will'.[103] The testatrix had the opportunity to express misgivings to the drafter of the disputed will and did not take it.

There are rightly some limits to the court's sympathy towards carers, however, even if nuanced judgments have to be made on the facts of particular cases. In *Schrader v Schrader*,[104] a comparatively rare case where undue influence was made out, the purported 2006 will of Jessica Schrader left (aside from some minor

[97] ibid [110].
[98] See the text accompanying nn 82–88 above.
[99] *Bateman v Overy* [2014] EWHC 432 (Ch).
[100] ibid [152] (John Male QC).
[101] *In the Estate of Wilkes* [2006] WTLR 1097 (Ch).
[102] ibid 1127.
[103] ibid 1128.
[104] *Schrader v Schrader* (n 57 above).

items) her house to her son Nick, and the residue in equal shares to Nick and her other son Bill, albeit that the residue was ultimately of little value. Her previous 1990 will treated the residue in the same way, but made no specific gift of the house. The judge found that Nick had feelings of hatred towards his brother, as well as an unjustified feeling that they had been treated unequally by their parents throughout their lives.

Nick gave up work and moved into Jessica's house to look after her after she suffered a fall in 2005. The will-writer who took instructions for the 2006 will recalled that:[105]

> Jessica informed her that she wanted to alter the distribution of her estate because Nick had sold his house [though it was in fact sold by his trustee in bankruptcy] and moved in with her and was contributing towards the cost of maintaining her house, and she wanted to ensure that he had somewhere to live after her death.

That said, Mann J found that although 'he was a caring son who tended to his mother's needs', he had a 'short fuse' and that 'his physical presence and personality around the house would be likely to produce a significant degree of subservience in an anxious, dependent, increasingly frail elderly lady in his care'.[106] The judge considered it 'entirely plausible that he would get cross with her from time to time and that she should be anxious about him and anxious to please'.[107]

The factors that Mann J held to give rise to his inference of undue influence were:[108] Jessica's vulnerability as a lady in her mid-90s who was more uncertain after her fall (notwithstanding that she had testamentary capacity); her dependence on Nick which, although not total, meant that she 'would have been very worried about his moving out and ceasing to look after her'; the engagement of a will-writer rather than her previous firm of solicitors, for which the reasons (given by Nick) were found to be unsatisfactory; the inaccuracy in Jessica's understanding of the reasons for Nick's house being sold, which was likely to have been caused by Nick; the fact that Nick's way of thinking provided the only identified reason why Jessica would have changed her will; Nick's own anxiety (as he saw it) to 'even up' the provision made for Bill and himself; his misleading attempts to distance himself from the will's preparation; his failure to disclose the existence of the 2006 will until steps were taken to prove the 1990 will; and the fairly blunt attempt made by the will-writer to establish whether or not there was any undue influence in the case. Mann J admitted that it was 'not possible to determine any more than' the general sowing of ideas and taking advantage of vulnerability, in particular: 'the precise form of the pressure, or its occasion or occasions', but he was also confident that 'it is not necessary to do so' in order to find undue influence.[109]

[105] ibid [59].
[106] ibid [56].
[107] ibid.
[108] ibid [97].
[109] ibid [98].

Judges have also scrutinised claims about the beneficiary of a disputed will actually being a carer in the first place. In *Re Edwards (deceased)*,[110] for example, Lewison J found that the sole beneficiary of the impugned will of Mrs Edwards, the testatrix's son Terry, had the opportunity to exercise undue influence because he took her back home against medical advice and had tried to push his brother John out of the house on the day that the will was executed, and that the testatrix was 'frail and vulnerable, and frightened of Terry'.[111] Lewison J also found that Terry had taken this opportunity on the basis that there was:[112]

> no other reasonable explanation for Mrs Edwards having levelled ... false accusations [concerning theft and putting her in a home to die] against John and [his wife]; and for having given ... a palpably inadequate and false explanation to [the drafter of the will] of the reasons for changing her will.

Interestingly for present purposes, Lewison J drew his conclusion partly in the light of the fact that Mrs Edwards justified the change to her will on the basis that Terry 'look[ed] after [her] and [did] [her] washing and clean[ed] the house and [did] everything', but that this was in the judge's analysis 'plainly untrue'.[113]

Judges appear to be adopting a careful and relatively evenhanded approach to undue influence claims in relation to testamentary dispositions in favour of carers, albeit that their approaches are heavily fact-sensitive. That said, it is certainly not easy to make out an allegation of undue influence and there is something of an academic consensus that this situation is undesirable.[114] The next section (3.2) considers the extent to which care situations shed light on whether perceived deficiencies in the current law should be remedied through the application of a presumption of undue influence.

3.2. Carers and a Presumption of Testamentary Undue Influence

It has been seen that there is no presumption of testamentary undue influence. This contrasts with the situation in *inter vivos* situations, where a relationship of trust and confidence, coupled with a gift[115] judged to 'call for explanation', gives rise to a presumption of undue influence.[116] This obliges the recipient of the gift

[110] *Re Edwards (deceased)* (n 52 above).

[111] ibid [55].

[112] ibid.

[113] ibid [50].

[114] Ridge (n 75 above); Burns (n 42 above); Mason (n 4 above), Kerridge (n 4 above); *cf* P Vines, 'Challenging the Testator's Mind by Challenging Lifetime Transactions: *Bridgewater v Leahy* as Back-door Probate Law?' (2003) 10 *Australian Property Law Journal* 53.

[115] The doctrine also applies to contracts.

[116] See especially *Royal Bank of Scotland v Etridge (No 2)* [2001] UKHL 44, [2002] 2 AC 773; *Hammond v Osborn* (n 47 above).

to adduce positive evidence that the gift was in fact the result of an exercise of free will, usually—but not necessarily—by citing the provision of independent legal advice.[117] The relevant relationship of trust and confidence can arise either because it belongs to a recognised category of such relationships, or because particular circumstances of the parties produced one.[118]

The effect of the distinction between *inter vivos* and testamentary cases was to some extent illustrated in *Cattermole v Prisk*.[119] While Judge Norris QC considered that one *inter vivos* gift to a carer raised the presumption of undue influence because there was a relationship of trust and confidence and the gift called for explanation (albeit that an earlier one did not), he held that testamentary undue influence by the same person had not been made out. The distinction has persisted in spite of the fact that *inter vivos* transactions found to have been procured by undue influence can otherwise, of course, have a profound effect on ultimate testamentary dispositions.[120]

Ridge has been critical of the distinction between *inter vivos* and testamentary undue influence (which are historical in origin, given the different approaches of the chancery and probate courts), arguing that the factual situations to which they apply are 'virtually indistinguishable'.[121] Even after extensive consideration of the arguments in favour of the application of the *inter vivos* doctrine to testamentary dispositions, however, she admits that 'the case for reform is not clear-cut'.[122] Mason has been more single-minded in advocating the extension of the *inter vivos* presumption to testamentary cases,[123] but his arguments have been specifically and forcefully refuted by Kerridge.[124]

The justification for the distinction between the *inter vivos* (equitable) and testamentary (probate) doctrines was considered by the Privy Council in *Craig v Lamoureux* in 1920, where it was emphasised that 'a will, which merely regulates succession after death, is very different from a gift inter vivos, which strips the donor of his property during his lifetime'.[125] There was thus

> no reason why a husband or a parent, on whose part it is natural that he should do so, may not put his claims before a wife or a child and ask for their recognition, provided the person making the will knows what is being done,

albeit that '[t]he persuasion must of course stop short of coercion, and the testamentary disposition must be made with comprehension of what is being done'.[126]

[117] See eg *Inche Noriah v Shaik Allie Bin Omar* [1929] AC 127 (PC).
[118] *Royal Bank of Scotland v Etridge (No 2)* (n 116 above).
[119] *Cattermole v Prisk* (n 37 above).
[120] See eg *Simpson v Simpson* [1992] 1 FLR 601 (Ch); Vines (n 114 above).
[121] Ridge (n 75 above) 617.
[122] ibid 639.
[123] Mason (n 4 above).
[124] Kerridge (n 4 above).
[125] *Craig v Lamoureux* (n 48 above) 356 (Viscount Haldane).
[126] ibid 357.

Conversely, Klinck has suggested that a presumption of undue influence is *more* justifiable in the testamentary context because 'exploiters might be more inclined to refrain from depredations in the *inter vivos* context by the very fact that their victims might still be alive and be able to expose them',[127] and it thus seems that he would go further than Mason in this respect. For his part, Kerridge is adamant that '[t]here *is* a distinction between inter vivos gifts and testamentary dispositions, and it makes no sense to attempt to treat them in the same way'.[128] One reason that Kerridge considers the two situations distinct is that the nature of the influence itself differs between two types of claim: the testamentary concept 'implies pressure', while the *inter vivos* concept 'does not' and rather suggests 'affection'.[129] Kerridge's description of undue influence *inter vivos* might invite criticism,[130] but it is clear that he regards the presumption as a particular and important distinction between the testamentary and *inter vivos* versions. He argues, with reference to *Wyniczenko v Plucinska-Surowka*,[131] that presumed undue influence might involve a presumption against the beneficiaries under an *earlier* will, ie the 'wrong' will, in circumstances where close relatives have been excluded from a later will which was procured by someone with a much shorter-term relationship with the testator.[132]

Burns notes a number of problems with such a presumption.[133] These include that a presumption could be used strategically to procure the grant of probate in relation to an earlier will at odds with a testator's intention at death and the fact that the testator is by definition not alive to give evidence. This is also true by the time many *inter vivos* undue influence claims are litigated,[134] and Vines has suggested that

> the distinction between the doctrines and the choice of when those doctrines should be used should focus more on the reasons for the distinctions between the doctrines, such as who is available to give evidence, than on technical distinctions between them.[135]

The 'major problem' with extending a presumption to the probate context, in Burns' view, is that the presumption 'might be used to defeat the true intention of the testator on the basis of whether the testator did or did not act in accordance with "social norms"'.[136] In spite of her sympathy to the similarity between

[127] DR Klinck, 'Does the Presumption of Undue Influence Arise in the Testamentary Context?' (2005) 24 *Estates, Trusts & Pensions Journal* 125 at 137.

[128] Kerridge (n 4 above) 129.

[129] ibid 133.

[130] He apparently avoids, for example, a clear distinction between actual and presumed undue influence *inter vivos*.

[131] *Wyniczenko v Plucinska-Surowka* (n 79 above). It is interesting that Kerridge criticises Mason's suggestion that testamentary and *inter vivos* situation should be treated in the same way with reference to this decision, given that the undue influence allegation per se was specifically abandoned in the case (at [4]).

[132] Kerridge (n 4 above) 134–35.

[133] Burns (n 42 above) 469–70.

[134] See eg *Hammond v Osborn* (n 47 above).

[135] Vines (n 114 above) 63.

[136] Burns (n 42 above) 474.

inter vivos and testamentary situations, Ridge similarly concedes that 'the discretionary nature of equitable undue influence might encourage judges to fall back on what they perceive to be cultural norms in order to determine the validity of a testamentary gift, rather than deciding each case on its merits',[137] as they do relatively carefully under the current law in England and Wales.

Burns also accepts that '[i]t might be argued that the gift in favour of care-givers or housekeepers to the disadvantage of the relatives is inexplicable "by the ordinary motives by which people act"', but that 'there may be good reasons why the testator decided to leave substantial assets to such persons, although the testator may not have articulated these reasons in the will or supplementary documentation'.[138] Whatever the potential problems with Kerridge's analysis of undue influence *inter vivos*,[139] his general thesis is convincing. As he puts it, 'the equitable [undue influence *inter vivos*] doctrine is designed to prevent those for whom the donor has high regard or affection from taking advantage', but such people are 'precisely the people for whom one would expect him to make provision in his will',[140] and a deceased person's property must be devolved somehow. While Kerridge's argument could be employed against a later-arriving carer and in favour of family members excluded from a later will, in the present author's view it could also favour a carer.

As Burns puts it, moreover, '[u]nlike an *inter vivos* transaction, the provisions in the will cannot improvidently affect the testator during his lifetime (except to the extent that the testator may know that the will does not reflect his true desires)'.[141] Mason points out that this argument 'fails to take account of other victims who may have been the natural beneficiaries under the Will had the testator not been unduly influenced in making his Will',[142] but the disadvantaging of oneself is a rather more objective means of measuring whether a disposition 'calls for explanation'. It is also an important one in the particular context of care. In *Hammond v Osborn*, the defendant carer conceded that the gift to her of over 90 per cent of her charge's assets called for explanation.[143] Ward LJ nevertheless emphasised that the gift divested him of 'practically all of his free capital',[144] and was 'an act of generosity wholly out of proportion to the kindness shown to [the donor]',[145] and that '[h]e may have needed more care in the future and would not have been able to afford it'.[146]

137 Ridge (n 75 above) 639.
138 Burns (n 42 above) 474.
139 See n 130 above.
140 Kerridge (n 4 above)134; *cf* Ridge (n 75 above) 628–29.
141 Burns (n 42 above) 469 (footnotes omitted).
142 Mason (n 4 above) 118; see also Ridge (n 75 above) 627–28.
143 *Hammond v Osborn* (n 47 above).
144 ibid [35].
145 ibid [58].
146 ibid [35]; see also *Niersmans v Pesticcio* [2004] EWCA Civ 372, [2004] WTLR 699.

The present author has previously admitted that, despite the fact that carers per se are not in a category of relationship which will automatically be considered one of trust and confidence, the circumstances of a care scenario make it likely that carers and care recipients will nevertheless be in such a relationship where a significant amount of care is provided.[147] A similar admission would have to be made if the presumption of undue influence were extended to testamentary cases. The author has also emphasised the importance of applying the 'calling for explanation' criterion rigorously in *inter vivos* cases, so that deserved voluntary dispositions can be upheld, and he has criticised the apparent reluctance to do so evident in some Australian cases.[148]

It has been seen that the judiciary have taken account of the testator's convincing motives to benefit carers in several cases considered in the previous section, and *Cattermole v Prisk*[149] demonstrates that they can also do so to prevent the presumption of undue influence from arising in *inter vivos* cases. Nevertheless, the application of that requirement inevitably becomes much less certain—and much more subject to difficult value judgements—when a judge is asking whether property that must inevitably be disposed of should have gone to others than those specified in a will, such as to raise a presumption of undue influence. Care might well be considered a good explanation for a testamentary gift by the judiciary, but it is unclear whether there is any particular advantage of considering it as part of a presumption rather than simply as evidence establishing whether undue influence was present on the balance of probabilities.

Moreover, while Bell sees the view that the absence of a presumption is unproblematic (because the testator is not personally disadvantaged) as 'consistent with the traditional English emphasis on freedom of testation',[150] he is mindful of the fact that—as Mason is clearly aware[151]—the Inheritance (Provision for Family and Dependants) Act 1975 enables certain individuals to apply for provision out of an estate, quite irrespective of the relevant will.[152] Family members in genuinely necessitous circumstances might well be able to be secure provision for themselves, even when they have been excluded from a will caused by unproven undue influence. This is not a comprehensive or ideal solution, not least because family provision rests on different principles than giving effect to the free intentions of a testator.[153] It is also significant that Ridge attempts to use family provision legislation as a possible *justification* for the imposition of a 'testamentary influence' presumption. She argues that it demonstrates that interests in estates extend

[147] *Informal Carers and Private Law* (n 1 above) 230.
[148] ibid 230–34.
[149] *Cattermole v Prisk* (n 37 above).
[150] Bell (n 50 above) 579.
[151] Mason (n 4 above) 119.
[152] On family provision, see Rebecca Probert's contribution in Ch 2 of the present volume, discussing recent reform to the regime.
[153] See eg *Informal Carers and Private Law* (n 1 above) 141.

beyond the testator and that it reduces the social acceptability of lobbying testators (on which several early authorities on testamentary undue influence were based). Even if these suggestions seem rather indirect,[154] the Act could—in addition—be seen as a reminder that the law in some respects interferes *more* with the disposition of property on death when compared to *inter vivos* situations, but the difficulties surrounding whether a gift 'calls for explanation' in a testamentary context remain.

In any case, the Act does reduce the potential for injustice caused by the absence of a presumption, and a presumption itself risks injustice in the other direction. It may be very difficult to rebut a presumption of undue influence by showing that the testator received independent advice, for example, given that it is by definition too late to provide it,[155] particularly since the beneficiary of the disputed will may be unaware of the gift (unlike in *inter vivos* situations).[156] In *Schomberg v Taylor*,[157] for instance, it is notable that, in pronouncing against the later will, the judge could have negated the legacy for a carer who was not a party to the undue influence and in fact was enlisted by the deceased in order to protect her from it. The beneficiaries of the earlier will (the testatrix's sons), however, had admirably agreed to respect the legacy, even if the later will was not upheld.

Burns has identified difficulties with Kerridge's alternative suggestions that presumptions be applied based on involvement in the will-making process.[158] She therefore advocates the Canadian approach of changing the definition of undue influence, the evidence that can be relied upon to prove it, and the standard of proof. For example, an appropriate modern English appellate case could clearly confirm the equivalence of actual undue influence *inter vivos* and testamentary undue influence; the approach to costs where undue influence is alleged could be changed; or judges could simply be more interventionist in response to the evidence presented. But whatever the preferable solution, it is clear that informal care situations do not lend weight to calls for the presumption of undue influence in *inter vivos* situations to be extended to testamentary ones.

4. Conclusion

This chapter has argued that testamentary dispositions in favour of informal carers are in principle perfectly understandable in light of the social context, and should

[154] Ridge (n 75 above) 634.
[155] ibid 629–30.
[156] *Parfitt v Lawless* (n 49 above) 469.
[157] *Schomberg v Taylor* (n 51 above).
[158] Burns (n 42 above) 478–79, commenting on the suggestion in R Kerridge, 'Wills Made In Suspicious Circumstances: The Problem of the Vulnerable Testator' (2000) 59 *CLJ* 310, remade in Kerridge (n 4 above) 129.

not be set aside lightly on grounds (for example) of supposed undue influence. As Norris J rightly recognised in *Wharton v Bancroft*, claims of undue influence and similar can be 'a cry of anguish dressed up in legal language'.[159] Judges have given consideration to testators' legitimate motivations, albeit adopting a nuanced and fact-sensitive approach. While there may be force in the argument that it is too difficult to demonstrate successfully that a will has been procured by undue influence, the chapter has also argued—with particular reference to informal care situations—that any difficulties should not be resolved through the simple extension of the presumption of undue influence which equity applies to cases of *inter vivos* dispositions. *Inter vivos* and testamentary dispositions are different in principle, even if they sometimes produce comparable results in practice. In particular, any attempted application of the requirement that a disposition 'calls for explanation' is likely to be problematic due to the difficulties involved in establishing relevant criteria.

[159] *Wharton v Bancroft* (n 92 above) [85].

9

What Is Left of the Non-Delegation Principle?

LIONEL SMITH*

1. Introduction

In 1944, the House of Lords held in *Chichester Diocesan Fund & Board of Finance Inc v Simpson*[1] that, outside of the field of charitable bequests, a testator cannot delegate the power to select who will benefit from his estate. This holding has never been called into question at the level of the Court of Appeal, let alone at the level of the House of Lords or the Supreme Court. If taken seriously, this principle would seem to exclude the possibility of giving personal representatives, or other persons, discretionary powers relating to the distribution of the estate. And yet, not only were such powers taken to be valid before 1944, but a significant number of decisions afterwards have held that such powers can be created, and indeed there is no limit on how wide they can be; a testator may create a 'general' power, which allows the donee of the power to distribute the relevant property to any person or among any persons in the world.[2]

What, if anything, is left of the non-delegation principle? Some have suggested that there is no such principle in English law, which seems to come very close to saying that *Chichester Diocesan Fund* was wrongly decided, or at least that the House of Lords expressed itself very poorly indeed. This chapter argues for a more nuanced interpretation. It begins with a discussion, in Section 2, of the decision in *Chichester Diocesan Fund*. Section 3 looks at how the decision has been treated

* The author thanks Birke Häcker, Roger Kerridge and Ian Williams for valuable comments on an earlier version of this chapter.

[1] *Chichester Diocesan Fund & Board of Finance Inc v Simpson* [1944] AC 341 (HL). The case (hereinafter '*Chichester Diocesan Fund*') will be discussed in more detail in Section 2 below.

[2] In this chapter, I adopt the widely accepted terminology according to which a 'general' power allows the donee (holder) of the power to appoint the relevant property to anyone, including himself; a 'special' power allows appointment only among defined objects, who may be identified by name or by description; a 'hybrid' or 'intermediate' power allows appointment to anyone except one or more excluded persons, who may be identified by name or by description.

subsequently; this includes an examination of several decisions, in a range of jurisdictions, which have held that wide discretionary powers can be created in a will. It also includes some discussion of a smaller number of decisions which have applied the holding in *Chichester Diocesan Fund* to invalidate testamentary provisions. Section 4 then aims directly to address the question whether any non-delegation principle exists in the common law. Here it is suggested that there is an important core to the non-delegation principle, illustrated by the principle that the act of making a will cannot be delegated. This Section describes how the validation of wide testamentary powers of appointment can be understood against the backdrop of developments in the law of trusts. Finally, the conclusion in Section 5 aims to synthesise the seemingly contradictory propositions that the common law does, and does not, allow a testator to delegate his will-making power.

2. The Non-Delegation Principle in the House of Lords

Many jurists are aware that Caleb Diplock, who died in 1936, left a will in which he directed his executors to distribute the very substantial residue of his estate among 'such charitable institution or institutions or other charitable or benevolent object or objects in England' as they should, in their discretion, select; and that this disposition was held to be void by a majority of the House of Lords, leading to an intestacy of the residue.[3] This, in turn, led to further litigation relating to the restitutionary liabilities of the entities that had received funds from the executors.[4]

Why was it void? An examination of the speeches reveals at least three possible answers. One is that it was too uncertain. While 'charitable' has a legal definition, 'benevolent' does not, and the conjunction 'or' had the effect that the disposition allowed the residue to be applied to purposes that were benevolent but not charitable. Since 'benevolent' has no legal definition, the disposition was too vague to be legally effective, regardless of whether in fact the executors should choose to dispose of the property only among charitable institutions. This reasoning is found in all four of the majority speeches.[5] Another line of reasoning, appearing

[3] *Chichester Diocesan Fund* (n 1 above). Less well-known is that Caleb Diplock was notorious during his life as a miser, and that while he had no children, his grandfather had 31, many of whom emigrated. It was the relations in Australia who challenged the disposition, and one author relates that it was a Melbourne lawyer who spotted the significance of the fateful 'or': CE Morris, 'The Testament of Caleb Diplock' (1948) 65 *South African Law Journal* 578 at 580.

[4] *Re Diplock* [1948] Ch 465 (CA), aff'd *Ministry of Health v Simpson, sub nom In re Diplock* [1951] AC 251 (HL); see also T Akkouh and S Worthington, '*Re Diplock* (1948)' in C Mitchell and P Mitchell (eds), *Landmark Cases in the Law of Restitution* (Oxford, Hart Publishing, 2006) 285.

[5] *Chichester Diocesan Fund* (n 1 above) 348: 'void for uncertainty', and 349: 'too vague' (Viscount Simon LC); 350: 'too uncertain' (Lord Macmillan); 364: 'benevolent' is 'too vague' (Lord Porter); 371: the court could not execute a trust for 'benevolent' objects because 'what is benevolent the court knows not' (Lord Simonds). Lord Wright dissented.

in two of the majority speeches, is based on the rule that a trust for charitable purposes must be exclusively charitable, or, what is the same thing, that English law does not generally allow trusts for non-charitable purposes.[6] Again, since there can be benevolent purposes which are not charitable, the disposition seemingly attempted to create a purpose trust that was not exclusively charitable.[7] But a third line of reasoning, also found in all four of the majority speeches, is arguably the most prominent. It is based on the principle that a testator may not delegate his will-making power. Viscount Simon LC said:[8]

> The fundamental principle is that the testator must by the terms of his will himself dispose of the property with which the will proposes to deal. With one single exception [a wholly charitable bequest], he cannot by his will direct executors or trustees to do the business for him.

Lord Macmillan said:[9]

> the law, in according the right to dispose of property mortis causa by will, is exacting in its requirements that the testator must define with precision the persons or objects he intends to benefit. This is the condition on which he is entitled to exclude the order of succession which the law otherwise provides. The choice of beneficiaries must be the testator's own choice. He cannot leave the disposal of his estate to others. The only latitude permitted is that, if he designates with sufficient precision a class of persons or objects to be benefited, he may delegate to his trustees the selection of individual persons or objects within the defined class. The class must not be described in terms so vague and indeterminate that the trustees are afforded no effective guidance as to the ambit of their power of selection.

This reasoning allows some delegation, subject to a requirement of the definition of a determinate class. Lord Porter said: 'The testator must make his own will and not leave his executors to make their choice of the objects of his bounty, subject to this, that a general gift to charity will be upheld'.[10] Finally, Lord Simonds said:[11]

> It is a cardinal rule, common to English and to Scots law, that a man may not delegate his testamentary power. To him the law gives the right to dispose of his estate in favour of ascertained or ascertainable persons. He does not exercise that right if in effect he

[6] The disposition of the residue was not a pure testamentary direction to the executors, but was in the form of a will trust: see the longer extract from the will in the first instance judgment, reported at [1940] Ch 988 (Ch) 988–89, or in the judgment of the Court of Appeal, reported at [1941] Ch 253 (CA) 253–54. Although the structure is commonly used, there is some conceptual difficulty with a will trust that (like this one) includes a direction to pay the deceased's debts. The reason is that the liabilities of the estate have priority over any directions as to the assets, and the constitution of a will trust is a direction as to the assets: see L Smith, 'Scottish Trusts in the Common Law' (2013) 17 *Edinburgh Law Review* 283 at 300–303.

[7] *Chichester Diocesan Fund* (n 1 above) 364–67 (Lord Porter), 370–71 (Lord Simonds).

[8] ibid 348.

[9] ibid 349.

[10] ibid 364.

[11] ibid 371.

> empowers his executors to say what persons or objects are to be his beneficiaries. To this salutary rule there is a single exception [that is, wholly charitable objects].

It is not easy to answer the question, what is the *ratio decidendi* of this decision? Fatal uncertainty is not the same problem as violating a principle that forbids delegation, and neither is the same as infringing a rule against non-charitable purpose trusts. It is possible for a particular testamentary disposition to fall foul of all three of these; it is not difficult to imagine dispositions that violate each of the three of them without violating the other two, or that violate any two without violating the third. As a matter of positive law, when a decision has more than one *ratio decidendi*, each of the *rationes* is binding on inferior courts.[12] At the same time, no decision finally determines the rule that it stands for; that determination can only be made by later courts, through an examination of what legal norms the judges in the earlier case decided were applicable to the facts they considered relevant, seen in the light of other pertinent decisions, both preceding and succeeding the earlier decision.[13]

3. Subsequent Treatment of the Non-Delegation Principle

In some jurisdictions, there was a legislative response to the decision of the House of Lords, aimed at allowing similarly worded dispositions to be validated as charitable.[14] In New Brunswick, the legislation came too late to save a disposition that was worded similarly to the one in *Chichester Diocesan Fund.* The Supreme Court of Canada invalidated a residuary bequest 'for charitable, religious, educational or philanthropic purposes'.[15] The majority, after referring to the House of Lords decision as governing the case, founded the result on the rule against delegation:[16]

> The fundamental principle is that a testator must, by the terms of his will, himself dispose of the property with which the will proposes to deal. He may not depute that duty to his executors or trustees, save in the case of a gift for charitable purposes, when he may depute the selection of the charities.

[12] R Cross and J Harris, *Precedent in English Law*, 4th edn (Oxford, Clarendon Press, 1991) 81–84.

[13] ibid 72–75.

[14] The English legislation (Charitable Trusts (Validation) Act 1954) only applies to instruments taking effect before it came into force. Some other jurisdictions have generally applicable legislation aimed at validating such dispositions. For citations and criticism, see DWM Waters, M Gillen, and L Smith, *Waters' Law of Trusts in Canada*, 4th edn (Toronto, Thomson/Carswell, 2012) 801–5.

[15] *Brewer v McCauley* [1954] SCR 645 (SCC).

[16] ibid 649 (Kellock J, with whom Estey, Cartwright and Fauteux JJ concurred). Rand J stated (at 647) that the holding in *Chichester Diocesan Fund* (n 1 above) was that 'the purported bequest was invalid as being uncertain'.

A few years earlier, in *Tatham v Huxtable*,[17] the High Court of Australia had also invalidated a testamentary provision as violating the principle against delegation. The decision was by a 2:1 majority, Latham CJ dissenting. The disposition was interpreted as providing that the executor was authorised to distribute the residue among (a) those who had already received legacies, or (b) those who, in the opinion of the executor, 'have rendered service meriting consideration by the testator'. A wider range of cases was discussed in the judgments than had been addressed in *Chichester Diocesan Fund*, including two English decisions, one decided before and one after *Chichester Diocesan Fund*, in which wide powers of appointment in wills had been held valid.[18] Kitto J in the High Court stated that general powers were valid because the donee of the power could appoint to himself and therefore was placed 'for all practical purposes in the position of beneficial owner of the property'.[19] He said that special powers could be valid in line with the words of Lord Macmillan quoted above; that is, if there is a determinate class. On this basis, he concluded that the disposition was invalid. Even if it permitted the executor to benefit himself, it was not sufficiently wide to qualify as a general power. Fullagar J concurred in the result, questioning the correctness of the two English cases in which powers were upheld.

Some years later, the High Court invalidated a disposition that was in the form of a power over the residue with only one object, a charitable entity.[20] The judges who held it invalid apparently took the view that it was not a special power (which could have been valid under *Tatham v Huxtable*) because it had only one object. The reasoning is rather difficult to follow; as Barwick CJ said, in his reasons for holding the disposition valid,

> I am unable to find any reason why a discretionary power to appoint to a named person should be in any worse case than such a discretionary power to appoint amongst a named class to whom no gift is made by the will.[21]

But the disposition was held invalid as violating the rule against delegation.

In 1955, the Supreme Court of New Zealand (as it then was) in *Re McEwen* upheld a will that gave a general power of appointment to the executors.[22]

[17] *Tatham v Huxtable* (1950) 81 CLR 639 (HCA).

[18] *Re Park* [1932] 1 Ch 580 (Ch); *Re Jones* [1945] Ch 105 (Ch). *Re Park* was not mentioned in *Chichester Diocesan Fund* (n 1 above). In neither case was the power a fully general one, but it was very wide in both.

[19] *Tatham v Huxtable* (n 17 above) 654.

[20] *Lutheran Church of Australia, South Australia District Inc v Farmers' Co-operative Executors and Trustees Ltd* (1970) 121 CLR 628 (HCA). The High Court divided 2:2, and the decision of the Supreme Court of South Australia, that the disposition was invalid, was affirmed. The case is noted by JF Keeler, 'Delegation of Testamentary Power' (1971) 4 *Adelaide Law Review* 210.

[21] *Lutheran Church of Australia v Farmers' Co-operative Executors and Trustees Ltd* (n 20 above) 637. See the criticism in IJ Hardingham, 'The Rule Against Delegation of Will-Making Power' (1974) 9 *Melbourne University Law Review* 650 at 658–61.

[22] *Re McEwen* [1955] NZLR 575 (NZSC). This was a decision of the first instance superior court, which became the High Court in 1980. The current Supreme Court, established in 2004, is the highest appellate court in New Zealand.

The power specifically authorised the executors to appoint to themselves, and named the testator's son as the taker in default. The power was challenged as violating the anti-delegation principle. This argument may have been inspired by an article of DM Gordon, who noted in 1953 that a wide and general principle against delegation was inconsistent with the creation of powers of appointment in wills, even though such powers had been upheld in many cases over the years.[23] Gordon argued that a general non-delegation principle would invalidate all such powers, however wide or narrow the class of appointees might be, since the creation of any power of appointment is a kind of delegation. After reviewing a range of cases, Gresson J stated that a general power could be consistent with an anti-delegation principle on either of two grounds: first, that a power was not a delegation of the relevant kind, so long as the objects are certain; secondly, that a *general* power is so close to ownership that it amounts to an outright disposition of the property.[24]

More recent cases have gone in the same direction. In *Re Nicholls*,[25] the testatrix was a member of a missionary religious group. In relation to the distribution of the residue of her estate, she directed her executor to 'follow the dictates and directions given to him from time to time by Carson Cowan', who was a member of the same group.[26] This was held to create a general power of appointment held by Cowan over the residue.[27] The Court noted that it was accepted that such a power could be created *inter vivos*, and that as a matter of practice, such powers had been created in wills for centuries. The next of kin, however, contended that the principle against delegation did not permit the creation of such a power.

The Court began its analysis by observing that it was conceded that there was no binding decision invalidating a bequest creating a general power.[28] After reviewing

[23] DM Gordon, 'Delegation of Will-Making Power' (1953) 69 *LQR* 334, cited in *Re McEwen* (n 22 above) 578.

[24] *Re McEwen* (n 22 above) 581–82. The second ground reflects the reasoning of Kitto J in *Tatham v Huxtable* (n 17 above).

[25] *Re Nicholls* (1987) 57 OR (2d) 763 (Ont CA).

[26] Two other persons, also members, were named as alternatives in the event of Cowan's predeceasing the testatrix. In the event, however, Cowan had given directions to the executor, and the executor applied to the court for directions on the validity of the disposition.

[27] There was an issue as to whether the disposition naming Cowan (and the others) imposed an obligation on him, but it was held only to create a power, even though the will did not name any taker in default. Since a power is by its nature not obligatory, there must be someone who will take in default of its exercise. Presumably the taker in default of the residue was the next of kin, even were the power to be held valid, as it was. This was stated to be the position in an earlier case quoted in *Re Nicholls* (n 25 above) [15], namely *Higginson v Kerr* (1898) 30 OR 62 (Ont HC) 68. The same analysis was adopted by Hutley JA in *Horan v James* [1982] 2 NSWLR 376 (NSWCA) 378–79, although confusingly the judge also seemed to say that the estate trustees had a duty to exercise the power. Mahoney JA indicated (at 383) that it was agreed that the power was a 'trust power' (now usually called a discretionary trust), which means that the trustees were obliged to distribute to the objects and had a power only to select among them, not as to *whether* to distribute. Of course, where the disposition obliges the donee to distribute the property, there is no need for a taker in default.

[28] There was no general power either in *Chichester Diocesan Fund* (n 1 above) or in *Brewer v McCauley* (n 15 above). Note that *Brewer v McCauley* was not actually mentioned in *Re Nicholls* (n 25 above).

a range of cases, the Court stated that a general power could be consistent with an anti-delegation principle on the two grounds that had been identified by Gresson J in *Re McEwen*.[29] The Court went on to hold that since the authorities were unclear, the matter should be decided on the basis of 'principle or policy'. It held that there was no reason to think that a testamentary general power was any more problematic than one created *inter vivos*, and that the principle of freedom of testation pointed in the direction of validity. No valid reason had been shown to limit that principle. In particular, the suggestion that a general power was inconsistent with the policy of the Wills Act was rejected.[30]

In 1991, Hoffmann J (as he then was) decided *Re Beatty*.[31] The testatrix gave her executors and will trustees a power over her personal chattels, and over the sum of £1.5 million, which allowed them to appoint these assets to anyone during a period of two years. Subject to that, these assets would fall into the residue. The personal chattels included 'a very valuable collection of paintings'.[32] The validity of the powers was challenged by the residuary legatees. Hoffmann J held that because the powers were fiduciary, they were not general powers in the traditional sense; they were, he said, intermediate or hybrid powers.[33] As in *Re Nicholls*, it was conceded that such powers can be created *inter vivos*, but counsel relied on the statements in *Chichester Diocesan Fund* for the existence of a distinct rule that forbids delegation in the making of a will.

Hoffmann J said that it was 'hard to imagine' that Lord Simonds (and presumably the other Law Lords in the majority) intended to cast doubt on 'the validity of testamentary powers of appointment, whether special, general or intermediate'.[34] Any such rule would itself be vague and uncertain. Hoffmann J referred to some of the Australian cases, and *Re Nicholls*, and reached the conclusion that 'a common law rule against testamentary delegation, in the sense of a restriction on the scope of testamentary powers, is a chimera, a shadow cast by the rule of certainty, having no independent existence'.[35]

There was a thorough review of the case law and commentary in the British Columbia case of *Tassone v Pearson*.[36] Leaving out some complications, the will

[29] See the text accompanying n 24 above.

[30] This was the principal argument of Gordon (n 23 above). Fullagar J in *Tatham v Huxtable* (n 17 above) 649 also stated that the creation of testamentary powers was inconsistent with the Wills Act. In Ontario, the equivalent legislation to the English Wills Act 1837 was Part I of the *Succession Law Reform Act*, RSO 1980, c 488, now RSO 1990, c S.26.

[31] *Re Beatty* [1990] 1 WLR 1503 (Ch).

[32] ibid 1505.

[33] Another clause provided that the trustees could exercise their powers notwithstanding their having a personal interest in the mode of its exercise. In reliance on this, the three trustees had given themselves £10,000 each (ibid 1506). Hoffmann J said that the clause in question 'arguably' permitted this (ibid), but the validity of these gifts was not in issue apart from the validity of the powers.

[34] ibid 1507.

[35] ibid 1509. A similar argument was made in ID Campbell, 'The Enigma of General Powers of Appointment' (1955–57) 7 *Res Judicatae* 244 at 251–53, and later by P Creighton, 'Certainty of Objects of Trusts and Powers: The Impact of *McPhail v Doulton* in Australia' (2000) 22 *Sydney Law Review* 93 at 116.

[36] *Tassone v Pearson* 2012 BCSC 1262.

provided 'I devise all the residue of my estate to be distributed as seen appropriate by my executor', the underlined words being printed in a form, the other words in manuscript. The parties agreed, and the judge accepted, that this amounted to the grant of a general power of appointment to the executrix.[37] Following *Re Nicholls* and *Re Beatty*, the general power was upheld.

However, not every decision has tended towards the extirpation of the principle against non-delegation. The Australian position was left unclear by the High Court decisions discussed above. In *Horan v James*,[38] the testator attempted to create a testamentary power that was wide, but was not general. The New South Wales Court of Appeal applied *Tatham v Huxtable*[39] to hold that it was invalid, but one of the judges expressed strong reservations about the coherence of the law.[40] In *Gregory v Hudson*,[41] the same Court stated clearly that only the High Court could address the issue. Even so, the court held valid a testamentary provision that directed the residue to be distributed to the trustees of a pre-existing trust, where the terms of that trust were widely discretionary, including a power to add beneficiaries. Such a testamentary provision, it was held, did not involve any delegation of testamentary power.[42] Beginning with Queensland in 1981, the majority of Australian jurisdictions have now abolished the rule by statute, to the extent that it relates to testamentary powers and discretionary will trusts.[43]

Two Canadian decisions have invalidated widely discretionary testamentary dispositions. In *Prendergast Estate v British Columbia (Public Trustee)*,[44] the relevant disposition provided that

> If there is any residue of my Estate after distribution according to my instructions then I direct my Executor and Trustee to distribute the rest and residue of my Estate as he, in his absolute discretion deems fit, including payment to himself or to his spouse.

[37] It is not stated who would be the taker in default—presumably the next of kin: see n 27 above.

[38] *Horan v James* (n 27 above).

[39] *Tatham v Huxtable* (n 17 above).

[40] *Horan v James* (n 27 above) 381 (Hutley JA); see also 382 (Glass JA). As explained above (n 27 above), however, the disposition was agreed to be obligatory, so it was not a power at all in the usual sense; it gave a power of selection only.

[41] *Gregory v Hudson* (1998) 45 NSWLR 300 (NSWCA).

[42] The Court of Appeal suggested (ibid 310–12) that the power in *Horan v James* (n 27 above) may have been valid, but did not clearly state its view of the scope of the rule as it relates to testamentary powers. Young J, at first instance in *Gregory v Hudson* (1997) 41 NSWLR 573 at 586, attempted to summarise the law. He said there is a rule against creating testamentary powers, but that it has exceptions inasmuch as a power will be valid if it is in favour of charity, if it is general, or if it is special and the class of objects is precisely defined. He also held that the rule was not violated when property was given to a pre-existing trust, nor, apparently, where secret or half-secret trusts are used. This summary was said to represent the law of South Australia in *Lines v Lines* [2003] SASC 173 at [36], where the non-delegation principle invalidated a testamentary disposition in favour of a named trust which was not constituted at the death of the testatrix, but was to be constituted by her husband's will.

[43] See the Queensland Succession Act 1981, s 33R: 'A power or a trust, created by will, to dispose of property is not void on the ground that it is a delegation of the testator's power to make a will, if the same power or trust would be valid if made by the testator, by instrument, in the testator's lifetime'. Similar provisions are in the New South Wales Succession Act 2006, s 44; Victoria Wills Act 1997, s 48; Tasmania Wills Act 2008, s 58; Australian Capital Territory Wills Act 1968, s 14A; Northern Territory Wills Act 2000, s 43.

[44] *Prendergast Estate v British Columbia (Public Trustee)* [1986] BCJ No 1106 (BCSC) para 8.

In a brief judgment, McKay J in the British Columbia Supreme Court referred to *Chichester Diocesan Fund* and to the statement of the non-delegation principle in *Brewer v McCauley*,[45] and held:[46]

> In this case the testator did not, by the terms of his will, himself dispose of the residue. He gave to [the executor] an absolute discretion as to the disposition … The clause is, on the face of it, void for uncertainty and the residue must be distributed as on an intestacy.

In *Re Balfour Estate*,[47] the deceased again used a form. He named his daughter executrix. The only dispositive provision was this: 'Whatever Brenda Goll my daughter decides is O.K. if anyone else doesn't like it too bad'. Gerein J also cited *Brewer v McCauley* and held that the words quoted[48]

> do not constitute a disposition in favor of Ms. Goll. Equally, they do not constitute a disposition in favor of anyone else. They do nothing more than deputise Ms. Goll to distribute the estate property. The result is that there is no testamentary disposition which in turn precludes any finding of testamentary intention.

4. What, If Anything, Is Left of the Non-Delegation Principle?

This review shows that, since *Chichester Diocesan Fund*, most of the cases in which the non-delegation principle has been invoked involved testamentary powers. As things stand, in England and Wales, in New Zealand, and in Ontario and British Columbia, it has been decided that very wide testamentary powers are permissible. The same is true in the Australian jurisdictions that have intervened by statute.[49] For South Australia and Western Australia, the law is somewhat unclear: general powers, the widest of all, are valid, but less wide powers may not be. One question that has to be addressed, however, is whether the non-delegation principle goes beyond issues about the creation of testamentary powers, or indeed whether it stands entirely apart from such issues.

In determining the scope of the non-delegation principle, if indeed one exists, it is natural to aim first to try to understand its normative basis. If we understood why the principle exists, it would tell us something about its scope, including, for example, whether it should invalidate powers. But efforts in this regard have not been notably successful. Some have argued or assumed that the principle flows

45 *Brewer v McCauley* (n 15 above).
46 *Prendergast Estate v British Columbia (Public Trustee)* (n 44 above).
47 *Re Balfour Estate* (1990) 85 Sask R 183 (QB).
48 ibid 184–85.
49 See n 43 above.

from the Wills Act.[50] But this argument, which was rejected in *Re Nicholls* and *Re Beatty*, has been effectively refuted.[51] The Wills Act stipulates requirements as to form; it did not create testamentary capacity, and there is no reason to think that it delimits such capacity. Moreover, the formal requirements are not applied by the Act to privileged wills, and no one has suggested that the anti-delegation principle does not apply to privileged wills.[52]

There is a general rule that one to whom a discretion is delegated may not, in turn, delegate it, in the absence of specific authority.[53] But it has never been suggested, to my knowledge at least, that a person's will-making power is held as a delegated discretion. Lord Macmillan once described testamentary capacity as a 'privilege', implying that it followed from this that it could not be delegated.[54] But it does not follow as a matter of logic; some reason is needed.[55] Testamentary capacity is not obviously any more of a privilege than the capacity to dispose of one's property *inter vivos*, and clearly delegation is permitted in *inter vivos* dispositions.

Some judges in formulating the principle have implied that it is because the testator is disinheriting her next of kin that she must do so personally.[56] Again, if

[50] This is the argument by Gordon (n 23 above), who took it to the logical conclusion that there could be no exception for charitable purposes. It was also deployed by Fullagar J in *Tatham v Huxtable* (n 17 above) 649.

[51] Particularly by Hardingham (n 21 above) 664–68, who acknowledges FC Hutley, 'The Delegation of Will-Making Powers' (1956) 2 *Sydney Law Review* 93. This is the same person who—as Hutley JA—criticised the state of Australian law in 1982: see n 40 above and the accompanying text.

[52] Hutley (n 51 above) 94–95. In England and Wales, privileged wills do not need to be signed, and may even be oral: see R Kerridge (assisted by AHR Brierley), *Parry and Kerridge: The Law of Succession*, 12th edn (London, Sweet & Maxwell, 2009) 55–59. In Canada, however, although privileged wills may not require witnesses, they generally still require signing by the testator or by another in the testator's presence and by his direction: eg Ontario *Succession Law Reform Act*, RSO 1990, c S.26, s 5. With different scopes as to which testators qualify, the possibility for privileged wills to be unsigned or oral is preserved in Nova Scotia (*Wills Act*, RSNS 1989, c 505, s 9) and in Newfoundland and Labrador (*Wills Act*, RSNL1970, c W-10, s 2(2)). In most Australian jurisdictions (in all but South Australia, Tasmania, and the Australian Capital Territory), privileged wills have been abolished: N Peart, 'Testamentary Formalities in Australia and New Zealand' in KGC Reid, MJ de Waal, and R Zimmermann (eds), *Comparative Succession Law: Testamentary Formalities* (Oxford, Oxford University Press, 2011) 329 at 334, fn 25.

[53] This principle operated to invalidate an exercise of a fiduciary power in *Re Hay's Settlement Trusts* [1982] 1 WLR 202 (Ch).

[54] *Attorney-General New Zealand v New Zealand Insurance Co* [1936] 3 All ER 888 (PC) 890.

[55] In the vocabulary of Hohfeld's fundamental legal conceptions, it is a 'power' not a 'privilege': WN Hohfeld, *Fundamental Legal Conceptions as Applied in Judicial Reasoning*, 3rd printing with new foreword by AL Corbin (New Haven CT, Yale University Press, 1964). A Hohfeldian 'privilege' allows one to do what would otherwise be unlawful, and such privileges (such as a licence to occupy land, to practise a profession, or to drive a car on public highways) are usually personal and non-delegable. A Hohfeldian 'power' is an ability to change legal relations, and testamentary freedom is such a power. Hohfeldian powers are frequently delegable.

[56] Viscount Haldane in *A-G v National Provincial and Union Bank of England* [1924] AC 262 (HL) 268: 'a man cannot disinherit his heirs by giving away his property unless he really gives it away; he cannot leave it to some one else to make a will for him'. In *Houston v Burns* [1918] AC 337 (HL) 343, he said, that 'by the law of Scotland, as by that of England, a testator can defeat the claim of those entitled by law in the absence of a valid will to succeed to the beneficial interest in his estate only if he has made a complete disposition of that beneficial interest. He cannot leave it to another person to

this is not simply an article of faith, some reason for it seems to be required. Why must it be done personally, when so many other legal acts can be done through another? Moreover, it seems slightly odd to conceptualise a will as disinheriting the next of kin, at least in the common law, where the intention of the testator is considered to be of primary significance.[57] It is more typical to consider intestacy as a backup regime that is called upon when—and precisely because—the testator has failed to make a valid will. In that perspective, it seems counter-intuitive to conceptualise a will negatively, as an instrument of disinheritance, rather than positively, as an exercise of testamentary capacity.[58]

In order to understand what is left of the principle in the modern common law, it seems more useful to start from such cases as can be found in which it actually operates, and then to attempt to articulate a sound basis for the principle.

4.1. Complete Delegation of Will-Making

Assume that a person said to another, 'write a will for me, and whatever you write, I will sign it and have it witnessed'. The first person signs the document without knowledge as to its contents. The law appears to say that this instrument, even if properly executed, is not a will. This was decided as a question of law, on a pleading point, in *Hastilow v Stobie*.[59] The defendant, challenging the will, pleaded (among other pleas) that the testator, 'at the time he signed the said pretended will, did not know and approve of the contents thereof'.[60] The plaintiff demurred to this

make such a disposition for him'. See also Lord Macmillan in *Chichester Diocesan Fund*, cited in the text accompanying n 9 above, who refers to a valid will as 'exclud[ing] the order of succession which the law otherwise provides'.

[57] Eve J was reported to have said 'I shudder to think that in the hereafter I shall have to meet those testators whose wishes on earth have been frustrated by my judgments': (1941) 60 *Law Notes* 26, alluded to by Lord Atkin in *Perrin v Morgan* [1943] AC 399 (HL) 415.

[58] One could wonder whether the opposite perspective had civilian roots. Most civilian systems have some form of forced heirship; in Scots law, this takes the form of 'legal rights' over moveable property. Lord Macmillan was a Scottish Law Lord; as for Viscount Haldane, he was born and educated in Scotland, and the first of the two cases in which expressed himself in these terms, *Houston v Burns* (n 56 above), was an appeal from Scotland. The Scottish government published a Consultation Paper on the Law of Succession on 25 June 2015 that asks about the reform of legal rights. For comparative studies of testamentary powers, see eg JEC Brierley, 'Wills—General Powers of Appointment in Wills—Bare Powers and Trust Powers—Ontario and Quebec Compared: *Re Nicholls; Royal Trust v. Brodie*' (1990) 69 *Canadian Bar Review* 364; R Zimmermann, '*Quos Titius voluerit'—Höchstpersönliche Willensentscheidung des Erblassers oder 'power of appointment'?* (Munich, CH Beck, 1991). Quebec is an interesting case because it has a largely civilian system of private law, but with full freedom of testation engrafted since 1774. Despite this, Quebec law does not allow general powers of appointment, either *inter vivos* or in wills. Brierley argued that this is due to a different conception of ownership. The civil law is less willing to allow the incidents of ownership to be disaggregated and held by more than one person; a person holding a general power over property is not the owner of that property, but holds one of the most significant elements of ownership: see JEC Brierley, 'Powers of Appointment in Quebec Civil Law' (1992–93) 95 *Revue du Notariat* 131 and 245, especially at 138–39.

[59] *Hastilow v Stobie* (1865) LR 1 P & D 64.

[60] ibid 64.

plea; his counsel submitted that a testator 'may adopt and execute a will made by another person, without knowing its contents, or, knowing them, without entirely approving them'. Sir JP Wilde rejected the demurrer and held that the plea was valid.[61] He stated that 'a will is the act of a man's own intelligence and volition'.[62] One could say that this illustrates the core, at least, of a non-delegation principle.

To test whether it is a testamentary principle, assume that the same thing happened with a deed. A person says to another, 'whatever you write, I will execute as a deed'. Then assume that the second person produces a document, and the first person complies with the formalities required for execution as a deed, intending the document to take effect as a deed. Would a court treat this instrument as effective? It is difficult to see why it would not. It is not a case of *non est factum*. This doctrine is said not to apply where a person executes an instrument carelessly;[63] a fortiori, it would not apply in our example, where the person executes it deliberately. Neither is there a mistake or other vitiating factor.

If in such a case the will is invalid, but the deed (and presumably a written parol contract) is valid, then there would be an independent testamentary principle, requiring a will to be the personal creation of the testator. As Sir JP Wilde stated in *Hastilow v Stobie*, such a result could indeed be seen to follow from the definition of a 'will' as a personal act.

4.2. An Attorney Cannot Make a Will

It has been said that there is a principle of the common law that an agent or an attorney, no matter how wide his authority in relation to dealings with property, cannot make a will on behalf of his principal. This would be a genuine testamentary principle. If I grant authority to my agent to execute deeds on my behalf (which requires a grant in the form of a deed),[64] then my agent can validly execute such deeds on my behalf, even though I am unaware of their contents and existence until a later time. And of course, the same is true in relation to parol contracts or gifts. If, however, the widest grant of authority does not allow the execution of

[61] Rightly or wrongly, the plea of lack of knowledge and approval has apparently evolved since then to become a general plea that subsumes a range of defects of execution; it was referred to as 'the classic fudged ground of lack of knowledge or approval' in R Kerridge, 'Undue Influence and Testamentary Dispositions: A Response' [2012] *Conv* 129 at 140. This is why I do not discuss it further. My aim is to determine whether there is a principle that stands apart from such other issues as capacity, fraud, undue influence, and mistake. In *Hastilow v Stobie* (n 59 above), it was held that it did stand apart, since the decision was that 'lack of knowledge and approval' was legally independent, as a ground of challenge, from such issues as incapacity and undue influence. The fudging came later. See also Penelope Reed's contribution in Ch 7 of this volume, discussing the relationship between testamentary incapacity and lack of knowledge and approval.

[62] *Hastilow v Stobie* (n 59 above) 67.

[63] *Saunders v Anglia Building Society, Gallie v Lee* [1971] AC 1004 (HL); *Marvco Color Research Ltd v Harris* [1982] 2 SCR 774 (SCC).

[64] P Watts and FMB Reynolds, *Bowstead and Reynolds on Agency*, 20th edn (London, Sweet & Maxwell, 2014) (hereinafter '*Bowstead & Reynolds*') art 10 at [2-040]–[2-041].

a will, then we appear to have identified a principle that is confined to the testamentary context.

Moreover, it would not simply be a special case of the principle discussed in the previous section. As in the situation discussed there, the principal or grantor, whose attorney purports to make a will for him, has no knowledge of the contents of the instrument in question. Yet here we are in a situation in which the principal or grantor does not purport to execute the instrument herself. It is executed by the attorney. Although the principles cover different situations, they could be based on the same underlying idea: that it is inherent in the definition of a 'will' that it is willed by the testator personally.

It is somewhat difficult, however, to find direct authority for the existence of the principle regarding attorneys.[65] Some light is shed in the context of statutory provisions that allow the creation of 'continuing', 'enduring', or 'lasting' powers of attorney, which remain effective after the grantor loses legal capacity. For example, in some jurisdictions including England and Wales, the court is granted by statute a power to make a will on behalf of an incapacitated person.[66] Since this grant is not limited to cases in which an attorney has not been validly appointed, its existence seems to presuppose that even where there is an attorney, he or she cannot make a will.

In Canada, it is in this context that the principle regarding attorneys has come to the surface in recent years. There is a range of estate planning transactions that the attorney might wish to implement, which might reduce the taxation burden on the estate of the grantor without necessarily changing the destination of the property. Canadian courts have suggested that this is not possible if the transaction is testamentary in character, precisely because it is not possible for an attorney to execute a testamentary instrument.[67]

In Ontario, the principle regarding attorneys is in the legislation;[68] but courts in other Canadian provinces have taken the Ontario provisions to be declaratory of the common law. The latest Canadian word on this question is the decision of

[65] No such principle appears to be mentioned in *Bowstead & Reynolds* (n 64 above), including in art 6, which discusses acts that may be done through an agent. The article says that an agent may not do an act that a principal is required to do in person, but there is no discussion of wills.

[66] Mental Capacity Act 2005, s 18(1)(i). Although, by s 16(2)(a), the court can in many cases appoint a 'deputy' to act in relation to the matters listed in s 18, the power to make a will is specifically excepted by s 20(3)(b), so that only the court can exercise the power in s 18(1)(i).

[67] Canadian courts apply the established test that an instrument is testamentary if it depends for its 'vigour and effect' on the death of the grantor: *Cock v Cooke* (1866) LR 1 P & D 241. For some nuance, see however *Baird v Baird* [1990] 2 AC 548 (PC) and the analysis in R Scane, 'Non-Insurance Beneficiary Designations' (1993) 72 *Canadian Bar Review* 179 at 182–91.

[68] *Substitute Decisions Act*, 1992, SO 1992, c 30, s 7(2): 'The continuing power of attorney may authorise the person named as attorney to do on the grantor's behalf anything in respect of property that the grantor could do if capable, except make a will'.; s 31(1): 'A guardian of property has power to do on the incapable person's behalf anything in respect of property that the person could do if capable, except make a will'. The former provision governs voluntarily created powers of attorney; the latter governs court-appointed guardians of property: see E Musyj and J McKim, 'Can an Ontario Attorney for Property Engage in Estate Planning?' (2014) 34 *Estates, Trusts & Pensions Journal* 79.

the British Columbia Court of Appeal in *Easingwood v Cockroft*,[69] in which Saunders JA said, for the court: 'It is clear, I consider, that an attorney may not make a testamentary disposition'.[70] But now we find ourselves in a strange logical circle. What was the basis for this proposition? The very statements of Lord Macmillan and Lord Simonds in *Chichester Diocesan Fund* that were set out above, and that have been effectively ignored by subsequent courts as dicta; the text of Gordon,[71] which is clearly a minority view, as it would forbid all testamentary powers of appointment; and the Wills Act, which—as we have seen—imposes only formal requirements. The court also referred to an earlier British Columbia decision at first instance, which recognised the principle.[72] In that case, the judge relied on a legal education document that stated that a person may not make a will through an attorney.[73] That document provides an endnote which states: 'This proposition seems obvious'. The author goes on to observe that the Wills Act requires the testator to sign the will; alternatively, the testator may direct another person to sign, but this must be in the testator's presence and by his direction.[74]

Although it was suggested above that the Wills Act cannot provide a sound basis for a wide anti-delegation principle that would prohibit testamentary powers,[75] one might thus argue that its formal requirements can explain why an attorney cannot create a will: a will can be validly signed by another, only if that other signs in the presence of the testator and by his direction.[76] However, if this is the basis of the rule against will-making by an attorney, it is a rule of pure form.[77] It seems

[69] *Easingwood v Cockroft* 2013 BCCA 182. The court held that the *inter vivos* trust that had been created by the attorney was within his authority, but articulated the principle against testamentary dispositions by attorneys.

[70] ibid [49].

[71] Gordon (n 23 above); the Court also referred to Hardingham (n 21 above).

[72] *Desharnais v Toronto Dominion Bank* (2001) 42 ETR (2d) 192 (BCSC), rev'd on other grounds (2002) 9 BCLR (4th) 236 (BCCA).

[73] P Renaud, 'Taking Instructions' in Legal Education Society of Alberta, *Enduring Powers of Attorney; Dependent Adults; Living Wills* (Edmonton, LESA, 1991) 141 at 149. This book is a set of materials prepared for seminars for practitioners, which took place at the time the relevant Alberta legislation was coming into force. The book also includes (at 1–140) the Report of the Alberta Law Reform Institute on enduring powers of attorney, which preceded the Alberta legislation. The Report seems not to mention will-making by attorneys.

[74] See also DD Oosterhof, 'Alice's Wonderland: Authority of an Attorney for Property to Amend a Beneficiary Designation' (2002) 22 *Estates, Trusts & Pensions Journal* 16, where the principle regarding attorneys is discussed at 18–19. For the proposition that a will must be executed personally, Oosterhoff cites Renaud (n 73 above) and refers also to the requirement of the testator's presence when the will is signed by another. Oosterhoff also suggests that the fiduciary duty of an attorney is inconsistent with the possibility of will-making by an attorney.

[75] See nn 50–52 and the accompanying text.

[76] Wills Act 1837, s 9; similar provisions exist in most cognate statutes.

[77] This would imply that the rule against will-making by an attorney would not apply to privileged wills, where such wills do not need to be signed, or can be made orally (see n 52 above). Still, it would be unusual for a testator who was qualified to make a privileged will to have also created a very broad power of attorney, or indeed for an attorney, who was qualified to make a privileged will, to do so on behalf of his principal during the time that he was so qualified. Depending on the jurisdiction, the qualification to make a privileged will typically involves being in actual military service, or being a mariner at sea.

more plausible that it is a rule of substance: wills cannot be *made* by attorneys, but where a will needs to be *signed*, this requirement can be satisfied through the signature of another if this is done in the testator's presence and at his direction. In other words, the possibility of signing in the presence and at the direction of the testator does not *constitute* the rule against will-making by an attorney; rather, that possibility is simply a limited exception to the requirement of signing by the testator, where such signing would otherwise be required.

If the rule against will-making by an attorney is a rule of substance, then it must be based on the notion that a will is, by definition, a personal act. We will return in the conclusion to the question whether such a definition can be squared with the ability to create wide testamentary powers.

4.3. Contests and Lotteries

Charles Millar died in 1927, leaving a will in which the residue was to go to the Toronto woman who, in the 10 years following Millar's death, should give birth to the most children.[78] The disposition was attacked as contrary to public policy; it was upheld, without any suggestion that the testator had delegated his will-making power.

In *Bowen Estate v Bowen*,[79] the testatrix directed her executors to conduct a lottery to choose among six named persons. The person selected by chance was to receive a diamond ring. The court held that this was a valid direction. The judge referred to *Re Nicholls* and stated that in the case at bar, there was no delegation since the trustees had no decision to make.

It does seem correct that this is not a case of delegation in any normal sense of the word, and nor was there delegation in *Re Millar Estate*. But if the non-delegation principle, or whatever is left of it, is based on the idea that a will is, by definition, a personal decision of the testatrix as to the disposition of her property, these cases might be considered problematic. These are not simply cases in which a beneficiary was identified by description, as in 'my eldest child who survives me'. In these cases, the recipient was not identifiable at the moment of death, but only later, through the process established by the testator.

4.4. Powers and Duties

Finally it is necessary to address the cases on powers. A wide reading of the non-delegation principle would make it impossible to create testamentary powers. The clear trend of the case law, however, is in favour of allowing them.

[78] *Re Millar Estate* [1938] SCR 1 (SCC). He also left one share in a brewing company to each Protestant minister in Toronto: *Re Millar* [1927] 3 DLR 270 (Ont SC).

[79] *Bowen Estate v Bowen* (2001) 42 ETR (2d) 1 (Ont SC).

One of the recurrent arguments, in the cases and in the commentary, is that since a person can create wide powers in an *inter vivos* instrument, it seems inconsistent to say that this cannot be done in a will.[80] Of course, the estate of a deceased person is not a trust of the kind that is created *inter vivos*.[81] But it is inevitable that drafting practices that are adopted for trusts will also be used—if possible—for wills, especially since most wills operate entirely through a trust structure.[82]

Trust drafting practices have evolved since the 1960s, in the direction of the use of wider and wider discretionary powers held by trustees. This has been assisted by the relaxation of the standards for certainty of objects for powers: it is only necessary that one must be able to say, of a given postulant, whether he or she 'is or is not' a member of the class of objects.[83] This is the standard of 'individual ascertainability'. And in *Re Beatty*,[84] Hoffmann J said that, at least as it related to testamentary powers, all there was to the anti-delegation principle was the requirement of certainty of objects.

Of course, not all of the cases mentioned above involved powers. Some involved duties imposed on the executors. But if we take our cue from Hoffmann J, how much of the law can be explained as based simply on the requirements of certainty, or of other legal principles that stand apart from any non-delegation principle? In *Chichester Diocesan Fund* and in *Brewer v McCauley*,[85] the executors or trustees were *obliged* to distribute the property, not merely empowered to do so. In my view, the only way that *Re Beatty* can be reconciled with *Chichester Diocesan Fund* is by focusing on the obligatory nature of the disposition in the earlier case, since the holding in the later case is that a testamentary *power* can be as wide as the testator wishes.

The House of Lords decided in *McPhail v Doulton*[86] that the test for certainty of objects in relation to a discretionary trust is almost the same as for a power. A discretionary trust in this context does not mean a trust structure in which the trustees, or others, hold discretionary dispositive powers; it refers more narrowly to a particular disposition in a trust, one that *obliges* the trustees to distribute property but gives them discretion as to who, within a group or class, shall receive.

[80] The Australian legislation (n 43 above) adopts this argument as a legislative technique, authorising the creation of any power in a will that would be valid *inter vivos*.

[81] See Smith (n 6 above), where it is argued that the estate is a trust with a different conceptual structure, namely that of the trust that is known to Scots law, in which the trustee has multiple capacities and patrimonies, and where the beneficiaries are creditors of the trustee in his capacity as such and only in relation to the assets held in the trust patrimony.

[82] Recall that this was the case in Diplock's will (see n 6 above). In other words, even if there were different rules for trusts and wills, testators could invoke the 'trusts' rules by creating testamentary trusts, which is what they already usually do. On general principle, it seems it would be difficult to justify different rules for settlements (ie trusts created *inter vivos*) and will trusts, both being merely different kinds of trusts.

[83] *Re Gulbenkian's Settlement* [1970] 1 AC 508 (HL); *Re Hay's Settlement Trusts* [1982] 1 WLR 202 (Ch).

[84] *Re Beatty* (n 31 above). As mentioned above (n 35 above), this argument was also made decades earlier by ID Campbell.

[85] *Brewer v McCauley* (n 15 above).

[86] *McPhail v Doulton* [1971] AC 424 (HL).

The law is that the test for certainty of objects is the same as for powers—individual ascertainability—but with a superadded requirement of 'administrative workability'. This requirement could be understood to mean that the class must not be so wide that there is no rationally defensible way in which the obligation to distribute the property could be implemented. Another way of explaining it is that when the class becomes enormously wide, an obligation to distribute property among the members of that class becomes, effectively, a non-charitable purpose trust.[87]

This may be enough to explain some of the cases mentioned earlier in which testamentary dispositions were invalidated. Consider again *Chichester Diocesan Fund* and *Brewer v McCauley*. If it be correct that in these cases there was an obligation to distribute the property in question, then, since there was no restriction to charitable objects, there would seem to be two possible interpretations. One is that the will trustees were obliged to distribute the property, as they saw fit, among everyone in the world. Although there can be general *powers*, a trust to distribute, with objects so wide, falls foul of the requirement of administrative workability. And if we follow the logic that the certainty requirements developed in the law of trusts apply to testamentary dispositions, we would say also that a similar obligation imposed upon a personal representative must equally be invalid.[88] Alternatively, a more likely interpretation is that they were obliged to distribute the property for purposes that were not exclusively charitable; in that case, these dispositions could be understood to have failed due to the rule against non-charitable purpose trusts.[89] And indeed, bringing both interpretations together, we have noticed that an obligation to distribute among the members of an enormously wide class can actually be seen as an attempt to create a non-charitable purpose trust.[90] On this view, then, the ratio decidendi of *Chichester Diocesan Fund* could be articulated in the following terms: an obligation imposed on a personal representative (or a

[87] *R v District Auditor No 3 Audit District of West Yorkshire Metropolitan County Council* [1986] RVR 24 (Div Ct).

[88] As mentioned above (n 5 above), all of the judges in the majority in *Chichester Diocesan Fund* referred to uncertainty as a fatal problem with the disposition. This interpretation also helps us to understand the comments of Lord Macmillan (set out in the text accompanying n 9 above), which some courts in the cases on powers have struggled with; he required a 'defined class' and said that '[t]he class must not be described in terms so vague and indeterminate that the trustees are afforded no effective guidance as to the ambit of their power of selection'. In relation to powers, subsequent courts have largely ignored this (except in Australia); it does not seem to square with the possibility of creating a general power. But if, as his reference to 'power of selection' implies, Lord Macmillan was discussing an *obligation* to distribute, where the only discretion is as to who gets what, then his remarks could be seen as discussing a version of the requirement of administrative workability.

[89] Two of the judges in *Chichester Diocesan Fund* referred to this principle (see n 7 above). It seems to be widely accepted that a *power* for a non-charitable purpose is valid (but see the reservations expressed in L Smith, 'Understanding the Power' in W Swadling (ed), *The Quistclose Trust: Critical Essays* (Oxford, Hart Publishing, 2004) 67). Even so, such a power must be subject to a requirement of certainty in relation to the definition of the purpose. This, however, stands apart from the rule against non-charitable purpose trusts, which—outside of some exceptions—are invalid no matter how certain the purpose.

[90] See n 87 above and the accompanying text.

will trustee) to distribute property must, if it is not exclusively charitable, comply with the same standards for certainty of objects as an *inter vivos* discretionary trust, namely individual ascertainability with the superadded requirement of administrative workability.[91]

Similarly, in both *Prendergast Estate v British Columbia (Public Trustee)*[92] and *Re Balfour Estate*,[93] the correct interpretation of the will may well have been that the executors were obliged—and not merely empowered—to distribute the property to anyone in the world, as they saw fit.[94] As a discretionary trust, such a disposition would be invalid for administrative unworkability, and so perhaps it only makes sense to treat it as invalid when it takes the form of an obligatory direction to an executor. Again, the 'trust power' that was invalidated in *Horan v James*[95] was, in fact, an obligation to distribute the property with a power of selection; that is, a discretionary trust.[96] A nineteenth-century Irish case also sheds light on this. In *Fenton v Nevin*,[97] the will stated, 'I will my executors shall apply the [residue], if any, as they see fit'. It was argued that this created a general power, but it was held rather to be obligatory, partly because it is more difficult to read such a disposition as creating a power when there are two executors than when there is one.[98] As an obligatory disposition, it was too vague to be enforceable and it was held void. If general *powers* can be created, the only way to explain why such a provision should be invalid is as infringing the principle that requires administrative workability in the case of an *obligation* to distribute.

If, in relation even to obligatory provisions, the real concern is one of certainty (in the sense that includes administrative workability), it would seem to follow that even an obligatory testamentary direction could give quite a lot of discretion to executors. As many cases including *Chichester Diocesan Fund* make clear, an obligation on executors to apply property to 'charitable purposes' is valid; it is

[91] If this be the *ratio*, then the extensive references to the non-delegation principle must be read as addressing only cases in which the testator imposes an obligation to distribute the relevant property. This seems justifiable inasmuch as that was the case before them.

[92] *Prendergast Estate v British Columbia (Public Trustee)* (n 44 above).

[93] *Re Balfour Estate* (n 47 above).

[94] In *Tassone v Pearson* (n 36 above), Fitzpatrick J suggested (at [58]) that *Prendergast* was incorrectly decided. It is true that if the disposition in *Prendergast* created a general power, then the two cases could not be distinguished. However, the language of the will (see the text accompanying n 44 above) rather suggests an obligation.

[95] *Horan v James* (n 27 above).

[96] See the discussion in n 27 above. It must be said, however, that Mahoney JA expressly considered (at 383–84) the question of administrative workability and found that it was satisfied in the case of an obligation to distribute among everyone in the world except testator's wife and the trustees themselves. I agree with Creighton (n 35 above) 107 that the judgment is flawed on this point. Mahoney JA purported to follow two English cases that validated wide powers, namely *Re Manisty's Settlement* [1974] Ch 17 (Ch) and *Re Hay's Settlement Trusts* (n 84 above), but both of these involved powers, not discretionary trusts.

[97] *Fenton v Nevin* (1893) 31 LR Ir 478.

[98] ibid 486. In the context of an obligation to distribute, but one which gave discretion as to the recipients, *Horan v James* (n 27 above) 378 provides a drafting solution: if the trustees could not agree, each was given an individual power over one half of the residue. Presumably this could work for a power of appointment as well.

certain, even though it gives a very wide discretion. Further, if the trend is towards applying the same certainty standards to wills and will trusts as to *inter vivos* trusts, then wide discretion would also be possible in relation to an obligatory disposition for persons, so long as it satisfied the requirement of administrative workability. Imagine that we took the discretionary trust of the income in *McPhail v Doulton*[99] and turned it into a residuary bequest: the executors are obliged to distribute the residue, as they see fit, among 'any of the officers and employees or ex-officers or ex-employees of the company or to any relatives or dependants of any such persons'. If discretions can be created in relation to testamentary duties as well as testamentary powers, it would seem that this should be a valid disposition.

We have seen, however, that there seems to be more to the non-delegation principle than a concern about certainty. The rule forbidding attorneys to make wills—if it is a substantive rule—shows this, as does the rule against executing a will that someone else has created. In the following conclusion, I will attempt to answer the question posed in the title of this chapter.

5. Conclusion

Taking all of this together, it seems that the common law does not have a strong non-delegation principle. It is permissible to create a will in which another person is empowered, or even obliged, to make discretionary decisions as to the destination of the testator's property. The tenor of the case law is that such discretions can be very wide indeed, and still be valid. Moreover, it is permissible to make a will in which the destination of the property is determined by chance, or by the actions of competitors in a competition created by the testator.

What the common law does have for wills, it seems, is an authorial principle. You must be the author of your will, even if you choose to author a will that creates powers, discretions, lotteries, or contests. Your will must express *your* will. This is why a testator cannot make a will without knowing what it contains, however much he may wish to do so, and even though he could be bound by other legal acts without knowing their contents. This is also why a will cannot be made by an attorney, however wide his authority, and even though such an attorney can bind a principal to other legal acts. Unlike other legal acts, a will must be the personal creation of the testator.

If such a principle seems to be in an irreconcilable tension with the possibility of creating testamentary discretions, it may be useful to bear in mind the classic distinction between a court sitting 'as a court of probate', to decide whether an instrument can take effect as a will, and a court sitting 'as a court of construction',

[99] *McPhail v Doulton* (n 86 above).

to construe an instrument that has been proved to be the testator's will.[100] The authorial principle operates in the former setting, not in the latter; the converse is true for rules about certainty that apply in relation to testamentary discretions.[101] Again, you must make your own will; whether you did so is a question for the court of probate. Once your will is proved, it must be construed, discretions and all; in construing it, the court of construction may need to apply the rules about certainty, and these may invalidate the discretions that you tried to create.

The tension between the authorial principle and the acceptance of wide testamentary discretions may be a creature of the mixed history of the common law of succession.[102] The authorial principle is an old one, rooted in canon law or in Roman law, whereas wide discretions are a creature of the common law and its disposition towards the liberty of the subject.[103] One practical example of how this tension can play out is *In the Goods of John Smith.*[104] The testator had executed a will and a codicil. He then executed a second codicil, that included the words, 'I give my wife the option of adding this codicil to my will or not as she may think proper or necessary'. The wife, who was the executrix, decided not to add this codicil, and applied for probate of the will and the first codicil. Lord Penzance granted the application, holding that 'the intention of the testator in this case was lawful'.[105] I would disagree. Conditional legacies are everyday fare, but the testator's aim was that the executrix should have the power to decide what should be provable as the testator's will. This, in my view, is contrary to the authorial principle, and the correct holding (which would have led to the same result) was that the second codicil was void.[106]

[100] In the modern world, of course, the same court usually performs both functions, but it remains important to bear in mind the conceptual distinction, for example in relation to rectification: M Cullity, 'Rectification of Wills: A Comment on the *Robinson* Case' (2012) 31 *Estates, Trusts & Pensions Journal* 127; see also *Tatham v Huxtable* (n 17 above) 651 (Kitto J).

[101] See Hutley (n 51 above) 94; Hardingham (n 21 above) 668.

[102] On this mixed history, see Smith (n 6 above) 297–99.

[103] The English law of testate succession was originally entirely ecclesiastical law, which was often influenced by Roman law: the ecclesiastical courts had jurisdiction over wills of personal property, and estates in land (over which the jurisdiction lay with the common law courts) could not be the subject of a will until the Statute of Wills 1540.

[104] *In the Goods of John Smith* (1869) LR 1 P & D 717 (Ct P).

[105] ibid 719.

[106] In JR Martyn, M Oldham and others, *Theobald on Wills*, 17th edn (London, Sweet & Maxwell, 2010) 7, the authors say that a testator cannot leave it to another to decide whether an instrument shall take effect as a will. The holding in the *Smith* case is said to be 'probably' the law, which suggests a doubt; and after explaining that the second codicil was not proved, the authors say: 'It does not follow that it could have been proved if she had wished it.' This might be based on a view that the executrix was able to decide to exclude it, but not to decide to include it; but it might also be based on a view that the second codicil was void.

In my view, then, there is a principle against delegation of will-making power, although it is narrower than suggested by the speeches in *Chichester Diocesan Fund.* The heart of it is captured by a passage in Swinburne:[107]

> Likewise by these Words, *our Will*, are excluded those Wills which depend of another Man's Will. Wherefore if the Testator should refer his Will to the Will of another; as if he should say, I give thee Leave and Authority to make my Will … yet this Will is void in Law. For as thy Soul is not my Soul, so thy Will is not my Will, nor thy Testament my Testament.

[107] H Swinburne, *A Treatise of Testaments and Last Wills, Compiled out of the Laws Ecclesiastical, Civil, and Canon; as also out of the Common Law, Customs and Statutes of this Realm*, 5th edn (London, E & R Nutt and R Gosling, 1728) 11. Swinburne's references are difficult to decipher, but some of them are to *ius commune* commentators of Roman law (especially Bartolus and Baldus). Part of this passage was cited in *Hastilow v Stobie* (n 59 above) 68, without reference to any particular edition of Swinburne.

10

Pension Death Benefits: Opportunities and Pitfalls

ALEXANDRA BRAUN*

1. Introduction

The will is not the only instrument available to pass wealth on death in England and Wales. For instance, survivorship operating on the death of a joint tenant, and the *donatio mortis causa*, can function as a means for benefitting someone on death. The same is true of trusts, life assurance policies, statutory nominations and private pension schemes. For this reason, in the United States, these mechanisms are generally referred to as 'will-substitutes',[1] ie instruments that, like wills, transfer wealth on death, but do so outside traditional probate procedures. It is true that these mechanisms operate like wills in that they allow for wealth to pass with effect on death whilst remaining revocable up until that moment. However, the term 'will-substitutes' does not quite capture their essence because these mechanisms often complement wills, without operating as a 'substitute'.[2] Indeed, due to the asset-specific nature of most of them, frequently a will is still required or desirable. In addition, these instruments can often do more than a will: they are capable of pursuing a number of additional functions and are at times also more sophisticated.[3]

The term 'will-substitute' is not normally used as a term of art on this side of the Atlantic, where there is little scholarly debate about the transfer of wealth on

* The author would like to thank Victoria Coleman for assistance with the research, Prue Vines for help with Australian sources, and David Pollard, Dan Schaffer, and Lionel Smith for invaluable comments on an earlier draft of this chapter. The author is further grateful to the Alexander von Humboldt Foundation for funding a sabbatical leave during which parts of this chapter were written and to the John Fell Fund for funding research assistance for this chapter.

[1] JH Langbein, 'The Nonprobate Revolution and the Future of the Law of Succession' (1983–84) 97 *Harvard Law Review* 1108 at 1109.

[2] A Braun and A Röthel, 'Exploring Means of Transferring Wealth on Death', ch 16 in A Braun and A Röthel (eds), *Passing Wealth on Death: Will-Substitutes in Comparative Perspective* (Oxford, Hart Publishing) (hereinafter '*Will-Substitutes*') VII.B, 364–66.

[3] ibid.

death outside probate.[4] I have argued elsewhere that England and Wales have not experienced a non-probate revolution in the same way that the United States have.[5] Nevertheless, in recent years, a substantial amount of wealth seems to have been passed on death through ways other than wills and intestacy, such as life assurance policies, private pension schemes and survivorship operating on death of a joint tenant of real property, bank accounts or annuities.[6] Other instruments popular in the United States,[7] such as transfer-on-death (TOD) registrations of securities or automobiles, payable-on-death (POD) bank accounts, and transfer-on-death deeds of land, do not seem to be available in England and Wales, and revocable trusts are apparently not as popular.[8]

In the United States, the primary rationale behind the use of 'will-substitutes' is the desire to avoid probate, so as to reduce fees and delays in the administration of the estate and to maintain privacy.[9] Due to differences in the probate procedure, probate avoidance does not represent a major incentive in England and Wales. Tax considerations would seem to be much more important, as well as the fact that nowadays wealth is simply invested differently.[10] In other words, wealth is frequently saved in financial investments that normally permit a transfer of wealth on death with methods that obviate the need for a will.

This contribution focuses on the functioning of private pension schemes as a vehicle for the transfer of wealth on death in England and Wales. It analyses what benefits can be passed on the death of a member of such schemes and how recipients of death benefits are determined. In particular, it examines the nature of pension nominations and how they operate, and questions whether they provide an effective and reliable estate planning device.[11]

[4] Exceptions are G Miller, *The Machinery of Succession*, 2nd edn (Aldershot, Dartmouth Publishing Co Ltd, 1996) chs 14–17; C Sawyer and M Spero, *Succession, Wills and Probate*, 3rd edn (London and New York, Routledge, 2015) ch 2; R Kerridge (assisted by AHR Brierley), *Parry and Kerridge: The Law of Succession*, 12th edn (London, Sweet & Maxwell, 2009) 1–5 (hereinafter '*Parry and Kerridge*').

[5] For details, see A Braun, 'Will-Substitutes in England and Wales', ch 3 in *Will-Substitutes* (n 2 above), 51.

[6] Other mechanisms are statutory nominations and *donationes mortis causa*.

[7] For a discussion of the devices most common in the US, see JH Langbein, 'Major Reforms of the Property Restatement and the Uniform Probate Code: Reformation, Harmless Error, and Nonprobate Transfers' (2012) 38 *ACTEC Law Journal* 1 at 10; MB Leslie and SE Sterk, 'Revisiting the Revolution: Reintegrating the Wealth Transmission System' (2015) 56 *Boston College Law Review* 61, and T Gallanis, 'Will-Substitutes: A US Perspective', ch 1 in *Will-Substitutes* (n 2 above) 9. There is no agreement, however, as to which instruments are most relevant from an economic perspective.

[8] Braun (n 5 above) II, 53. They are, however, common in off-shore jurisdictions: see C McKenzie, 'Having and Eating the Cake: A Global Survey of Settlor Reserved Power Trusts: Part 1' (2007) *Private Client Business* 336 at 339.

[9] Langbein, 'The Nonprobate Revolution' (n 1 above) 1116. See also Gallanis (n 7 above)11–12 who mentions further reasons.

[10] Braun (n 5 above) IV, 71 ff.

[11] The effect of the payment of pension death benefits on third parties, such as creditors, family members and dependants, has been dealt with elsewhere: see Braun (n 5 above) III. D and E, 66–69.

2. Using Pension Schemes to Transfer Wealth on Death

2.1. Types of Schemes and Death Benefits

There are two main types of private pension schemes available in England and Wales: occupational pension schemes and personal pension schemes. Personal pension schemes are always defined contribution schemes, while occupational pension schemes take the form of a defined benefit (DB), a defined contribution (DC) (which is more common), or a hybrid scheme that provides a combination of DB and DC benefits. A person can be a member of both a personal pension scheme and an occupational scheme.

Although the primary purpose of such schemes is to provide for the retirement of the scheme member, they can also benefit someone on the death of the member. The type of death benefit payable varies considerably, depending on the nature of the scheme and on whether or not the member dies before or after retirement. Where the member dies before retirement, pension schemes usually provide death benefits in the form of a lump-sum payment, a dependant's pension or a combination of both. By contrast, where the member dies after retirement, some death benefits may be payable in the form of a guaranteed pension. In this case, if the member dies before the end of the guaranteed period, any remaining payments will be paid to the member's estate, to be distributed according to the will or intestacy rules. Defined benefit schemes will often pay a proportion of the pension the member was receiving when he died to his spouse or children. If, upon retirement, the member has invested the pension pot in a drawdown pension or an annuity, more benefits may be payable on death.

There are two main types of annuities: guaranteed term annuities and joint-life annuities. In the case of the former, the insurance company will make the payments for a guaranteed period,[12] even if the member dies, while in the latter case, the payment is made for the life of the survivor. Drawdown pensions are more flexible in that a death benefit can be provided to dependants in the form of a drawdown pension, a lump-sum payment or an annuity. In addition, in 2006, value protection annuities became available, which, in the event of death, provide a return of any unpaid capital as a lump-sum.

Thus, pensions offer a variety of different possible ways of passing wealth on the death of the member and sometimes the amount of money passed is significant. For instance, in the case of occupational pension schemes, lump-sum payments

[12] Before April 2015, the guaranteed period was for up to a maximum of 10 years, but under the new rules the period is no longer restricted.

are normally calculated as a multiple of the member's yearly earning at the time of death, or a multiple of four times the annual salary or greater. Most personal pensions will pay the full value of the pension fund so that the amount can be considerable.[13] In some instances, both a lump-sum and a dependant's pension of up to two thirds of the member's prospective pension, plus return of the member's contributions with interest, is payable.[14]

2.2. Attractiveness of Pension Schemes for the Transfer of Wealth on Death

While personal pension schemes were introduced in 1988,[15] occupational pension schemes have been available longer,[16] though gaining in popularity especially in the course of the twentieth century. Together with homes, today pensions often represent a household's most significant financial asset.[17] The most recent figures show that, in 2012, £2,405 billion was invested in private pension funds.[18]

The primary reason why someone joins a private pension scheme is to arrange for his or her retirement and, in particular, to provide for cases of old age or ill health. Although, at least in DB schemes, members are concerned about what their scheme will provide to their loved ones on their death, estate planning is not necessarily a key consideration for members. However, providing benefits to the same or next generation through a pension scheme offers certain advantages. Since pension death benefits generally pass outside probate, without entering the estate of the deceased, creditors cannot easily get a hold of them and the powers of the courts under the family provision legislation do not usually extend to them.[19] Moreover, pension death benefits offer certain tax advantages that other 'will-substitutes' do not necessarily enjoy.[20] In this respect, recent changes to the tax

[13] In determination *Childs-Hopkins* (K00663) the lump-sum amounted to £96,000, in *Wheeler* (PO-267) £150,053, and in *Tompkins* (J00510) £562,600.

[14] For details, see Office for National Statistics, *Occupational Pension Scheme Survey Annual Report 2011*, chs 5 and 6.

[15] Finance Act 1987. The immediate predecessors of personal pension schemes were Retirement Annuity Contracts.

[16] P Thane, *Old Age in English History. Past Experiences, Present Issues* (Oxford, Oxford University Press, 2000) 250 at 381–82; CG Lewin, *Pensions and Insurance before 1800* (East Linton, Tuckwell, 2003).

[17] In 2012–14, aggregate total wealth (including private pension wealth) of all private households in Great Britain was £11.1 trillion, and private pension wealth was the largest component, accounting for 40%. See *Total Wealth, Wealth in Great Britain, 2012–14*, ch 2. See also the English Law Commission's report on *Intestacy and Family Provision Claims on Death* (Law Com No 331, 2011) 145, para 7.99.

[18] This amount represents an 8% increase from £2,230 billion in 2011: 'Funds held in Life and Pension Products in 2012', *Association of British Insurers Data Bulletin*, November 2013, 2.

[19] Property in relation to nominations pursuant to an enactment may be included: *Goenka v Goenka* [2014] EWHC 2966 (Ch). This represents, however, an exception, as most private sector occupational pension schemes are not created by enactment. For further details see Braun (n 5 above) III.E, 67–69, and *Tolley's Pension Law*, Issue 85 (September 2014), D3-86-7.

[20] For details, see Braun (n 5 above) IV.C, 71–73.

regime applicable to death benefits of DC schemes have provided an even greater incentive for using such schemes as a means of benefitting someone on death.[21]

The primary rationale behind the reforms was to provide greater flexibility to members as to how they can access their pension savings once they reach the age of 55, ie as a lump-sum, pension, annuity, or drawdown pension. Up until recently, when a member of a defined contribution scheme retired, he or she could take 25 per cent of the defined contribution pot as a lump-sum tax-free; while the remainder, if taken as a lump-sum, was subject to onerous taxes. Depending on the scheme, the effect of pension legislation was that the member had to invest the remaining 75 per cent by purchasing an annuity, a drawdown pension, or a combination of the two.[22] Since April 2015, members can draw down their entire pension once they reach the age of 55, and are no longer forced to invest their pensions in annuities or drawdown pensions.

Conversely, other changes introduced by the 2015 pension reform have been aimed at persuading members to pass their wealth onto the same or next generation. Prior to the reform, a deceased member's defined contribution pension could be paid out as a lump-sum tax-free if the member died before the age of 75 and before he or she had touched his or her pension pot. Otherwise, if the member was over the age of 75 when he or she died, or had already started to take benefits from his or her pension pot, it was taxed at 55 per cent. This 55 per cent tax charge was abolished with effect from 6 April 2015. Under the new legislation, whether or not tax is payable on a lump-sum depends only on the age of the member when he or she dies. If the member dies before the age of 75, his or her beneficiary can take the whole pot as a tax-free lump-sum, or use it to provide a regular pension through a flexi-access drawdown arrangement or annuity, both of which are tax-free. If the member dies after the age of 75, the beneficiary can take the whole pot as a lump-sum, but it will be taxed at 45 per cent (although the government is expected to review this). With effect from 6 April 2016, if the defined contribution pot is used to provide a pension (through a drawdown arrangement or by purchasing an annuity), it will be taxed at the beneficiary's income tax rate. If the beneficiary chooses to take regular smaller lump-sums, they too will be taxed as income.[23]

In addition to these tax incentives, the new regime facilitates a transfer of certain death benefits to anyone chosen by the member. For instance, joint-life annuities can now be passed on to any chosen beneficiary, and not just to the spouse, the civil partner, or a dependant. And, whereas under the old rules the option to take

[21] On 21 April 2015, HMRC updated its Inheritance Tax Manual (IHTM) due to changes that resulted from the Taxation of Pensions Act 2014 (in force from 6 April 2015). The guidance IHTM17052 (*Pensions: IHT charges: General power over death benefits*) confirms that death benefits will only be treated as part of the member's estate for IHT purposes if the scheme provider is bound to pay the benefits in a particular form in accordance with the member's directions.

[22] Lifetime annuities were often best suited for those with a smaller pension fund. See *Tolley's Tax Guide 2012–13*, at 341, and Pensions Policy Institute, *Briefing Note No 61*, (December 2011).

[23] These changes do not apply to NEST (National Employment Savings Trust), a defined contribution workplace pension scheme set up by the Labour Government in 2008.

a pension from a drawdown scheme of a deceased member was only available for their dependants, now any beneficiary can take a pension from such a scheme, in addition to a lump-sum.

Whilst it is true that these reforms have made the transfer of wealth through defined contribution schemes more attractive, in England and Wales, besides there being an annual allowance for relief on pension contributions, there is also a lifetime cap allowance for payments made into a pension.[24] The cap for the tax year 2015–16 was £1.25 million, reduced from £1.5 million in 2013–14 and falling to £1 million from 6 April 2016. Although theoretically one can invest more in a pension scheme, tax is charged at 55 per cent on the amount exceeding the cap when the money is taken out. This imposes a considerable restriction on pensions as an effective 'will-substitute', especially for higher earners.

3. The Distribution of Pension Death Benefits: Potential Problems

The pension death benefits described above are not transferred by will, but are paid out by the trustees or scheme administrators in accordance with the rules of each scheme.[25] The benefit is distributed by a will or intestacy rules only where the payment is made to the deceased's estate. While some death benefits (typically the pensions element) are payable to the spouse, children and dependants (as defined), lump-sum benefits tend to be payable to one or more persons in a beneficiary class. Generally, both occupational and personal pension schemes allow members to nominate a beneficiary or beneficiaries by filling in a particular nomination form. Such nominations typically serve two purposes: they add someone to the potential class, where they would otherwise not be included, and they indicate how the lump-sum should be distributed.

Pension nominations are similar to wills, in that they take effect on death and are usually revocable up until that moment. Exactly how they work and what they require depends, however, on each scheme. For instance, each scheme prescribes a different set of formality rules for the nomination and revocation of a beneficiary and varying definitions of the beneficiary class for the purposes of distributing the lump-sum death benefit. And while in some schemes the trustees must pay in accordance with the member's nomination, in most schemes, the trustees will take the nomination into account, but are not obliged to pay in accordance with it

[24] In the US and Canada, there is no flat-amount lifetime cap as in England and Wales, but there are yearly limits on how much can be contributed. The limits depend on a person's yearly income, and differ from one type of retirement account to another.

[25] Depending on whether or not the scheme is trust or contract-based, distribution takes place through trustees or scheme administrators. When reference to trustees is made, this chapter intends to refer to trustees and scheme administrators.

or, if specified, in accordance with the proportions that the deceased member had indicated. England and Wales thus lack the kind of uniform statutory framework that regulates pension nominations in other common law jurisdictions.[26] Instead, regulation is largely left to those who draft the schemes.

This raises a number of potential problems, which, from the perspective of the member of the scheme, render pension schemes a somewhat unreliable estate planning device. First, the lack of standardised rules for nominations creates uncertainty and leaves room for mistakes when nominations are made or revoked. Further, the exact legal nature of nominations remains undetermined. It is conceptually uncertain whether they should be treated as lifetime or testamentary dispositions, or even as dispositions at all. It is, therefore, unclear whether the provisions applicable to wills should be extended by analogy to nominations. For instance, while marriage usually revokes a will, it does not automatically revoke a pension nomination,[27] unless of course this is stipulated by the scheme. An additional problem is that the way in which nominations and wills interact is uncertain. For example, what happens if a member of a scheme tries to revoke a pension nomination in a later will?[28]

Another significant problem from the perspective of the members of pension schemes is that their wishes may not be fulfilled. Even though the member is usually permitted to nominate a beneficiary, unlike in the case of wills, the member's choice may be limited by the rules of the scheme to certain classes of persons. Dependants' pensions can only go to those falling within the class of 'dependants', as defined by the Finance Act 2004,[29] and pension schemes can restrict the choice of beneficiaries of lump-sum benefits. What is more, as mentioned earlier, unlike in other common law jurisdictions, such as the United States and Canada, and to a certain extent also Australia,[30] in England and Wales, nominations of most schemes are not, in principle, binding upon the trustees, who can decide to distribute the benefit to someone other than the nominee.[31] For this reason, pension nominations are often described as mere letters of wishes.

[26] Many Canadian provinces have legislation regulating beneficiary designations. For instance, in Alberta, the Wills and Succession Act, SA 2010, c W-12.2, includes specific provisions dealing with beneficiary designations. Interestingly, these provisions seem to have their roots in the English legislation on statutory nominations: see RE Scane, 'Non-Insurance Beneficiary Designations' (1993) 72 *Canadian Bar Review* 178 at 192. Australian statutory law also regulates nominations: see Section 6 below.

[27] In *Baird v Baird* [1990] 2 AC 548 (PC), the testator's marriage did not revoke the nomination.

[28] See Section 5.1.1.2 below.

[29] Finance Act 2004, s 167 and sch 28, para 16, as added by sch 10 of the Finance Act 2005, para 26, which extends the definition of 'dependant' to a person who was married to a member when the member first became entitled to a pension under the pension scheme.

[30] For Australia, see Section 6 below. For the US, see Gallanis (n 7 above), and for Canada, see A Campbell, 'Will-Substitutes in Canada', ch 2 in *Will-Substitutes* (n 2 above), as well as L Smith, 'Will-Substitutes and Creditors: Canada and the US', ch 12 in the same book.

[31] An exception is, for example, represented by nominations within the NEST scheme mentioned in n 23 above.

Furthermore, under some schemes, for pensions paid out in the case of death after retirement, the amount of the survivor's benefit can be reduced or stopped altogether, depending on the age difference between the spouses or the length of their marriage. Also, since the legal right to equality following the Civil Partnership Act 2004 applies only to services rendered after 2005, some schemes may restrict payments to a surviving civil partner so as to reflect only the period of the deceased member's pensionable service since 5 December 2005.[32]

Finally, and linked to the non-binding nature of nominations, the payment of death benefits can be slower than expected, as trustees can take up to two years to reach a decision.[33] Thus, to summarise, the transfer of wealth on death through pension schemes may not be problem-free and poses its own challenges.

4. The Elusive Nature of Pension Nominations

4.1. Introduction

As noted earlier, the legal nature of nominations under a pension scheme is arguably unclear, at least where the trustees have no discretion and must follow the direction of the member. According to Megarry J,[34] pension nominations are 'odd creatures', and therefore difficult to qualify.[35] Nonetheless, establishing the nature of pension scheme nominations is important in order to determine whether or not they fall within the scope of current succession rules, and in particular those applicable to wills. If pension scheme nominations are classified as testamentary dispositions, both mandatory rules (those concerning formalities) and default rules (those concerning construction, automatic revocation, forfeiture, and so on) could apply.

In England and Wales, questions as to the nature of pension nominations and whether they are testamentary, have, thus far, only been addressed in relation to the formality requirements established in section 9 of the Wills Act 1837, and only in two decisions, both of which are somewhat inconclusive as to the conceptual

[32] *Innospec Ltd and others v Walker (Sex Discrimination: Sexual Orientation)* [2014] UKEAT 0232/13/1802. The Employment Appeal Tribunal found that the discrimination suffered by the member was not unlawful and, on appeal, the Court of Appeal confirmed the validity of the exception to equal treatment. See *O'Brien v Ministry of Justice & Walker v Innospec and others* [2015] EWCA Civ 1000.

[33] The two-year period has been removed by the Finance Act 2011 for deaths where the member is over 75.

[34] *In re Danish Bacon Co Ltd Staff Pension Fund* [1971] 1 WLR 248 (Ch) 257.

[35] Counsel in ibid 256 defined them as 'sui generis, with some of the characteristics of an appointment under a power, some of the characteristics of a will, and some of the characteristics of a donatio mortis causa. As Alice said, "curiouser and curiouser"'. Scane (n 26 above) 179 speaks of 'mysterious juridical creatures' and in *Re Cairnes (deceased)* [1983] 4 FLR 225 at 228, Anthony Lincoln J defined them as 'a hybrid concept'.

nature of pension nominations.[36] Section 9 requires that a valid will be made in writing and signed in the presence of two witnesses. Section 1 of the Wills Act 1837 provides that 'the word "will"; shall extend to a testament, and to a codicil … and to any other testamentary disposition'.[37] In theory, therefore, the formality requirements apply to 'testamentary dispositions'. However, the legislature does not tell us what a 'testamentary disposition' is, nor does it explicitly extend the Wills Act 1837 to pension nominations, or exempt them from its scope.[38] In fact, the issue of what constitutes a testamentary disposition continues to remain controversial, and not just in this context.[39] For the purposes of this chapter, it suffices to note that the prevailing view since *Cock v Cooke* seems to be that any legal act that purports to make a transfer that takes effect only upon death (and which is therefore ambulatory) and that is revocable up until that point is a testamentary disposition, and therefore should comply with the formalities in section 9.[40]

4.2. The Position of the Courts

The first case in which the applicability of section 9 was addressed in relation to a pension nomination was the High Court decision in *In re Danish Bacon Co Ltd Staff Pension Fund*.[41] It is important to note that at the time of this case, it was not yet as common for trustees to have full discretionary powers over the distribution of death benefits, and nominations were generally binding on the trustees. In that case, the rules of a company's staff pension scheme provided that the fund passed to the personal representatives unless the member appointed (in the approved form) a nominee. A member who had appointed his wife later wrote a letter to one of the trustees asking him to amend the original application form. The trustee complied with the instructions. Once the member had died in service, the question arose as to whether the original nomination was still valid or whether there was a later nomination in favour of the person mentioned in the letter. Megarry J

[36] The question as to the applicability of s 9 of the Wills Act 1837 has further arisen in relation to joint bank accounts: see *Young v Sealey* [1949] Ch 278 (Ch).

[37] As to why the phrase 'any other testamentary disposition' may have been included, see DD Oosterhoff, 'Alice's Wonderland: Authority of an attorney for property to amend a beneficiary designation' (2002–03) 22 *Estates, Trusts & Pensions Journal* 16 at 23.

[38] In contrast, statutory nominations are expressly exempt from the scope of the Wills Act 1837: see *Parry and Kerridge* (n 4 above) 4.

[39] On the meaning of the terms 'will' and 'testamentary disposition', see G Elias, *Explaining Constructive Trusts* (Oxford, Clarendon Press, 1990) 87–95; J Ritchie, 'What is a Will?' (1963) 49 *Virginia Law Review* 759; and Oosterhoff (n 37 above). The issue has also arisen in relation to secret trusts: see P Critchley, 'Instruments of Fraud, Testamentary Dispositions and the Doctrine of Secret Trusts' (1999) 115 *Law Quarterly Review* 631, who reminds us that there may be more than one legal usage of the term 'testamentary'.

[40] In *Cock v Cooke* (1866) LR 1 P & D 241 at 243, Sir JP Wilde stated that irrespective of the form 'if the person executing [the instrument] intends that it shall not take effect until after his death, and it is dependent upon his death for its vigour and effect, it is testamentary'. See also *Jarman on Wills*, 8th edn (London, Sweet & Maxwell, 1951) vol 1, 26.

[41] *In re Danish Bacon* (n 34 above) 256.

held that in both the nomination and the letter, there was sufficient substantial compliance with the requirements of the scheme rules and that the nomination was, therefore, valid. He was further asked to address the question of whether the nomination represented a testamentary disposition requiring compliance with the formalities set out in the Wills Act 1837.

Megarry J concluded that the statute had no application. In the absence of relevant authority, he referred to case law dealing with statutory nominations, which although being testamentary,[42] expressly fall outside the scope of the Wills Act 1837.[43] According to Megarry J, the reason why statutory nominations do not fall under section 9 of the Wills Act 1837 is that they take effect by force of the statute that regulates them. He was of the view that, although the pension nomination featured certain testamentary characteristics, these did not suffice to make it a testamentary document and thus did not trigger the application of section 9 of the Wills Act 1837. However, we were not told exactly what was missing save that the ambulatory nature and revocability of the nomination were considered to be insufficient.[44] In Megarry J's view, the pension nomination operated by force of the provisions of the trust deed and not as a testamentary disposition by the deceased.

Almost 20 years on, similar arguments were employed by the Privy Council in *Baird v Baird*, which dealt, however, with a different type of nomination.[45] Here a company established a pension scheme in which the funds were vested in trustees and the scheme was administered by a management committee. Under the rules of the scheme, the benefits were not assignable. On the death of a member of the scheme while employed by the company, payment would be made to such a person or persons as the member had nominated, or, in default, to the member's widow, widower or estate. Though binding, unlike in *In Re Danish Bacon Co*, the nomination, revocation and alteration required the management committee's consent. The member nominated a beneficiary and the nomination was approved by the company, but the nomination failed to comply with the provision relating to the execution of a will in section 42 of the Wills and Probate Ordinance (Law of Trinidad and Tobago) 1950.[46] The member subsequently married but died before retirement without having revoked or varied his nomination. Both his widow, as his personal representative, and the nominated beneficiary claimed the benefit payable under the scheme. At first instance, the High Court of Trinidad held that the nominated beneficiary was entitled to the benefit and the Court of Appeal of Trinidad upheld that decision. The case reached the Privy Council, which dismissed the appeal.

[42] Hence, Farwell J in *In re Barnes* [1940] Ch 267 (Ch) felt that the doctrine of lapse applied to a nomination made under the Industrial and Provident Societies Acts 1893 to 1928.

[43] See text to n 38 above.

[44] For a similar critique, see WJ Chappenden, 'Non-Statutory Nominations' [1972] *Journal of Business Law* 20 at 24, who points out that had the nomination been attested, it would have been admitted to probate (as happened in *Re Baxter's Goods* [1903] P 12).

[45] *Baird v Baird* (n 27 above).

[46] Which prescribed the same requirements as s 9 of the Wills Act 1837.

Lord Oliver of Aylmerton, delivering the judgment for the Judicial Committee, declared that whether or not the provisions relating to wills applied to nominations made under modern pension schemes depended on the provisions of the individual scheme.[47] Like Megarry J, Lord Oliver was of the view that not every revocable instrument which creates interests taking effect on the death of the person executing the instrument, is necessarily a will, and like Megarry J, he did not clarify what renders a document a truly testamentary disposition. Instead, he drew an analogy between the power of a member of a pension scheme to make a nomination and a revocable power of appointment under a settlement *inter vivos.* He saw the analogy in the fact that the power to make a nomination 'disposes of no property of the appointor, for the proprietary interest of the estate of the appointor is one which arises only in default of appointment and in the event of there being no surviving widow'.[48] Thus, Lord Oliver saw the pension scheme just like any other lifetime declaration of trust or settlement containing provisions for the destination of the trust fund after the death of the principal beneficiary. For this reason, he rejected the analogy Megarry J saw with statutory nominations, on the basis that such nominations concerned the post-mortem disposition of funds which were the 'absolute property of the disponer and capable of being dealt with by him during his lifetime entirely, without reference to any nomination which he might have signed'.[49] In other words, the applicability of the formality requirements for wills was excluded because the member of the pension scheme could not freely dispose of the property during his lifetime,[50] as was the case in the Canadian Supreme Court decision in *Re MacInnes* (distinguished by the Privy Council).[51]

Finally, Lord Oliver added that, in any event, the nomination in *Baird v Baird* lacked the essential character of being freely revocable that is typical of testamentary dispositions, as the nomination required the consent of the management committee.[52] Thus, the Privy Council's decision seems to have turned primarily on the types of powers that the member of the pension scheme had during his lifetime, while the fact that, in this instance, he could not freely revoke the nomination seems to have played only a secondary role.

What consequences thus ensue for other nominations? In *Baird v Baird* the Privy Council did not exclude the possibility that other pension nominations

[47] *Baird v Baird* (n 27 above) 561.

[48] ibid 557. This reasoning evokes the words of Megarry J in *In re Danish Bacon* (n 34 above) 255, where, while dealing with the question of the applicability of s 53(1)(c) of the Law of Property Act 1925, the judge stated that in the case of pension nominations, the deceased deals with something which *ex hypothesi* could never be his.

[49] *Baird v Baird* (n 27 above) 557.

[50] This was criticised by G Kodilinye, 'Pension scheme nominations and the Wills Act' (1990) 54 *Conv* 458 at 461, who favours focusing on the intention. The intention argument was employed also by Hughes J in *Re MacInnes* [1935] 1 DLR 401, who relied on *Cock v Cooke* (n 40 above) and *Robertson v Smith and Lawrence* (1870) 2 P & D 43, which dealt, however, with a codicil.

[51] *Re MacInnes* (n 50 above) was not cited or referred to in *In re Danish Bacon* (n 34 above).

[52] *Baird v Baird* (n 27 above) 558.

could fail, due to a lack of compliance with section 9 of the Wills Act 1837, where the member has a full power of disposition during his lifetime over the amount standing to his or her credit under the scheme. However, a member will hardly ever have a full power, given that section 91 of the Pensions Act 1995 imposes several restrictions on assignability (and surrender) of rights under occupational pension schemes, and that, in the case of personal pension schemes, similar restrictions can be imposed by the scheme rules.[53] In other words, by preventing assignability during lifetime, most pension nominations will automatically fall under the reasoning in *Baird v Baird*, and the application of section 9 of the Wills Act 1837 will be excluded.[54] Even where the interest is assignable, it is probably unlikely that a court would stray from the decision in *Baird v Baird*.

Moreover, since nowadays most pension schemes confer discretionary powers on the trustees, and nominations are treated as non-binding letters of wishes, in those cases it is not the member but the trustee who ultimately determines who receives the death benefit. In fact, this analysis undermines the analogy between pension nominations and wills and 'solves' the problem of the formality requirements.

4.3. Between Testamentary and *Inter Vivos* Dispositions

In the two decisions discussed above, the validity of the pension nomination was upheld despite them not complying with the Wills Act 1837. Although this article does not aim to solve the complex issue of what constitutes a testamentary disposition, the question remains as to whether the arguments employed by the courts to exclude the application of section 9 of the Wills Act 1837 are convincing.[55] We know that statutory nominations fall outside the Wills Act 1837 because specific legislation says so, but can a pension scheme attribute powers to distribute wealth on death without having to comply with the Wills Act 1837?[56]

It is certainly true that in the case of pension nominations the benefits usually move directly from the fund to the nominee, without entering the estate of the deceased. This may be important when considering the position of creditors and

[53] In any case, an assignment under a registered pension scheme would be treated as an unauthorised payment: Finance Act 2004, s 172.

[54] To be on the safe side, David Pollard suggests that 'any binding direction by the member compl[y] with the attestation requirements of the Wills Act': D Pollard, *The Law of Pension Trusts* (Oxford, Oxford University Press, 2013) 137, fn 16.

[55] On the difficulty of reconciling the reasoning in *Re MacInnes* (n 50 above) with that in *In re Danish Bacon* (n 34 above), see R Atherton, 'Nominations and testamentary dispositions' (1991) 65 *Australian Law Journal* 49 at 52–53.

[56] For criticism, see Chappenden (n 44 above) 24 as well as WF Nunan, 'The Application of the Wills Acts to Nomination of Beneficiaries Under Superannuation or Pension Schemes and Insurance Policies' (1966) 40 *Australian Law Journal* 13. Both consider nominations under pension schemes to be testamentary dispositions, although the latter article was written prior to the decisions in *In re Danish Bacon* (n 34 above) and *Baird v Baird* (n 27 above).

the applicability of the family provision legislation, as well as inheritance tax. But it is not necessarily clear why this would be relevant to the consideration of whether to impose formality requirements for wills on nominations. Further, from the perspective of succession, rather than trust law, it is not self-evident why the nature of a member's powers over the pension fund during his or her lifetime, and thus whether or not the member can assign his or her interest in the scheme, should matter in determining the applicability of section 9 of the Wills Act 1837.[57]

By definition, the member of a pension scheme has no claim to a death benefit that only crystallises once he or she is dead. That said, where the nomination is binding, the member has a power to dispose of it and, in the case of lump-sum payments, the benefit can be of significant value. The exercise of this power takes effect on death, and until then, can always be revoked. If we applied the reasoning of Sir JP Wild in *Cock v Cooke*,[58] a nomination of this kind would be testamentary in nature and section 9 would come into play, especially where, as in *In re Danish Bacon*, the nomination was also freely revocable. In other words, in *Cock v Cooke* the focus was placed on the time at which the disposition should take effect, and not on the nature of the right disposed of.

Given that binding nominations are functionally similar to wills, we should probably ask ourselves what the purposes of the formality requirements for wills are and whether the same goals need to be pursued in the context of pension schemes. This is not to say that the formalities applicable to wills should necessarily extend to pension nominations. Pension schemes usually require nominations to be in writing and signed by the member, although only few require attestation (which is essential for wills).[59] One could argue that these formalities suffice.[60] In fact, there may well be policy reasons for exempting pension nominations from the formalities required for wills, as is the case, for instance, with statutory nominations, even though the amount that can be disposed of through a pension nomination is usually higher than the amount disposable through a statutory nomination.

Such an approach would be in line with legislation in some Canadian provinces, which tend to impose a lower threshold of formalities for similar beneficiary

[57] The argument advanced by Scane (n 26 above), whereby a beneficiary designation is testamentary only where the beneficiary receives the identical beneficial interest, as the plan holder held immediately before death, seems equally unconvincing.

[58] *Cock v Cooke* (n 40 above).

[59] Although nowadays some schemes allow for electronic nominations to be made, the Electronic Communications Act 2000 makes provision for the use of electronic signatures.

[60] It is interesting to note that complaints to the Pensions Ombudsman in which undue influence or duress was alleged, or where doubts as to the capacity of the member expressing the nomination have been voiced, seem relatively rare. For exceptions, see *Goodland* (D12153), where the member had been seriously ill. In *Massie* (L00463/M00159/60) the complaint was rejected despite the fact that the form was in the partner's handwriting. In *McGovern* (J00031), the complainant (father) questioned the soundness of the death-bed nomination on grounds of incapacity, but the Ombudsman found there was insufficient evidence to prove it.

designations.[61] The drafters of the American Uniform Probate Code also chose to regard pension plans, individual retirement plans, and employee benefit plans (and other 'will-substitutes') as non-testamentary for the purposes of formalities.[62] They took the view that they were unable to identify policy reasons for applying the formalities applicable to wills to 'will-substitutes',[63] and, therefore, concluded that the Statute of Wills only requires probate transfers to comply with its formalities and does not require non-probate ones to do so. However, it is important to note that, for purposes other than formalities, the prevailing position in the United States is to treat pension nominations as the functional equivalent of wills.[64]

In England and Wales, the question as to whether pension nominations are to be seen as testamentary for the purpose of default rules has not yet been addressed, and it remains unclear whether rules, such as those concerning capacity, lapse, forfeiture, automatic revocation, construction, and rectification, should apply, at least to binding pension nominations, as well as other 'will-substitutes'.[65] Where trustees are provided with discretion in distributing the death benefit, some problems, such as those that arise in case of lapse or re-marriage, can easily be solved, as the nomination is not binding on the trustees and they can re-distribute the benefit. Still, the disadvantage of this approach is that each case is treated differently and that discretion creates the risk of uncertainty. And, in any event, the problem persists where nominations are binding on trustees such that the question of the conceptual nature of pension nominations remains an important one.

5. Non-Binding Pension Nominations: Advantages and Problems

In England and Wales, the reason why most private pension schemes provide trustees with discretion to choose the beneficiary of the lump-sum death benefit is to avoid any risk that the payment will be treated as part of the member's estate for

[61] See Scane (n 26 above) 193 and Smith (n 30 above). According to Oosterhoff (n 37 above) 32, this legislation was a reaction to the Canadian Supreme Court decision in *Re MacInnes* (n 50 above), and was intended to prevent future beneficiary designations from failing for non-compliance with the formality requirements for testamentary dispositions. In Australia too, formality requirements are usually lower, except where the nomination is meant to be binding: see Section 6 below.

[62] Section 6-101 of the Uniform Probate Code (as amended in 2000).

[63] In the comment to s 6-101 UPC, at 726, it is reported that: 'the evils envisioned if the statute of wills were not rigidly enforced simply do not materialize'. For details see Gallanis (n 7 above).

[64] As a consequence, certain default rules are now extended to 'will-substitutes'. See Gallanis (n 7 above).

[65] For details, see Braun (n 5 above) III.C, 65. The common law rules on forfeiture applicable in case of unlawful killing would seem to apply to pensions, though there is little authority: see *Glover v Staffordshire Police Authority* [2006] EWCA 2414 (Admin), discussed by Ian Williams in Ch 3 of this volume. See further I Greenstreet, 'Murder most horrid and other crimes and misdemeanours—what crimes do you have to commit to lose your pension?' (2002) 93 *British Pension Lawyer* 15 at 16 ff.

the purposes of inheritance tax.[66] That said, providing trustees with discretion also has other advantages. For instance, it allows trustees to address instances where a pension scheme member has omitted to update his or her nomination,[67] which can lead to cases of 'accidental succession'.[68] Nominations are often made when a person is first employed, and is not, therefore, focused on succession, and it is possible that with time the member forgets that he or she made a nomination and who the nominee was. Further, discretionary powers avoid problems created by invalid nominations and permit trustees to deal with instances in which the nominee predeceases the member of the scheme or has unlawfully killed the scheme member. Granting the trustees discretionary powers also avoids the question (much debated in Canada) of whether an attorney under a lasting power of attorney, or a court-appointed deputy, can revoke a nomination.[69] Nevertheless, providing discretion to trustees to distribute death benefits also creates a number of problems, which we will now consider.

5.1. Exercising the Discretion

5.1.1. Range of Interests and Criteria to Consider

When deciding how to distribute death benefits, trustees must act in accordance with the provisions of the pension scheme, which establish who falls within the category of potential beneficiaries, While some schemes allow trustees to choose only among a certain category of potential beneficiaries, many allow for a wider range of potential beneficiaries, including personal representatives, spouses and civil partners, ancestors/relatives, nominee(s) indicated by the member, those benefitting under the member's will, anyone financially dependent on the member, and, sometimes, also any person entitled to an interest in the member's estate.

In order to gain a full picture of those falling within the frame of potential beneficiaries, it is necessary for trustees to carry out investigations, although it is not always clear how extensive these must be. For instance, should the enquiry of the width of the class depend on the amount of money involved,[70] and should it

[66] Pollard (n 54 above) 137; R Kerridge, 'Testamentary Formalities in England and Wales' in KGC Reid, MJ de Waal and R Zimmermann (eds), *Comparative Succession Law, vol 1: Testamentary Formalities* (Oxford, Oxford University Press, 2011) 305 at 307; Miller (n 4 above) 335; R Kandler, 'Occupational pension schemes. Lump-sum death benefits: Tax issues', Linklaters, September 2013. Recent changes to the HMRC Manual indicate that any nomination that is binding triggers IHT, irrespective of who is the beneficiary: see n 21 above.

[67] For a good example, see *Wagenbichler* (83186/1).

[68] For the US, see E Sterk and MB Leslie, 'Accidental Inheritance: Retirement Accounts and the Hidden Law of Succession' (2014) 89 *New York University Law Review* 2.

[69] Oosterhoff (n 37 above). See also the Final Report No 104 on 'Beneficiary Designation by Substitute Decision Makers' produced by the Alberta Law Reform Institute (ALRI).

[70] In *Wagenbichler* (83186/1), the Pensions Ombudsman found that investigations were proportionate to the sum involved and its value to the potential recipients.

perhaps be less extensive where the nomination is recent?[71] Here general rules concerning the exercise of the trustees' discretion apply.[72] Certainly, trustees should not make a decision until they are apprised of all the facts, nor should they have a pre-conceived idea of whom they are going to benefit. In other words, they should not limit themselves to following the nomination,[73] but must actively investigate and make reasonable enquiries.[74]

Once it is established who counts as a potential beneficiary the next question is how to distribute the death benefit. Again there are no clear criteria, and general trust principles come into play. Trustees of pension schemes seem to be investigating whether there is anyone financially dependent on the deceased, but the determination of what constitutes 'financially dependent' can be difficult. For instance, it is unclear whether the fact that two persons were living together is in itself a sufficient criterion.[75] Also uncertain is the extent to which other sources of income of the potential beneficiary, such as a dependant's pension, should be taken into account.[76] According to the Pensions Ombudsman, trustees should refrain from guessing what the member's 'presumed wishes' might have been.[77] Also, they should keep a paper trail, as failing to give reasons for rejecting a claim may be seen as maladministration.[78]

Whatever decision they take, trustees are required to balance the interests of all the potential beneficiaries, including those of potential future beneficiaries.[79] This does not mean that they have to produce equal benefits of equal value to all beneficiaries, or that their decision must be fair. As was stated by the Court of Appeal in *Edge v Pensions Ombudsman*, provided that the trustee's decision is made properly, the trustee can prefer some beneficiaries over others.[80] A decision is made properly if the trustees have acted in accordance with the relevant scheme provisions, taken into account relevant factors, and ignored irrelevant considerations.[81] Further, they must not come to a perverse decision, ie a decision to which no reasonable

[71] See text to n 87 below.

[72] GW Thomas, *Thomas on Powers*, 2nd edn (Oxford, Oxford University Press, 2012) 482; *Beau D'Aulnay* (H00533), in which the trustees relied on *Re Gestetner* [1953] 1 Ch 672 (Ch).

[73] *Kemp* (84427/1); *Young* (PO-1758), *Earle* (76674/4). See also text to n 128 below.

[74] *Thomas on Powers* (n 72 above) 480; *Young* (PO-1758).

[75] One could be a dependant without ever living with the deceased: see *Stephens v Michelin Pension Trust* [2006] EWHC 1640 (Ch) [19].

[76] *Hendry* (85218/1).

[77] *Earle* (76674/4). See also *Blakeburn* (K00892).

[78] *Curran* (74746/1); *Moreland* (PO-2087); *Childs-Hopkins* (K00663); *Kennedy* (F00948/49/50); and *Pensions Ombudsman Annual Report 2001–2002*, 7 (D Laverick). See further D Hayton, 'Pension trusts and traditional trusts: drastically different species of trusts' (2005) 69 Conveyancer and Property Lawyer 229 at 235, and R Walker, 'Some Trusts Principles in the Pensions Context' in AJ Oakley (ed), *Trends in Contemporary Trust Law* (Oxford, Clarendon Press, 1996) 123 at 129–30.

[79] The content of the 'best interest' rule and the extent to which it emerges from the decision in *Cowan v Scargill* [1985] Ch 270 (Ch) 287–88 is, however, controversial: see GW Thomas, 'The duty of trustees to act in the "best interests" of their beneficiaries' (2008) 2 *Journal of Equity* 177. On the view that the rule should be avoided, see Pollard (n 54 above) ch 9.

[80] *Edge v Pensions Ombudsman* [2000] Ch 602 (CA).

[81] ibid 627 (Chadwick LJ).

body of trustees could arrive or which is discriminatory.[82] But it is not always clear what exactly is meant by relevant or irrelevant,[83] and what amounts to a perverse decision.[84]

5.1.1.1. The Role of the Nomination

Where trustees have absolute discretion in the distribution of the death benefit, the nomination simply represents one of many factors that they must consider.[85] In practice, however, they will almost invariably follow a nomination,[86] especially if it is very recent.[87] This is good news for the members and nominees, though they can never be certain. Also, it potentially exposes trustees to complaints.[88] Even where the nomination is not recent, trustees cannot simply ignore it.[89]

Trustees are less likely to abide by a nomination where the member's circumstances have changed after the nomination was signed. For instance, when someone has nominated their parents at a time when they were not yet married or before becoming a parent themselves, trustees might find it reasonable to think that the person had forgotten to update their wishes. The same is true when the member has nominated the spouse but later separates or divorces.[90] However, whether the lack of a new nomination should necessarily be read as an accidental oversight is unclear. After all, '[t]he member may have intended to leave the nomination form as originally completed and this should be borne in mind'.[91]

[82] *Associated Provincial Picture Houses Ltd v Wednesbury Corporation* [1948] 1 KB 223 (CA) 228–31. On the use of public law concepts in the pensions context, see J Evans, 'Challenging trustee decisions: differing approaches to the supervision of the exercise of trustee's powers' (2012) 26 *Trust Law International* 55. See further *Pitt v Holt* [2013] UKSC 26; [2013] 2 AC 108 at [11] and *Braganza v BP Shipping Ltd* [2015] UKSC 17; [2015] 1 WLR 1661.

[83] Irrelevant matters were considered in *Crisp* (D11512).

[84] In making these decisions trustees are afforded a wide margin of discretion: *Pitt v Holt* (n 82 above) [73]. See *Elson* (F00859) for an example of a case where the Pensions Ombudsman concluded that the decision was perverse because the trustees should have ignored the nomination. Conversely, in *Horwood* (J00013) the decision was considered perverse because the trustees failed to take into account an unsigned invalid will that the member had made in contemplation of his suicide.

[85] Exactly what weight trustees should give to the member's wishes is not much discussed in legal literature: D Pollard, 'Pension Trusts: The Position of Spouses and Dependants' (2002) 16 *Trust Law International* 74. In *Winterstein* (76288/1), the trustees thought that the starting point should be the nomination unless there was a good reason not to follow it, and that was considered to be wrong by the Pensions Ombudsman.

[86] Law Commission, *Second Report on Family Property: Family Provision on Death* (Law Com No 61, 1974) para 213; *Tolley's Pension Law* (n 19 above).

[87] *Dudley* (M00489) and *Montgomery-Di Vito* (K00020).

[88] See Section 5.2 below.

[89] *Wagenbichler* (83186/1); *Williams* (J00373).

[90] In *Askew* (PO-4823). the nomination was made at a time when the couple was not yet separated. In *Childs-Hopkins* (K00663), the member nominated her parents before becoming engaged. See also *McNee* (PO-2780/PO-4183), where the parents were nominated but the member had since had a son, and *Gilliland* (PO-4043) where the member had a son after the nomination was made.

[91] Pensions Ombudsman, *How to avoid the Pension Ombudsman*, available online via: pipin.webplus.net/howtoavoidpo.pdf (last accessed 20 November 2015) 33. This problem arose in *McNee* (PO-2780/PO-4183), in which the Ombudsman held that the trustees wrongly assumed that the member's wishes had changed after the child was born. In *Redford-Gyseman* (J00400), the trustees assumed that as the

The answer to the question is particularly difficult where the scheme has sent out annual reminders to update the form.[92]

Occasionally, trustees do not follow the nomination, despite the fact that the circumstances have not changed,[93] in which case the decision may well be found to be perverse. Thus, irrespective of whether or not the circumstances have changed, in certain instances, the decision of the trustees may go against the express wishes of the member and, where that is the case, a complaint is likely to be lodged by the nominee.[94]

5.1.1.2. The Role of the Will

Another issue concerns the role of a will in the decision-making process of trustees. Wills cannot, in principle, dispose of pension death benefits, and they are not binding on the trustees.[95] However, a problem arises where there is a will in which the testator indicates who should take the pension death benefits, and that indication conflicts with an earlier or later pension nomination.[96] This raises questions as to whether or not the wish expressed in the will should be taken into account and whether or not it should prevail over the wish expressed in the nomination, especially when the nomination predates the will.

Although such cases are likely to be rare, similar problems can emerge when the will does not mention the pension death benefits. For instance, one issue that has arisen is whether the content of the will should guide the trustees' decision about the distribution of the pension death benefits. In other words, should the nomination be distributed in accordance with an existing will, so that those benefitting under the will receive the pension death benefits as well, or should trustees assume that the member intended for the person benefitting under the pension scheme not to take also under the will? A glance at Pensions Ombudsman determinations reveals that the position of trustees (and the Ombudsmen) on this point varies. While in some cases trustees take into account the fact that one person is benefiting from a will or another source[97] (such as a dependant's pension or property

nomination was made when the policy was taken out, that is to say many years prior to the death of the member, she had overlooked the need to update it when she got divorced.

[92] *Dudley* (M00489).

[93] *Worseley* (J00280).

[94] See *Elson* (F00859) and *Montgomery-Di Vito* (K00020). In the latter case, the member had made two nominations, both times naming his second wife, and indicated reasons why he did not want other people to benefit. Notwithstanding that, the lump-sum was paid to the father, the former wife, and to a settlement for the son.

[95] *Dudley* (M00489).

[96] In *Batten* (L00054), the trustees followed a will which preceded a nomination on the basis that the will was legally binding and the nomination was not, even though it was not clear whether the will dealt with the pension and/or the lump-sum death benefit. In *Moreland* (PO-2087), the will was made after the nomination and the trustee followed the will. See also *Morton* (77828/2), in which there was a later will.

[97] *Askew* (PO-4823). For a case in which a court award under the family provision legislation had influenced the decision of the trustee, see *Bailey* (N00495).

jointly owned) as a reason for not awarding them a lump-sum death benefit, in other cases they completely disregard other sources of funding.[98] This can make estate planning very difficult.

5.1.2. *Asking Too Much of Trustees?*

We have seen that the exercise of discretionary powers of trustees over death benefits may lead to unwelcome results from the perspective of scheme members and their nominees. However, even for trustees the current situation is often unsatisfactory, as the exercise of discretion in this particular context is not an easy endeavour,[99] especially where the scheme is complex and the number of members, and thus the number of potential beneficiaries of the death benefits, is high. Exercising this discretion may involve posing delicate questions about the nature and solidity of the deceased member's personal relationships, as well as the financial situation of potential beneficiaries.[100] Sometimes it may even require scrutinising medical records. This is because trustees need to build up a picture of the member's life, as well as the lives of those eligible to receive the death benefit. Such enquiries are potentially intrusive and as such trustees might be reluctant to enquire.[101]

Complainants and potential beneficiaries usually have to supply details of how they hold properties, whether they have been made redundant, whether they are receiving a pension themselves, how they have contributed to the joint household, and what the member may have paid for on their behalf, and, at times, this information may conflict.[102] Colleagues and friends too often present trustees with information that risks amounting to mere speculation and opinion,[103] and trustees must be careful not to rely on third-party hearsay or partial information.[104] It can be difficult to determine how to use this information and how to balance the need to provide information about their decision, at the request of the complainant, against the need to preserve the privacy of the persons who may be entitled to the benefit.[105]

Thus, one question that the current state of the law raises is to what extent courts should require trustees to act as quasi-detectives to uncover facts relevant to the exercise of their power.[106] The Pensions Ombudsman has expressed the view that

[98] *Williams* (J00373).

[99] This is acknowledged in the *Pensions Ombudsman Annual Report 2005–2006* at 17 (D Laverick) and in the *Pensions Ombudsman Annual Report 2007–2008* at 17 (T King).

[100] *Pensions Ombudsman Annual Report 2007–2008* at 17 (T King). See *Horwood* (J00013), where the member's relatives were quite derogatory about the widow, alleging that she had had an affair.

[101] *Earle* (76674/4). The Ombudsman held that it would not have been too invasive to enquire into the potential beneficiaries' financial circumstances.

[102] *Kennedy* (F00948/49/50); *Crossan* (82784/1).

[103] *Ashe* (N00730).

[104] *Gooch* (PO-627).

[105] This is acknowledged in *R* (P00883).

[106] Evans (n 82 above) 65.

there is a limit to what can be expected from trustees,[107] and this was confirmed by Lindsay J in *Stephens v Michelin Pension Trust*.[108] Trustees cannot know at all times who is within and who is outside the class of potential beneficiaries. Where exactly the limit lies is difficult to tell, and trustees, keen not to expose themselves to Ombudsman criticism, might over-compensate with costly, time-consuming, and intrusive enquiries before making a decision.

That said, it would also seem that in some cases trustees simply reach their conclusions without following the appropriate procedure,[109] or without acquiring the full picture.[110] In other words, sometimes trustees do not investigate whether or not a person falls within the category of beneficiaries,[111] or they base their decision entirely on oral evidence.[112] The good news for trustees is that it is actually quite difficult to challenge their decision successfully (though reputational damages are not excluded),[113] but this leaves scheme members and potential beneficiaries in a vulnerable position. Moreover, it causes cost to the scheme in terms of legal advice and can postpone the ultimate decision for months, even years, whilst the Ombudsman process concludes.

5.2. Role and Powers of the Pensions Ombudsman

The Pensions Ombudsman may investigate and determine any complaints alleging injustice (in the form of financial loss or disappointment) as a result of maladministration by the trustees.[114] Complaints can be brought by actual and potential members as well as actual or potential beneficiaries of a scheme, including a widow/widower, surviving civil partner, or surviving dependant of a member who has died.[115] In principle, such complaints must be brought within

[107] *Childs-Hopkins* (K00663).

[108] *Stephens v Michelin Pension Trust* (n 75 above) [10].

[109] *Kennedy* (F00948/49/50).

[110] *Miller* (G00545 & 6). Sometimes the trustees may not make proper enquiries because they know the member and his or her family personally: see *Smith* (D10683).

[111] *Ellaway* (80200/1).

[112] *Curran* (74746/1).

[113] Generally speaking, only where there is compelling evidence that the decision was flawed will the Ombudsman intervene: see text to n 135 below.

[114] The post of Pensions Ombudsman was created by the Social Security Act 1990, but is currently governed by ss 145 ff of the Pension Schemes Act 1993, as amended by the Pension Acts 1995 and 2004. Although s 146 of the Pension Schemes Act 1993 had provided the Pensions Ombudsman with the power to investigate cases in which trustees exercise discretion over the distribution of death benefits, until Dr Julian Farrand took office in 1994, the Pensions Ombudsman did not investigate such complaints: *Edge v Pensions Ombudsman* (n 80 above). Nowadays, the Pensions Ombudsman's competence extends to personal pensions as well. See the *Pensions Ombudsman Annual Report 2002–2003* (D Laverick). The Financial Ombudsman is also competent for some complaints, but anything concerning the administration and management of plans usually falls within the competence of the Pensions Ombudsman.

[115] Pension Schemes Act 1993 s 146(7).

three years, although the Ombudsman has discretion to accept out-of-time complaints.[116]

In the absence of a definition of 'maladministration' in the Pension Schemes Act 1993, the term has been interpreted as having an open-ended meaning and as covering bias, neglect, inattention, delay, incompetence, ineptitude, perversity, turpitude and arbitrariness.[117] However, as mentioned earlier, the Pensions Ombudsman may only intervene where it can be shown that the power was not exercised for the purpose for which it was given, that proper consideration was not given to relevant matters, or that irrelevant matters were taken into account. More specifically, in the words of Julian Farrand, the Pensions Ombudsman can interfere with the exercise of a discretionary power

> if: (1) the wrong question has been asked; (2) the trustee has misdirected itself in law (ie made an incorrect construction of the rules); or (3) the decision was perverse (ie a decision which no reasonable trustee would have taken).[118]

Where that is the case, the Pensions Ombudsman can remit the decision to the trustees.

Generally speaking, death benefits are not an uncommon source of complaint to the Pensions Ombudsman.[119] One reason for that might be the increased complexity of family arrangements. For example, for people who remarry for a second or third time, or who cohabit with a new partner, the cases show that problems can arise between the new partner and the children of the first marriage,[120] or the new partner and the separated or divorced spouse, or the estranged partner.[121] In fact, in several Ombudsman determinations, the member was cohabiting with a new partner, but had not obtained a divorce from their previous partner.[122] The determinations further reveal that disputes can develop between the estranged partner and the parents[123] or siblings of the deceased.[124]

Complaints about maladministration in the exercise of discretionary powers are sometimes lodged when the nomination is not followed.[125] More frequently,

[116] Personal and Occupational Pension Schemes (Pensions Ombudsman) Regulations 1996, reg 5(3). For an example see *Legal & General Assurance Society Ltd v Pensions Ombudsman* [2000] 2 All ER 577 (Ch).

[117] *R v Local Commissioner for Administration for the North and East Area of England, Ex parte Bradford Metropolitan City Council* [1979] QB 287 (CA) 311 (Lord Denning MR); *Miller v Stapleton* [1996] 2 Pens LR 67; [1996] 2 All ER 449 (QB).

[118] *Montgomery-Di Vito* (K00020).

[119] *Pensions Ombudsman Annual Report 2001–2002* (D Laverick) at 38 and *Annual Report 2010–2011* (T King) at 17. In 2014–15, 7,3% of all closed investigations concerned death benefits.

[120] *Hughes* (L00713); *Holmes & Coulson* (P00664 & 5); *McElhaney* (F00125); *Evans* (Q00894 and Q00895); *Northmore* (N00436); *Massie* (L00463/M00159/60).

[121] *Hendry* (85218/1); *Froggett* (N01351), and *Parsons* (P00184).

[122] *Dewhurst* (H00527) and *Miller* (G00545 & 6).

[123] *Osborne* (Q00664). The *Pensions Ombudsman Annual Report 2003–2004* (D Laverick) also mentions determination no L00331/2.

[124] *Dudley* (M00489).

[125] See n 93 above. When the member filled in a new nomination form, there may be a conflict between the nominees of the earlier and the later nominations. See *Massie* (L00463/M00159/60) and *Friday* (M01138).

however, the Pensions Ombudsman is asked to investigate whether discretion was exercised in a careful manner.[126] Trustees are sometimes accused of: failing to undertake a reasonable enquiry;[127] overlooking more deserving beneficiaries;[128] failing to ask the right questions;[129] or basing their decision on insufficient information and evidence.[130] Occasionally, complaints also concern delays in the payment of the death benefit.[131]

Even though the percentage of cases was higher in the years 2010–14 than in previous years, overall comparatively few of the cases dealing with death benefits concern the exercise of discretion in relation to lump-sum payments.[132] One reason for that may be that some of the problems are solved through internal dispute resolution procedures (IDRP).[133] In fact, the Pensions Ombudsman will generally only investigate complaints that have already been heard through the scheme's own IDRP, or from complainants who have sought the assistance of the Pensions Advisory Service. On the other hand, the relatively limited number of complaints may also indicate that the majority of pensions trustees are doing a good job. The overall low figures may further be a result of the fact that, although Pensions Ombudsmen sometimes criticise the behaviour of trustees, they do not necessarily remit the decision for reconsideration.[134]

While the Pensions Ombudsman can direct trustees to review their decision, the Court of Appeal's decision in *Edge v Pensions Ombudsman* made it clear that the Pensions Ombudsman should not second guess the trustees' decisions and that, unless manifestly unreasonable, the trustees' decisions should not be disturbed.[135] Even if the Ombudsman remits the decision back to the trustees, the latter may not change their decision. In this context it is interesting to note that while in the early cases trustees were hardly ever required to reconsider their decisions, from 2006 the number of cases remitted back to trustees has increased. This might be due mostly to the fact that some Pensions Ombudsmen have been more

[126] A complaint that too much weight was placed on the nominations was raised in *Kennedy* (F00948/949/950), and *Elson* (F00859).

[127] *Hercberg* (82431/2); *Winterstein* (76288/1) and *Young* (PO-1758).

[128] See text to n 73 above; *Young* (PO-1758); *Hendry* (85218/1); *Lang* (F00092); *Miller* (G00545 & 6).

[129] *Kemp* (84427/1) and *Harrison* (PO-2759).

[130] *Ellaway* (80200/1); *Earle* (76674/4); *Gooch* (PO-627), *Crossan* (82784/1).

[131] *Phipps* (80253/2); *Lang* (F00092); *Barnicoat* (PO-5763), and *Parizad* (82720/2). Where payment takes place after two years, it may be classed as an unauthorised payment and, therefore, subject to a tax charge.

[132] Usually between two and nine determined cases a year, out of between 900 and 1,000 cases completed every year by the Pensions Ombudsman.

[133] Trustees or managers of an occupational scheme are required by law to put in place procedures for internal dispute resolution: ss 50, 50A and 50B of the Pensions Act 1995, as inserted by s 273 of the Pensions Act 2004 (as amended).

[134] For an example in which the Ombudsman did not change the decision, despite the fact that it seemed perverse, see *Montgomery-Di Vito* (K00020). Although the Pensions Ombudsman felt that the decision had made a 'mockery of the expression of wishes form' and that the trustees had not made extensive enquiries into the financial situations of the potential beneficiaries, he did not think there was evidence of maladministration.

[135] *Edge v Pensions Ombudsman* (n 80 above).

interventionist than others.[136] In addition to remitting the decision to the trustees, the Ombudsman can also award compensation for financial loss and distress, but the amount awarded is usually between £500 and £1,000, except in exceptional circumstances.[137] Thus, all in all, the Pensions Ombudsman's powers and the scope of his intervention are relatively limited.

If the Ombudsman adopts a decision in the complainant's favour, and the trustees do not carry out his instructions, the complainant can apply to court to enforce the decision. The decision of the Ombudsman can be appealed to the High Court, but only on a point of law.[138] An appeal may only be worthwhile if the benefit in question is of significant economic value. In any event, it would seem that a court could not make a decision in place of the trustees' decision, but that it could simply remit the decision back to the trustees.[139]

6. The Australian Experience: Some Lessons?

At this point it is interesting to take a brief look at developments in Australia, where superannuation schemes are compulsory.[140] Unsurprisingly, therefore, pension schemes represent the primary 'will-substitute' in Australia.[141]

As is the case in England and Wales, in Australia usually superannuation benefits cannot be transferred through a will. However, since 1993 Australian superannuation schemes can include binding death benefit nominations.[142] Although not all superannuation funds offer the possibility of making a binding nomination, where the fund provides this option, the member may give notice requiring the trustee to provide any death benefits (in the form of a lump-sum or income stream) to a nominated person, which can be either the legal personal representative or a dependant of the member. For this purpose, 'dependant' is defined as including 'the spouse of the person, any child of the person and any person with whom the person has an interdependency relationship'.[143] An interdependency relationship

[136] Tony King, who was Pensions Ombudsman between September 2007 and May 2015, was more likely to direct trustees to reconsider their decision. In about 74% of the cases he heard, the complaint was upheld.

[137] *Swansea City Council v Johnson* [1999] Ch 189 (Ch) [205] (Hart J). See also the recent *Pensions Ombudsman's Factsheet on Redress for Non-financial Injustice* of 3 July 2015, available online via: www.pensions-ombudsman.org.uk/2015/07/redress-for-non-financial-injustice/ (last accessed 20 November 2015).

[138] Pension Schemes Act 1993, s 151(4), as amended by Pensions Act 1995 s 157.

[139] Hayton (n 78 above) 243.

[140] For self-employed persons, there are self-managed super funds (SMSF) with slightly different rules.

[141] N Peart and P Vines, 'Will-Substitutes in New Zealand and Australia', ch 5 in *Will-Substitutes* (n 2 above). Recent figures speak of $1.94 trillion at the end of the December 2014 quarter: Superannuation Statistics, February 2015.

[142] Section 59(1A) of the Superannuation Industry (Supervision) Act 1993 (Cth) (effective from 31 May 1999) (hereafter 'SIS Act').

[143] SIS Act 1993 s 10.

is usually described as a close personal relationship between two persons who live together, where one or both provides for the financial and domestic support and care of the other. This means that, at least as far as the choice of beneficiary of the lump-sum payment is concerned, the choice is more restricted in Australia than in England and Wales. The reason for that seems to be that the purpose of superannuation schemes in Australia is primarily to provide income on retirement to a member and his or her dependants.[144] As a consequence, it may be difficult, for instance, to benefit a partner who does not live with the member and who is, therefore, not considered to be financially dependent.[145]

In order for a nomination to be binding, members must comply with certain formalities, which are similar to those required for wills. The nomination (including a revocation notice) must be in writing, signed and dated by the member in the presence of two witnesses (who are over the age of 18 and who are not nominated to receive a benefit in the notice). It must further contain a declaration signed and dated by the witnesses stating that the notice was signed by the member in their presence.[146] If a member completes a binding death benefit nomination in the correct form, the trustees must distribute the death benefits to the nominated beneficiary and they have no discretion to vary or override it. If no binding nomination is made, or the nomination is not made in the required form, the trustees can distribute the pension as they wish, so long as it is fair and reasonable, which is different from the criteria applied by trustees of English pension schemes.[147] Binding nominations only last for three years, or for a shorter period if the scheme specifies so, with the time period running from the day the nomination was first signed or first confirmed by the member.[148] After three years, the nomination is no longer binding and the trustees can distribute the superannuation to anyone they wish, as is the case with any non-binding nominations.

Among the advantages of the Australian approach, is the fact that where the member intends the nomination to be binding, the distribution is made according to his or her wishes and is potentially made more quickly. This way estate planning is easier and trustees do not have to make difficult decisions, which they may be ill-equipped to make. The fact that the member has to renew the nomination every three years also ensures that it is not outdated.[149] Also, because

[144] See Determination D13-14/076 [2013] SCTA 153.

[145] See Determination D13-14/144, where the trustees overturned a binding nomination on the grounds that the nominee had not lived with the deceased member.

[146] Superannuation Industry (Supervision) Regulations 1994 (Cth) reg 6.17A (hereafter SIS Regulations). In light of the decision of the Supreme Court of Queensland in *Munro v Munro* [2015] QSC 61, it would seem that the requirements for binding nominations do not apply to self-managed super funds (SMSFs).

[147] See the text to n 80 above.

[148] SIS Regulations reg 6.17A(7). The Australian Taxation Office has recently announced that the lapse of binding nominations after three years would not apply to self-managed super funds (SMSF), so that those binding nominations simply continue unless they are formally revoked by the superannuant.

[149] Pension schemes usually send out a reminder about updating the nomination and usually all the member has to do is to confirm it.

legislation establishes one set of formalities applicable to all binding nominations, there is less scope for uncertainty or mistakes. Moreover, if a member thinks their circumstances may change, a non-binding nomination remains still possible.

7. Conclusion

This chapter has shown how pensions can operate as a mechanism for benefiting others on the death of the member of a pension scheme. At the same time, it has also identified problems with the current state of the law that may render pension schemes less suitable as a reliable instrument for estate planning. We saw that pension nominations raise wider questions, such as what makes an instrument 'testamentary', and whether pension trusts should be treated like any other trust. However, the purpose of this chapter has been to focus on more specific issues dealing with the distribution of pension death benefits.

Most of the problems addressed stem from the fact that England and Wales lack a statutory framework to regulate pension nominations. Each scheme has its own rules with different sets of requirements and procedures, and this creates uncertainty as to the prerequisites for the validity of nominations and their revocation, the legal nature of such nominations, as well as their interaction with the law of wills, and with dispositions in a will.[150] In the absence of a statutory framework, such questions are tackled on a case-by-case basis. The problem with this approach is that the outcome can vary greatly in each case and is, therefore, unpredictable. It is submitted that if legislation were passed, along the lines of legislation in other common law jurisdictions, a number of these issues could be resolved.[151] Legislation could establish standardised formality requirements for nominations, clarify their nature, and decide upon the applicability of default rules regulating succession, as well as the interaction with dispositions in wills.

In addition, legislation could be an opportunity to deal with the second set of problems discussed in this chapter, which is the widespread practice of paying death benefits at the discretion of the trustees. While discretionary powers of trustees have certain advantages, such as tax privileges and increased flexibility,[152] it is questionable whether these outweigh the member's lack of control over the distribution of the benefits and the lack of certainty created by the discretion, which affects, in particular, the distribution of lump-sum death benefits.

[150] A *donatio mortis causa* cannot be revoked by a subsequent will: *Jones v Selby* (1710) Pre Ch 300, 24 ER 143. The same is true of a statutory nomination: *Parry and Kerridge* (n 4 above) 5.

[151] Interestingly, in the *Pensions Ombudsman Annual Report 2005–2006* at 4–5, David Laverick suggested developing a common approach through a limited number of model schemes, dealing also with other aspects of pension schemes.

[152] See Section 5 above.

Although it is true that trustees tend to follow nominations, where nominations are not binding, members of a pension scheme cannot rely on the fact that the nominee will receive the death benefits, which ultimately affects their planning.[153] And even though a complaint can be presented to the Pensions Ombudsman, his powers are of a relatively limited nature. Might it not, therefore, be preferable to release trustees from having to 'negotiate their way through a potential minefield of competing interests',[154] and to offer scheme members the option of making a binding nomination?[155] After all, on balance the current situation is unsatisfactory not just for members and their families, but also for trustees, with the potential that concerns about the correct distribution of benefits may lead to higher insurance costs for pension schemes. Although one could argue that other discretionary trusts, too, pose similar problems, pension schemes differ in that often the member does not choose the scheme and is not able to choose the trustees.

Making nominations binding of course has tax implications. But surely, if the government wishes to avoid the possibility of death benefit payments being subject to inheritance tax, this could be achieved in other ways.[156] After all in the Canadian provinces, where beneficiary designations are binding, they nevertheless enjoy tax-benefits, and the same is true of Australia.[157] Although the lack of flexibility in the case of binding nominations may give rise to other problems, many could be solved through specific provisions addressing, for instance, cases of lapse and forfeiture, and the consequences of marriage. And by requiring regular and express confirmation of the nomination, the risk of 'accidental succession' can be mitigated. Furthermore, distribution in accordance with the wishes of the member would be more in line with the principle of testamentary freedom, which underpins succession law.[158] This argument finds further support in the fact that the member has himself paid into the scheme, and has in a sense already provided consideration for the death benefit payments,[159] which represent some form of deferred remuneration.

[153] Jane Irvine, the Deputy Ombudsman Pensions Ombudsman, in *Oliver* (77373/1) stated: 'A pension scheme member should not rely on the prospective award of a discretionary death benefit when making a will or other financial arrangements'.

[154] This was also suggested in the *Pensions Ombudsman Annual Report 2006–2007*, 4–5 (D Laverick).

[155] This is already the case with nominations made in the context of the NEST scheme: see n 23 above.

[156] *Pensions Ombudsman Annual Report 2005–2006* at 5 (D Laverick). The government has launched a consultation on whether there is a case for reforming tax relief on pensions: CM 9102 entitled 'Strengthening the incentive to save: a consultation on pensions tax relief' (8 July 2015).

[157] Campbell (n 30 above). For Australia, see Peart and Vines (n 141 above). However, in Australia, there is no estate tax imposed.

[158] And potentially the rule against non-delegation of testamentary powers to the extent to which it still exists after *Re Beatty (deceased)* [1990] 1 WLR 1503 (Ch). For a discussion of the principle, see Lionel Smith's contribution in Ch 9 of this volume.

[159] As noted by Sir Nicolas Browne-Wilkinson VC in *Imperial Group Pension Trust v Imperial Tobacco* [1991] 1 WLR 589 (Ch) 597. See also *Finch v Telstra Super Pty Ltd* [2010] HCA 36.

11

Estate Planning for Businesses

EMMA CHAMBERLAIN

1. Overview

On death a person's estate is potentially chargeable to inheritance tax at 40% if it exceeds £325,000 in value.[1] However, the prevalence of many exemptions, in particular spouse exemption, business property relief and agricultural property relief, means that in many cases no tax is payable on death. As Kay and King put it, inheritance tax is ridden with loopholes that favour 'the healthy, wealthy, and well-advised'.[2]

Inheritance tax (IHT) has been remarkably stable in structure since 1986, with no change having been made since that date to the flat rate of 40%. John Major increased the exemption for business property and agricultural property from 50% to 100% in 1992. After that, the Labour Government did little to change the tax apart from introducing a transferable nil rate band between spouses and between civil partners. This contrasts with the capital gains tax (CGT) regime, which has been subject to major restructuring and changes in rates at least once every 10 years.[3]

Inheritance tax was introduced in 1986 to replace capital transfer tax. The main difference was to exempt most lifetime gifts from inheritance tax, provided that the donor survived for seven years. Unlike estate duty, inheritance tax provides a complete spouse exemption, so that no tax is payable on property passing to the surviving spouse on death. This is one of the major reasons why it raises relatively little revenue. In 1895–96, the £14 million raised from death duties

[1] And it should be remembered that spouses and civil partners can hand on their own unused nil rate band to the other spouse or civil partner, so that on the death of the last spouse or civil partner to die, the tax-free inheritance tax threshold is potentially £650,000.

[2] JA Kay and MA King, *The British Tax System* (Oxford, Oxford University Press, 1990) 107.

[3] For example, the Finance Act 1998 introduced taper relief and abolished retirement relief, and the Finance Act 2008 abolished taper relief and introduced entrepreneurs' relief. Changes in rates occurred from 40% before 1998, to 18% in 2008, to 18% (lower rate) or 28% (higher rate) in 2015.

represented about 35% of Revenue taxes. By 1968, estate duty produced only £382 million—about 5.8% of total Revenue receipts. In 2013–14, it was levied on 28,000 estates, representing 4.9% of all deaths. Inheritance tax receipts are estimated at £3.4 billion in 2014–15 and are expected to rise to £6.4 billion by 2019–20. By contrast, capital gains tax is now £5.4 billion. The average inheritance-tax-paying estate is worth £875,000, made up of £190,000 worth of cash, £253,000 worth of shares and bonds and £329,000 worth of residential property.[4]

In the absence of any change, inheritance tax receipts are expected to rise by an average of around 11% a year, simply because of an increase in asset values. However, the introduction of the new main residence nil rate band (announced in the July 2015 Budget) will reduce the number of estates with an inheritance tax liability, keeping the total number of estates paying inheritance tax at around 6%. Since 2010, some significant changes have been made to the inheritance tax regime, with a lower rate of tax if more than 10% of the net estate is left to charity, restrictions on deduction of loans taken out by foreign domiciliaries and on the purchase of business or agricultural property, and the phasing in of a main residence allowance of up to £175,000 per individual. However, the legislation governing the taxation of businesses and farms has been left relatively unchanged. Nevertheless, there has been considerable litigation in recent years: at 100% the reliefs are very valuable and worth fighting over. The cost of agricultural property relief has increased from £195 million in 2008–09 to £370 million in 2012–13; the cost of business property relief has increased from £150 million to £385 million over the same period. Moreover, these are probably underestimates, as they do not take account of lifetime gifts.

This chapter discusses the scope of business property relief (BPR) in the context of estate planning. It is not a detailed technical discussion for practitioners, and the purpose of the discussion is to highlight the anomalies and rather arbitrary effects of these reliefs.[5] For reasons of space, I have focused primarily on business property relief, but similar observations could also be made of agricultural property relief (APR). The overall conclusion is that the current reliefs are not good value for money and are both complex and arbitrary in effect. Tax reliefs also have profound practical effects for clients who are advised as to the best estate and succession planning strategy to adopt. Their complexity means that people are generally advised to leave their business properties or farms on discretionary trusts in their wills, and to rely on their trustees to sort out any problems after their deaths with the aid of a letter of wishes and a tax manual. That in turn can lead to ambiguities, disputes and litigation.

[4] Office for Budget Responsibility, *Economic and Fiscal Outlook—March 2015*.

[5] For detailed technical discussion of the applicability of the reliefs, see E Chamberlain and C Whitehouse, *Trust Taxation and Estate Planning*, 4th edn (London, Sweet & Maxwell, 2014), as well as C Whitehouse and E Chamberlain (eds), *Dymond's Capital Taxes*, looseleaf edn (London, Sweet & Maxwell, 2015).

Many other countries also offer some relief for businesses on death, including Ireland and Germany. However, none of these are based on the simple proposition that if a person has owned a qualifying business for two years by the time of her death, it is entirely tax free, irrespective of what happens subsequently. In Germany and Ireland, for example, the business must be retained for a minimum length of time after death to qualify for the exemption, on the basis that the purpose of the relief is to preserve jobs inside small family businesses and to secure continuity.[6] The policy objective is presumably similar for the UK, and yet here there is no rule requiring a minimum period of ownership after death. No doubt such a rule would distort normal commercial behaviour if the heirs proved unable to run the business but were forced to keep it for tax reasons. On the other hand, it could be said that requiring someone to hold the business until their death is equally likely to distort behaviour.

The rather arbitrary tax consequences of business property relief are illustrated by the following examples. These demonstrate that there is a strong incentive to keep the business or agricultural property until death, and to acquire it two years before death.

Example 1

(a) Phyllis, a widow, is the sole owner of a family trading company worth £10m. The shares show a gain of £10m as they have a minimal base cost. She is fed up with working so hard. She sells the business, paying capital gains tax after entrepreneurs' relief at 10%. The net sale proceeds are £9m. The shock of retirement causes her to die a year later. 40% inheritance tax of £3.6m is payable on her death on the net sale proceeds. Her heirs therefore take away £5.4m.

(b) Mo is also the sole owner of a family trading company. She decides to continue trading, even though she knows that all of her family want her to sell. Mo knows that she has to keep the business until her death in order to obtain business property relief. She enters a sale agreement under which the purchaser is granted an option to buy the company a week after Mo has died. On her death, there is no inheritance tax. The option is exercised, and Mo's executors sell to the purchaser. No capital gains tax is due as the shares are re-based to market value on death. Mo's heirs take away £10m.

[6] Note that the German business property relief regime, contained in §§ 13a, 13b *Erbschaftsteuergesetz* (ErbStG), is currently in the process of being reformed, after it was declared to be unconstitutional by the Federal Constitutional Court: BVerfG (17.12.2014) BVerfGE 138, 136; NJW 2015, 303.

(c) Emma sells her main house for £10m. She moves into a nursing home and invests all of the sale proceeds in AIM-listed trading shares and farming land which is contract farmed. After two years she dies. The sale proceeds are free from tax. The heirs take £10m.

(d) Roger is also fed up with work and decides to sell his company to a rival unlisted trading company. He is offered cash, shares or loan notes. If he receives cash or loan notes, the same result occurs as in (a) above. If he receives shares in the acquiring company, these will, under the Taxation of Chargeable Gains Act 1992 (hereinafter 'TCGA 1992'), sections 126–136, be identified with the shares in the company that Roger previously owned. His period of ownership of the new shares is treated as including his period of ownership of the original company shares. The effect is that he can claim business property relief on the new shares. Roger can receive preference shares with a fixed right to dividends (akin to loan notes) that have a guaranteed capital value to avoid any risk in the new trading company. On his death, the capital gain he has rolled into the preference shares is wiped out and the shares qualify for full business property relief. His heirs will then be in the same position as Mo's heirs in (b) above.

(e) Roger could alternatively settle the shares on a trust prior to sale from which he is wholly excluded from benefit. If the trustees then retain the shares and the company sells the underlying trading business and reinvests the proceeds in let properties, there is no clawback of relief on Roger's death within seven years.[7]

Further difficulties arise from the very different types of business and farming structures used: a business may operate as a sole trader, partnership, limited liability partnership or incorporated entity; it may also be held in a family trust. The rules are slightly different for each structure. Many businesses are family run and often adjustments have to be made, typically with parents handing over control and ownership to their children. There are problems when one child works in the business, but the parents want the other child to receive some value. What if they leave all the business to the working child who then sells up immediately after their death? The use of a trust in a parent's will to hold the business property is often the suggested solution, but then the trust has to be administered and run after death. That leads into a further area of tax complexity.

Moreover, the rules are not aligned between capital gains tax and inheritance tax. Generally the inheritance tax reliefs are more generous, not least because, once

[7] Inheritance Tax Act 1984 (hereinafter 'IHTA 1984'), s 113A(3A(b)).

available, the relief is at 100% and uncapped. At best, entrepreneurs' relief exempts the first £10m of gains on a disposal of a business and the tax rate is 10%.

The arbitrariness of the reliefs seems to encourage complex structures and tax avoidance. Perhaps now is the right time to take a long hard look at business property relief and agricultural property relief and to simplify the whole regime.

2. Basic Conditions

2.1. Minimum Ownership Required

In the case of both agricultural property and business property relief, a minimum ownership period has to be satisfied before the relief is available. In the case of business property relief, a two-year period is required; in the case of agricultural property relief, section 117 of the Inheritance Tax Act 1984 imposes a minimum period of ownership or occupation, which is two years when the agricultural property is occupied by the transferor, and seven years when occupied by the owner or another (eg when the land is let). Where business property or farms are replaced, there are various rules to deal with this. Moreover, even the basic minimum ownership period rule is subject to anomalies. For example, it is arguable that it is not necessary to own the shares in a *trading* company for two years to qualify for relief, and that it suffices to own the shares for two years even if the company has been trading for a shorter period.

Example 2

Chris owns shares in a company that holds mainly let property. He has owned the company shares for many years. About six months before his death, he decides to start trading after selling the let properties. The company is a trading company at his death. It is a matter of debate as to whether the shares qualify for full relief.[8]

In the case of both reliefs, the business or farm must be run on a commercial basis and with a view to making a profit.[9]

[8] IHTA 1984, s 106.

[9] See *Grimwood-Taylor v Inland Revenue Commissioners* [2000] STC (SCD) 39, [2000] WTLR 321.

2.2. Types of Business

Any interest in a business (sole trader and partnerships), any unquoted shares (including AIM-listed shares), quoted shares which give control (50%), securities (loan notes) which give control (50%), land used for the purposes of a business of which the transferor had control or of a partnership where he was partner (50%), and land used by a life tenant in his business (generally 100%) can potentially qualify for business property relief.[10] The rules governing these different categories of property are complex.

Example 3

(a) Ray owns 40% of the shares in Gardening Hambridge Ltd (a garden centre) and his wife owns a further 5%. The remaining 55% of the shares are in a family discretionary trust set up by Ray's father, under which Ray and his wife can benefit. Ray personally owns the premises used by the company. On Ray's death, the IHT position is as follows:

  i. 100% relief will be available on the value of Ray's shareholding (assuming that the other conditions for relief, eg two-year ownership, are met);
  ii. to obtain 50% relief on the value of the land, Ray needs to control the company. His wife's shares are taken into account (they are related property: IHTA 1984, section 269(2)), but that still leaves him short of the necessary control (more than 50%) to get relief on the property. If, however, the trustees were to appoint Ray an interest in possession in 6% of the shares, then that would give him control.

Note:

  i. it does not matter that Ray's interest in possession is not 'qualifying' for IHT purposes: section 269(3) attributes the votes of shares comprised in a settlement 'to the person beneficially entitled in possession to the shares'; Ray is beneficially entitled to an interest in possession, even though he is not deemed to own the underlying property;
  ii. there is no requirement that Ray must have controlled the company throughout the two years before his death. He must have owned the land etc for this period, but the appointment of the 6% can occur just before his death;

[10] IHTA 1984, s 105(1).

iii. the appointment of the interest in possession for Ray is a 'nothing' in IHT terms: the 6% shareholding will not be taxed on Ray's death.

(b) Ray could transfer the land into the company and obtain 100% relief on the land, but then he will have to pay stamp duty land tax (SDLT) and capital gains tax (CGT).

2.3. Types of Qualifying Business

Business property relief is not available 'if the business … consists wholly or mainly of one or more of the following, that is to say, dealing in securities, stocks or shares, land or buildings, or making or holding investments'.[11]

The inheritance tax legislation does not define an investment business, but some guidance may be obtained from *Cook v Medway Housing Society Ltd*, in which Lightman J defined 'investment' as 'the laying out of moneys in anticipation of profitable capital or income return', and further commented that:[12]

> In determining what is the business of a company … it is necessary to have regard to the quality, purpose and nature of the company and its activities, and this includes the full circumstances in which the relevant assets are acquired and retained, including the objects clause in the memorandum of association of the taxpayer and the objects of a society … as revealed in its rules. It is relevant to have regard to the actual activities carried on by the taxpayer at the relevant date, but if these are viewed without regard to the taxpayer's past history or future plans they may give only a partial or incomplete picture. The critical question is whether the holding of assets to produce a profitable return is merely incidental to the carrying on of some other business or is the very business carried on by the taxpayer.

It is in this area that there has been much recent tax litigation. 'Mainly' means more than 50%. So if a business is 51% trading and 49% investment, then full relief is obtained even on the investment assets. If the position is reversed, no relief is obtained. So depending on where the 51% line lies, relief may or may not be available on a portfolio of let properties. However, it is not always easy how to determine what is mainly trading or investment. Over what period of time do you judge the position?

[11] IHTA 1984, s 105(3). Note the 'mixed business' cases, especially *Farmer v Inland Revenue Commissioners* [1999] STC (SCD) 321; *George and Loochin (Executors of Stedman, deceased) v Inland Revenue Commissioners* [2003] EWCA Civ 1763, [2004] STC 147; and *Brander v HM Revenue & Customs* [2010] UKUT 300 (TCC), [2010] STC 2666.

[12] *Cook v Medway Housing Society Ltd* [1997] STC 90.

Example 4
Archer is a farmer who farms land on which there are also let cottages and industrial units. In terms of turnover and employee time, the farming income exceeds the letting income. In terms of profit and asset value, however, the reverse is true. Is relief available?

The case law tells us to look at the matter 'in the round'[13] when assessing such situations, but this is not always easy. Caravan parks and mobile homes have been a particular battleground, with some cases giving relief and others not. The Court of Appeal decision in the *Stedman* case[14] is the most authoritative business property relief case, but the *Brander* case[15] is the most helpful in relation to landed estates. The latter case concerned a Scottish landed estate of 1900 acres with 26 let cottages. It is notable for a number of surprising conclusions, in particular the view taken by the Upper Tribunal that the fact that the capital value of the investment properties comprised in the estate was nearly double that of the non-investment assets, was not a factor which needed to be given much weight, since it was not envisaged that the property would be sold. The Tribunal emphasised that it was the overall nature of the business that must be considered. It confirmed that it is necessary to have regard to the period leading up to the date of the transfer, and not just to the position at the date of death. The length of the period depends on what is appropriate for the particular business.

The disparity between obtaining business property relief and only agricultural property relief is starkly illustrated by the *McClean* case.[16] Here the deceased had 33 acres of farmland which she had inherited from her husband in 1983. She let the land under grazing agreements with local farmers. The land was zoned for development and when the deceased died, the agricultural value was only £165,000, but its market value was £5.8 million. Agricultural property relief was available, but only on the agricultural value of the land. If business property relief was available, then the whole market value could be exempt from tax. The question was whether the grazing agreements constituted a letting business or a trading business. Around 100 hours per annum was spent in weed control, fence maintenance, litter and damage control and drainage and water works. However, it was concluded that although a business, this was not a trading business, as it did not involve the selling of a grass crop but simply the letting of land, even if on a

[13] *Farmer v IRC* (n 11 above).
[14] *George and Loochin (Executors of Stedman, deceased) v IRC* (n 11 above).
[15] *Brander v HMRC* (n 11 above).
[16] *McCall and Keenan (Personal Representatives of McClean, deceased) v HM Revenue & Customs* [2008] STC (SCD) 752, [2008] WTLR 865; aff'd [2009] NICA 12, [2009] STC 900.

non-exclusive basis. According to the Special Commissioner (whose judgment was affirmed on appeal):[17]

> The activities of the business do not involve the cutting of the grass and the feeding of it to the cattle but simply making the asset available so that the cattle may live and eat there: the income arises substantially from the making available of the asset not from the other activity associated with it or from selling separately the fruits of the asset: that is the business of holding an investment, and it was the main activity of this business ... [It is not] like a 'pick your own' fruit farm where after months of weeding, fertilising, spraying and pruning, customers are licensed to enter to take the produce and pay by the pound for what they take away: in the business of letting the fields there was less in preparatory work, the fields were let for the accommodation of the cattle as well as for the grazing and the rent was paid by the acre rather than by the ton of grass eaten: it was not a business consisting of the provision of the grass but of the provision of the (non-exclusive) use of the land.

There are a number of other types of 'mixed' businesses where problems can arise in determining whether it is investment or trading. For example, consider property development where land is often retained for long-term development plans and in the meantime let out. Is this business mainly trading or investment?

A question of this sort was considered in the *Piercy* case.[18] The company had been established for property development and had large holdings of land for which it received substantial amounts of rent until it could obtain the right planning permission; the lets were generally short term in nature. For corporation tax purposes, it was generally classified as trading. However, HMRC considered this to be irrelevant, contending that the receipt of substantial rents meant that business property relief was not available. The Special Commissioner concluded otherwise, holding that the business of the company involved marshalling sites for development with a view to selling the finished developments. Critically in that case, land was held as trading stock and, even though it produced a rental income, there was no evidence that it had been appropriated as a fixed asset. Business property relief was therefore available.

Money-lending can raise similar issues. This activity was the subject of a decision in favour of the taxpayer in the *Phillips* case,[19] where one of the taxpayer's companies had made a series of loans to other connected property companies. The Special Commissioner concluded that money-lending could be either an investment or a trading activity, depending on the particular facts. The facts of *Phillips* perhaps did not justify the conclusion that the money-lending was trading activity, as the lending activity was relatively slight and not particularly commercial, but HMRC appeared to lose the case because they wrongly argued that the money-lending must have been an investment activity because the money lent was

[17] ibid (first instance) [98] and [103].

[18] *Executors of Piercy (deceased) v HM Revenue & Customs* [2008] STC (SCD) 858, [2008] WTLR 1075.

[19] *Phillips and Phillips (Executors of Phillips, deceased) v HM Revenue & Customs* [2006] STC (SCD) 639, [2006] WTLR 1281.

used by the borrower for investment purposes. The Special Commissioner quite rightly concluded that this was wrong and said that one must look at the nature of the money-lending business and not at the nature of the borrower's business.

Lock-up garages, car parking lots, and holiday lets[20] are also businesses that often have a high 'investment element' in terms of being dependent in some way on land, while there is simultaneously some service element suggesting that they can be regarded as trading activities.[21]

The all or nothing nature of business property relief means that the stakes are high.

Example 5

A company, Miller Ltd, runs a timber business on some valuable land near Slough. The family find the timber business less and less profitable, but the land is very valuable, being zoned for development in the area. As long as the timber business is carried on from the land, there is 100% relief. If the timber business ceases and the land is let or not used in any business, there is no BPR.

Suppose Miller Ltd decides to let out some of the offices and continue the timber business from the other offices. Is the business mainly investment or not? The answer will determine the availability of BPR. The company must be careful to ensure that the company is still mainly trading when its activities are looked at 'in the round'.

Consider the position if Miller Ltd has two properties, owned by separate subsidiaries. On Property 1 they carry out the timber trade. Property 2 is let out to local businesses. Property 1 is definitely more valuable, and so the holding company is mainly the holding company of a trading group and Property 1 will qualify for relief. However, because Property 2 is held in a separate subsidiary which is not itself mainly trading, no relief will be available on Property 2, although relief is available on Property 1 (IHTA 1984, section 111). If the two companies are amalgamated into one subsidiary, however, full BPR can be obtained on both properties because overall the company is mainly trading.

[20] See *HM Revenue & Customs v Lockyer and Robertson (Personal Representatives of Pawson, deceased)* [2013] UKUT 050 (TCC), [2013] STC 976.

[21] See eg *Trustees of David Zetland Settlement v HM Revenue & Customs* [2013] UKFTT 284, [2013] WTLR 1065, and *Best v HMRC* [2014] UKFTT 077 (TC), [2014] WTLR 409, both concerning let business and industrial units with a high service element. This was still not enough to get the taxpayer relief, as the real value was in the lets.

Consider the position if Miller Ltd has an interest in three trading companies in which it holds a 50% stake. These are not 51% subsidiaries and are therefore regarded as investments. No relief is available. Partnerships also create particular anomalies. If an asset is only used by a partnership, but is not partnership property, only 50% relief is available. If the partnership is a limited liability partnership and holds a trading company, no relief is available. But if the individual owns shares in a company which enters into a trading partnership, then relief is available.

Is any of this justifiable in policy terms? HMRC naturally do not want to give business property relief on cash businesses. So section 112 of the Inheritance Tax Act 1984 disallows relief to the extent that the asset is not used in the business or required for future use. The aim is to stop people dumping personal assets such as yachts and pictures and vintage cars into a trading company and claiming business property relief. However, section 112 is not straightforward. For example, it is by no means clear that cash is in fact an excepted asset at all. If I inject cash into my company and the company invests it in let property, one would accept that the let property is an investment asset, but it is not an excepted asset. It is being used in a business carried on by the company to produce a return. The question then is whether the company is mainly trading or investment. However, if the cash is left on current account, presumably it is an excepted asset. But if the cash is placed on the money market, then the cash is producing a return of interest. Why is this any less of a business than property letting?[22]

3. Some Oddities

3.1. Trusts

As noted at the start of this chapter, the complexity of business property relief and agricultural property relief means that people are often encouraged to hold the assets in trust. This is not only or even mainly for tax reasons. Parents are unlikely to want to give all the value of the business to one child. Dividing the shares of a company between several children and grandchildren may encourage disputes. Leaving all the shares or the farm to the child who runs the business may be very unfair. That child may sell up shortly after her parents' deaths and pocket all the proceeds. So the parent is forced to consider using a trust to hold the business or shares.

[22] See *Barclays Bank plc v Inland Revenue Commissioners* [1998] STC (SCD) 125.

There are many anomalies to watch out for when using trusts to hold business property or farms. The following discussion will highlight a few points.

Most trusts nowadays are relevant property trusts subject to inheritance tax at up to 6% on each 10-year anniversary and on capital distributions from the trust. Relevant property trusts are now likely to include most trusts set up in lifetime and all discretionary trusts made on death. Differences arise between exit charges arising before and after the first 10-year anniversary.

In the case of an exit charge arising in the first 10 years from the date when the property was settled, the rate of charge is calculated by reference to 'the value, immediately after the settlement commenced, of the property then comprised in it'.[23] This means that even though property qualified for business property relief on the way into the trust (assuming the donor had owned the property for at least two years), there is no reduction for business property relief or agricultural property relief if the trustees sell the property in the first 10 years and distribute the proceeds.

Example 6

Adam settles property qualifying for 100% BPR in 2009. In 2014, the business is sold and the cash distributed amongst the beneficiaries. An exit charge arises (maximum 6% and in this case less, as the property has not been in trust for the full 10 years). How is this calculated?

It might be thought that the IHT exit charge will be nil, on the basis that the value of the property originally settled was—after 100% relief—nil. However, as noted above, IHTA 1984, section 68 (which deals with the rate of tax before the first 10-year anniversary), provides that the rate is calculated by reference to value, ignoring BPR/APR, and hence the distribution of cash may attract an exit charge. If the trustees had distributed the property before sale, while it still qualified for BPR, then there would be no inheritance tax charge. Note that the trustees would have had to own it for two years in order to qualify for relief on a distribution.

However, if business property owned by trustees qualifies for relief on the 10-year anniversary, there is no inheritance tax payable on a later distribution of the sale proceeds for the next 9.9 years! This is because the exit charge is no longer calculated by reference to the value of the property, but by reference to the rate of tax charged at the 10-year anniversary.

[23] IHTA 1984, s 68(5)(a).

Example 7

As above, except that the trustees hold the business property until 2020 before selling it. They distribute the proceeds of sale in 2021. The tax position is as follows:

1. at the time of the 10-year charge in 2019, the value of the property in the settlement benefited from 100% relief, so that the amount on which tax was charged at the 10-year anniversary will be reduced to nil;
2. the sale of the shares by the trustees gave rise to a CGT charge with no entrepreneurs' relief. The trustees could have appointed a non-qualifying interest in possession to one of the beneficiaries who worked in the business, and provided that this beneficiary owned at least 5% of the shares personally, the trustees could at the beneficiary's option claim a share of her entrepreneurs' relief. The trustees could appoint non-qualifying interests in possession to many different beneficiaries working in the business. Provided each beneficiary owns at least 5% personally, the trustees can (if the beneficiary agrees) claim entrepreneurs' relief of up to £10m per beneficiary. The appointment of the interest in possession is a nothing in inheritance tax terms. The interest in possession can be revocable and so, after the sale, the interest in possession can be revoked and the proceeds appointed to another beneficiary;
3. the calculation of the exit charge in 2021 will depend on the rate charged at the time of the last anniversary. As this was nil, no tax is payable.

3.2. Lifetime Gifts

The legislation attempts to deal, not entirely successfully, with the position if someone gives business or agricultural property away and then dies within seven years. In these circumstances, should there be relief or not? What happens if the donee has stopped farming or running the business? The general principle is that if the donee is not farming or running the business by the time the donor dies within seven years, the relief should be clawed back, but the legislation does not always succeed in achieving this. Note that if the donor survives for seven years and the donee has sold the business, there is no clawback.

Example 8
Emma gives Luke a minority holding of unquoted shares which qualify for BPR at the date of the gift. Emma dies within seven years, and tax becomes chargeable on the failed potentially exempt transfer (PET). If Luke has sold the shares before Emma's death and banked the proceeds, the relief will not be available, subject only to the possibility of replacement relief under IHTA 1984, section 113B, which is very restrictive. Similarly, the relief will be denied where, though Luke has retained the shares, they have acquired a full Stock Exchange listing before Emma dies. However, if Luke has retained the shares but the company remains unlisted albeit changed in nature, eg has become an investment company, there is no clawback of relief. This means that Luke should not sell the company shares if he receives an offer. Instead, he should sell the underlying trading business, and the company can then invest the proceeds in let property! See also Example 1(e) above.

3.3. Deathbed Planning

An elderly taxpayer may own a qualifying trading business but hold spare cash outside the business, or she may have made loans to the business (which do not attract relief). In these circumstances, what can be done to increase the available business property relief? If the taxpayer is a partner, then she should consider capitalising any loans, so that her partnership share is enhanced. A two-year period does not need to run from the date of capitalisation.

Provided the taxpayer has owned a partnership share (however small) for two years, the fact that she may acquire a large share does not matter. Full business property relief is available on the entire enhanced share immediately after capitalisation of the loan.

A similar approach can be used in relation to shares in the family company.[24] If money is invested by way of a rights issue, then business property relief can be obtained in the cash immediately, provided of course the company can use the cash in its business or invest it. (See Example 1 for the options if the taxpayer wants to sell up but preserve business property relief.)

[24] See *Vinton and Green (Executors of Dugan-Chapman, Deceased) v HM Revenue & Customs* [2008] STC (SCD) 592, [2008] WTLR 1359. See *Vinton v Fladgate Fielder (a firm)* [2010] EWHC 904 (Ch), [2010] STC 1868.

4. Estate and Succession Planning with Business Property

As noted above, there is a strong incentive to keep business and agricultural property until death, given the valuable reliefs available and the fact that there is a tax-free step-up for capital gains tax purposes on death. Here the drafting traps are numerous. Estate and succession planning is important, but rarely simple.

For example, a will establishing a nil rate band discretionary trust and leaving residue to the surviving spouse will not generally operate in the way that is often intended by the deceased if she owned property attracting 100% business or agricultural property relief. The problem is that part of the benefit of the business or agricultural property relief will accrue to the nil rate trust—ie the trustees will receive more than £325,000 (in 2015–16), but not the whole value of the business property—and the remainder of the relief will be attributed to property passing to the spouse and so will be wasted.[25]

Example 9

Andrew left a nil rate band legacy in the form set out below to his daughter and the residue to his spouse when he died on 1 January 2016. His assets include property eligible for BPR worth £500,000 out of a total estate of £1 million. The deceased made no lifetime transfers and so a full nil rate band is available.

> 'I give to my daughter such sum as at my death equals the maximum amount which could be given by this will without inheritance tax becoming payable on my estate'.

How much will the daughter take? £325,000? No, the legacy will be reduced by multiplying it by the reduced value of the estate (after deducting any specific gifts qualifying for relief 'R') divided by the unreduced value of the estate (after deducting any specific gifts qualifying for relief 'U').

Accordingly, the daughter will take £650,000, the IHT value of which will be reduced to £325,000, thereby being covered by the deceased's nil rate band as follows:

$$\text{£}650{,}000 \times \frac{\text{£}500{,}000\,(\text{R})}{\text{£}1{,}000{,}000\,(\text{U})} = \text{£}325{,}000$$

This may or may not be what the testator intended.

[25] See IHTA 1984, s 39A.

'Two bites at the cherry' arrangements are common, although since 2013 they are less attractive if the surviving spouse cannot buy the business property outright with cash, as the deductibility of loans to acquire business property is now restricted.

Example 10

Assume that a husband (H) owns a farm qualifying for 100% APR and worth £1m. It is envisaged that his wife (W) will take over the business after his death, but if he leaves her the farm, APR will be wasted. Consider therefore the following:

(i) the farm is left to his daughter D. IHT is not payable because of the relief;
(ii) after his death, the farm is sold to W, with D receiving £1m in cash;
(iii) once W has owned the farm for two years, APR will be available on her death (hence, 'two bites at the cherry');
(iv) if desired, D can also be given a cash legacy of the nil rate sum.

Note in connection with the above:

(i) SDLT will be payable by W on the acquisition of an interest in land (although on the farmland at the lower commercial property rates);
(ii) there is no clawback of APR or BPR if the property is sold (however soon!) after H's death;
(iii) if it is desired to protect W's position, she could be given an option to purchase the farm in the will.

Difficulties arise if W has insufficient money to purchase the farm for £1m. If all or part of the purchase price is left outstanding as an interest-free loan from the daughter, then the effect of IHTA 1984, section 162B, will be to deduct the liability against the value of the farm before relief. So then the relief is effectively wasted.

It is often difficult to determine whether a business will qualify for full relief or some part of the business will be restricted. Even if full relief is available now, perhaps the business will change in nature following the drafting of the will. A possible solution is as follows. Let us assume that a testator wants to leave his business property to his children if it attracts relief, but otherwise to his spouse. The will therefore is drafted to:

(i) establish a discretionary trust; and
(ii) settle the business or agricultural property with no qualification such as 'provided that it shall qualify for IHT relief'. This will be a specific gift of the

> property within section 39A(2) of the Inheritance Tax Act 1984 and, because tax will be at stake, HMRC must consider the availability of the relief. Note that it should not just say 'all my business property'. It should name the business or the company specifically and leave it on discretionary trusts.

Alternatively, the testator could leave the whole of his residuary estate into discretionary trust and make no mention of business property relief. The disadvantage of this course is that inheritance tax has to be paid upfront before probate can be obtained. Clearly, assets such as the main residence will not qualify for any relief and are therefore better going outright to the spouse or on interest-in-possession trusts for her. An appointment can be made to the spouse before the grant of probate to ensure that this part of the estate is exempt and therefore free of inheritance tax, as there is reading back under section 144 of the Inheritance Tax Act 1984 (see immediately below). The balance of the estate that is believed to qualify for business property relief can then be retained on discretionary trusts and the position debated with HMRC.

The advantage of using a discretionary trust is that appointments out of the trust within two years of death will fall within section 144 of the Inheritance Tax Act 1984 and will be read back into the will for inheritance tax purposes. It is, therefore, possible, once the APR/BPR position has been agreed with HMRC, to take a view on the future of the trust. For instance, if full relief is given, then either the trust may continue for the benefit of surviving spouse and children, or the property could be appointed to chargeable persons outright (eg to children or grandchildren). But, if relief is not available, then an appointment to the surviving spouse of the chargeable property can be made within two years of death. Spouse exemption is then obtained (as the appointment is read back under section 144 and treated as a gift to the spouse by the testator). The surviving spouse can always make lifetime gifts and survive for seven years. There will be no capital gains tax payable on the lifetime gifts, as the gain has been wiped out on the first death.

If the business property is retained in trust on the first death, some more planning can be done later. For example, if residue is left on discretionary trusts on death, the business property can be appointed into a sub-fund which is retained on discretionary trusts, and the chargeable property (such as the house or quoted shares or cash) appointed within two years of death on a sub-fund within the same trust for the surviving spouse, which is a qualifying interest-in-possession fund with spouse exemption. Each sub-fund is part of the same trust. If the surviving spouse becomes ill or elderly, the trustees then do an appropriation, swapping business property for chargeable property of equivalent value. There is no inheritance tax event on the swap, provided the assets are of equal value; no disposal for capital gains tax purposes, as it all takes place within the same trust; and no stamp duty land tax event either. After two years, the surviving spouse can qualify for business property relief again!

5. Conclusions and the Future

One must question whether these sorts of reliefs, loopholes and anomalies can really be justified. Do they actually achieve the policy objectives of preserving farms and businesses, or would more targeted, focused and principled reliefs be preferable? Should there be some sort of cap on the relief or some requirement that the business or farm has to be held for a minimum period after death, or does this simply distort commercial decision making even more?

Business property relief and agricultural property relief are becoming increasingly expensive reliefs. They make estate and succession planning complex. I suggest that they should be examined critically, with the policy objectives in mind, to determine whether there are better ways of achieving the same goal. Maybe inheritance tax itself should be abolished and instead capital gains tax should operate on death. Here the capital gains tax position is more targeted and focused. That is the subject of a separate discussion, however.

In the Gospel according to St Luke 12:20, we find these words: 'You fool! This very night your life will be demanded from you. Then who will get what you have prepared for yourself?' It might justifiably be said that it is very difficult to know 'who will get', at least in relation to business property or agricultural property. Perhaps 100% relief on a business on death is not a God-given right, but at least the taxpayer should know what the position is, without having to instruct an expensive tax adviser before and after death.

INDEX